D1476745

PHANTASMAL MEDIA

PHANTASMAL MEDIA

An Approach to Imagination, Computation, and Expression

D. Fox Harrell

The MIT Press
Cambridge, Massachusetts
London, England

MIT Press books may be purchased at special quantity discounts for business or sales promotional use. For information, please email special_sales@mitpress.mit.edu.

This book was set in Adobe Garamond and Gotham by the MIT Press. Printed and bound in the United States of America.

Cover image composed from a photograph of *In the Hood* (sweatshirt hood, dimensions variable; David Hammons, 1993) and a Turing Machine (Cbucklely, licensed under a Creative Commons Attributions Share Alike 3.0 Unported license).

Chapter 3 epigraph: Complete panel ("All media of communication . . . *mind to mind*") from *Understanding Comics* by Scott McCloud. Copyright © 1993, 1994 by Scott McCloud. Reprinted by permission of HarperCollins Publishers.

Chapter 4 quotation: "Walking Around" by Pablo Neruda, translated by Donald D. Walsh, from *Residence on Earth*, copyright ©1973 by Pablo Neruda and Donald D. Walsh. Reprinted by permission of New Directions Publishing Corp.

This book draws on several articles and chapters published previously, including the following: "Agency Play: Expressive Dimensions of Agency for Interactive Narrative Design," in *Proceedings of the AAAI 2009 Spring Symposium on Narrative Intelligence II*, 156–162 (Menlo Park, CA: AAAI Press, 2009) (with Jichen Zhu); "Cultural Roots for Computing: The Case of African Diasporic Orature and Computational Narrative in the GRIOT System," *Fibreculture* 11 (adapted from *Proceedings of the 7th Digital Arts and Culture Conference*, 157–168 [Perth, Australia; Curtin University of Technology, 2007]); "Toward a Theory of Phantasmal Media: An Imaginative Cognition- and Computation-Based Approach to Digital Media," *CTheory*, September 2, 2009; "Phantasmal Fictions," *American Book Review* 31 (6) (September/ October 2010); 4–6.

Library of Congress Cataloging-in-Publication Data

Harrell, D. Fox.
Phantasmal media : an approach to imagination, computation, and expression / D. Fox Harrell.
    pages   cm
Includes bibliographical references and index.
ISBN 978-0-262-01933-0 (hardcover : alk. paper)
1. Computers and civilization. 2. Creation (Literary, artistic, etc.) 3. New media art. I. Title.
QA76.9.C66H38   2013

303.48'34—dc23

2012051759

10 9 8 7 6 5 4 3 2 1

to
my father
and
my son,
who give me
light
to see
&
my wife,
who gives me
water
to grow

CONTENTS

PREFACE

The imagination is at the root of many things we see as social reality. A "phantasm" is a particular pervasive kind of imagination, one that encompasses cognitive phenomena including sense of self, metaphor, social categorization, narrative, and poetic thinking. This type of imagination influences almost all our everyday experiences, across diverse domains of experience, including art, entertainment, commerce, culture, and power relationships. This book presents an approach to understanding and designing computing systems that evoke these ubiquitous and often-unseen phantasms—with special attention paid to revealing oppressive phantasms and creating empowering phantasms.

Self-Reflection and Nostalgia

This book grew out of a childhood idea. Television, everyone said, was already compromised—it rotted minds and turned people into couch potatoes. So I wondered if there would be any way that I could help whatever medium came next to play a more ethical role in society. I cannot say that this book lives up to the dream that musing sparked. Yet this book might be considered a step in pursuing a more mature vision rooted in that early dream, with its dual aims of helping people see the unconscious forces that shape media images and helping them use computational media—the next media after television, one could say—to affect society for the better.

As a teenager, I learned of college majors such as "logic and computation," "symbolic systems," and "cognitive science." How wonderful it sounded to combine computer science with fields such as philosophy, mathematics, and psychology. Those majors also all involved artificial intelligence (AI). What a dangerous-sounding area of study—all wrapped up in the aesthetic sensibility of a computer game I loved called *Neuromancer.* By earning a hybrid computer science/mathematics/philosophy degree at the same time as a degree in art (which included learning to work with images, text, sound, video, computer-based media, and more), I would not have to leave any of my educational interests behind. As a small step before crossing the country to attend the university where I executed this plan, I joined a special-interest AI group with the engineers and academics of San Diego. I was the only youth, and a different tint and shade than the other members; I suffered a few askance looks, meanwhile their spouses offered me cookies.

In college, pursuing research in interactive narrative or AI agents seemed to be the best way to blend art and science. Interactive narrative research would allow the computer to help people tell stories set in dynamic worlds from multiple perspectives—we could see the world through the eyes of others in imaginative realms where tender moments constantly decay and die or memories emerge like old bones from tar pits. Research on AI agents would allow programmers to implement characters that have their own lives—characters who represent different modes of thinking. Artificial Intelligence is concerned with topics such as representing meaning, so artificial intelligence–based art seemed like the most artful of computer science fields. At Carnegie Mellon University, I was fortunate to be in a place where such research was pursued.

I chose interactive narrative from those possibilities; my path seemed set. Yet the types of meaning I was interested in were mostly left out of all that I encountered in that area. I felt that most of the work I saw in interactive narrative was focused on a single goal: the Holy Grail seemed to be immersing ourselves in virtual worlds and participating in stories as main characters. I had a passion for a different kind of question: could a computer help people imagine in new ways? When taking an introductory course on the history of art and civilization framed exclusively through the lens of European history, I daydreamed of implementing fantastic interactive narratives on the computer that incorporated what I was learning, creating scenes like this:

> Rising from the depths of a lake filled with thinned white oil paint, I encounter
> specters with faces that looked like Caravaggio's chiaroscuro figures, exaggerated

shadows, intense and ecstatic gazes. I encounter other ghosts, long and stream-lined like Brancusi's sculptures. Touching them transforms me; I am a spooky conglomeration of trans-European hobgoblins, cherubs, and Flemish nobles in a fluid white demesne. As I approach the surface, feeling more and more buoyant, I make one final choice that will ultimately determine my own image, reflected back down at me from the water's impending surface I see myself. I now look like . . .

Unusual daydreams like that were rooted in a reactionary sentiment[1] to a reoccurring experience I had: I was simultaneously inspired by, and excluded from, the cultural milieu in which I was immersed. My own interests in engaging intellectual and artis-tic traditions from a breadth of cultures were engaged only on the periphery—a single reading in a conceptual art course here, an independent study there. The transformative and inspiring references I found on my own during late nights in libraries were not part of the cultural canon. In computer science, interactive narra-tive research started with a limited range of types of interaction, rather than attempt-ing to implement customized forms of interaction suitable to the meanings at hand. I asked myself: if poets can create finely crafted works based on evocative imagery, why should I not use the computer to create interactive narratives filled with evoca-tive, poetic imagery, like the previously mentioned daydream? Much of the technol-ogy was already available: one could use a fluid dynamics model to simulate the viscous liquid of the translucent white lake, ray-tracing to address diffusion and refraction effects, a virtual camera to simulate movement continuously upward along the z-axis, and European art historical images as skins for 3D graphical models for nonplayer characters (NPCs), and one could build a simple finite-state machine to track how a player character transforms based on which NPCs it encounters. Sure, the models do not generalize, but could not that technology express the *meaning* and *subjective experience* I wished to convey through metaphor and narrative?

Beyond such abstract musings, I also had a different set of more conventional research questions. Could one algorithmically retell stories from multiple cultural perspectives? What about with different feelings? Different imagery? Could all of this be accomplished with the power, nuance, and imagination of a book such as Ralph Ellison's *Invisible Man*? Ellison's critically acclaimed novel continues to have an impact on U.S. society and has entered into the canon of world literature. It compels readers to share the experience of navigating an imaginative world of social invisibil-ity, of being on the margins. The novel weaves together profound social critique, experimentation with prose style and narrative structure, imaginative (even border-line science-fiction) events, and verbal imagery. When I read research papers and books about interactive narrative, the development of computational models engaged with imaginative and social meaning (modes of expression akin to Ellison's) was not considered a research aim. In short, I wanted to focus on content and content creation. Doing so meant really coupling representations of *meaning* (able to address issues of theme, social empowerment, emotion, culture, and aesthetics) with appropriate AI and interaction models. It was a focus that was not en vogue.

A breakthrough came when I discovered that some cognitive scientists were interested in the types of meaning that I was seeking. Mark Turner's book *The Literary Mind* was not computationally oriented, yet he wrote on topics such as narrative, parable, metaphor, and blending concepts. This book, and the books in cognitive linguistics to which it led me, connected the idea of artistic thinking to everyday thought and life. I learned that these research topics were the domain of the area of *cognitive semantics*—a subfield of cognitive linguistics, which is in turn a subfield of cognitive science. The field was little recognized in the AI, mathematical logic, and analytic philosophy I knew, nor was it commonly cited in my art training. I encountered criticisms about the field and from the field and defenses from those criticisms all around. I had unwittingly walked onto a battlefield within linguistics. Regardless, these were kindred spirits whose topics supported my needs. My challenge, then, was to figure out how this field's insights could be combined with the AI and logic that I knew well (and against which the cognitive semantics researchers so often seemed to argue) and then applied to artistic and cultural aims.

Urgently seeking, I came upon a theory called *algebraic semiotics*, invented by a computer scientist and mathematician named Joseph Goguen, whose research group was called the Meaning and Computation Laboratory at the University of California, San Diego (UCSD), a kindred spirit with whom I began to correspond. Algebraic semiotics combines insights from the area of algebraic semantics in computer science with semiotics and applies them to topics such as user interface design and cognitive science. Algebraic semiotics is unique as a theory because Joseph was always careful to discuss the limitations of mathematical-computational formalisms at the same time he was using them to think about and model the most poetic types of thought and language. Furthermore, UCSD was an oasis for cognitive semantics. Gilles Fauconnier, another visionary thinker about thought, was also there. Joseph, whose work investigated mappings in mathematics (among a multitude of other subjects), was friends with George Lakoff, whose work addressed one of the main types of meaning

I sought to learn more about: metaphor—mappings in cognition. Though loathe to return to beautiful, oppressive San Diego, where I grew up, to the very campus my parents attended, I went to UCSD to apprentice with Joseph. It was fortunate and tragic. We found great synergy and he embraced me as his Ph.D. student in computer science and engineering. However, he died before we could finish our work—just days after an international symposium held in his honor (occasioned by the publication of a Festschrift on Joseph's work called *Algebra, Meaning, and Computation*). Chapter 4 of this book is a tribute to Joseph's work. I hope it will help others see what I found so profound about algebraic semiotics.

Joseph was always a strong supporter, yet he finally conveyed to me a deep appreciation of the value and depth of my vision when we successfully developed a modest conceptual blending algorithm (which we later named Alloy) that I used to author a program capable of generating a new poem every time it was used. When I was invited to speak at a conference focused on issues of technology and social power relationships (with a feminist bent), I presented the system and its implementation to help make the argument that accounts of race and ethnicity needed to move beyond binary oppositions and instead focus on subjective and dynamic experiences. A year later, I sketched out an architecture diagram to generalize the operation of that first interactive poem, which grew into the GRIOT system.

The GRIOT system is a computer program developed as a platform to support the implementation of works of interactive narrative, poetry, and related types of interactive multimedia expression. It is a research system, a project initiated to explore a set of ideas about how to make storytelling on a computer more improvisational. In particular, central challenges were to develop technology focused on composing content that is meaningfully different each time and theory to explain just what "meaningfully different" means. It turned out that the outcome was not specifically focused on narrative, but rather on phantasms: outcomes of the more general aspects of imaginative cognition that include narrative imagining, poetic discourse, and figurative thinking.

Realizations and Hopes

Ultimately, I realized that AI-based narrative was not my main interest. Some of my work at the time looked like (interactive) surreal poetry; other work was more straightlaced user interface design, though driven by user values. Though some work was highly narrative, other work was more metaphorical and associative (and, I hoped, evocative). Yet I realized that there was one strand that went through all of it: the imagination.

I deeply believe that the human capacity to imagine is our greatest means to freedom. I do not believe that great art and forms of culture should deal with only lofty issues of life, death, love, and beauty. I do believe in the functional value of art to change society and minds—and to understand how they should change. At the same time, I am concerned about social ills encountered in everyday life: violence, atrocities of war, small acts of unkindness, prejudice. These are not unique concerns; they are powerful phenomena that all sensitive people care about. I see these topics as part of everyday life, just like death, love, and beauty. Furthermore, I also see that the ways we conceive of these very real social ills are shaped by the human imagination. The ultimate function of the kind of cultural production I am interested in, whether one calls it art or engineering, is to reveal and shape the combination of imagination and real-world experiences that oppress or empower.

The focus on phantasms prompted and revealed by media is both an outcome of this journey and a lens through which others can begin to see my perspective on all of these topics. One of the things I work hardest at is making sure that my ideas are synthesized into a coherent whole rather than remaining discrete interests. I constantly chart, map, and plan ideas. This book has been a great challenge of synthesizing, charting, mapping, and planning, all wrapped up in the word *phantasm*. This topic is, perhaps, unheeding of many trends of current art practice and may seem rather "soft" to many engineers and scientists. Understanding and designing computing systems to prompt the imagination poses several challenges. In computer science, where researchers often prove ideas through making systems with techniques and technologies that rapidly become dated, one challenge is to produce theory that stands the test of time. Cognitive science is a field in which researchers propose theoretical models that also will one day be superseded by new theories with more rigorous empirical grounding as we learn more about the brain. Furthermore, this book is interdisciplinary and draws upon a range of ideas that I encountered and pursued as rigorously as I could, not only through traditional paths of achieving academic expertise but additionally just through reading and life experience (remember, that was part of the plan).

Despite these challenges, I hope that the book will be useful for researchers and other interested people who want to think about the computer, imagination, social reality, and cultural expression from a new perspective. I have given some attention to making the book useful in a practical way as well as presenting new theory. Each chapter of the book offers a clear set of constructs (a model) that should be useful for enriching understanding and guiding design of computing systems.

I also realize a flaw of my childhood dream: the medium alone is not what is ethical or unethical. The computational medium that I work in, which has indeed come after television, is connected to a complex web of previous media, culture, behavior, preexisting power relationships, and more. From one perspective, I submit this book to you as a wistful, probably doomed, love letter—hoping for an "I love you too" (your theories make sense, and open up new possibilities), but I am prepared for my ideas to receive the fate of all words of unrequited lovers. That is, even if it ends up not laying a blueprint for the future, I strive for this book to be good poetry.

More assertively, I would say that this book is a manifesto arguing that great expressive potential of computational media comes from their ability to construct and reveal what I call phantasms. It argues for the importance of cultural content, diverse worldviews, and social values in computing. Designing and analyzing such epistemic functions of computational media is key to unleashing their expressive power. The expressive function of phantasms, those blends of cultural ideas and sensory imagination that the computer can so effectively conjure, is not restricted to purely aesthetic dimensions. More substantively, phantasmal media can express and construct the types of meaning central to the human condition.

ACKNOWLEDGMENTS

This book was completed with gratitude to, and in memory of, Joseph A. Goguen, gardener of algebraic flowers.

Nick Montfort has been a true friend and colleague—his insight, support, and wit have been invaluable. James Paradis has deeply engaged my material, emphasized that style is content, offered unwavering support, and shared his taste for edgy and soulful jazz—for all this and more, I thank him. Grant Malcolm offered exceptional feedback that helped me properly tend Joseph Goguen's mathematical flora—I thank him for helping me consider both the Wet and the Dry. I also thank Michel DeGraff, who engaged my ideas regarding cultural computing and shared examples where cultural computing and mathematics are flourishing, and where they are necessary. I appreciate the anonymous reviewers whose insights helped the book grow, and my editor Doug Sery for securing them and for his ongoing support and belief in my ideas.

Kenneth Manning has been a wonderful supporter and mentor, sharing his oracular wisdom with me over the years. Wesley Harris has graciously and consistently reiterated his belief in the importance of my work. Patrick Winston has been an excellent colleague and mentor in computer science and a fellow believer in the power of narrative. I thank each of them sincerely for their advice since I arrived at MIT.

Several people have been kind and wise supporters and inspirations over the years. Janet Murray's work has long been an inspiration, and she is a true leader; I'll always cherish her friendship and advice. Michael Mateas has been a true inspiration;

I have had the benefit of his pioneering the way with his visionary work combining AI and art. Noah Wardrip-Fruin has been a wonderful friend who believed in my ideas early on; his scholarship and generosity are both profound. Simon Penny, artist, roboticist, and sailor, I thank for sharing with me his immense wisdom regarding the divides and synergies between art and engineering. Steve Kurtz makes theory ring true in everyday life and is a true fighter for empowerment who inspires me. Arthur and Marilouise Kroker are gracious and poetic thinkers who have catalyzed a community and personally shown me longstanding support. Mary Bryson's intellectual waters run deep and implacably cool, yet it is the accompanying warmth of her spirit that has made her support so special. Henry Lieberman's broad, humanistic approach to AI is powerful in its applications; his kindness and support over the years have been truly meaningful. Erik Loyer is one of the most amazing artists I have ever encountered; his expressive fluency with code has inspired me—I thank him for the insight he has given me about his practice. Johnny Golding has initiated a powerful nexus of art and technology; I thank her for that and also for the fact that she does so in a community where it matters.

There are numerous colleagues in the various academic communities I participate in whom I would like to thank for the conversations we have shared and the powerful ideas they pursue: Jeremy Douglass, Mark Marino, Mary Flanagan, Ayoka Chenzira, Lev Manovich, Jane Prophet, Phoebe Sengers, Pamela Jennings, Elizabeth Losh, Alondra Nelson, Gilles Fauconnier, Espen Aarseth, Eric Zimmerman, and Ian Bogost.

I would like to thank each of the students of the Imagination, Computation, and Expression Laboratory at MIT and previously at Georgia Tech. Chong-U Lim's contributions as a Ph.D. student have been invaluable. Additionally, Sonny Sidhu, Jia Zhang, Ayse Gursoy, Dominic Kao, Christine Yu, and Greg Vargas have all contributed to lab projects at MIT and have been a pleasure to work with. In particular, let me thank some of the first graduate students whom I was honored to have graduated: Jichen Zhu, Kenny K. N. Chow, and Daniel Upton—I learned a great deal from each of them. I also particularly thank Ayoka Chenzira (who has deep insight into art and media), Jisun An (who is a brilliant graphic designer), and the many other students who took the ICE Lab Project Studio Course at Georgia Tech for their contributions to early lab projects.

At past institutions where I was a student, I also thank the following professors for their guidance toward my degrees as advisors, committee members, or mentors:

Jeremy Avigad, Geoffrey Voelker, Victor Vianu, Frank Lantz, John Sturgeon, and Herbert Olds.

I thank the faculty, students, and staff of the MIT Comparative Media Studies Program. I also thank those in the Computer Science and Artificial Intelligence Laboratory. I appreciate the past support of the Georgia Institute of Technology School of Literature, Communication, and Culture; Carnegie Mellon University School of Art and Department of Philosophy; and the University of California, San Diego, Department of Computer Science and Engineering. I appreciate each of my fellow board members of the Electronic Literature Organization. I convey my goodwill to all those I have kindly engaged within the digital arts and culture, creativity and cognition, and computational creativity communities.

I thank the following institutions for their generous support: the National Science Foundation, the National Endowment for the Humanities, the Ford Foundation, and the National Endowment for the Arts.

Dayasagara Basil Harrell; Douglas Harrell Sr.; Diane Harrell; Alana Harrell; Anika Harrell; Elan Harrell; Jason Ryan Harrell Diaz; Shantinath Veeragoudar; Sarojani Veeragoudar; Veerendra Veeragoudar; and the Harrell, Williams, and Veeragoudar families I thank with love.

Sneha Veeragoudar Harrell, for more than I can convey here and more than she knows, I thank with love and devotion.

INTRODUCTION

1

DEFINING PHANTASMS

The dream, you see, had not been vivid with voices and colors, with faces and passions, with actions and artifacts you could haul back through sleep's black currents into the wakeful sun, then to ponder them like a full story, smiling over its absurdities, wondering at its glories, now and again this part or that falling away as you recognized what had been loaned it by past adventure or future hope. Rather it had been a gray, lazy, hazy froth of recall and fancy just under the film of consciousness, so that waking was like that thinnest of surface's parting at which drowsing and waking merged.

—Samuel R. Delany, *Return to Nevèrÿon*

When they approach me they see only my surroundings, themselves, or figments of their imagination—indeed, everything and anything except me.

—Ralph Ellison, *Invisible Man*

The term "phantasm" may summon, for some readers, mental pictures of ghosts, spooks, apparitions, and specters. In this book, however, it does not refer to such supernatural or paranormal entities but rather to the result of a particular type of thought; a phantasm is the result of human imaginative cognition. This book explores how computers can play a role in the creation and revelation of these imagined entities.

Phantasms are a combination of imagery (mental or sensory) and ideas. A phantasm is not simply the result of a specific neurobiological process; rather, the term "phantasm" describes a broad type of subjective cognitive phenomenon. The breadth of the term is useful because the idea of the phantasm poses a challenge to the way that many people view human experience. It is a challenge to the idea that human thought, especially thought regarding society and culture, reflects a "real" and objective world. The importance of the concept of the phantasm to challenge conventional understandings of human experience can be expressed by a simple observation: *much of what humans experience as real is based upon the imagination.*

Before offering a definition of the term "phantasm," I shall start with a few examples that illustrate ways in which phantasms combine images (mental or sensory) and ideas. These examples will help you gain a greater sense of the nature of phantasms, thus setting a foundation for an investigation into their creation and revelation using computers.

Much in our conceptions of the world—from our senses of selves and others to social ills and other everyday experiences—can be seen as phantasms, as results of the imagination. For example:

Self   Each of us has a self-image (maybe more than one). This self-image can be composed of personality traits, fashion, categories such as gender or ethnicity, biology and physical appearance, affectations, mannerisms, and more. A self-image is not just a concrete sensory image, like the result of looking at a photograph. It is a combination of immediate and/or remembered sensory perception (of how one looks, sounds, smells, etc.) and sociocultural ideas. Along with a sensory impression of how she looks, a woman might think, "I am an American woman, but with a hard-edged European style; I'm not stereotypically American or stereotypically feminine." This thought is combined with ways of behaving toward objects and others in specific situations. That thought about oneself, influenced by social and cultural norms and externalized through situated behavior, is a phantasm—a combination of a mental image and ideas.

Other   In order to communicate, we all try to make sense of other people. Some people do this by trying to relate others to preexisting social categories. "Oh, you are from France," you exclaim to your colleague in philosophy. At that same time, your mind brings forth images of crêpes and the smell of the air in Versailles, along with your admiration of a certain dense and exuberant style of academic writing that you think of as French critical theory. "You are not like other Californians," you say to your niece, comparing her with your impression of what Californians are like as a group. The combinations of mental and sensory images (including the immediate perception of the physical appearance of the person standing in front of you) and ideas (whether based on stereotype or previous experience) prompted by the words "France" or "Californian" are phantasms.

Social ills   When we hear about social ills such as slavery or genocide, we often have visceral internal reactions accompanied by strong mental images. The phrase "slavery in the United States of America" might invoke embodied emotional responses. You might feel shame or anger, imagining the notorious scene from the film *Gone with the Wind* in which the character Prissy admits, "I don't know nothin' 'bout birthin' babies!," guilt or sadness imagining a torturous iron human collar from a history textbook you read as a child, or indignation or envy as you imagine the big house of a southern plantation and think, "My ancestors were there, not me—why should I feel ashamed/angry/guilty/sad?" Any such mental image that is based in your envisioning of a historical or current event that you did not experience directly and is imbued with your associated subjective emotional and intellectual impressions is a phantasm.

Everyday experience   We all have everyday experiences that are simultaneously understood within broader stories. The real-world experience of looking up at a certain type of balcony might prompt you to imbue the scenario at hand with deeper significance. You might imagine calling up to your lover on the balcony, as you just saw in a scene from a filmic adaptation of Shakespeare's *Romeo and Juliet*. Alternatively, you might imagine the sober importance of your life's mission as you look up at the balcony, recalling the tragic balcony you saw in photographs where civil rights leader Martin Luther King Jr. was assassinated. The results of either of those mappings of imagery and ideas—which you previously experienced through media such as film, television, photography, and books—onto your immediate sensory perception of the balcony at hand are phantasms.

Selves, others, social ills, and everyday experiences such as described thus far are not the only kinds of phantasms. Much of human thought depends on these phantasms; to the extent that people ever imaginatively extrapolate to fill in gaps in our first-hand experiences, we are building phantasms. Indeed, the term "phantasm" is intended to function in much the same way as the term "concept" does. Yet a phantasm is more specific than the cognitive science notion of a concept in three distinct ways (which can be seen in the preceding examples). First, phantasms incorporate immediate, remembered, or elaborated sensory perceptions that I call images. Hence, "image" in this sense does not refer only to immediately perceived vision but rather refers to any mental or sensory impression, whether based on something at hand, remembered, or imagined. Second, phantasms combine that image with ideas or, more precisely, with ideas based in particular worldviews. That is, phantasms imbue images with connotative meanings based in some worldview beyond that which is apprehended perceptually. Third, these connotative meanings are semivisible. That is, within the worldview in which they are based, phantasms seem natural and uncontroversial. Phantasms are revealed only when compared to concepts and images grounded in multiple worldviews. For individuals whose worldviews correspond to those in which the phantasm is based, the assumptions underlying a phantasm's connotative meaning are invisible. But from other worldviews or perspectives, the assumptions underlying the connotative meaning of the phantasm are clear and obvious. For example, to someone who has never heard of France, the highly stereotypical association of the country with crêpes and complicated philosophical theory would be obviously visible as a strange conflation of a place with ideas. But for those familiar with this phantasm of France, merely saying "He's French" conveys those additional meanings invisibly.

The philosophical emphasis of the concept of the phantasm is the contention that much of what people experience as real is based on the imagination.[1] Selves, other people, social ills like slavery, and everyday experiences are real. People experience them. Phantasms, which conflate ideas and images that need not be related, thus have a significant real-world impact as they become, to some extent, self-fulfilling prophecies. They are made real by the imagination. Although there is no denying the brutal reality of social ills such as slavery, much of what shapes that reality is perception and consequent human reaction. The idea of the phantasm does not deny the experiential reality. It does, however, claim that there is an important, underexamined relationship between those experiential realities and the basic human processes of imaginative cognition.

Selves, others, social ills, and everyday experiences are all aspects of the human condition. What these examples show is that the human imagination partly defines the human condition. As such, the philosophical orientation of the concept of the phantasm is toward analyzing the roles that the types of imaginative feats involved in *narrative imagining*, closely related to what others have called *poetic thought*,[2] play in constructing the social and cultural experiential realities of people (Gibbs 1994; Lakoff and Turner 1989). Furthermore, you shall see that media can be designed in such a way as to structure and prompt phantasms. Media can also help in the process of sharing these phantasms throughout groups of people (I shall later call these socially entrenched phantasms "cultural phantasms"). In particular, this book focuses on computer-based media and their potential to create and reveal phantasms.

Illustrating and Defining Phantasms

A series of simple examples will lead up to a formal definition of "phantasm." When encountering an image such as the one shown in figure 1.1, many people immediately recognize it as a sign meaning "woman" or "women"—for example, on the door to a lavatory.

FIGURE 1.1
An everyday sign represents "women."

If one thinks about it, one can infer the meaning by reasoning that in some societies women tend to wear clothing that resembles that abstracted silhouette, but for most people reading this book, no such conscious reasoning process was needed to understand the basic meaning of the image. Even individuals who do not assume that such clothing is or should be restricted to a single gender can make meaning of the sign without consciously reasoning about it. People who understand the sign draw upon the cultural worldview of women that includes beliefs about how women present themselves in public. That rich array of cultural knowledge includes the specific concept that a dress is an iconic, gender-specific type of clothing. In the case of the sign in figure 1.1, this concept is distributed onto the actual image itself. The result is a phantasm, an image integrated with cultural knowledge and beliefs (which may be traditional, stereotypical, or otherwise representative of an ideology). The meaning is immediate and uncontroversial for those who subscribe to the cultural worldview that the concept integrated in the phantasm is drawn from. Figure 1.2 illustrates this phantasm.

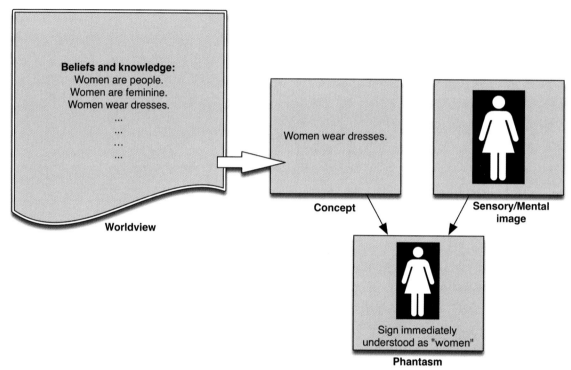

FIGURE 1.2
Everyday images can be phantasms.

However, other signs are also used to represent women. The image in figure 1.3, designed at the Indian Institute of Technology for use in public hospital systems, depicts a woman wearing a South Asian sari and earrings. In such settings, the sign represents "women," though in settings where saris are uncommon garb it would seem to represent something else, perhaps "Indian women" (the idea of "Indian women" itself being a phantasm, as many women in other countries such as Bangladesh, Mauritius, and the United States also wear saris).

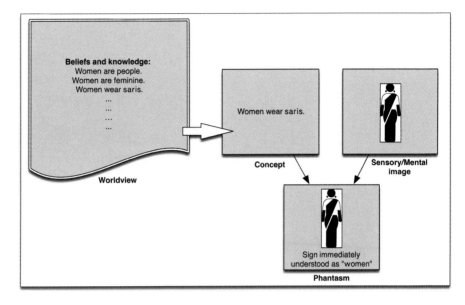

FIGURE 1.3
Another everyday image for "women" (left) is also a phantasm (right).

Even in many communities in South Asia where the sari is still familiar—for example, where other garb is preferred due to religious affiliations—the sign in figure 1.3 might represent something other than just an icon for "women." Consider also the example of another sign for "women" used in the Southwest Asian country of Oman. Just as with the other "women" signs, the Omani sign shown in figure 1.4 shows another phantasm for "women."

FIGURE 1.4
Another everyday sign that represents "women."

Of course, some people might be aware of multiple worldviews that provide the conceptual bases for phantasms in the previous examples. Some people might even be aware of other worldviews that assert, for instance, that any cultural worldview of how women dress as a monolithic group will result in a stereotyped sign for women. Awareness of these contrasting worldviews renders the phantasm visible. The contrast between these three different signs intended to indicate "women" can be used to illustrate how phantasms, which often operate invisibly because they are immediately understood and uncontroversial in meaning in their native cultural settings, can be revealed through their contrast with multiple phantasms based in other worldviews and images. Revealing a phantasm means making conscious the awareness of the cultural worldview from which the phantasm is drawn, rather than off-loading meaning onto the image itself for immediate apprehension. This process of revealing a phantasm is depicted in figure 1.5, in which the phantasm is shown as no longer immediately and uncontroversially understood.

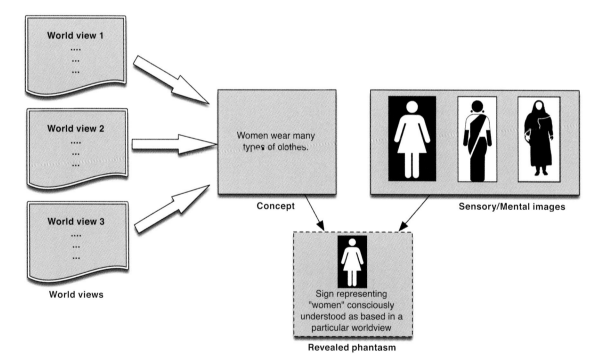

FIGURE 1.5

A phantasm representing "women" is *revealed* or *made visible* by integrating knowledge and beliefs from multiple worldviews.

A *revealed phantasm* is one that an individual consciously understands to be based in a subjective worldview. This worldview can be individual (in the case of fantasies in someone's mind) or shared widely within or across cultures, as shall be explored later in this book.

I shall now refine the nomenclature for describing worldviews, concepts, and images in turn. A cultural worldview includes the knowledge and beliefs of a culture and the values they entail. In this book, the term *epistemic domain* is introduced to refer to an abstracted, structured description of salient aspects of worldviews for a purpose at hand. Epistemic domains are abstract because they represent idealizations of units of semantic content. Epistemic domains are structured because they represent systematic subdivisions of semantic content. Indeed, in chapter 3 you shall see that they are possible to describe informally, semiformally (e.g., using a markup language), or formally (e.g., using first-order logic as is common in AI systems). They are called *domains* because they inherit the meaning of the term from cognitive science, in which "domain" refers to conceptual information about some subdivision of the world. The word "epistemic" in the term *epistemic domain* is used because these structured descriptions are used to express knowledge and beliefs, which are topics explored in the branch of philosophy called *epistemology*.

In order to construct a phantasm, a particular concept that I call an *epistemic space* is drawn from the epistemic domain. The epistemic space is a smaller, more concise packet of information (called a mental or conceptual space in cognitive science) for making meaning of a situation at hand. A sensory or mental image, the *image space*, is then integrated with an epistemic space. The result is a *phantasm space* or a *phantasm*. Phantasms can then be integrated with other epistemic spaces, image spaces, and/or phantasms to result in new compound phantasms (which could in turn be integrated into further compound phantasms, and so on). Figure 1.6 illustrates that general structure of a phantasm along with the terms just introduced.[3]

The term "epistemic domain" as used here does not refer to any particular way of structurally expressing worldviews using particular informal or formal mathematical means of description. Particular forms of representation such as frame data structures in computer science, diagrams in the cognitive science theories of meaning construction, or natural language descriptions in ethnographic accounts from sociology can all be used to describe epistemic domains, depending on the analytical purpose at hand. Furthermore, it is extremely important to note that epistemic domains are not intended to exhaustively describe worldviews or to claim that such a structure is sufficient for nuanced social analysis.

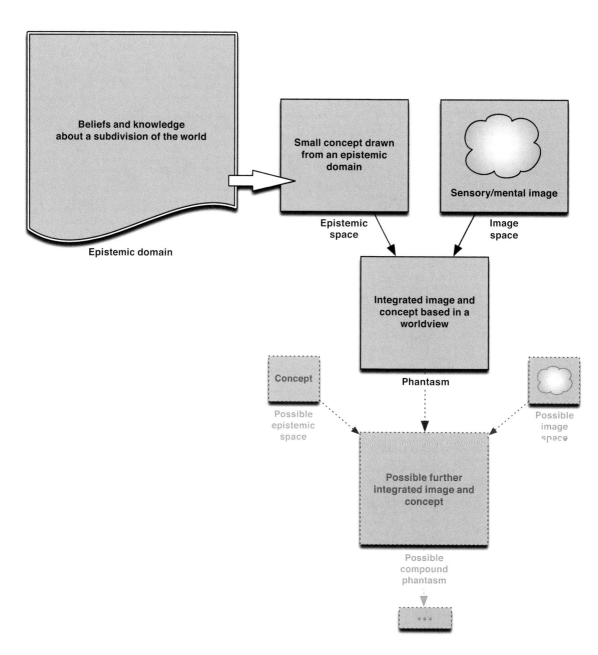

FIGURE 1.6
Phantasms share the depicted general structure.

To illustrate the concept of an epistemic domain in more detail, consider the results of the classic study published by Kenneth B. Clark and Mamie P. Clark in the 1930s and 1940s (Clark and Clark 1947). In this study, African American (then called "Negro") children were given requests related to two pairs of nearly identical—but differently colored—dolls, as shown in figure 1.7. Some of those requests were intended to help understand the children's preferences such as "give me what you like to play with," "give me the doll that looks nice," and "give me the doll that looks bad."

FIGURE 1.7
In the Clark study, African American children were required to choose between two color variations of otherwise identical dolls.

The results were striking, for example 67 percent of the 253 participants chose the pale, blue-eyed, blond doll to play with, 59 percent selected the pale doll as looking "nice," and 59 percent selected the brown, brown-eyed, black-haired doll as looking "bad." The study has been often duplicated and the implications of the children's preferences have been well explored. The study also included requests of the children intended to elicit racial identifications from the children. The children were given requests such as "give me the white doll," "give me the colored doll," and "give me the Negro" doll (using the racial category terms that were most prominently used at the time). The children selected the brown doll 93 percent of the time when the "colored" doll was requested and 72 percent of the time when the "Negro" doll was requested. The children selected the pale doll 94 percent of the time when the "white" doll was requested. To put it simply, a major interpretation of the study's results is that the children's preferences reflected a cultural worldview that includes the racist beliefs that "white" people are "preferred" and "look nice" whereas "colored" or "Negro" people "look bad." In general, the children had internalized negative self-conceptions.

I shall use this interpretation of the Clark study's results to illustrate a phantasm. To do so, consider the salient elements of a particular U.S. racial worldview leading to this interpretation. These elements include thoughts about people, the racial labels used in the experiment, the differences in physical features highlighted by the experiment, and the types of preferences elicited by the experiment. A complete epistemic domain would include more than just the salient elements of the experiment, such as other labels that might be used for race, historical facts, and knowledge of contradictory preferences related to race. There are many ways that this interpretation of a particular U.S. racial worldview that informed the children's preferences could be described in a systematic, structured way.[4] In figure 1.8, the racial worldview is informally described as an epistemic domain. For the illustrative purposes at hand, figure 1.8 highlights the salient elements related to the argument, some ways that those elements might be distinguished as different sorts of things, and knowledge or beliefs held about those elements. Figure 1.8 presents such information in a structured way, using the term "sort" to refer to what type of thing different elements of the worldview are. A particular sort of element is an attribute, which provides information about other elements of other sorts. Readers might consider skimming figure 1.8 first to gain a sense of the kind of information it conveys and returning to it later to explore its details to engage in more thorough analysis of the Clark experiment example.

Figure 1.8 emphasizes the binary set of races (with two labels for one of the races, namely colored and Negro), people, dolls, and attributes such as "looks nice" or "looks bad." This particular format is not required for describing this worldview as an epistemic domain, and indeed it is overly simplifying. However, the aim here is to use the example to convey key concepts and terms en route to defining phantasms. Take the example of a child who considers the white doll to "look nice." In this case, an epistemic space, such as the one shown in figure 1.9, is drawn from the U.S. racial worldview epistemic domain discussed previously.

For a majority of the children in the study, seeing the two dolls and the contrast between them prompted a phantasm. When asked to select a doll that looks nice, a child's sensory perception of the doll (the image space) was tightly integrated with concepts that they have about real people in society (the epistemic space). The children identified a doll as white and recognized the features that they associated with an idealized whiteness as "looking nice" without having to reason about their preferences. They off-loaded part of their sense-making processes onto the image space; the sensory experience of the white doll immediately looked nicer to such children in the

Salient Aspects of a Particular U.S. Racial Worldview		
Elements	Sorts of elements	Knowledge and beliefs about elements
Person	Person	All human beings are people.
Hair	Person-part (component of a person)	Typical humans have hair.
Eyes	Person-part	Typical humans have eyes.
Skin	Person-part	All humans have skin.
Preferred	Person-attribute (relational attribute associated with people)	Some people can be preferred.
Looks nice	Person-attribute	Some people can look nice.
Looks bad	Person-attribute	Some people can look bad.
Looks nice (blond hair)	Person-part-attribute (relational attribute associated with people-parts)	Blond hair looks nice.
Looks nice (blue eyes)	Person-part-attribute	Blue eyes look nice.
Looks nice (pale-toned skin)	Person-part-attribute	Pale skin tones look nice.
Looks bad (black hair)	Person-part-attribute	Black hair looks bad.
Looks bad (brown eyes)	Person-part-attribute	Brown eyes look bad.
Looks bad (brown skin)	Person-part-attribute	Brown skin looks bad.
White person	White-person (subsort of person)	White people are not Negroes. White people are not colored people.
Negro person	Negro-person (subsort of person)	Negroes are colored people (they share all characteristics of colored people). Negroes are not white people.
Colored person	Colored-person (subsort of person)	Colored people are Negroes (they share all characteristics of Negroes). Colored people are not white people.

FIGURE 1.8

An interpretation of a particular U.S. racial worldview revealed by the Clark study can be abstracted and summarized in a simple, structured format.

White Person "Looks Nice" Concept		
Elements	Sorts of elements	Knowledge and beliefs about elements
White person	White-person (subsort of person)	White people are not Negroes. White people are not colored people.
Looks nice	Person-attribute	Some people look nice.
Looks nice (blond hair)	Person-part-attribute (relational attribute associated with people-parts)	Blond hair looks nice.
Looks nice (blue eyes)	Person-part-attribute	Blue eyes look nice.
Looks nice (pale-toned skin)	Person-part-attribute	Pale skin tones look nice.

FIGURE 1.9

A concept associated with a white person drawn from a particular U.S. racial worldview reveals values about attributes that "look nice."

same uncontroversial way that the children would say it looked like a baby or that it had arms and legs. In this sense, the "nice-looking doll" is a phantasm such as that depicted in figure 1.10.

Although in the case of the Clark study, the phantasm represents the social ill of racism, not all phantasms have to do with social identity categories and not all phantasms serve to oppress. Phantasms can also be used to create innovative and empowering possibilities. I shall now describe a computer-based case of one such empowering phantasm. The phantasm in this case is a new conception and image of radical Jewish music and musicians presented on a record label's website.

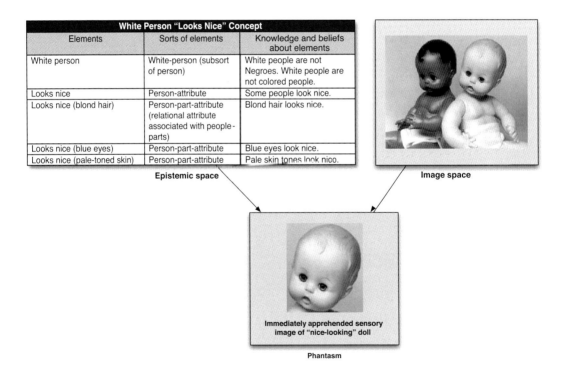

FIGURE 1.10
This interpretation of the Clark study is a phantasm.

Tzadik Records has released a series of recordings under the label "Radical Jewish Culture," which is the basis of this new conception and image for Jewish music (Zorn 2012). Tzadik Records is an "avant-garde and experimental music" record label that was founded in 1995 by award-winning composer, improviser, and musician John Zorn. The record label uses as its logo צ, the eighteenth letter of the Hebrew alphabet, which Hebrew speakers sometime pronounce as *tzadik*, which means "righteous one" in Hebrew. The verbal imagery evoked by the text descriptions and the consistently elegant graphical imagery used in their online presentation combine to create a "group identity" phantasm that enables new radical cultural possibilities for Jewish composers and musicians. Such a phantasm is not composed of one specific graphical or verbal image but is rather distributed onto a number of design elements that constitute an immediately recognizable holistic sense of an identity. It is a phantasm that contrasts strongly with a former phantasm casting Jewish music and musicians as traditional and culturally conservative. The cultural possibilities enabled by the Radical Jewish Culture phantasm have been described on the label's website as "Jewish music beyond klezmer: adventurous recordings bringing Jewish identity and culture into the 21st century" (Zorn 2012).

The Radical Jewish Music series features music by artists such as saxophonist Steven Bernstein (a New York City artist whose music is rooted in what was called the "downtown" music scene), The Cracow Klezmer Band (a Polish group whose music is a melancholy and experimental extension of klezmer music), and John Zorn himself (e.g., his Masada project consisting of "special arrangements for small ensembles of strings, keyboards and clarinets" performing "compositions expanding the Jewish tradition"). Even just examining the small sample of three cover images and descriptions of albums by these artists on the website, one can find several emergent themes, including Jewish culture, cross-cultural experimentation, mysticism, tradition, and history. Furthermore, there are uniformly elegant design elements on the website and images of album covers, one minor example of which is a gold stripe near the bottom of the images upon which the album titles are written. These themes, along with the selected album cover images and quotations that evoke them, are summarized in figure 1.11.

John Zorn's essay introducing the Radical Jewish Culture series provides evidence that these common themes were chosen to aid in the creation of an empowering phantasm (Zorn 2012). The essay starts with a quotation by Gershom Scholem, a noted scholar on Jewish mysticism. This quotation argues that "much of what is best in current Jewish consciousness" is indebted to a "treasure hunt within tradition." That is, people look for what is valuable within traditional culture and create vital

Analysis of Three Albums on the Tzadik Records Website			
Artist and album	Album cover	Quotations from Tzadik album descriptions	Themes evoked by album descriptions
Steven Bernstein: *Diaspora Blues* (2002)		cantorial melodies	Traditional Jewish music
		moving ballads	Emotion; Popular music
		hypnotic grooves	Slight mysticism; Popular music
		free jazz	Experimental music
The Cracow Klezmer Band: *De Profundis* (2000)		the secret connection between the Gypsies [sic] and the Jews	Obscure knowledge; Cross-cultural connections
		dynamic original compositions	Experimental music
		creative arrangements	Experimental music
		Jewish Renaissance	New Jewish culture
John Zorn: *Bar Kokhba* (1996)		dark, passionate, evocative music	Emotional music; Edgy music
		Jewish tradition	Jewish culture
		Jewish music	Jewish culture

FIGURE 1.11

A small sample of albums in Tzadik Records' Radical Jewish Culture series reveals several themes. Images © Tzadik, Hips Road.

current innovations even if those innovations are expressed outside the framework of orthodox traditions. Zorn creates an analogy between Jewish music and both jazz music rooted in African American culture and European classical music, both of which he sees as having undergone a series of radical transformations and growth.[5] At the same time, Zorn is clear in asserting that the "Jewish music" promoted by the Radical Jewish Culture series does not simply mean any music performed by a Jewish person. Rather, the Radical Jewish Culture series is intended to support musicians with experimental and avant-garde practices who articulately negotiate some relationship in their practices to the histories and traditions of Jewish culture. All of these elements of Zorn's essay reinforce the earlier identified themes of cross-cultural experimentation, mysticism, tradition, and history.

I can now describe the structure of the phantasm evoked by the visual and verbal imagery used on the Tzadik Records website. For Zorn, there is an epistemic domain that captures an expansive worldview of Jewish culture that includes aspects that are variously traditional, experimental, secular, and orthodox. From this, Zorn selected a subset of aspects of his holistic view of Jewish culture that he considers to be radical and appropriate to Tzadik Records. The verbal and visual elements of the website are designed to prompt epistemic spaces for the Tzadik vision of radical Jewish culture (such as described in figure 1.11) in the minds of individuals looking at the site.

With enough exposure, one might even immediately associate the concepts captured by such an epistemic space with the verbal and visual imagery that is immediately recognizable as part of the Tzadik Radical Jewish Culture series, such as the consistent graphic style or descriptive terminology. In such a case, Tzadik Records has created a phantasm that is illustrated by figure 1.12.

Such a phantasm is empowering because it creates new visions and possibilities for self-determination. As a Jewish musician performing a diversity of experimental music, a large subset of which early on was seen as developing an African American tradition of jazz music, Zorn might have faced some struggle reconciling social expectations for a musician of his identity with his own musical aspirations. In the Radical Jewish Culture series, Tzadik Records has created not only opportunities for the publishing of music that is in line with the aspirations of Zorn and other like-minded musicians but also an image that reinforces the idea of the Jewish musician as a radical innovator. Such an image can serve to reinforce the self-conceptions of those excluded from, or stigmatized by, traditional worldviews (such as perhaps Jewish musicians playing straight-ahead jazz) and open up new possibilities for those who are in the process of defining their own self-conceptions.

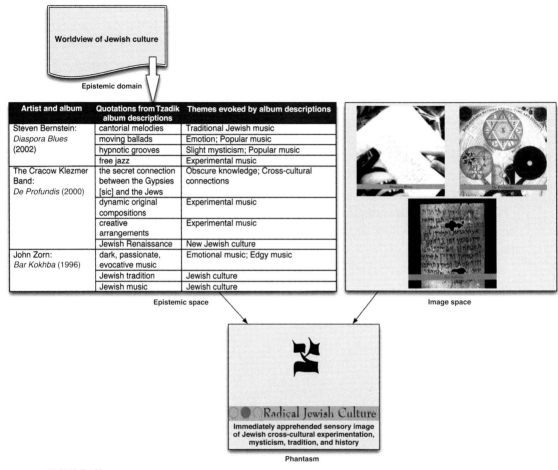

FIGURE 1.12
Tzadik Records has created an empowering phantasm of radical Jewish culture. Images © Tzadik, Hips Road.

When used for making sense of the world, phantasms inherit the ideological assumptions, biases, or innovations of the epistemic spaces (and hence epistemic domains) that they are drawn from. The ideological assumptions, biases, or innovations can be empowering or disempowering. They can serve to reinforce other existing phantasms or engender new ones. They can be highly individual or broadly entrenched within and across cultures. Finally, they can be revealed as subjective, highlighting the role of the imagination in the construction of many of the things people accept as "real" in individual and social realities.

Phantasmal Media: The Roles of Phantasms in Imagination, Computation, and Expression

Recall that this chapter started with the statement that the computer can play a role in the creation and revelation of phantasms. This statement means that computing systems (working in conjunction with people, with other artifacts, and in particular situations) can play a part in prompting the imaginative cognition processes that result in phantasms. There is already a history of using the computer to explore cognition. The field of artificial intelligence was founded based on the idea that human cognition could be modeled using a computer. However, the early days of AI focused on rational thought as the key type of human intelligence to model. Early AI researchers also believed that human intelligence could be reduced to formal models implementable on a specific type of computer architecture (abstractly defined by a Turing machine[6]). Whereas the field of artificial intelligence was founded on the basis of trying to emulate rational human intelligence, this book instead explores the following question:

How can one better understand and design computing systems that effectively prompt human imagination in the forms of narrative imagining and poetic thought (e.g., metaphor, theme, emotional tone, narrative, social categories, and imaginative worlds)?

A few of the terms in this question should be elaborated upon. The word "effectively" might seem to imply that prompting human imagination is an optimization problem in which one could measure how well a computer prompts the imagination. Such is not the case. It is important to first realize that all objects in the world are capable of evoking imaginative processes. Considering this, "effective" means that computing systems should prompt people to engage in a process of meaning construction that could be seen as a dialogue between the system authors' intentions, the users' life experiences and understandings, and the broader sociocultural knowledge of both system authors and users. This dialogue should be one that authors, users, and other parties alike would generally agree is constructive, meaningful, and to some degree mutually intelligible. Additionally, there is an aesthetic dimension to such meaning construction that must be taken into account that involves issues like affect, formal structure, beauty, convention, and culture. This type of definition of "effective" will seem woefully inadequate to some traditional scientists and engineers. At the same time, it will seem strangely mechanical to some traditional humanities researchers and artists because the definition is intended to encapsulate a process of determining the "effectiveness" of works that is usually negotiated through processes such as conversations between people, professional and informal criticism, purchasing patterns (in the cases of commodified fine art and popular cultural media), and assessing novelty, quality, and how the work influenced subsequent works. To summarize these processes, "effectively" refers to the ability to engage with the subjective, cultural, and critical dimensions of human imagination. Indeed, this book's title, *Phantasmal Media*, refers to the ways that computational media can be used for the subjective, cultural, and critical aims of prompting humans to generate both individual and shared combinations of sensory imaginative impressions and ideology.

Moving toward our focus on computational media, I shall describe how a diversity of types of creative and cultural media expression including literature, film, and computer games prompt and reveal phantasms—each with implications for computational media that prompt and reveal phantasms more generally. Consider first Jean Toomer's hybrid prose and poetry book *Cane*, which offers a lyrical portrait of the rural South in the United States (Toomer [1923] 1969). *Cane* is one of the most celebrated works to have emerged from the African American cultural movement of the 1920s and 1930s known as the Harlem Renaissance. The work and the movement from which it emerged existed in a complex relationship to the European American literary establishment of the time because of the existing systems of criticism, publication, patronage, prejudice, and nuances related to the identities of authors and audiences alike.

Cane jumps from poetry to prose with abandon, constructing powerful phantasms in part through humanizing lyrical verbal imagery creating portraits of African American life in the southern United States. For example, Toomer's short story "Becky" tells the tale of an outcast, with its refrain "Becky was the white woman who had two Negro sons. She's dead; they're gone away. The pines whisper to Jesus. The Bible flaps its leaves with an aimless rustle on her mound" (Toomer [1923] 1969, 8). Placing the reader in a role that takes part in the collective responsibility for the fate of Becky's sons, the story contains the following passage:

> We, who had cast out their mother because of them, could we take them in? They answered black and white folks by shooting up two men and leaving town. "Goddam the white folks; goddam the niggers," they'd shouted as they left town. Becky? Smoke curled up from her chimney. Nobody noticed it. A creepy feeling came over all who saw that thin wraith of smoke and felt the trembling of the ground. Folks began to take her food again. They quit it soon because they had a

fear. Becky if dead might be a haint, and if alive—it took some nerve even to mention it. (Toomer [1923] 1969, 11)

The sons' curse, "Goddam the white folks; goddam the niggers," cuts against readers who identify with either side of the racial binary opposition set up by Toomer. In conjunction with his verbal imagery, Jean Toomer's quote in Ana Bontemps's introduction to an edition of *Cane* suggests some of the epistemic domains he drew upon in writing such passages, stating:

> Racially, I seem to have (who knows for sure) seven blood mixtures: French, Dutch, Welsh, Negro, German, Jewish, and Indian. Because of these, my position in America has been a curious one. I have lived equally amid the two race groups. Now white, now colored. From my own point of view I am naturally and inevitably an American. I have strived for a spiritual fusion analogous to the fact of racial intermingling. Without denying a single element in me, with no desire to subdue one to the other, I have sought to let them function as complements. I have tried to let them live in harmony. Within the last two or three years, however, my growing need for artistic expression has pulled me deeper and deeper into the Negro group. And as my powers of receptivity increased, I found myself loving it in a way that I could never love the other. It has stimulated and fertilized whatever creative talent I may contain within me. A visit to Georgia last fall was the starting point of almost everything of worth that I have done. (Toomer [1923] 1969, vii–ix)

Cane reveals phantasms because it simultaneously draws concepts from epistemic domains that engage diverse worldviews, including the perspective of an African American person in the rural South, the aesthetic sensibilities of the literary establishment's vanguard of the time, and Toomer's own position as a self-described multiracial insider-outsider in both arenas. In chapter 3 is an example of a computational media–based approach to engaging such phantasms, the AI-based poetry called "The Girl with Skin of Haints and Seraphs," which both prompts and reveals the imaginative origins of phantasms regarding racial binaries.

Another example from literature can be found in Samuel R. Delany's award-winning books of science fiction and fantasy, which are notable for their use of a combination of imaginative world-building, poetic language, experimental structure, and genre-fiction tropes to create highly sophisticated analyses of real-world themes such as identity, sexuality, slavery, and liberation. In other words, he uses verbal imagery to construct and reveal phantasms. Delany's imaginative short story "The Tale of Gorgik" from his *Tales of Nevèrÿon* series constructs a new phantasm for what it means to be civilized and challenges more conventional phantasms for the same. The story uses a swords-and-sorcery world as a setting in which readers first encounter the character Gorgik, an ex-sailor's son with humble beginnings and with a glorious future as Gorgik the Liberator—emancipator of slaves for whom a metal collar is both a symbol of physical oppression and sexual liberation. Gorgik eventually experiences life across a range of social strata, including being enslaved in a brutal mine, indulging a noblewoman as her courtesan, and ultimately becoming a rare truly civilized man (Delany [1979] 1993). "The Tale of Gorgik" draws from epistemic domains for freedom fighting, black masculinity, subaltern sexualities, and the notion of civilization itself to create a specific phantasm of the civilized man. Delany describes Gorgik as "this dark giant, solider, and adventurer, with desires we've not yet named and dreams we've hardly mentioned, who could speak equally of and to barbarian tavern maids and High Court ladies, flogged slaves lost in the cities and provincial nobles at ease on the country estates" (Delany [1979] 1993, 78). By valorizing Gorgik's ability to speak "of and to" all equally, Delany's story prompts a phantasm integrating the image of Gorgik (a "dark giant") with the idea of being able to engage people across all social strata. This notion of being civilized undermines a conventional phantasm that attributes being civilized only to a privileged ruling class whose members are neither giant, nor dark, and who usually have others soldiering and adventuring for them (Delany [1979] 1993). The fantasy story helps readers understand a real-world social issue. It is the issue that people immersed only in the limited worldviews of their own social strata are ultimately trapped by their own phantasms because they can engage with and understand only people in their narrow social milieus rather than with people across the spectrum of human experience. In chapter 5 is an example of computational media practice based on comparatively engaging phantasms of culture and civilization, namely Guillermo Gómez-Peña's artwork that explores the relationship of computer technologies to Latin American and other cultures.

Akira Kurosawa's famous film *Rashomon* (see figure 1.13) is an example of constructing and revealing phantasms in cinema. *Rashomon* is based on Ryunosuke Akutagawa's 1922 short story "In a Grove," the story of a brutal rape and murder that is told and retold from a variety of perspectives, each of which could be considered to be constructed of a series of phantasms (Akutagawa 1999; Kurosawa 1950). This telling and retelling makes *Rashomon* a good example of how phantasms can be

FIGURE 1.13
Kurosawa's *Rashomon* is a film in which the meaningful difference between
multiple narratives reveals the phantasms of different characters.

revealed when juxtaposed with other phantasms. The central event—the rape and
murder—is narrated from vantage points set in the epistemic domains of the ostensible victims, the perpetrator, and a bystander. Each character expresses a phantasm
that constructs a different image of the other characters, conveying who is innocent
or to blame, who is brave or craven, and who is telling the truth or lying. Meaning is
constructed as a blend of the concrete knowledge that the event did take place and
the shifting, conflicting reports given by the characters amid a cinematic forest scene
dappled by shadow and light. The conflicts between the epistemic spaces drawn from
different points of view are used to help reveal the phantasms that imbue the filmic
image of the violent incident with a pathos-laden idea that truth is absent in the irrational world of humans, as exemplified in the following dialogue from *Rashomon*:

Priest: If men don't trust one another, then the earth becomes a hell.
Commoner: Right. The world's a kind of hell.
Priest: No! I don't want to believe that!
Commoner: No one will hear you, no matter how loud you shout. Just think.
Which one of these stories do you believe?
Woodcutter: None makes any sense.
Commoner: Don't worry about it. It isn't as if men were reasonable.
(Kurosawa 1950)

In the examples of works created with the GRIOT system (as discussed in chapters 3 and 6 particularly), and as demonstrated in the examples of *Terminal Time* and *Blue Velvet* in chapters 7 and 8, computational media can use meaningful differences between instances to expressively prompt and reveal phantasms.

It is worthwhile to note here that implementing dynamic experiences that result in meaningful difference is one of the great potentials of computational media. Besides prompting phantasms for art and entertainment (as in computer games) or more utilitarian purposes (as in scientific simulation), computing systems can help *reveal* phantasms. Many computer games allow players to play through stories in multiple ways to compare the results in the endings, such as in the computer role-playing game *Fallout 3*. In games like this, a player might want to know the difference in the outcome of a game based on the sacrifices he or she is willing to make versus those he or she allows others to make (see figure 1.14). If each of these endings is set in a different worldview—that is, drawn from a different epistemic domain and accompanied by different images—the endings have the power to reveal phantasms. I mention another example of a computer game that prompts phantasms—in this case, one expressing notions of life and death—when discussing the computer game *Passage* in chapter 4.

FIGURE 1.14
The game *Fallout 3* tracks the player character's "karma" and uses it to depict the player character's moral state using an icon (left); the contents of the game's ending montage, composed of elements such as an image focused on a nostalgic photo of the player character and his or her father (right), is determined in part by the character's moral state. Images © Bethesda Softworks.

Similarly, computer-based scientific simulations can reveal phantasms by allow-ing people to compare the results of starting the system running with different vari-able values. For example, research in geography has tackled the simulation of riots in ways that reveal "a range of configurations, characters, events, environments, and so on" (Torrens 2012). Such work constitutes a virtual space in which such researchers can explore a complex socio-behavioral system (rioting) and model changes of human emotions in groups over time (see figure 1.15). Such software has social implications for better understanding real-world issues such as the relationships between police

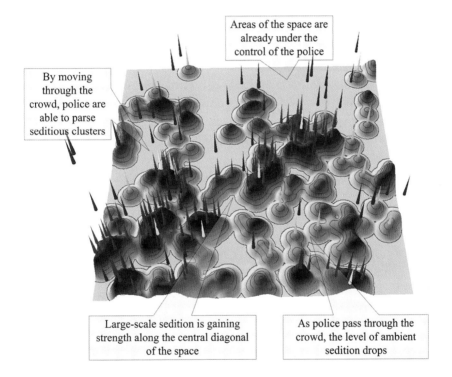

FIGURE 1.15

Research in geography has revealed aspects of rioting using simulation methods based on a geostatistically generated riot model. The colors indicate the following "emotions": relatively high level of grievance (red), relatively moderate level of grievance, tending toward high (yellow), relatively low level of grievance (dark blue), relatively moderate level of grievance, tending toward low (light blue), in addition to a color for police (gray). All of the "emotions" shift as the simulation runs; this graphic is one space-time slice (Torrens and McDaniel 2013).

and other individuals in riot/rebellion situations, along with the roles that subjective factors such as emotions may play in such situations. The types of meaningful difference exhibited by computer games and scientific simulation software are just small instances of the ways in which computational media can help reveal phantasms.

Selves, others, social ills, and everyday experiences, as mentioned earlier in this chapter, along with emotions, culture, beauty, gender, race, privilege, civilization, and power as revealed through these examples of expressive media, are all, in part, feats of human imagination. It bears repeating that imagination is not just "in the head." As the examples of phantasms thus far have illustrated, imaginative cognition involves the body, due to reliance on sensory perception and motor action in the case of interactive systems, other people, artifacts, environments, and immediate situations at hand. Yet as broad as the concept of the phantasm is, it does not refer to all forms of imagination. One advantage to asking a research question focused on understanding and designing computing systems that effectively prompt phantasms is that the question is not limited to addressing just one type of computing system. Although the concept of phantasmal media is especially useful for developing expressive computing systems such as videogames, computer-based artworks, social media applications, and interactive narratives, it is also useful for analyzing and developing more utilitarian computing applications. Later in this book, I discuss how computing systems used for tasks such as for commerce or productivity can also prompt phantasms—integrated epistemic spaces and images spaces immediately apprehended for a purpose at hand.

The definition of "phantasm" described in this chapter is not meant to be exhaustive in articulating the imaginative processes involved in making meaning from computational media. Yet it should be sufficient to provide orientation toward our dual goals of *understanding how computing systems prompt phantasms* and *developing computing systems that can both reveal insidiously oppressive phantasms and prompt positively empowering phantasms alike*. Let us turn our attention now to a more in-depth examination of the roles that computers play in prompting humans to construct and reveal phantasms.

2

IMAGINING AND COMPUTING PHANTASMS

The operations of narrative, like those of mathematics, cannot differ all that much from one people to another, but what can be constructed on the basis of these elementary processes can present unlimited combinations, permutations, and transformations.

—Italo Calvino, *The Uses of Literature*

This book argues that computational media play roles in constructing ideas that we unconsciously accept as true and constitutive of reality yet are in fact imaginatively grounded constructions based in particular worldviews. This view is well explicated by experimental writer Italo Calvino in his essay/lecture "Cybernetics and Ghosts," quoted in the epigraph (Calvino 1982b). Calvino argues that a computing system can play a combinatoric game of words and sentences but cannot produce a revolutionary form without acknowledging the "ghosts" of social values (Calvino 1982b). Calvino's argument rings true in light of insights from cognitive science. That is, understanding the ways that phantasms can be produced using a computer involves bolstering two dimensions of understanding. First, it means better understanding the human imaginative cognition processes that produce social values and, more specifically, phantasms, as well as the related concepts of epistemic domains, epistemic spaces, and image spaces. Second, it requires a better articulation of different computational approaches to prompt them—namely, ways to use computing for subjective, cultural, and critical ends. This chapter shall investigate the two dimensions in turn.

Imagining Phantasms: The Cognitive Basis of Phantasms

This book subscribes to three important observations emerging from cognitive science. The first observation is that cognition is always situated in particular social and cultural contexts (Lave and Wenger 1991). This observation informs the concepts of epistemic domains and spaces, which, as you shall see, very often represent aspects of social and cultural worldviews. The second observation is that cognitive processes may be distributed across aspects of environments, including artifacts, members of social groups, and even time (Hutchins 1996, 2000). This observation informs the concept of image spaces, in which thought is offloaded onto the sensory impressions of an environment (or mental images based on such sensory impressions). The third observation is that "the same neural and cognitive mechanisms that allow us to perceive and move around also create our conceptual systems and modes of reason" (Lakoff and Johnson 1999, 4). This observation informs the concept of phantasms, which integrate perceptual and conceptual thinking. In short, *the concepts introduced in this book are grounded in a perspective that cognition is situated, distributed, and embodied*. This perspective implies that phantasms, as they are outcomes of processes of imaginative cognition, are situated, distributed, and embodied.

To the extent possible, the concept of the phantasm is based only upon accepted empirical results about the mind/brain complex. Adopting this approach for understanding and designing computing systems is also a paradigm shift in computer science research. The technical approach to phantasmal media to be explored later in this book does not attempt to implement a model of creativity (human or computer). Instead, it aims to provide a language for representing the human author's expressive intentions along with users' interactions and phantasms. That is, the goal is to enable human authors to construct phantasmal media works that are informed by accounts of sensory imagistic and conceptual thinking from cognitive science and its subfield of cognitive linguistics.

The cognitive linguistics enterprise offers several theories that provide descriptive accounts oriented toward the types of thought that involve phantasms. As such, let us start by characterizing relevant aspects of the cognitive linguistics enterprise at large before mentioning finer grained concepts. The cognitive linguistics enterprise is dedicated to investigating "the relationship between human language, the mind and socio-physical experience" (Evans, Bergen, and Zinken 2006, 1). In very general terms, the cognitive linguistics enterprise centralizes the fact that language is in service of "constructing and communicating meaning" and provides a window into human cognitive processes (Fauconnier 1999, 96). It is characterized by a rejection of earlier formal approaches to linguistics and by a collection of shared philosophical commitments. Two key philosophical commitments of cognitive linguistics have been described as the "Generalization Commitment" and the "Cognitive Commitment" (Evans, Bergen, and Zinken 2006). The Generalization Commitment refers to a commitment to understanding and describing general principles of human cognitive processes of meaning making. This commitment has led cognitive linguistics researchers to focus upon commonalities among language phenomena and the application of successful methods of investigation to language phenomena at as general a level as is possible. The Cognitive Commitment refers to the goal of finding principles underlying meaning construction in accordance with known and accepted results about the mind/brain complex from a range of disciplines (Evans, Bergen, and Zinken 2006). This commitment challenges cognitive linguistics researchers to ensure that new results "present convergent evidence for the cognitive reality of any proffered model of explanation—whether or not this research is conducted by the cognitive linguist" (Evans, Bergen, and Zinken 2006, 7). Specifically, models of meaning construction should reflect results from the component disciplines of cognitive science such as psychology, neuroscience, philosophy, and artificial intelligence. The approach in this book takes seriously the generalization and cognitive commitments. Additionally, it sometimes uses humanities- and arts-based arguments to address nuanced issues of subjectivity, culture, and critical engagement with the human condition. Hence, the approach here differs from cognitive linguistics endeavors in that rather than focusing on better understanding the human mind, the focus is on better understanding and designing effective computing systems that prompt phantasms and affect real-world social structures.

From this perspective, phantasms are constructed as an outcome of imagination at a number of interrelated levels of cognition, described by philosopher Colin McGinn as (1) percept, (2) memory image, (3) imaginative sensing, (4) productive image, (5) daydream/dream, (6) possibility and negation, (7) meaning (cognitive imagination), and (8) creativity/expressivity (McGinn 2004). The levels of *sensory imagination* and *conceptual imagination* are especially relevant to understanding phantasms. McGinn reminds us: "Sensory imagination employs sensory elements, much as perception does—though, as we have seen, these elements must not be conflated. Cognitive imagination employs conceptual elements, much as thinking does: these elements are not intrinsically modality specific, and combine to form propositional contents. What is in common is the general faculty that works on these elements—the imagination"

(McGinn 2004, 129). Phantasms are products of the imagination that are constructed at the nexus between sensory-imagistic and conceptual thinking. Research in cognitive linguistics can help describe in more detail what is meant by this nexus of sensory imagistic mental processes and the processes of conceptual thinking. A major way that this type of sensory-conceptual, phantasmal thinking is applied is in service to narrative imagining or poetic thought.

The concepts of narrative imagining and poetic thought can be illustrated by drawing upon two quotations. The first quotation, by linguist Roman Jakobson, is as follows: "Poetics deals with problems of verbal structure, just as the analysis of painting is concerned with pictorial structure. Since linguistics is the global science of verbal structure, just as the analysis of painting is concerned with pictorial structure. Since linguistics is the global science of verbal sytructure, poetics may be regarded as an inegral part of linguistics" (Jakobson 1981, 18). Jakobson's poetics addresses what he calls the "poetic function" of verbal art, a concept not limited to forms that are considered to be poetry (Jakobson 1960). For him, expressive linguistic phenomena and their analyses are seen as within the domain of inquiry of linguistics. The second quotation, from a study by cognitive scientists Vyvyan Evans, Benjamin K. Bergen, and Jörg Zinken, is as follows: "Models of language and linguistic organization proposed should reflect what is known about the human mind, rather than purely aesthetic dictates such as the use of particular kinds of formalisms or economy of representation" (Evans, Bergen, and Zinken 2006, 6). For Evans, Bergen, and Zinken, all linguistic phenomena are observable manifestations of human cognitive processes (Evans, Bergen, and Zinken 2006). Taken together, the two quotations suggest that expressive linguistic phenomena are observable manifestations of human imaginative cognitive processes. Because this book is ultimately focused on computational media that may or may not possess all of the chracteristics of expressive linguistic forms such as narrative or poetry from stricly language-oriented traditions, the view of narrative and poetics taken here is necessarily broad, also addressing image-oriented thought.

According to the cognitive linguistics perspective here, narrative imagining (and its component structures and processes) provides basic semantic "building blocks" from which more elaborate forms of expression can be created and made sense of. As there is no consensus definition of the term "narrative" and related terms such as "story," I should further clarify what is meant here by the word "narrative" in the term "narrative imagining." Within cognitive science, Mark Turner (1996) has described stories as dynamic interactions of events, actors, and objects, a quite minimal model aimed at capturing the skeletal pattern underlying narrative imagining. This definition parallels the minimal literary theoretic definition provided by narrative theorist Manfred Jahn (2005), in which stories are sequences of events involving characters, with events including both natural and nonnatural happenings. Jahn also presents a minimal definition of narrative as story that is presented via media. Serving the very broad conception of narrative thinking here, this book shall accept Turner's view of story and at times focus on the presentation of such stories through media. However, in doing so one must realize that it is quite a general description of narrative that would need to be augmented when analyzing the rich conventions, innovations, and meanings expressed in any specific cultural media form. In order to define the building blocks of narrative imagination and poetic thought more precisely in terms relevant to defining phantasms, let us discuss the components of phantasms from the perspective of cognitive linguistics.

The Cognitive Basis of Epistemic Domains

Looking more closely at the cognitive linguistics notion of the domain and several related concepts will assist in explicating the concept of an epistemic domain. Informed by both Ronald Langacker's and George Lakoff's uses of the term "domain," Timothy Clausner and William Croft have produced an excellent synopsis of the notion. They write, "A central principle of cognitive semantics is that concepts do not occur as isolated, atomic units in the mind, but can only be comprehended (by the speaker as well as by the analyst) in a context of presupposed, background knowledge structures. The most generic term for this background knowledge structure is domain" (Clausner and Croft 1999, 2). Additionally, a *domain* can be defined "as a semantic structure that functions as the base for at least one *concept* profile" (6).

The term domain is also closely related to the term "frame." Clausner and Croft's discussion highlights a difference between frames and domains by citing Charles Fillmore's earlier work on *semantic frames* (Fillmore 1985). The primary distinction is that frames are more structured than domains, which were often represented simply as lists of "experientially associated concepts" (Clausner and Croft 1999, 2). This distinction highlights the structural orientation of the concept of frames, which was influenced by the definition of the frame introduced in artificial intelligence research by Marvin Minsky (1975). In artificial intelligence research, a *frame* is a type of data structure used to describe information about the world on the basis of subdivided information about situations (facts about objects and hierarchically structured types of events). Though there are overlaps between the terms "domain" and "frame," generally "frames" refer to more specific and tightly interconnected collections of concepts, such as "toys," which might include dolls, building blocks, and so on, with dolls being further subdivided into categories like action figures, dress-up dolls, and baby dolls, each with relations describing facts such as that action figures, dress-up dolls, and baby dolls each have two legs. In contrast, "domains" generally refer to broader collections of concepts such as "law," "race," or "art."

A final term related to both frames and domains is the *idealized cognitive model* (ICM). The term provides a similar function but is oriented toward a focus on cognition situated in particular contexts. Clausner and Croft refer to idealized cognitive models as being developed by George Lakoff "to describe how the background knowledge for some concepts, such as bachelor and mother, involves an idealized model of experience, and that some categorization problems (e.g., Is the Pope a bachelor?, or Who is the 'real' mother if birth, genetics, nurturance, marriage, or genealogical conditions of maternity diverge?) arise from a mismatch between the ICM and a more complex reality" (Clausner and Croft 1999, 2). The focus on external realities with the concept of the ICM is perhaps closest to the intended application of the concept of the epistemic domain with its focus on worldview. Epistemic domains are intended to highlight issues of individual subjectivity and cultural knowledge and beliefs as they relate to one another. Integrating aspects of the definitions of domain, frame, and ICM in light of this focus, I shall define an epistemic domain as a semantic structure for a worldview that functions as the base for at least one epistemic space.

The Cognitive Basis of Epistemic Spaces

There are several cognitive science theories relevant to the concept of epistemic spaces. Conceptual metaphor theory proposes that the understanding of many basic abstract concepts relies upon metaphorical thinking and analogy, and that metaphorical thinking arises from embodied human experience of the world (Johnson 1987; Lakoff and Johnson 1999; Varela, Thompson, and Rosch 1991). George Lakoff, Mark Johnson, Mark Turner, and others have studied metaphor as mappings from one concept, which they call a "conceptual space," to another. These researchers have shown that there are many basic metaphors that people use to express everyday concepts (Lakoff and Johnson 1980; Lakoff and Turner 1989). These basic metaphors are often structured by image schemas, "skeletal patterns" that recur in motor-sensory experiences such as "Motion along a Path," or "More Is Up" as expressed respectively by metaphors such as "Life Is a Journey," or "Good Is Up." Epistemic spaces are akin to such everyday concepts, with the distinction that they are based in particular worldviews. Paralleling the comparison between epistemic domains, as the term is used here, and the more general term "domain," *epistemic spaces are conceptual spaces that represent aspects of worldviews*. In other words, epistemic spaces are smaller scaled concepts drawn from epistemic domains. Furthermore, just as concepts can be mapped onto one another in the case of metaphor, epistemic spaces can be mapped on to one another as well.

Conceptual blending theory builds upon Gilles Fauconnier's theory of mental spaces and elaborates insights from metaphor theory (Fauconnier 1985, 2006; Fauconnier and Lakoff 2011; Fauconnier and Sweetser 1996). Fauconnier and Turner's conceptual blending theory describes the means by which concepts are integrated, guided by "uniform structural and dynamic principles," both in everyday thought and in more complex abstract thought such as in literary arts or rhetoric (Fauconnier and Turner 2002). Conceptual blending networks are composed of concepts (described as "conceptual spaces") and "mappings" between them. Blending can be used to describe metaphors as well as to describe combinations of concepts that are more complex than a single metaphor. Conceptual blending theory has been criticized as using ad hoc and overly broad explanations (Gibbs 2000). Conceptual blending theory has also been defended regarding the same as mining for "golden-events" (exemplary phenomena resulting in a theory that comprehensively covers even challenging cases) and being supported by a convergence of data from psychology, AI, sociology, literature, and philosophy (Coulson and Oakley 2000). Regardless of the state of this debate, conceptual blending theory provides an account that can help explain how epistemic spaces and image spaces are integrated to result in phantasms. It also offers a structured descriptive language for such phenomena, aspects of which are even amenable to formalization and implementation (which I have used for building interactive and generative multimedia narrative and poetry systems). Fauconnier and Turner assert that the process of blending is structured by sets of "constitutive" and "governing" principles that exert pressure to produce optimal blends. The constitutive principles describe the structure of conceptual integration networks and the process of blending, while the governing principles optimize emergent structure in the blends all "other things being equal" (Fauconnier and Turner 2002). These principles hold for articulating the constraints under which epistemic spaces can be integrated both with other epistemic spaces and also with image spaces.

Conceptual metaphor and blending theories can help in understanding narrative imagining and poetic thought such as mentioned earlier. Narrative imagining and poetic thought rely upon a host of cognitive operations, including sequence recognition and construction, categorization of objects and events, projection of image schemas, and more. The metaphor and conceptual blending processes discussed previously play central roles (Turner 1996). For example, blends can integrate input spaces from different, even clashing, organizing frames; such blends are called "double-scope blends" (Fauconnier and Turner 2002). When these input spaces represent story elements, the blended results are "double-scope stories" (Turner 2003). Such blends can be multiplied, as Turner has shown with several examples of double-scope stories featuring an astounding succession of blending operations in which characters magically, metaphorically transform from one entity to another (Turner 2003, 2004). One of his examples is the song "O, Magali" from Frédéric Mistral's *Mireille*, which contains a sequence in which a suitor pursues the object of his affection, only to have her transform into a different entity to escape him. He transforms to capture her; she transforms to escape again, and so on in a spiraling competitive conversation:

> —If you become a fish, I will become a fisherman.
> —Well then I will become a bird and fly away.
> —Then I will become a hunter and hunt you.
> —Then I will become a flowering herb in the wild.
> —Then I will become water and sprinkle you.
> —Then I will become a cloud and float away to America.
> —Then I will become the sea breeze and carry you.
> (Turner 2003, 136)

Turner's account of "O, Magali" and similar stories is especially useful here because it considers how such work can possibly achieve meaningful impact upon users as they project these metaphorical narratives onto the real-life experiences of phenomena like courtship. In the case of "O, Magali," a phantasm is prompted that refers to a type of aggressive courtship. An epistemic space drawn from an epistemic domain about courtship is blended and reblended with a series of image spaces evoked by verbal imagery about fishing, hunting, flower gardening, the sky, and so on.

Empirical research in cognitive linguistics suggests that the ways humans generate and express epistemic spaces through language and media are only the observable result of processes in which humans draw upon "a vast array of cognitive resources" involving "innumerable models and frames, set up multiple connections, coordinate large arrays of information, engage in creative mappings, transfers, and elaborations" (Fauconnier 1999, 96). It is this array of cognitive resources that underlies the construction of phantasms. Gilles Fauconnier has referred to these process of meaning construction as "backstage cognition" and asserts that backstage cognition includes specific phenomena such as "viewpoints and reference points, figure-ground/profile-bases/landmark-trajector organization, metaphorical, analogical, and other mappings, idealized models, framing, construal, mental spaces, counterpart connections, roles, prototypes, metonymy, polysemy, conceptual blending, fictive motion, [and] force dynamics" (Fauconnier 1999, 96). The assertion that many aspects of backstage cognition are based upon shared cognitive structures or operate on the basis of general principles is referred to as "operational uniformity" (Fauconnier 1999). On this basis, the cognitive linguistics approach to defining phantasms can be seen as a philosophical and methodological acceptance of empirical evidence suggesting operational uniformity for such a wide range of cognitive phenomena.

A convergence of research supports understanding the bases of epistemic spaces in cognition; this research includes the following observations cited by Fauconnier:

> Backstage cognition operates in many ways uniformly at all levels. . . . Narrative structure (Saunders & Redeker, 1996), in signed and spoken languages, and of course many aspects of non-linguistic cognition. Metaphor builds up meaning all the way from the most basic levels to the most sophisticated and creative ones (Lakoff & Turner, 1989; Grady, Oakley, & Coulson, 1999). And the same goes from metonymic pragmatic functions (Nunberg, 1978) and mental space connections (Fauconnier & Sweetser, 1996; Liddell, 1996; Van Hoek, 1997) . . . Conceptual blending and analogy play a key role in syntax and morphology (Mandelbilt, 1997), in word and sentence level semantics, and at higher levels of reasoning and rhetoric (Coulson, 1997; Robert, 1998; Turner, 1996). Similarly, we find force dynamics and fictive motion (Talmy, 1985, 1998) operating at all levels. (Fauconnier 1999, 100–101)

Readers unfamiliar with these concepts should focus on these examples as illustrating a convergence of approaches and data supporting the notion of backstage cognition in processes involved in phantasm construction—ideas that are commonly accepted by cognitive linguists. Although these examples represent a convergence of data in light of the commitments of cognitive linguistics, our understandings of the cognitive science basis of phantasms must continually develop as new evidence comes in, new theories are generated, and further groundings in neuroscience are discovered.

As mentioned previously, although the approach in this book accepts the cognitive and generalization commitments, ultimately it is the arts and humanities that best describe nuanced issues of subjectivity, culture, and critical engagement with the human condition. Hence, the approach here differs from cognitive linguistics endeavors in that rather than trying to produce scientific results to better understand the human mind, instead the focus is on *using cognitive science results to provide better understandings to guide design of effective computing systems that prompt phantasms and impact real-world social structure*. As such, epistemic spaces represent a structured way of looking at conceptual spaces focused on worldview because it allows for such critical engagement with individual and social understandings of the world.

The Cognitive Basis of Image Spaces

It is possible now to begin a more detailed discussion of the aspect of phantasms called image spaces. Visual studies researcher W. J. T. Mitchell (1987) has stated that "fantasmata" are conscious mental images that constitute a range of meaning phenomena. They are imaginative meanings, but crucially are not restricted to language. They can refer to embodied sensations, cultural contexts, and more abstract ideas. Certainly, engaging with media artifacts often involves the mental work of interpretation. Yet the focus of the concept of phantasmal media is on types of computing systems that prompt narrative and poetic thinking to better understand phenomena in the world. Mitchell (1987) has argued that mental images are closely related to visual images and verbal images as well. He argues that "contrary to common belief, images 'proper' are not stable, static, or permanent in any metaphysical sense; they are not perceived in the same way by viewers any more than are dream images; and they are not exclusively visual in any important way, but involve multisensory apprehension and interpretation" (Mitchell 1987, 13–14).

Mitchell's conception of images builds on ideas of the philosopher Ludwig Wittgenstein, who famously has argued that mental images of things people communicate to others, such as shapes, colors, and sounds in the world, are all based on our actual sensory experiences of shapes, colors, sounds, and so on (Wittgenstein 1965). Mitchell's argument acknowledges that this is a controversial assertion and that mental images and physical images seem to be quite different from one another on the surface. His argument also acknowledges the difficulty of proving the assertion because mental images are not directly observable (as physical images and writing are):

Two things must immediately strike the notice of anyone who tries to take a general view of the phenomena called by the name of imagery. The first is simply the wide variety of things that go by this name. We speak of pictures, statues, optical illusions, maps, diagrams, dreams, hallucinations, spectacles, projections, poems, patterns, memories, and even ideas as images, and the sheer diversity of this list would seem to make any systematic, unified understanding impossible. The second thing that may strike us is that the calling of all these things by the name of "image" does not necessarily mean that they all have something in common. It might be better to begin by thinking of images as a far-flung family which has migrated in time and space and undergone profound mutations in the process. (Mitchell 1987, 9)

Having described this family of images, illustrated in figure 2.1, Mitchell observes that the various branches of this "family" tree are each studied by individual academic fields. For example, psychologists and philosophers might study mental imagery, while art historians study graphical and sculptural images.

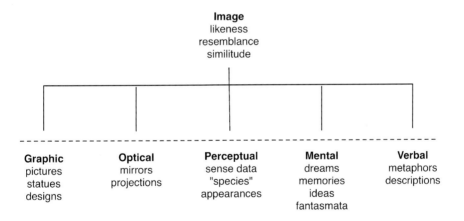

FIGURE 2.1
W. J. T. Mitchell has diagrammed a family of images as shown here (Mitchell 1987, 10).

However, there is a blurred boundary that can be revealed between all of these types of images. Mitchell states that

> perceptual images occupy a kind of border region where physiologists, neurologists, psychologists, art historians, and students of optics find themselves collaborating with philosophers and literary critics. This is the region occupied by a number of strange creatures that haunt the border between physical and psychological accounts of imagery . . . the fantasmata, which are revived versions of those impressions called up by the imagination in the absence of the objects that originally stimulated them. (Mitchell 1987, 10)

Image spaces, as defined in this book, are "fantasmata" and their relations in Mitchell's family of images that work in conjunction with conceptual thinking in the form of epistemic spaces. In other words, image spaces describe cases in which sense-making processes have been *distributed* onto images. In such cases, images act to provide representations that support human imagining. These representations involve not only cultural structure (such as I would say is provided by epistemic spaces) but also, as cognitive scientist Edwin Hutchins argues, material structure. In other words, image spaces allow us to consider how the forms of images trigger further imaginative processes.

Important in understanding how phantasms involve both concepts and images in the world is the idea of distributed cognition: the notion that human thinking depends on and is structured not only by individuals' physical bodies, but also by the environments in which those bodies are acting. In this view, images in the world and actions of other agents in the world shape thought. The notion of distributed cognition, as described by Hutchins, asserts that material structures like marks or diagrams, called "material anchors," can provide us with stable images for complex mental operations. Examples of this are calculations made on paper or navigation with a compass (Hutchins 1996, 2005). For example, when using a compass, it is not necessary to hold a mental image of a dial in one's mind. One can merely watch the needle move and the compass dial can be its own representation. People can think using the world as its own representation, and the structure found in the world in turn shapes their thinking: in this manner, material images shape phantasms. Hutchins's arguments for material anchors mainly focus on human-performed instrumental and operational tasks, so his material anchors have to be stable and faithful representations of the elements to be manipulated in the cognitive process. Hutchins explains:

Reasoning processes require stable representations of constraints. There are two principal ways to achieve stability in conceptual models. First, the conceptual models that anthropologists call cultural models achieve representational stability via a combination of intrapersonal and interpersonal processes. Second, the association of conceptual structure with material structure can stabilize conceptual representations. This is an old and pervasive cognitive strategy. Conceptual blending theory provides a useful framework for considering the joint contributions and mutual constraints of mental and material structure. Projecting material structure into a blended space can stabilize the conceptual blend. I call an input space from which material structure is projected into a blend a 'material anchor' for the blend. The term material anchor is meant to emphasize the stabilizing role of the material structure. (Hutchins 2005, 1555)

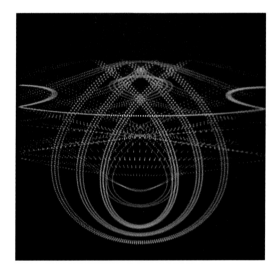

FIGURE 2.2
John Whitney's analog computer-based work "Arabesque"
presents dynamic patterns (Whitney 1975).

The notion of image spaces builds upon this idea but also acknowledges that the material structures of external objects perceived in the world can be inherited by the structures of mental or verbal images.

The notion of a material anchor alone may be insufficient to account for cases in which the medium is dynamic or the sense-making processes are not task specific and clear beforehand, such as in engaging with computer-based art forms. Take the example of computer animation. Animated visual images transgress the boundary between the material and the imaginative. They build upon viewers' motor-sensory perceptions and evoke embodied understandings of sensations. When engaging with a work like John Whitney's early computer animation "Arabesque" (1975), shown in figure 2.2,[1] a great deal of meaning-making happens at the level of the image space.

In "Arabesque," colorized lines dance and twirl around each other in a striking pattern while companied by a seductive soundtrack. Taking pleasure in the colorful patterns on the screen is a type of direct perceptual apprehension captured by the notion of the image space. Kenny Chow and I have argued that neuroscientific results can also help in understanding how people make meaning from works like "Arabesque" (Chow and Harrell 2009b). While being careful not to overstate these claims, results regarding the activation of brain structures known as mirror neurons have had profound implications in understanding the relationship between doing and seeing. These results have suggested that when perceiving a performed action in a moving image, the viewer's interpretation relies upon unconsciously recalling corresponding sensorimotor knowledge from a repertoire of her or his own embodied experiences (Rizzolatti and Sinigaglia 2008). The viewer's potential understanding of the sensuous undulation of the lines in "Arabesque" as being like dancing is prompted by immediate sensory experience in light of previous experiences of dance. This kind of visceral understanding largely takes place at the immediate, or even preconscious, level—requiring minimal cognitive effort.

Kenny Chow and I introduced the term *elastic anchor* to describe material artifacts that specifically evoke imaginative processes through their dynamic material forms (Chow and Harrell 2009b). *An elastic anchor is a dynamic material anchor that holds information in place, but not in shape.* As Hutchins did when he highlighted the role of the compass in mental processes involved in navigation at sea, we start by asserting that there are important relationships between material images and mental images. For elastic anchors, the subtle difference between the visceral sensation represented by the animated image and the mental image engenders nuanced types of imagination. Elastic anchors are especially adaptable and elaborative because a user might interpret his or her motor input differently each time depending on the feed-back provided by the work. For an interactive system, animated feedback often defines, or redefines, the meaning of the motor input action that triggered it.

In summary, elastic anchors are characterized by the following properties:

• Material-based imagining: they consist of material images.

• Imagination triggering: they "hold" dynamic information or sensation in place for perceivers, yielding imaginative images.

• Action inviting: they "invite" perceivers to take motor action, such as interaction using a graphical user interface.

• Motor-sensory connecting: they constitute iterative motor-sensory feedback loops, such as those in sketching of architectural designs, pencil testing of hand-drawn animation, engaging in shadow play, or previewing real-time computer animation.

• Spatiotemporal patterning: when the motor-sensory feedback loop runs spontaneously and continuously, as in computer animation, they provide not only spatial and structural patterns, but also temporal patterns.

Chow and I argue that material-based imagination is pervasive in today's computational media (Chow and Harrell 2009b), and I assert here that they are at the core of understanding how many subjective computing systems convey meaning.

When analyzing computational media, understanding the nature of elastic anchors is useful because it can help account for the dynamic natures of image spaces in computational media. However, what is needed to more completely account for the types of phantasm prompting and revealing computational media focused upon here is the new concept of the *phantasmal anchor*, building upon the terms "material anchor" and "elastic anchor." The difference is that in the case of a phantasmal anchor, material-based imagination can also be internalized and rehearsed through mental or verbal imagery based on prior experience of dynamic material structures. In such cases, the imagination is not offloaded onto the environment but rather the constraints from the environment (static or dynamic) have been internalized, yet are still processed like sensory imagination rather than conceptual imagination. Because image spaces can be material, elastic, and phantasmal anchors, they support the notion of image here that spans Mitchell's entire family of images from graphic to verbal. Phantasms are produced when conceptual information from epistemic spaces is distributed onto (or one could say "integrated with") image spaces, whether they are static graphics, dynamic animations, or mental or verbal images prompted by reading a website or playing a computer game.

The Subjective, Cultural, and Critical Natures of Phantasms

I now take a moment to reiterate the definition of phantasms in updated terms. *Phantasms are blends of epistemic spaces and image spaces through backstage cognition processes; these processes operate at the levels of both sensory imagining and conceptual thought and occur in understanding aspects of the world ranging from basic events to complicated forms, such as work in the arts.* Based on the focus of this book, let us turn our attention to understanding the subjective, cultural, and critical natures of phantasms. The concept of the phantasm focuses attention on social and cultural illusions in which people are all immersed.[2] In the work of Gilles Deleuze (1990), the phantasm often seems to oppress and confine people; you shall see later in this book that phantasms can be used to both oppress and empower. Indeed, senses of identity, community, and values, which often become quite divisive, arise from the phantasmal. Yet constructing learning to recognize phantasms and to create new and empowering ones, akin to what linguist Otto Santa Ana (2002) calls "insurgent metaphors," can help design media with empowering and critically aware aims. Such ideas reveal that phantasmal media are not limited to the potentially disempowering effects of indoctrinating with the mainstream values of the privileged in society, but they also can produce empowering effects by constructing plays of ideas in order to question or even change social order for the better.

For example, normative social categories of nationality, gender, or profession are constituted by epistemic domains. The epistemic spaces drawn from these epistemic domains are not based in sets of objective characteristics but are imaginative and metaphorical constructions that define "normal" behaviors and appearances. The mental images that people then associate with those imaginative constructions are phantasms. The fallout is that social norms are defined by these phantasms. To give a brief example, a norm reinforced by this type of process could be the mental image of a sober engineer informed by the idea that "all engineers lack understanding of the arts." In this case, the norm is constituted by a phantasm for a nonartistic engineer, ignoring the existence of art-oriented engineering applications and practitioners in the broader epistemic spaces. Yet, more important for those of us interested in empowerment than computing system's participation in reinforcing normative idealized cognitive models, *computational phantasms* can also help attack the normative "ghosts" of misleading idealized cognitive models such as stereotypes and prompt the construction of more equitable alternatives.

Computing Phantasms

Prompting computational phantasms that can help disrupt oppressive social norms and empower people entails revealing the imaginative nature of social constructions that people navigate in everyday life. Image spaces give phantasms salience and sensory structure; however, the conceptual aspects of phantasms are what predominantly convey ideology. If a computer generates a phrase such as "race and gender," that phrase might prompt a user to imagine certain types of people. The phrase prompts phantasms, but the specific phantasms prompted are not fully determined. The phrase might simultaneously prompt one user to conjure up a network of ideas and impressions associated with unbridled liberalism, identity politics, minority subjects, marginal social issues, guilt, and indignation while prompting another user to conjure up clouds of ideas and impressions of oppression by the privileged, social justice, activist politics, people of color, positive diversity, and cultural awareness. Both are phantasms; they just come from differing political sides of the same social reality, which can be revealed only when looked at from multiple users' perspectives. Computers can improvisationally and dynamically combine media elements in new ways, at the same time as responding to user interaction, thus allowing the juxtaposition of phantasms necessary to make those phantasms visible. This process always involves both human interpretation of meaning and the limited types of formal symbol manipulation possible on a computer. Understanding and designing systems to negotiate this balance between ghostly, subjective human meaning-making and computational data structures and algorithms is the key to using the computer to prompt effective phantasms. Such meaning construction processes also underlie many uses of the computer for expressive purposes.

One of the first notable uses of the word "expressive" in high-profile computing research is the term "expressive AI" (and later "expressive intelligence") coined by Michael Mateas (2001) to refer to the use of AI techniques for artistic goals such as interactive drama. This concept builds upon the work of computer science practitioners interested in technologies to support the arts such as Joseph Bates, Bruce Blumberg, and Ken Perlin; it also tries to encompass the works of practitioners such as Harold Cohen, who described his autonomous painting system, Aaron, as actually learning, and George Lewis, who describes his autonomous and collaborative improvisational music system, Voyager, in more culturally situated terms based in aesthetic practices of the African diaspora (Bates 1992; Blumberg and Galyean 1995; Cohen 2002; Lewis 2000; Perlin and Goldberg 1996). Expressive computing research also has roots in the ideas of thinkers who describe expressive computational forms based in part on the characteristics of the medium (as described below) such as Espen Aarseth and Janet Murray (Aarseth 1997; Murray 1997). These ideas have been expanded upon by other researchers' ideas focused on the procedural nature of the medium, such as Ian Bogost's procedural rhetoric and Noah Wardrip-Fruin's expressive processing (Bogost 2007; Wardrip-Fruin 2009). The aim of this book is aligned with expressive AI and computing endeavors, but this book takes a cognitive turn focused on human imagination—again, with the understanding that cognitive science no longer explores only what is "inside the head" or how computers can model the mind.

I shall not argue in favor of any singular vision for how computer systems can be used more effectively for expression, nor shall I argue for a singular new or definitive genre or form of expressive computational narrative, poetry, virtual worlds, social media platforms, or any related type of computing system. Rather, I present a perspective on how one might better understand and design systems that negotiate the interplay between human meaning and machine information structure and processing so as to create new poignant, specific, novel, and creative forms of expression (and even to understand and design more utilitarian systems that have an impact on society). The computer is humble in its limited capability to capture and express the elusive world of human imagination. Human imagination is expansive, with blurry boundaries between conscious and unconscious meanings, between discourse and affect, and between sensory perception and mental imagery. This does not mean that the imagination cannot be increasingly apprehended through science. Yet science may never be able to predict or control imagination, even if scientists can understand and model an increasing number of its underlying processes and biological structures. Science's role is not to provide subjective interpretations of human cultural artifacts and ideas. Social, cultural, and aesthetic meanings will always be subjective issues, and it is important to choose the most appropriate means of addressing them. Understanding the roles of phantasms is important in finding ways to address these meanings.

Presenting the concept of phantasmal media as a lens through which to understand how computing systems can prompt the imagination, and thereby affect social reality, bears a set of risks. This goal is more intangible and more difficult to define than describing and theorizing a singular well-known media form such as Hollywood cinema, a set of related forms such as in computer gaming, or even a lofty cultural vision such as "technology to support international development." Rather, this book presents a way to think about the computer and its current and future roles in society. This approach centralizes culture and content. This approach is an invitation for others to consider how to centralize the roles of imaginative content and social reality in computing research and practices.

The concept of the phantasm is based in research accounts of cognition, art traditions across media, computer science, cultural theory, and social power relationships, synthesizing and reconciling concerns from each area. The argument in this book uses this theoretical and scientific grounding for both descriptive and prescriptive purposes; it uses an interdisciplinary theoretical framework to envision how the computer has an impact on our lives through analysis of examples from media forms such as literature, videogames, computer-based art, and commercial software systems, and it outlines a vision of how the computer can powerfully play a role in prompting the imagination and even empowering people in the future.

Beyond Characteristics of Computational Media

There are many ways to analyze computational media and how they can be used in imaginative ways. For this reason, it will be useful to highlight several important previous approaches, which in turn can illuminate the distinctions of the phantasmal media approach. One approach to analyzing computational media has been to describe material characteristics and affordances—that is, the qualities of objects that enable actions involving them (Gibson 1977)—of the computer as a conveyor of information and comparing its modes of information conveyance to those of other media. Yet in this book, the focus is on *how* the characteristics and affordances of computational media can be effectively deployed for expression. For example, the notion of *expressive epistemologies* to be introduced in chapter 3 enables examination of how diverse knowledge representation techniques can support subjective expression. This focus on *how computers can be used effectively for expression* instead of *what the characteristics of the computer are as a medium* is a contrast to some previous research that asks questions such as what makes the computer differ as a medium from film or the book. Likewise, the concept of *agency play* to be introduced in chapter 7 does not suggest only that user agency is a characteristic of the medium. Rather, it explores *how* the dynamics and scope of the relationship between the user and the system agency can be effectively designed to evoke aesthetic phenomena (Harrell and Zhu 2009). This expression-oriented perspective, however, is enabled only by the media-centric ("*what*") analyses that other theorists have ingeniously explored.

Approaches focused on describing the nature of the computer as a medium are important because of the observation that computational media have the facility to represent (if imperfectly and with differing materiality) other media forms ranging from the printed page to ancient games like Go (Hayles 1993). The term "metamedium" has been used to describe cross-medial relationships since Marshall McLuhan's early analyses, and these relationships have been articulated with greater nuance via the concept of remediation in the work of Jay Bolter and Richard Grusin (Bolter and Grusin 1999; McLuhan 1964). Bolter and Grusin explore complex persistences and tangled discontinuities between old and contemporary media as media forms emerge. Yet Bolter and Grusin have also critically examined this approach's historical antecedents, for example, by citing an essentializing view of painting focused on articulating the essence of the medium (due to Stanley Cavell, Clement Greenberg, and Michael Fried) that asserted "one of the defining characteristics of modernist painting is its insistence on acknowledging the conditions of its own medium" (Bolter and Grusin 1999, 58). That point of view might celebrate an abstract expressionist painting that treats paint "as paint" at the expense of a more figurative painting focused on myth and symbolism. Bolter and Grusin's discussion of that view of painting is useful because it reveals how perspectives focused on the characteristics of the medium can have the side effect of marginalizing works and viewpoints that do not seek to engage what are seen (by someone else's viewpoint) as the most essential aspects of the medium.

Three thinkers have been especially important in their efforts to describe the characteristics of computational media for the purposes of this book. The first of these, inspirationally influential in the field, is digital media theorist Janet Murray. Murray developed a set of characteristics of computational media. She also demonstrated these to be especially relevant for the analysis and production of interactive narrative systems (Murray 1997). She defined the four essential properties of digital environments as

• *procedural* and *participatory* (based on algorithmic processes and involving user action, which jointly give rise to *interactivity*), and

• *spatial* and *encyclopedic* (which jointly give rise to *immersion*).

In contrast, the second of these thinkers, art theorist Lev Manovich (2001), focused on computational media forms both narrative and otherwise, proposed a different set of characteristics of computational media in general:

• *numerical representation* (a computational media object can be described mathematically and is subject to algorithmic manipulation),

• *modularity* (computational media are collections of discrete samples, often with hierarchical structure),

• *automation* (computational media enable automation of aspects of creation, manipulation, and access),

- *variability* (computational media objects can be presented in multiple ways), and

- *transcoding* (making sense of computational media occurs at both machinic and cultural levels).

The third of these thinkers is game studies scholar Espen Aarseth, who, like Murray, was motivated to understand how literary concerns manifest themselves in computational media, and who devised a taxonomy for digital texts (broadly construing the term "text"; Aarseth 1997). Aarseth's variables take a starting point related to Manovich's principle of variability, which focuses on the ability of the computer to present media texts in various ways (the separation of form and content—with content often described as being composed of individual media elements called "assets"). Aarseth's focus is on describing the mechanisms by which information is generated or revealed and presented to users based on underlying information such as code and media assets. Based on these mechanisms, which he terms "traversal functions," Aarseth (1997) devised a set of seven variables to describe digital texts summarized as follows:

- *dynamics* (a text may be *static* or *dynamic* in several ways—with a fixed or variable number of assets),

- *determinability* (a text is *determinate* if presentation of elements always occurs in the same order; otherwise, the text is *indeterminate*),

- *transiency* (a text is transient if the passage of time causes it to be presented differently; otherwise, the text is is intransient),

- *perspective* (a text is personal if it requires the user to play a strategic role as a character in the world described by the text; otherwise, it is impersonal),

- *access* (if all possible presentations of assets are readily available to the user at all times, then the text is *random access*; otherwise, it is *controlled access*),

- *linking* (a text may be organized with *links* that are always available for the user to follow, *conditional links* that can be followed only if certain conditions are met, or neither),

- *user functions* (all texts feature a user function called *interpretation*; a text may also feature *explorative functions*, in which the user must decide which path to take, and *configurative functions*, in which presentation of assets is in part generated by the user's actions).

Murray's Principles of Digital Environments	Manovich's Principles of New Media	Aarseth's Variables for Describing Digital Texts
• Procedural • Participatory • Spatial • Encyclopedic	• Numerical representation • Modularity • Automation • Variability • Transcoding	• Dynamics • Determinability • Transiency • Perspective • Access • Linking • User function

FIGURE 2.3
Several important approaches to characterizing computational media forms are shown here.

Aaseth's approach is taxonomic, resulting in exactly 576 precise descriptions of the nature of digital texts. The rubrics of Murray, Manovich, and Aarseth are all summarized in figure 2.3.

There is significant overlap between the three rubrics. Murray's procedural property contains elements of each of Manovich's categories. In this regard, Manovich's characteristics can be said to refine the notion of the procedural nature of the medium. However, numerical representation and modularity also contribute to the encyclopedic nature of digital environments, so one cannot simply say that any of these approaches contains another within just one of its categories. Murray's encyclopedic property is enabled by increases in the capacity of data storage hardware, the economy of data representations, and the efficiency of accessing data. In contrast, Manovich's set of characteristics seems primarily concerned with the nature of software itself rather than Murray's more specific focus on digital environments—that is, Murray is more concerned with structure apparent to users, whereas Manovich's work moves closer to addressing the underlying computer code.

The properties and characteristics proposed by all three authors offer insights into general affordances offered uniquely by computational media for producing cultural artifacts. Each author's framework operates at a different grain size, and they vary in their degrees of specificity and adherence to categories used within computer science. Hence the frameworks are useful when taken together. It is important to combine the focus on the division between user experience and data/code of Aarseth with the more software-oriented analysis of Manovich and the user experience/digital environment–oriented analysis of Murray. However, the argument in this book is influenced less by top-down views of categorization that taxonomies represent than by an aim of accounting for how frameworks of media characteristics can be developed in order to yield specific types of insights regarding different types of media artifact, which can be considered at different levels of abstraction for different purposes. This less taxonomic approach is instead focused on thinking of *prototypical media examples*[3] that best exemplify the media phenomenon at hand for particular analyses. For example, broad grained arguments about how media assets can be modularly combined—say, rules for choosing which scene should come next in an interactive digital video—might benefit from an analysis of formal languages (quite abstract rule systems describing how data can be presented). Yet in order to analyze how a specific media production application might produce recognizable aesthetic sensibilities such as a "William Burroughs cut-up style" or a "Hollywood cinematic style," perhaps consideration of how the application's traits arise from the programming languages used to implement it would prove useful, as I have argued previously (Harrell 2004). To discuss richly narrative computer-based works, one might highlight a combination of the characteristics discussed by Murray and Aarseth.

The prototypical computational media form of interest to a literary theorist may be different than those that concern a computer scientist, so it is useful that the characteristics of computational media can be described at varying levels of specificity or technicality. This adaptable approach embodies an observation core to the phantasmal media perspective. Rather than attempting to supersede the accounts of Murray, Manovich, or Aarseth (and others), here I consider how such theories can be targeted and comparatively invoked to help in better understanding meaning making involving computational media. I aim to develop theoretical perspectives aimed less at defining characteristics and more at understanding *how computational media characteristics can be effectively used to prompt construction of imaginative and expressive meanings*, which is the aim here with the idea of phantasmal media.

Three Approaches to Phantasmal Media

Phantasmal media are media systems that prompt phantasms. This book focuses on computational phantasmal media systems, and hereafter in the book the term "phantasmal media" shall generally refer to computing systems (although thinkers interested in addressing other media may find the term useful as well). Ultimately, the ensuing discussion of phantasmal media here is about the artful nature of computing systems. Phantasmal media systems have the capacity to create new phantasms while prompting or challenging users' preexisting phantasms. A special way that the computer can serve this function is through its ability to model dynamic systems that enable active user participation. This modeling can be an especially powerful use of the computer to have an impact on society when system development is coupled with cultural and critical awareness. Phantasmal media forms offer powerful possibilities for affecting people's lives through construction of imaginative worlds that enable empowering, evocative, and critically challenging social transformation. My vision of the possibilities of phantasmal media puts aside distinctions between highbrow and lowbrow art. It also puts aside distinctions between "fundamental" and application-oriented computing research, because socially and culturally oriented aims do not involve just finding new uses for existing computing systems; instead, I call for actually implementing new socioculturally engaged systems.[4] It also puts aside discussions that seek to locate computational works in a trajectory of American/European succession of art movements and/or engineering research trends. Instead, it is a vision of how computing systems can facilitate new possibilities of catalyzing the human imagination while also attempting to understand the cognitive and social processes involved in these imaginings.

The concept of phantasmal media is also intended to help researchers think about system development in a new way. Just as a goal of developing higher-level programming languages is to allow computer scientists to think in terms of problems and solutions as opposed to algorithmic steps, a goal of this approach is to enable developers[5] to think in terms of a range of improvisational interactions that systems may engage in with users, rather than designing every interaction explicitly. This design-oriented part of the argument is a speculative aspect of the book, envisioning both expressive and utilitarian possibilities enabled by approaching computational media in this way.

The idea of phantasmal media is not purely about some idealized form of computing system. Many computing systems are already aimed at prompting what I call phantasms, especially the types of expressive computing systems being developed in areas such as gaming, computer-based art,[6] and computational narrative.[7] Currently, many researchers and developers of such systems are trying to figure out ways to dynamically structure building blocks for expression that consist of assets such as paragraphs, pages, bitmaps, sprites, scenes, video or audio files, or computer-generated imagery (CGI). In contrast, the concept of phantasmal media is intended to help facilitate researchers and developers thinking in terms of *meanings*. These meanings are then instantiated into data structures that are computationally amenable *in light of theoretical considerations concerning how they might prompt users' subjective phantasms.*

Algorithms become strategies for composing meanings in ways that structure output and help constrain the types of phantasms the system might prompt. Such algorithms often work behind the scenes of interfaces in a manner media theorist Wendy Chun describes as "invisibly visible" (Chun 2011, 10). Expressive computing system developers can create digital stories, poems, or games in which aspects of content, such as theme, plot, emotional tone, metaphorical exposition, or imagery, can vary improvisationally with user interaction (Harrell 2007c). In addition to the new meanings generated in each new single session, new meanings emerge from the contrast between multiple readings or play sessions. These new meanings can be composed in response (discrete or continuous) to user interaction.

A focus on technology is common in computing discussions, but here the orientation is toward meaning. The change from a focus on technology to an orientation toward human meaning offers system developers a useful perspective. It is a perspective focused on how users explore and co-create meaning in conjunction with narrative, poetic, or other imaginative computational forms of expression. User interaction can go beyond enabling manipulation of virtual objects, navigating through virtual spaces, in ways that are purely instrumental modes of interaction (for example, rotating an object or zooming in by moving a virtual camera). Users' actions can instead prompt emergent meaningful interrogation of the human condition through imaginative worlds they encounter. For example, actions such as opening a door, talking to a virtual character, or wading across a computer-animated brook could drive the generation of nostalgic memories (Zhu and Harrell 2008), change the emotional tone of a tale (Harrell 2006), or cause a poem to be conveyed using a new set of metaphors and/or images (Harrell 2005; Chow and Harrell 2009b).

Enabling meaningful forms of interaction is a motivation for the theoretical approach taken here, but it is necessary to be able to articulate what is meant by "meaning" in order to make it the basic building block for system design. One way to do this is by approaching computing through new perspectives that centralize meaning. Hence, phantasmal media are theorized in this book through an articulation of three approaches to computing. These are subjective computing, cultural computing, and critical computing.

Subjective computing research and practice entails focusing on direct experience of computing systems, which includes a focus on how computing systems affect users by prompting the imagination. A loose literary analogy for this approach can be found in Edgar Allan Poe's essay "The Philosophy of Composition," in which he argues that authors should seek to achieve a "unity of effect" through a systematic and logical approach to writing (Poe [1846] 2009).[8] This analogy should not be taken too far, however, because Poe's description of authoring his poem *The Raven* is so systematic that some believe it is satirical. Furthermore, fields such as literary theory, semiotics, and cognitive science alike all agree that it is impossible for an author to control what ideas a work will prompt users to imagine and that communicating via any medium is not a unidirectional transmission of ideas from author to reader. However, the analogy is useful in the sense that Poe's essay focuses on prompting the reader's imagination to result in subjective effects of interpretation. Subjective computing has this characteristic. For example, a subjective artificial intelligence system would be focused on prompting humans to interpret it as intelligent in some way.[9] This orientation is not due to a goal of trying to "fool" people into thinking that a system is intelligent; rather, it is based on the realization that any understanding of a computing system's operation is based in human perception and imaginative cognition. The idea behind subjective computing is that it is both an open and hard research question to address how computing systems play roles in prompting human imaginative cognition processes that allow us to interpret, understand, and make meaning of their operations.

Cultural computing research and practice focuses on rigorously understanding and articulating the groundings of subjective computing systems in culture. The challenge of defining culture will be engaged in chapter 5. It is now possible to say, however, that cultural computing requires realizing that all technical systems are informed by shared bodies of knowledge, shared practices, shared behaviors, and more. Even regular and reproducible empirical results (the type favored by science and engineering) are cultural products. Saying something is "cultural" does not mean it is "nonscientific." The term "cultural" just suggests attending to the traditions of thought and practice that ground methodological values of disciplines, including science, mathematics, and engineering, as is especially the case in interdisciplinary research areas focused on how humans and computers interact with one another or research areas that seek to invent computing systems to accomplish actions formerly reserved for humans (such as generating art). Furthermore, when creating subjective computing systems, one may find that cultural models outside of those currently privileged in computing practices might be fertile groundings for new and innovative results. Like the well-worn tale of European mathematicians importing the Hindu-Arabic numeral zero, sometimes it pays to look further afield! However, rather than celebrating the ability of mainstream computing researchers to learn from other cultural perspectives, instead one should say that computing research can be grounded in a diversity of cultural frameworks.

Critical computing research and practice focuses on the design and use of cultural computing systems in light of social phenomena. More specifically, critical computing entails critically assessing the potential of the technology being researched and developed to engender conceptual change in users and the potential of the technology to engender real-world change in society. Although this may sound somewhat grand, critical computing could entail something as simple as considering the needs and values of users and other stakeholders when analyzing or developing a computing system. The structures of computing systems are typically direct responses to stakeholder needs and values. However, one can be much more explicit about making the relationship between computational structure and human needs and values clear. Critical computing practices also include activist aims such as using computing systems to support the needs of the economically impoverished or to help engender better understanding of institutionalized practices of discrimination and bias.

These three approaches to computing are intended to help facilitate both design of new systems in the future and understanding of the effects of existing systems upon people's lives. These three approaches to computing call attention to roles of imagination, culture, and society in computing practices that are often overlooked and undervalued in traditional disciplines. Critical computing systems are built upon cultural computing groundings, which in turn are informed by subjective computing research aims (see figure 2.4).

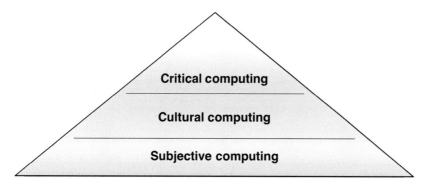

FIGURE 2.4
A pyramid shows the relationships between three new approaches to computing.

I shall briefly discuss each of these approaches in more depth in the following subsections, which include descriptions of several projects that I have created, or led creation of in my lab, and that illustrate the approach. These projects are not intended to be definitive of phantasmal media; some are no more than humble sketches of ideas implemented as computer programs as pedagogical exercises with my students. The examples are intended to help make the ideas here clearer, but they should not influence readers to think that the theoretical construct of phantasmal media and subjective, cultural, and critical approaches to computing are limited to the predominantly small-scale and artistic projects used as examples in the upcoming discussions.

Subjective Computing

Subjective computing research and development endeavors can use computing systems to construct a dialogue between the expressive goals of system designers and the imaginative experiences of users. Expressive "goals" are of a different nature than usability- or productivity-oriented goals. In fact, expressive content may be driven by intuition,[10] ambiguity, improvisation, or other subjective concepts. Expressive content does not need to be productive, useful, or even consciously understandable by users of such systems. The arts and humanities offer traditions of inquiry arising from such varied goals and for addressing both traditionally productive arts (such as works bordering on commercial design or even activist art) and introspective or philosophical endeavors (such as conceptual art). Addressing computing systems as subjectivity-oriented artifacts provides a clearer lens for analysis because it does not require artificial subdivision of the work according to disciplinary boundaries. The mathematical, computational, cognitive, and expressive elements of systems can be integrated with specific subjective content.

It is important in describing the notion of subjective computing here to acknowledge Sherry Turkle's influential work investigating a "range of new 'intersubjective' relationships" (Turkle 2004, 16) between humans and machines that have developed as computing has infiltrated everyday life, noting the difference between instrumental tool-oriented uses of computing and "relational uses" that treat computers as companions, prosthetic uses that treat them as extensions of the self, and more general everyday uses that treat technologies as objects to think with. From a user-centric perspective, Turkle writes, "Computer users are frequently more in touch with the subjective computer, the computer that does things to us, to our ways of seeing the world, to the way we think, to the nature of our relationships with each other.

Technologies are never 'just tools.' They are evocative objects. They cause us to see ourselves and our world differently" (Turkle 2004, 18). The phantasmal media concept is aligned with Turkle's notions, especially with her work focusing on new forms of identity enabled by emerging technologies. Yet, drawing upon an ethnographic and psychological perspective, Turkle's focus is often on interrogating the ways that these computational technologies serve as "evocative objects" that affect people's everyday lives through their interactions with them. In contrast, the orientation here also has a strong focus on the *design* of subjective computing technologies. A key observation informing subjective computing is that many similar imaginative-cognition processes are work in creative endeavors as diverse as the arts (Turner 2006), literature (Lakoff and Turner 1989; Turner 1996), practice of mathematics (Lakoff and Núñez 2000), and music (Lewis 2000; Zbikowski 2002). Subjective computing can emphasize the design of systems for these expressive uses, highlighting a third perspective on computing beyond the instrumental or Turkle's account of the intersubjective. Expressive computing practitioners often see the computer as a medium (or a set of media), as discussed earlier in this chapter. The practice of subjective computing in the design of phantasmal media entails understanding the use of computing to enable us to imaginatively express ourselves through forms including computational self-representations, narrative, and art.

As an example outcome of a subjective computing practice implemented using my GRIOT system for constructing phantasmal media, the multimedia fantasy artwork mentioned earlier called *Loss, Undersea* (see figure 2.5) blends computational representations of epistemic spaces describing undersea world concepts; the routinized, banal life of a worker in an information-oriented society; and associated emotional tones (Harrell 2006). These blended epistemic spaces are used to compose both verbal imagery (dynamically constructed poetry) and visual imagery (a dynamically constructed avatar) using a cognitive linguistics-based algorithm for conceptual blending. The combination of these blended epistemic spaces and dynamic image spaces results in the continuously varying emotional tone of a poem and avatar that are generated as output. In this example, a computational system has been implemented with the goal of generating an evocative phantasm focused on imaginative metaphor or emotional impact.

Starting from acknowledging the contextually situated, socially and technologically distributed, and humanly embodied nature of meaning, subjective computing requires system developers to consider which aspects of meaning can be represented formally within computing systems. It also requires designers to consider which

i get up , my mind , as always , a compassionate waker mind
the room has a liquid echo
reciting a pop song like a mantra while washing , i decide to

cleanse   scrub   soak   urinate

1) Lazy tone output instance:	2) Aggressive tone output instance:
no gills, no webbing between digits, it wouldn't be a watery grave, but a salt water life the day's initial action : I > **sleep** and feel like a lazy sleeping-beauty the indolent body atmosphere is a little heavy the day cannot begin without being clean, I need to > **soak** I think playful contented thoughts, then of the breakfast table you will recall the importance of hearty breakfast cuisine to > **munch** feeling tubes, staid again the sleeping-beauty, lazy atmosphere is a little heavy it is not a difficult job, I try to > **procrastinate** chilling and flimsy, my labor's reward too-satisfied, anxiety seeps under the door, through me, from me a sandwich, I must > **chit-chat** another soft lazy-goat lunch it's becoming a fish loser life the walk to the restroom is the nicest part of the workday again, I need to > **procrastinate** living my daily hours in this nasty ineffectual room an Atlantean aroma still at home an occasional television watcher, today I shall > **watch-tv** so goes the ice-hearted and lazy day ocean in the air, I feel lighter a rectangular cushion awaits I love you, good night crisp sheets fade to boring warmth	my head had been rock and my heart black lead, but somehow I would not perish in the watery clam, echinoderm world rousing from slumber to > **scratch** falling back to my pillow and blank ornery dreams a moment I become doormat fighting I never shower slowly, I just > **scrub** I think caring awesome thoughts, then of the breakfast table the air shimmers a bit in the dim cube for eating I > **devour** on toward my job the cave heavenly atmosphere is a little heavy always imagining, swim still at my desk, I must > **work-hard** a heavenly scary-place, a mean, weak job colors seem a bit duller today my lunch order is ready, I > **consume** uncaring angry, stuffed a lovely day work cave trench, whale fierce work, I must > **network** living my daily hours in this morning- person fierce room it's loser free, ever-changing days my room after the day where I shall > **fornicate** soon I'll be drowsy, seashell weaponly thoughts just like before, the day is done the tale of my every day good night

FIGURE 2.5

In *Loss, Undersea*, a dynamic character transforms (above) as shown in the silhouettes (above right). Two examples of poetic narrative text generated according to affective constraints (below). User input is entered by clicking on bubbles, but in the text version is indicated at the > prompt.

aspects of meaning should be left as intrinsic characteristics of media assets (e.g., a prerendered video rather than dynamically generated CGI).

The concept of subjective computing is naturally interdisciplinary, because it involves accounting for how humans make meaning cognitively, along with accounting for how computational systems can capture, and fail to capture, human meanings. *Loss, Undersea* does so using many of the theories mentioned earlier in this chapter, in particular building on (once again) cognitive science theories of how concepts are generated and mapped from one to each other from cognitive science (Fauconnier and Turner 2002; Lakoff 1987; Lakoff and Johnson 1980; Lakoff and Turner 1989), formal approaches to semiotics and cognition from computer science that acknowledge critical perspectives on artificial intelligence and do not attempt to reduce human cognition to computation (Goguen 1998), and cross-cultural and media theoretic approaches to expressive multimedia narrative, poetry, and other imaginative discourse forms (Gates 1988; Harrell 2006, 2007b, 2007c; Murray 1997).

Cultural Computing

Cultural practices and values are implicitly built into all computational systems. However, it is not common to develop systems with explicit engagement with, and foundations in, cultural practices and values aside from those traditionally privileged in discourse surrounding computing practices (Harrell 2007a). As mentioned previously, cultural computing entails engaging commonly excluded cultural values and practices to spur computational innovation and invigorate expressive computing research and practice. Such diverse ways of representing and manipulating semantic content and distinctive relationships between humans and computing systems can form the basis for new technical and expressive computing practices. Cultural computing also necessitates that developers reflect upon the challenges involved in making cultural values explicit in computing practices, rather than imputing them with essentialist characteristics (Biakolo 1999; Harrell 2007a; Ngugi 1998), stereotyping cultural production forms of particular cultures, or enabling cultural plunder.[11] Cultural plunder in this case means using diverse aesthetic traditions only to empower the culturally privileged, often implicitly "Western," materialistic, and production-oriented modes of thought that inform many engineering practices. In contrast, cultural computing means empowering technologies serving a plurality of worldviews.

Later in this book I shall explore an in-depth example of cultural computing. In the example, a notion of oral literature as it has been theorized and practiced by a set of theorists, most notably Ngugi wa Thiong'o, engaged with a diversity of aesthetic traditions from Africa and the African diaspora is shown as providing grounding for the GRIOT computational narrative system. Issues such as spatial situatedness, performativity, audience-performer interaction, and improvisation are just a few of the topics addressed by this analysis.

An example of a project built using GRIOT is the Generative Visual Renku (GVR) project, a collaborative project between Kenny Chow and me. GVR composes animated images based on both their visual characteristics and underlying meanings. GVR is a generative multimedia poetry project informed by research into the interplay between visual form (iconity) and conceptual metaphor by Masako Hiraga (building on Charles Saunders Peirce's work in semiotics) (Chow and Harrell 2009a; Hiraga 2005; Peirce 1965). This research looks at the ways in which visual icons can structure metaphorical meaning in a manner similar to Chinese characters used in forms of Chinese coauthored poetry and most notably in Japanese renku (or renga) poetry.

Coding Landscapes, Crossing Metaphors, a GVR installation artwork, is an interactive visual poem that functions as a meditation on the repetitive experiences of cityscapes as they intertwine with organic countryside environments (Higginson 1985, 1996, 2006). In *Coding Landscapes, Crossing Metaphors*, a character transforms to adapt to the terrain over which it walks (see figure 2.6).

The calligraphic iconic animations of a human character are dynamically composed by the system, guided by analogies between formalized epistemic spaces, expressing visual and conceptual constraints in response to user actions. These animated people are then placed into a fanciful topography articulating the nuanced interplay between organic (natural or hand-created) and modular (mass-produced or consumerist) artifacts that saturate our lives. The animated characters traverse the resultant topography and accumulate possessions based on the spaces they have journeyed through (e.g., hats with mouse ears after passing through an amusement park ride, or a camera after passing through a television). The iconic imagery is composed based upon underlying small-scale knowledge representation data structures describing the visual and structural aspects of the animation (images spaces) and conceptual content of the imagery (epistemic spaces). The poetic landscapes and character transformations generated by the system illustrate how visual meaning can also be subjectively represented in a manner that takes advantage of an underlying analogy-finding

FIGURE 2.6
In the GVR installation artwork *Coding Landscapes, Crossing Metaphors* (left), walking one's fingers along a touch pad results (middle) in a character walking across a generated landscape (right).

algorithm that structures such meanings dynamically. This dynamic reconfiguration of image, structure, and concept into culturally specific linguistic forms—all explicitly based on cognitive science research—is an example of cultural computing.

Critical Computing

The critical computing approach can help researchers and developers say something about, or do something within, the real world using computer systems. Perhaps at its best, critical computing can help in the laudable aim of facilitating the empowerment of people oppressed in some way. The critical computing approach helps researchers and developers move beyond just building utilitarian computing systems to considering the import of such systems with respect to issues such as social identity, power relationships, and political configurations. Science and technology studies researchers Geoffrey Bowker and Susan Leigh Star have articulated a brilliant motivating argument for doing so:

> Why should the computer scientist read African-American poets? What does information science have to do with race-critical or feminist methods and metaphysics? The collective wisdom in those domains is one of the richest places from which to understand these core problems in information systems design: how to preserve the integrity of information without a priori standardization and its often attendant violence. In turn, if those lessons can be taken seriously within the emerging cyberworld, there may yet be a chance to strengthen its democratic ethical aspects. (Bowker and Star 1999, 302)

Indeed failure to learn from that collective wisdom will result in the development of computing systems that create what media researchers Anna Everett and S. Craig Watkins call "pedagogical zones" reinforcing social issues such as racism and sexism (Everett and Watkins 2008, 158). Critical computing means that engineers, scientists, and other computing system developers can address social issues through technical solutions. Developers can be critically engaged with society through taking advantage of long traditions of thought about human empowerment offered by the humanities, arts, and social sciences.

The concept of critical computing is related in some ways to the earlier concept of critical technical practices introduced by Philip Agre. Critical technical practices represent a union between technical research and development, philosophy, and critical theory (Agre 1997). Agre's approach has influenced other technological fields beyond the area of AI in which he worked—for example, computer and information scientist

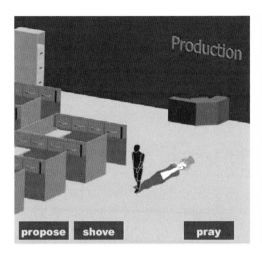

FIGURE 2.7
Chameleonia: Shadow Play is a prototype critical identity game in which an avatar and its shadow
(representing performed and imagined selves) dynamically transform, as does the cinematic presentation
of the scene, based on both player selected gestures and the current location they occur in.

Phoebe Sengers has developed and applied Agre's ideas to highly original approaches
to human–computer interaction (HCI) design of everyday computing applications,
such as for experiences in museums or using physically intimate devices such as hand-
held computers (Sengers et al. 2005). Many other researchers have approached this
project of cultural criticism, including Brian K. Smith's "Explanation Architecture"
research (Smith 2002), the Critical Art Ensemble's radical artwork and theory (Critical Art Ensemble 1993), Arthur and Marilouise Kroker's work in critical digital studies (Kroker and Kroker 2008), and Mary Flanagan's art and feminist theory based
approach to game design (Flanagan 2009). What all of these approaches share is a
focus on analysis and design of computing systems that are critically engaged with
human society. The approach here also takes a critical turn, implementing complex
computational systems to interrogate disempowering social constructions.

Several critical computing projects in my laboratory investigate and model social
identity phenomena across platforms such as games, social media, and virtual worlds.
This work addresses the ways that users of such systems imaginatively map aspects of
their real-world social identities, life stories, and senses of self onto technologies such
as player characters, online accounts, and avatars. One prototype system we implemented is a game called *Chameleonia: Shadow Play* (see figure 2.7). In this game, a

continuously walking player character transforms dynamically in response to both gestures (such as "beg" or "shove") and context (such as suburban or corporate scenes) while the character's shadow transforms differently in parallel. The player character, a representation prompting an image space that recalls a doll used by artists for figure drawing, enacts user-specified gestures representing the external (performed) self, while a more illustrative shadow continuously automatically transforms representing the socially constructed self. The difference between the two is inspired by W. E. B. Du Bois's classic definition of "double consciousness" (1903) in which a person's self-conception differs from the way society views her or him.

As the player character walks through the game's virtual world, the player selects actions for the character to perform. Based on these actions and the location at which they are performed, a number of effects take place. The shadow's transformation can be described as a dynamic phantasm guided by concepts associated with user-selected gestures associated with epistemic spaces representing concepts such as "commerce" or "aggression." The transforming shadow might look like a bazooka-toting cowgirl sipping a soft drink at one moment; after a series of actions, it might instead look like a gold-chain-and-pocketwatch-clad tycoon with stock charts bursting from a top-hatted head the next. The game is meant to suggest how people become both naturalized and marginalized in communities and social contexts. One of the major ways in which humans naturalize within communities is by displaying contextually appropriate gestures.

Another example is *DefineMe: Chimera*, a social networking application in which users collectively define phantasms representing each other through integrating epistemic spaces in the form of metaphorical profiles and image spaces in the form of avatars for one another (see figure 2.8). For example, if one user defines an epistemic space by entering "Kwame is a lion because he enjoys the shade" and another person defines an epistemic space by entering "Kwame is a peacock because he rarely flies," a phantasm in the form of a hybrid lion-peacock avatar for Kwame will be generated. The idea behind this project is that individuals' social identities are defined, in part, by other people. This observation is currently omitted from profile or character creation techniques in most social networking or gaming systems.[12] The *DefineMe* database[13] puts users into collectively generated categories. The system avoids some of the predefined categorization built into many social networking systems and is a critical computing exploration of several nuanced identity phenomena mentioned previously.

The unifying theme illustrated by these critical computing examples is the aim of revealing how many current identity representation systems replicate limited, static,

FIGURE 2.8
DefineMe: Chimera is a phantasmal media work in which users of a social networking site metaphorically define each other's profiles and the system generates chimerical avatars.

and often stereotypical notions of identity. Instead, phantasmal media can enable imaginative forms of identity to critique, and potentially improve, current models.

The Potential of Phantasmal Media for Expression

The overarching concept of this book is that *phantasmal media* operate at the intersection of imagination and computation. The theoretical framework developed in this book integrates research from cognitive science, formal approaches to semantics and semiotics in computer science, and sociology and cultural theory, and art practice. Through this framework, I examine how computing systems can prompt phantasms—that is, how they can function as phantasmal media.

The bulk of the book is structured by the three approaches to computing described earlier: part II, Subjective Computing; part III, Cultural Computing; and part IV, Critical Computing. Each of these parts of the book consists of a short introductory essay followed by two chapters. Part V looks at the implications of phantasmal media to more broadly affect the human condition through the agency and empowerment of users.

Imaginative cognition is powerful. Phantasmal media can prompt forms of imagination including fantastic blends of ideas, rich metaphors, social identities, and values that reinforce or challenge power relationships between people. Phantasmal media can support social empowerment through prompting us to imagine new ideas and by reinvigorating important old ideas. Many existing computing systems, however, often fail to support people's needs, dreams, and aspirations, and may even play roles in experiences that crush them. At their best, phantasmal media can help people seek our imaginative potentials. Empowerment through the imagination is not merely a matter of technological support. The end hope here is that these ideas can contribute to *imaginative visions, meaningful experiences, and expressive statements* that lead to real-world insight and action.

II

SUBJECTIVE COMPUTING

Although computers are often seen as objective machines, they can implement many types of subjectivity. Like other media, computational media can be used for human expression. Part II of this book provides a framework for better understanding and designing computational media that evoke a range of subjective, expressive phenomena. The phenomena to be discussed are important in both computing and culture at large.

In computing, one of the most venerable aims within AI is to implement forms of subjectivity. AI researchers continue to strive for methods to effectively make machines that can imitate subjective human behavior or that exhibit lifelike engagement with the real world. In everyday uses of communication media, the computer has allowed us to have subjective experiences in worlds distinct from our physical world. Unblinkingly, we use avatars to represent ourselves. Businesses and other institutions use data profiles to predict and determine our tastes and purchases. Families communicate using text, audio, images, and video across great distances over networks and in virtual worlds. In popular culture, computational media have been used for subjective aims ranging from the sentimental to the political. It has become a cliché to claim that videogames will become art when they can emotionally move players to tears. Many game designers strive to imbue games with emotion and many players appreciate such an effect when it occurs. In another arena, many people use the computer for social protest. Such uses promote subjective political viewpoints, whether of activists on the street using social media or hackers who practice radical computer-based art. Furthermore, many institutions deploy computers for surveil-lance of social media, desiring computers that can (simply put) distinguish the com-munication exchanges of the good guys from those of the bad guys.

Although any of these aims could be seen alternately as simplistic, admirable, passé, radical, or innovative, they all reveal human subjectivity that is intertwined with computational technologies. They reveal the deep cultural and subjective forces that drive much or all computer use. The two chapters that constitute part II of this volume present the concept of *subjective computing* to help explain how computing produces internal states of mind that we identify with subjectivity.

Chapter 3 explores how the structure of computational representations can impact imaginative worlds and prompt forms of imagination called *poetic phantasms* (meaningful mental imagery and ideas involving metaphor, narrative, categorization, etc.). In particular, *expressive epistemologies* are data structures that represent epistemic domains for the purpose of implementing computer-based imaginative worlds and prompting poetic phantasms. Besides offering new perspectives on expressive data structuring, subjective computing offers specific ways to help us analyze how com-puter systems express values. Chapter 4 serves this aim by developing the concept of *polymorphic poetics* as an approach to the analysis and design of computing systems. The term "polymorphic poetics" itself refers to the many forms that abstract concepts and data representing them can take in actual implemented computing systems and user interfaces. Polymorphic poetics addresses how computing systems express values through their structures. It provides a way of looking at how the choice of structures has an impact on how computing systems serve social and expressive needs. Although there are potentially other approaches to polymorphic poetics, chapter 4 presents the theory of *morphic semiotics* as a tool to describe how the abstract ideas behind com-puting systems are realized in actual implementations.

Chapter 4 is also a tribute to the work of Joseph Goguen, who invented the highly mathematical theory upon which the chapter's approach is based. The aim of this tribute is to develop a version of the theory accessible to researchers and practi-tioners from a greater range of backgrounds than mathematics and computer science. Morphic semiotics is shown in the chapter to help in analysis of systems ranging from an everyday utilitarian commerce website to a computer art game conceived of as a reminder of human mortality. The unifying factor in analyzing these systems is that their structures reveal their values.

Subjective computing provides ways to develop and precisely analyze how compu-tational media produce phantasms. Subjective computing, I argue, is based on both an interplay of data representations of imaginative meaning (expressive epistemolo-gies) and artful uses of mappings between meanings implemented in computational media (polymorphic poetics).

3

EXPRESSIVE EPISTEMOLOGIES

—Scott McCloud, *Understanding Comics*

Experience is the root of human meaning-making. Our experiences include basic sensory-motor encounters with the world such as moving a gaze across a surface or walking along a path (Lakoff and Johnson 1980); they also include many abstract situations that rely on common sense and acquired knowledge. For example, ethical decisions in everyday life, such as whether to verbally insult another person, may be made based on the common sense understanding that the action could provoke an altercation. Yet understanding a complex and artful response to a verbal insult, such as Adrian Piper's artwork *My Calling (Card) #1 (for Dinners and Cocktail Parties)* (1986–1990)—a cleverly written 3.5" × 2" card that she has distributed when receiving racist comments from people who incorrectly assumed that she is white (cases of inadvertently *passing* as white), may require acquired knowledge of topics like cultural politics and contemporary art (see figure 3.1).

Dear Friend,
   I am black.
   I am sure you did not realize this when you made/laughed at/agreed with that racist remark. In the past, I have attempted to alert white people to my racial identity in advance. Unfortunately, this invariably causes them to react to me as pushy, manipulative, or socially inappropriate. Therefore, my policy is to assume that white people do not make these remarks, even when they believe there are no black people present, and to distribute this card when they do.
   I regret any discomfort my presence is causing you, just as I am sure you regret the discomfort your racism is causing me.

FIGURE 3.1
Acquired cultural knowledge is required to make sense of Adrian Piper's work: Adrian Piper, *My Calling (Card) #1 (for Dinners and Cocktail Parties)*, 1986–1990. Performance prop: business card with printed text on cardboard. 3.5 in. × 2 in. (9.0 cm × 5.1cm). Collection Davis Museum of Wellesley College. © APRA Foundation Berlin.

Interpreting the meaning of *My Calling (Card) #1 (for Dinners and Cocktail Parties)* (1986–1990) and the transgressive nature of distributing it requires knowledge of aversive racism and its effects. Simultaneously, knowledge of conceptual and performance art practices is required to make sense of why the card is considered to be a work of fine art that has been displayed in galleries and museums across the world.

On a computer, basic motor-sensory experiences help us understand the meanings of our actions. When using word processing software, moving a cursor over a screen mirrors the ways that a user's eyes focus on specific words while moving a gaze across the screen. While playing a videogame, watching a character walking across a side-scrolling screen recalls our experiences of walking from one location to another. Similarly, acquired knowledge may also be necessary for making sense of experiences on a computer. The computer game *Grim Fandango* (1998) requires common sense to understand why the player character's predicament of being in a dead-end job is a bad situation (see figure 3.2). It also requires acquired knowledge of art and culture in order to recognize its Art Deco–style architecture and Mexican mythology–inspired setting. These observations should be self-evident; humans invented media to share experiences of many types of subjective meaning, and computers are no exception.

FIGURE 3.2
Recognition of the cultural references in the computer game *Grim Fandango* requires acquired knowledge.

For any medium, conventions have arisen to help us produce, use, and make sense of specific works. Each medium has its own manner of representing meaning. Each medium can play a role in meaning construction through a combination of social interactions, uses of objects in the world, and individual cognitive processes of conceptualizing. For example, computational media production may involve elements such as teams of developers, users, technical reports, computer programs, and reviews on blogs, which are all connected to one another (see figure 3.3).[1]

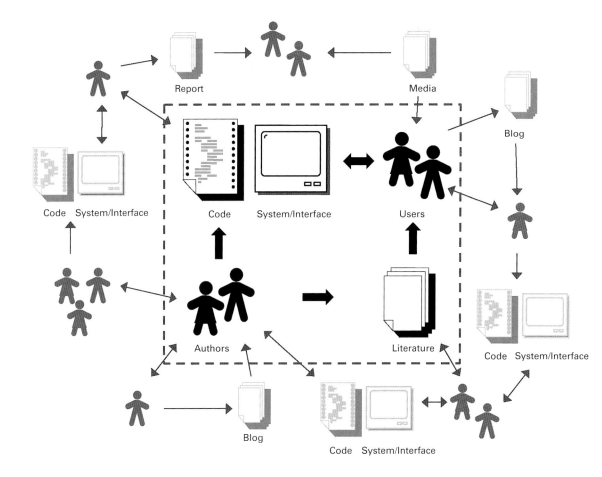

FIGURE 3.3
Meaning production in computational media occurs in an ecology involving individuals, artifacts, tools, and cognitive phenomena such as thinking metaphorically and inventing new concepts.

This chapter addresses how computational media represent, and can be designed to effectively convey, expressive meaning. "Expressive meaning" here refers to what I shall call *imaginative world and poetic phantasm construction*. The following discussion illustrates how computational media convey expressive meaning by drawing on examples both from long-standing media forms and more recent subjective computing systems. People can sustain long engagements with the imaginative worlds constructed by both videogames and literary works. Both Haruki Murakami's novel

FIGURE 3.4
The computer role-playing game *Alternate Reality: The Dungeon* models
characters in a fantasy world by attributing numerical statistics to a character's
abilities. It was an early game to include robust world modeling, including
day/night cycles, hunger, thirst, fatigue, an open world structure, and more.

Hard-Boiled Wonderland and the End of the World and the classic computer game
Alternate Reality: The Dungeon (see figure 3.4) create fantasy worlds that are eventually revealed to be constructed by high technology.

Programmatic music likewise is a type of music in which sounds are meant to
correspond to the world at large. Consider the song "Triptych: Prayer/Protest/Peace"
from *We Insist! Max Roach's Freedom Now Suite*. The song represents stages of the
African American civil rights movement. Beginning with Abbey Lincoln's wordless
solemn singing, the song shifts into screaming and finally to a last sighing breath.
Alban Berg's *Lyric Suite* could perhaps be considered a more obtuse type of programmatic music; hidden within its score is a secret message to his lover. A later section of
this chapter, "Imaginative World and Poetic Phantasm Construction," further articulates the types of expressive meaning central to phantasmal media.

Central to our description of computational approaches to represent and convey
expressive meaning is the concept of expressive epistemologies, the subject of the section that follows the one just described. In order to build two types of subjective
phantasm in a computational system, imaginative worlds and poetic phantasms,
knowledge has to be represented as computational data. The concept of expressive

epistemologies addresses the question of how different data representation models yield different subjective experiences for users. More specifically, the concept addresses how epistemic domains and spaces can be represented computationally in order to support expressive aims. Distinct from the way the terms are used in philosophy, the concept of an "epistemology" used here builds upon the concept of the epistemic domain introduced in chapter 1 and the definition of an "ontology" used in AI research. Yet expressive epistemologies have a greater focus on representing the *subjective knowledge of a system designer for expressive purposes* rather than providing objective specifications of what exists in some domain being modeled computationally as do ontologies. AI systems provide good test cases in this regard. Hence, a section introducing the concept of subjective AI comes next. AI systems often seek to exhibit phenomena such as computational *intentionality* (being *about* the real world) and computational *animacy* (being *lifelike* in some regards). These aims involve imaginative interpretation of system behavior by users just as much as innovative system design on the part of engineers. The term "subjective AI" can therefore be said to refer to AI systems that are also subjective computing systems.

This concept is developed in the subsequent section, "Expressive Epistemologies and the GRIOT System," a case study of a subjective AI platform and a system built using it that memorializes a tragic war. This latter system exemplifies a broader message, namely that representing subjective information computationally (an aspect of expressive epistemology design) must occur with great social sensitivity in light of real-world needs and values. That is, system development is not only an expressive act by system creators; it is an act that occurs within communities, each with their own sets of lived experiences, which extend even to the harrowing experience of war and its aftermath. System designers work less effectively, sometimes with socially detrimental effects, when they see themselves as separate from such communities and the meanings they generate. Rather, those meanings must drive system design down to the code level.

Imaginative World and Poetic Phantasm Construction

Imaginative world construction consists of modeling reality by drawing on subjective worldviews. That is, imaginative world construction consists of constructing phantasms that convey enough consistent imagery and information to evoke a coherent sense of a world. Phantasm construction consists of integrating component epistemic spaces and image spaces in ways that give structure to perspectives of reality. *Poetic phantasm construction* is the shaping of such phantasms in ways that hold aesthetic considerations as centrally important to meaning construction—for example, attending to the expressive qualities arising from skillful manipulation of attributes of diverse media forms such as word choice in literature; color and composition in graphic arts; pacing, staging, and movement in theater; and so on.

Imaginative world and poetic phantasm construction arise from poetic thinking, which was introduced briefly in chapter 1. It is a type of thinking that is the hallmark of the arts, though it has also shown to be fundamental to everyday life (Turner 1996). It is the type of thinking that allows us to tell stories. It is the type of thinking that allows us to envision the worlds conjured by novels. It is also the type of thinking that allows us to relate works of art to our lives and to understand the human condition better. Poetic thinking arises from cognitive processes giving rise to phenomena such as mental images, narrative, metaphor, analogy, parable, and indeed phantasms (Gibbs 1994; Lakoff and Turner 1989). When poetic thinking refers to objects resembling those in the real world, such as people in particular situations, it can be called *figurative thinking*. For reasons explained shortly, the subjective computing systems explored in this book largely are those that evoke figurative thinking. I shall continue to use the terms "poetic thinking" and "poetic phantasm" as well due to their greater generality.

This book argues, by way of the concept of phantasmal media, that one of the most promising directions in the design of subjective computing systems is to pursue effectively evoking figurative thinking with strong aesthetic considerations.[2] The focus on figurative thought in the phantasmal media approach to imaginative world and poetic phantasm construction is motivated by two facts. First, figurative thinking is fundamental to the imagination. Second, culturally influential forms of subjective computing such as games and social media are often figurative. For example, they allow us to explore simulated worlds or share our life stories with one another. Cognitive scientist Raymond Gibbs reminds us that

> human cognition is fundamentally shaped by various poetic or figurative processes. Metaphor, metonymy, irony, and other tropes are not linguistic distortions of literal mental thoughts but constitute basic schemes by which people conceptualize their experience and the external world. Since every mental construct reflects an adaptation of the mind to the world, the language that expresses these constructs attests to the continuous process of poetic thinking. (Gibbs 1994, 1)

Acknowledging the pervasiveness of figurative thinking in everyday life is a profound realization. Subjective computing systems, ranging from AI programs to games, evoke such poetic and figurative thought processes in ways unique to their media. Furthermore, they play profound roles in transforming our society's ideologies, for both good and ill. These reasons are the motivation for developing this chapter's account of how subjective computing systems play a role in constructing ideology. The type of ideology construction we look at here is that which occurs through the building of imaginative worlds and poetic phantasms. Designing data representations for imaginative worlds and poetic phantasms, especially using AI techniques for subjective ends, are explored in the next section.

Defining Expressive Epistemologies

The term *expressive epistemology* draws upon several earlier concepts. The way the term is used here (as a noun referring to a type of data structure) draws on the AI notion of an ontology, so we first shall discuss the origin of the term "ontology." In philosophy, ontology is well known as the branch of study concerning the nature of existence. It explores the nature of being in the world and how things in the world might be grouped into different classifications of existence. Building imaginative worlds using computers requires representing what it means for something to exist in those worlds. In computer science, representation of such knowledge is often accomplished in a highly structured way—for example, by including information about concepts and relations between them. Certain types of computational knowledge representation have come to be known as *ontologies*, a definition of the term distinct from its use in philosophy (Gruber 1995). Ontologies in computer science provide ways to specify conceptualizations of aspects of some domain. That is, they describe elements such as the objects, types of objects, attributes, relations, and events that exist in some world of operation (Sowa 2010). Though typically represented formally, ontologies can be represented informally; semiformally, such as with markup languages or morphic semiotics (an approach to be introduced in chapter 4); or very formally, such as with first-order logic. Such representations can then be used for purposes such as designing, combining, and deploying computer systems. Although ontologies need not be realized in a formal notation, the fact that they can be—and most often are—formally represented is an important reason why they are so useful.

Design of ontologies is a challenge for expressive system design because imaginative world construction is a subjective enterprise. It requires deciding what is meaningful to represent and how it should be represented. However, the focus shifts away from an objective representation of what exists and to a subjective representation of what is *known* and *believed* and how knowledge and beliefs constitute a worldview. In philosophy, epistemology has been defined as the study of knowledge and belief, along with issues of truth and justification of belief. Taking advantage of the precedent set by the way the term "ontology" becomes a noun in computer science rather than a branch of study, this chapter proposes the use of "epistemology" as a noun in computer science. The term has some advantages when discussing data specification for subjective content. Beyond its focus on knowledge rather than existence, the term "epistemology" has come to mean something akin to "worldview" in the area of social epistemology. For researchers in this field of study, there is "little or no use for concepts like truth and justification. In addressing the social dimensions of knowledge, they understand 'knowledge' as simply what is believed, or what beliefs are 'institutionalized' in this or that community, culture, or context. They seek to identify the social forces and influences responsible for knowledge production so conceived" (Goldman 2010). This social focus highlights the subjective and socially constructed nature of knowledge in a way that is useful for discussing data structures involved in imaginative world building. It is for this reason that the term "epistemology" is proposed as a new parallel to the computer science term "ontology" to refer to a specification describing an epistemic domain, representing what is known and believed in a conceptualization under a specific worldview. Rather than generally encoding what exists in a domain, as do ontologies, epistemologies are restricted to representing epistemic domains. *Expressive* epistemologies are intended to provide similar utility in designing and even implementing phantasmal media and are designed for subjective computing purposes. Expressive epistemologies can also be used as metadata to annotate multimedia assets and processes, in which case they describe the structure of image spaces.

An expressive epistemology can be more precisely defined as an epistemology (in the computer science sense defined previously) used in an expressive form of cultural production such as an artwork. The notion of expressive epistemology allows us to examine how data representation techniques can enable reflective and cultural engagement. Recall that the focus of this chapter is on exploring how meaning can be constructed formally by computing systems. Designing computational media works for artistic and subjective purposes poses different challenges than scientific and engineering agendas with easily definable goals. Yet the topic of subjective computing systems for expression has been explored by several important computational media scholars. I can now eleborate upon some of these explorations introduced briefly in chapter 2. Computer scientist and artist Michael Mateas, building on the work of computer scientist Joseph Bates, introduced the idea of *expressive artificial intelligence*. He uses the term to describe a type of AI that theoretically is agnostic about ideological battles in the field and in practice deploys an array of AI techniques to aesthetically affect users by any workable means (Mateas 2001). Media scholar and artist Noah Wardrip-Fruin generalized this idea in his book *Expressive Processing* (2009). Wardrip-Fruin focuses on works that are "born digital" and not mere recapitulations of forms in other media (Wardrip-Fruin 2009). His ideas explore the degree and visibility of *processing* (algorithmic) work that is carried out by an expressive system such as a game or computer artwork as it offers experiences to a user. Game studies scholar and game designer Ian Bogost's notion of *procedural rhetoric* offers a parallel approach that focuses on how such processes can be used to make an argument, often via simulation in his own games (Bogost 2007). The unifying factor in these theories is that computation serves the aim of subjective meaning-making.

Subjective meaning and computation are usually seen as incompatible, but this is not the case. AI researchers have long tried to produce systems to support or perform tasks that typically would be seen as requiring human intelligence to perform. In this regard, even the classic type of AI research now known as "good old-fashioned artificial intelligence" (GOFAI) could be considered to produce subjective computing systems. AI research in areas such as knowledge representation, expert systems, and semantic networks often focuses on developing complete and correct descriptions of some area of knowledge to support making inferences. Though these areas of knowledge may have varying degrees of specificity, a goal of such research typically entails developing systems that offer comprehensive understanding.[3] The results are systems with narrow expertise and the characteristic that "to solve a problem you almost have to know the answer already" (Russell and Norvig 1995, 22). An early example of such a project was the blood infection diagnosis expert system MYCIN developed at Stanford University in the 1970s by Ed Feigenbaum, Bruce Buchanan, and Edward Shortliffe (Russell and Norvig 2002). MYCIN produced successful diagnoses in its specific domain based upon rules (including certainty factors) acquired through extensive interviewing of experts. In contrast to systems such as MYCIN with a narrow and robust expertise regarding an explicitly defined goal, the design of systems that produce dynamic, subjective meanings that are both culturally acquired and individually idiosyncratic with surprising, novel inferences has not been the traditional focus of inquiry in AI research.

Interactive games and narratives and other subjective computing systems that capture diverse worldviews require knowledge representations that often must be scaled down to the size of small communities or even individual authors. The knowledge representations needed for large-scale systems based in traditional AI practices, like MYCIN, differ from those needed by interactive narratives, games, and other expressive subjective computing systems. These design aims can be contrasted with attempts to build totalizing large knowledge bases. The aims in building large-scale systems are appropriate for constructing rough inferences or for general applications such as commercial recommendation systems. Systems for such purposes include those for capturing general knowledge such as the WordNet, ConceptNet, or Cyc projects (Fellbaum 1998; Havasi, Speer, and Alonso 2007; Siegel et al. 2004). Yet such systems do not easily attend to the different types of knowledge produced by different communities. It is hard for such systems to facilitate reasoning across diverse domains of knowledge and worldviews.

A complementary approach is to provide techniques for authors to create their own highly individualized data representations of subjective information. These data representations need to be well structured so that user options are situated within their limiting contexts. Inventing effective strategies for designing and implementing these subjectively customized ontologies is a research problem shaped by aesthetic and cultural needs. Technical issues of efficiency are less central for this endeavor. The trade-off is that each system application requires a data representation, but results are likely to be more aligned with the system authors' intentions. Building upon this idea, the next topic to consider is the idea of a subjective data representation (expressive epistemology) and how it can be used for expression.

Expressive Epistemology Design

Implementing expressive epistemologies is challenging because representing a subjective and socially situated perspective on relevant knowledge in the world requires deciding what things are meaningful to a user and how they relate to other things represented with the data structures. Developers face a further challenge in that they must also decide how those meanings can be created through human interaction with the data structures. There are diverse approaches to building effective imaginative worlds computationally. To frame discussion of the challenges of this endeavor, let us consider a representational perspective trying to computationally represent human common sense. Computer scientists Robert Speer, Catherine Havasi, and Henry Lieberman have articulated this goal as teaching computers, "the concepts and relationships which underlie everything we know and talk about" (Speer, Havasi, and Lieberman 2008, 549). Speer, Havasi, and Lieberman developed AnalogySpace, a system to support reasoning over a large database of common sense knowledge (the ConceptNet system).[4] They write: "AnalogySpace distinguishes things people want from things people do not want. Concepts that fall in the "people want" direction include love, money, and vacation, while the opposite direction includes lose your keys and slavery" (1). The assertion in this quotation regarding what "people want," a result from AnalogySpace, is striking in several ways. It is impressively obvious, in the ways that commonsense knowledge should be. Yet common sense also suggests that the groupings contain items that most people would not relate to one another: the fundamental human qualities of wanting love and not wanting to be enslaved seem to dwarf the sundry scale of wanting to go on vacation or not wanting to lose one's keys.

Furthermore, the knowledge seems to be most applicable to general, "all things being equal" conditions. For example, someone having just broken an engagement might not want to fall in love again in that moment. Also, considering the prevalence of slavery in human history, certainly some people want slavery (e.g., slaveholders and traders). AnalogySpace and ConceptNet have captured a type of collective subjective knowledge based on the information submitted by the web volunteers who provided the knowledge base. The systems provide effective tools for making inferences based on such knowledge. At the same time, the projects do not seek to solve the problem of representing the type of idiosyncratic knowledge that is the hallmark of the arts. Handcrafted, individualized, and context-specific knowledge is avoided in favor of universals. Designing expressive epistemologies for subjective computing is a different problem.[5]

Deciding how ontologies should be structured is challenging, and it is no less the case with expressive epistemologies. Regarding ontologies, this observation has been articulated previously, including by researchers David Chalmers, Robert French, and Douglas Hofstadter, who state:

> Representations have been the object of much study and debate within the field of artificial intelligence, and much is made of the "representation problem." This problem has traditionally been phrased as "What is the correct structure for mental representations?," and many possibilities have been suggested, ranging from predicate calculus through frames and scripts to semantic networks and more. (Chalmers, French, and Hofstadter 1992, 172–173)

As discussed earlier, data representations for knowledge have ranged from fairly specific domains such as medical diagnosis to attempts to capture more general common sense. Chalmers and his colleagues cite the need for AI systems to address "entire complex *situations*, such as a love affair or a war," and argue:

> The traditional approach in artificial intelligence has been to *start* by selecting not only a preferred type of high-level representational structure, but also the data assumed to be relevant to the problem at hand. These data are organized by a human programmer who appropriately fits them into the chosen representational structure. Usually, researchers use their prior knowledge of the nature of the problem to hand-code a representation of the data into a near-optimal form. . . .
>
> Only after all this hand-coding is completed is the representation allowed to be manipulated by the machine. (173)

Two of the most influential systems related to general ontology construction are WordNet and Cyc.[6] Both of these systems have been noted as being largely dependent on hand-coded data. This issue can be addressed by means such as recruiting many users to enter information, as we have seen with ConceptNet. Yet, despite this difference, ConceptNet shares the concerns of WordNet and Cyc with large-scale general information representation (Liu and Singh 2004).

Yet, for expressive subjective computing systems, it is far from clear that general knowledge representation should always be the aim or that hand-coding is problematic. Consider the case of computational poetry generation in which a system's operation should result in construction of novel metaphors. Lakoff and Turner (1989) have described three approaches that poets have traditionally taken in creating and deploying metaphors that can be summarized as follows:

1. Versifying them in automatic ways, resulting in trite verse

2. Deploying them masterfully through combination, extension, and realizing them in striking imagery

3. Deploying them in unusual ways or destabilizing them by revealing their inadequacies for making sense of lived experience in the real world

The third case is especially intriguing, for such innovation is a hallmark of many exemplary artworks. I believe that in the case of phantasmal media works, generating uncanny, remarkable, and innovative mappings between epistemic spaces can result in exceptionally affecting and ideologically convincing phantasms. At the same time, unusual or destabilizing metaphors can reveal phantasms, because they may entail imagining alternate worldviews in which common sense under some normative worldview does not hold. Consider Thomas Hardy's classic poem "The Convergence of the Twain," by no means considered experimental, reflecting on the sunken ship the *Titanic*. When Hardy writes:

> Dim moon-eyed fishes near
> Gaze at the gilded gear
> And query: "What does this vaingloriousness down here?"
> (Hardy 1932, 288–289)

it is hardly common sense to imagine the striking imagery of fish with "moon" eyes querying each other on the hubris of humans and the invasion of their machines' debris into their demesnes. Yet incredibly nuanced interpretive ability would be required for a computer to generate or analyze such a metaphor. For example, it would be no trivial matter for an AI system to have the capacity to reveal that in the earlier verse:

> Over the mirrors meant
> To glass the opulent
> The sea-worm crawls—grotesque, slimed, dumb, indifferent.
> (Hardy 1932, 288)

the round shape of the mirrors prefigures that of the fishes' moon-eyes. It would be equally nontrivial for a computer to generate or analyze the dumb and indifferent sea-worm as setting the reader up for an unusual and striking contrast with the humanlike concern expressed by the fish.

Expressive epistemology design appreciates the possibilities of artists representing smaller-scale, individually subjective knowledge in ways that are amenable to generating striking, destabilizing, or otherwise expressive content. In other words, expressive epistemology design is about designing the ability of systems to prompt phantasms using data structures. The task becomes less one of reducing errors in output of the system and more one of designing subjectively oriented epistemologies that can take advantage of particular algorithms to result in instances of output with phantasm constructing effects for authors and users alike. The notions of *epistemic forms* and *epistemic games* of learning scientists Allan Collins and William Ferguson can help explicate this task (Collins and Ferguson 1993). A nice formulation of these ideas follows:

> An *epistemic form* is a target structure that guides the inquiry process. It shows how knowledge is organized or concepts are classified, as well as illustrating the

relationships among the different facts and concepts being learned. The completion or creation of the structure is the object of the epistemic game.

An *epistemic game* is a set of moves, entry conditions, constraints, and strategies that guide the building of the epistemic form. The rules may be complex or
simple, implicit or explicit.

Epistemic fluency is the ability to identify and use different ways of knowing,
including different epistemic forms and various epistemic games. It is the ability
to organize information into multiple patterns, to participate in multiple ways of
making sense of the world. (Sherry and Trigg 1996, 38)

Although ontologies in AI are not necessarily created to guide scientific inquiry, they
are akin in many ways to epistemic forms. If we flesh out the analogy, we can say
that creating an ontology is akin to an epistemic game. Creating an expressive epistemology requires epistemic fluency. To summarize, expressive epistemology design
requires the following:

1. *Epistemologies:* Ontologies for representing epistemic domains, which are
subjective worldviews expressed in terms of knowledge and beliefs. Expressive
epistemologies must be structured to support phenomena such as aesthetically
motivated concept generation, mapping, and inference.

2. *Epistemic formats:* Input formats for epistemologies suited to the computational
expertise of artists who use the systems.

3. *Epistemic semantics algorithms:* Algorithms for mapping, generating, or making
inferences between epistemologies using the knowledge base; these algorithms are
tuned for expressive goals (e.g., meaningful difference between instances of output,
providing multiple perspectives on scenarios, or producing surprising results within
specific social situations).

4. *Epistemic design processes:* Processes for producing works based on a research understanding of how users interpret output and designing for a range of interpretations (a
hallmark of art practice).

Some systems exhibit characteristics of expressive ontology design. Domike, Mateas,
and Vanouse's interactive video documentary generation system, *Terminal Time*
(2003), uses just a segment of the Cyc ontology to produce many variations of output
with differing rhetorical spin. Lev Manovich's work of database narrative, *Soft Cinema*
(2005), annotates videos that he collected and uses these annotations to generate

subjective stories, such as a story about his experience as an immigrant to the United States. *The Girl with Skin of Haints and Seraphs* uses my GRIOT system (Harrell 2005, 2007b) to generate many versions of a poem to destabilize and move beyond outmoded perspectives on social identity. All three of these are subjective computing systems that deploy expressive epistemologies. These examples illustrate that expressive epistemology design is not primarily a technical problem of knowledge engineering, but rather an issue of shifting developers' perspectives and aims. In AI, this shift is toward developing AI systems that result in particular interpretive phenomena for users. The next section ruminates on what such a project would look like by examining the notions of subjective AI, and of subjective computing more generally.

Subjective Artificial Intelligence

Stepping back a moment, we can call the problem of designing expressive epistemologies a *subjective AI* endeavor. Understanding computational media works as subjective AI systems entails more than just examining code functionality. It includes understanding how people communicate about such systems, how people interact with them, and how the systems relate to past media traditions. For example, even the most scientific, technical research papers often deploy metaphors to describe AI systems by using terms such as "creativity" or "learning" to describe what systems are doing. Furthermore, researchers are increasingly focusing on issues like embodied engagement and perception when building AI systems, a turn paralleled by media scholars acknowledging the role of materiality in computing (Hayles 2002; Kirschenbaum 2008). Examples include Rodney Brooks's (1991) "emergent behavior" approach to robotics and Paul Dourish's (2001) "embodied cognition" approach to interaction design. AI researchers also have attempted to create works in dialogue with well-established deployment media traditions. For example, David Cope's (2004) Experiments in Musical Intelligence (EMI) convincingly composes songs in the style of Mozart or ragtime music and Harold Cohen's (2002) rule-based AI system *Aaron* autonomously generates both figurative and abstract paintings. All of these endeavors reveal aspects of what subjective AI practice looks like.

Subjective AI contrasts with much of the current field of AI. Much of AI now has an engineering focus wherein innovative systems are most often understood as providing algorithmic heuristics or solutions for performing tasks that generally are considered to require human understanding to accomplish. However, both the original conception and the popular cultural understanding of the goal of AI see the field as aiming to create computational systems that actually are intelligent (or demonstrably seem to be). Rather than focusing on particular algorithms or data structures, the original aim instead focuses on implementing seemingly human engagement with the world or seemingly lifelike animacy. AI systems would be deemed successful according to this goal if they could, for example, participate in convincing, humanlike conversation or have physical bodies that move or even reproduce in patterns reminiscent of living creatures. The point is not that we should refocus on the original AI aims, but rather that we should recall the observation made at the start of part II of this book that many AI aims are subjective phenomena. Subjective AI research just makes this fact explicit and holds it as desirable at the same time as being self-critical about the limitations of AI techniques.

Subjective AI requires an integration of two analytical perspectives. First, we must distinguish between intentionality as humans construe it more generally (such as when we see a car as "not wanting to start") and intentionality explicitly designed in AI systems. Toward this end, Jichen Zhu and I have presented an analytical framework for understanding intentional systems[7] (Zhu and Harrell 2009; Zhu 2009). Second, we must distinguish between animacy as humans perceive it more generally and explicitly designed in AI systems[8] (Chow and Harrell 2009b; Chow 2010). In multiple papers with Jichen Zhu and Kenny Chow, we have addressed how developing systems that exhibit intentionality (aboutness) and animacy (liveliness) may have little to do with particular computational implementations. Rather, the phenomena arise from basic cognitive processes allowing humans to construe intentionality and animacy when we encounter them. Humans interpret inanimate artifacts as possessing intentionality in order to explain their behaviors. We also design artifacts that seem animate in order to imbue them with greater emotional salience, intimacy, and closeness to human behavior.

Expressive Epistemologies and the GRIOT System

Let us now turn to an example of a subjective AI platform, the GRIOT system,[9] to illustrate many of the concepts discussed. GRIOT is a subjective AI platform developed to implement works of interactive narrative, poetry, and related types of interactive multimedia expression (Harrell 2007b). The GRIOT system was developed in response to questions such as: Could a computer help tell stories from multiple character perspectives? What about multiple cultural perspectives? What about with different feelings? Different imagery? As such, GRIOT is a research system implemented to explore a set of ideas about how to make narrative and poetic expression on a computer more improvisational. A central challenge was to develop technology focused on composing content that is meaningfully different each time and theory to explain just what "meaningfully different" means. Here I would like to discuss GRIOT's implementation, the use of expressive epistemologies in GRIOT, and critical reflection about the system.

For systems made in GRIOT, the focus is not the individual output of one execution, but rather the variety of narratives and output that the code generates in response to user input. A conceptual blending algorithm called Alloy that can combine multiple epistemic spaces to produce new ones lies at the heart of GRIOT. Alloy generates blends of epistemic spaces drawn from epistemic domains, which are represented mathematically. These formal mathematical representations are based on Joseph Goguen's approach, called *algebraic semiotics*, which allows for precise descriptions of multimedia elements (and meaning-conveying systems more generally, as shall be discussed in chapter 4). Epistemic spaces are combined according to principles that produce "optimal" blends. Typically, this optimality results in "commonsense" blends, but for particular poetic effects, different criteria can be utilized that might instead be optimized to generate unexpected metaphorical blends.

GRIOT Case Analysis: *The Girl with Skin of Haints and Seraphs*

We can make clear GRIOT's functionality, and the role of expressive epistemologies in it, using an example implemented in it. *The Girl with Skin of Haints and Seraphs* is an interactive poem that was first implemented in a noninteractive form as the initial deployment of the Alloy algorithm for generative purposes within another system. It has been subsequently updated with each iteration of GRIOT, and it provides a good example for tracing through the execution of an interactive polymorphic poem. It is called a "polymorphic poem" because although some aspects of it are fixed, such as the narrative structure, the specific poem output is quite different with each execution. *The Girl with Skin of Haints and Seraphs* is a text-based system; other works produced with GRIOT involve multimedia elements such as animation or digital video, and I shall look at an example of such a work later in this chapter.

Thematically, *The Girl with Skin of Haints and Seraphs* is intended to convey limitations of simplistic binary views of social identity. In other words, it is intended to reveal phantasms focused on limited oppositions such as the highly stereotyped "black" and "white" identities exposed by the Clark study (Clark and Clark 1947) and the Toomer short story "Becky" (Toomer 1969) in chapter 1. *The Girl with Skin*

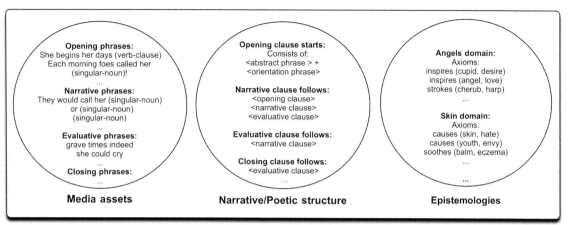

FIGURE 3.5
Authors using GRIOT must specify three components, as shown here.

of Haints and Seraphs does so by generating verbal imagery describing the life experiences of a girl with skin made from the binary opposites of angels and demons. Each particular execution of the polymorphic poem generates unexpected verbal imagery based on combining a data structure representing epistemic spaces that are drawn from the binary oppositional epistemologies representing blackness and whiteness, Africa and Europe, angels and demons, and an epistemology representing skin. In this way, any particular generated poem constructs a phantasm. However, running the polymorphic poem multiple times (the polymorphic poem itself can be run since it is a generative computational work with different output each time) reveals phantasms because each instance is grounded in different underlying expressive epistemologies and is illustrated using different verbal imagery.

The polymorphic poem's phantasm-revealing aim of exposing the dynamic nature of social identity can be described most clearly by looking at the way the program produces different poems with different novel metaphors each time it is run. Authoring in GRIOT requires the specification of three components such as illustrated in figure 3.5: (1) multimedia (including textual) assets, (2) a narrative/poetic structure, and (3) a set of expressive epistemologies related to the content of the assets (e.g., describing content or themes related to the assets).

Let us begin by looking at each of these components and how they relate to one another in order to create instances of output.

Textual Media Assets Used in *The Girl with Skin of Haints and Seraphs*

To start, a user enters a keyword that refers to one of the themes of the poem. The next line of the poem is then generated to incorporate that theme after it has been integrated with another theme selected by the system. If the word entered by the user is not recognized by the system as related to the poem's themes, the system chooses both themes to be integrated. The specifics regarding how these themes are represented will be explained in an upcoming subsection on expressive epistemologies in *The Girl with Skin of Haints and Seraphs.* For now, let us focus on the fact that the lines of text vary each time the poem is executed. Let us say that the user enters the keyword "Europe" at the > prompt. This keyword selects the "Europe stereotypes" theme, which could then be integrated by the system with another theme such as "whiteness," "angels," "blackness," "demons," "skin," or "Africa stereotypes." The first line would then be output, which might be

```
her tale began when she was infected with white female-itis
```

which integrates the "Europe stereotypes" theme with the system-selected theme of whiteness, or

```
she began her days looking in the mirror at her own pale-
skinned death-figure face
```

which integrates the "Europe stereotypes" theme with the system-selected theme of "demons," or any of a number of alternate phrases (there are fourteen templates for such opening phrases; when generated content is incorporated, there is an extremely large number of variations possible based on those fourteen templates). In the case of a text-based GRIOT work, such phrases are represented as assets that I shall call "phrase templates." An example of a phrase template is `(her tale began when (* g-verb-clause))` in the LISP computer language syntax of the implementation, in which the inner parenthesis is a variable called a wildcard (indicated by the initial asterisk in the parentheses) that gets instantiated with a verb phrase containing a past-tense transitive verb, such as `(was infected with (* g-singular-noun))`.

As an example of variation within a particular phrase due to wildcard replacement, among many other possibilities, the first line in the previous example could have also been either

```
her tale began when she was infected with tribal-warrior
spectre-itis
```

if the user- and computer-selected integrated themes were "Africa stereotypes" and "demons," or

```
her tale began when she was infected with black demon-itis
```

if the user- and computer-selected themes were "blackness" and "demons," depending upon how the phrase template was instantiated. That is, in one instance of output, a clause within the text might be instantiated based on combining epistemic spaces for stereotypes of whiteness and skin or whiteness in demons (as in the first two examples). It could also have been instantiated based on combining epistemic spaces for stereotypes of Africa and demons or blackness and skin (as in the latter two examples).

Simplifying the previous example, let us say that one set of phrase templates contains (her tale began when she was infected with (* g-singular-noun)-itis) in the LISP syntax of the implementation, in which the inner parenthesized statement is a variable that gets replaced with a generated noun cluster or a noun paired with a modifier. Exactly how the wildcard is replaced is determined by a combination of user input and the contents of the wildcard itself, to be explained shortly.[10] User input plays a role in wildcard replacement, as the user-entered keywords determine one of the domains to be used in constructing blends that will be used in template instantiation. After templates have been instantiated, subsequent templates are chosen according to the narrative (or poetic) structure of the work.

Narrative and Poetic Structure in *The Girl with Skin of Haints and Seraphs*

The initial implementation of an automaton to structure narrative clauses was relatively simple and was used to instantiate an adapted version of William Labov's (1972) empirical model of the narrative structure of personal experience from sociolinguistics. A formalization of this model is described in Goguen 2001. The format for specifying the automaton was designed in a way that was easy for a polymorphic poem author to specify.

Subsequent projects have necessitated the development of a more powerful machine to structure clauses, in particular to enable hierarchically organized and nested narrative structures. Toward this end, Joseph Goguen and I developed the Event Structure Machine; speaking technically, it is a probabilistic, bounded, stack transition machine[11] (Harrell 2006). The operation of the Event Structure Machine is centered on a primary "clause." The functioning of the Event Structure Machine can be understood by examining the components of these "clauses." A clause consists of a name, pair of integers, a subclause name, an exit-to clause name, and a read-flag, all surrounded by a pair of parentheses. A clause is to be interpreted as follows:

1. The <name> is a symbol used for referring to the clause type. This name can be anything and does not necessarily refer to specific clause types from various linguistic or narrative theories.

2. The <number-pair> consists of an integer indicating the minimum and maximum numbers of repetitions of the clause.

3. The <subclause> refers to the subsequent nested clause type to be selected.

4. The <exit-to-clause> refers to the subsequent clause type to be selected after all subclauses have been exhausted.

5. The <read-flag> determines whether user input is to first be read and taken into account when instantiating a phrase template of the selected clause type.

For example, the polymorphic poem *The Girl with Skin of Haints and Seraphs* (Harrell 2005) was implemented in the Event Structure Machine format as follows:

```
(structure

    (orientation-clause (1 1) () narrative-clause read)

    (narrative-clause (3 5) evaluation-clause coda-clause read)

    (evaluation-clause (0 1) () () n)

    (coda-clause (1 1) () () read))
```

A possible poem output by such an automaton would have the following structure (with clause names standing in for actual clauses):

```
    orientation-clause
    narrative-clause
        evaluation-clause
    narrative-clause
        evaluation-clause
    narrative-clause
        evaluation-clause
    coda-clause
```

The Girl with Skin of Haints and Seraphs (Sample Output 1)	The Girl with Skin of Haints and Seraphs (Sample Output 2)
> Africa	> evil
her arrival onto this earth was marked when	*every night she wakes covered with hate,*
first-born and charcoal-girl transforms to	*awe sweat*
impoverished-elder or charcoal-woman	> Europe
> Europe	*imperialist and girl thoughts taunted her*
she worked raising snow-queen original-lady	*as a teen*
children of her own	*serious times were here*
the young lady would prevail	> Africa
> demon	*drum spiked-tail vapor steamed from her*
a caress across her skin scares up demon	*pores when she rode her bicycle*
black	*in the rain*
> angel	> angel
her failure was ignoring her wings and	*when twenty-one she was a homely woman*
original-lady nature	*that was nothing lovely*
and she felt glad	> skin
> white	*tears ran relay races between her girl and*
as she grew older she saw entitlement	*European eyes and her*
defiance wrinkles upon her face	*ignorance, longing earlobes and back*
> juju	*she could laugh*
ebony-wood-like brimstone defines fetish	> angel
bedrock, the sign that let her know she	*her dreams were of cupid epidermis*
was finally really alive	*life was a sight gag*
	> demon
	so she resolved to find bat-wings and
	pointed-nose passion and be happy

FIGURE 3.6
The text here consists of two excerpts of poetic narrative text generated while running *The Girl with Skin of Haints and Seraphs.*

In this example, each "evaluation-clause" is nested under a "narrative-clause" and there are three repeats of each "narrative-clause, evaluation-clause" pair. Such structures can easily be elaborated to define more complexly structured output; for example, changing the event structure clause from `(orientation-clause (1 1) () narrative-clause read)` to `(orientation-clause (3 3) narrative-clause () read)` would result in output consisting of three full repetitions of the output structure in the previous example. Figure 3.6 shows examples of real generated output that incorporates blended concepts generated using Alloy (the LISP line breaks are left in so that clauses may be more easily distinguished). During execution, the user-entered keywords such as "Europe" or "Africa" select one of the epistemologies (representing themes) to draw epistemic spaces from in order to be blended; the system chooses the other epistemic space input to the blend.

Expressive Epistemologies in *The Girl with Skin of Haints and Seraphs*

It must be emphasized that the wildcard replacement in the templates does not occur simply by selecting text from a set prewritten fragments of English language. Rather, the inner parenthesized phrase is a variable that gets instantiated with a blend of epistemic spaces, which are logical axioms. The results of this blend, constructed using the Alloy conceptual blending algorithm, are then subsequently mapped to English phrases. In this manner, arguments of other templates are instantiated with elements from other epistemologies; hence it is a major subjective issue for the artist to choose the epistemologies appropriately.

We can now discuss how expressive epistemologies are used for wildcard replacement. The expressive epistemologies used in *The Girl with Skin of Haints and Seraphs* consist of four elements. These are a set of data types (also known as "sorts"), a set of constants of those data types, a set of logical axioms, and a set of relations between constants that are constrained by the axioms. We saw earlier when discussing possible different generated lines that using different themes such as "Europe stereotypes," "Africa stereotypes," "demons," "angels," and so on would result in different output. As an example, figure 3.7 provides a sketch of an epistemology representing the epistemic domain of "angels." In the table, the format "Data type: constant name" is used to indicate the data types of particular constants; capitalization indicates data types rather than proper nouns. Axioms set constraints for relations, in this case indicating the data types they can be defined on. Points of ellipses are used where there are many more elements in a given row that have been omitted for the sake of brevity (the actual epistemology included much more information).

Expressive Epistemology for Angels			
Data types	Constants	Axioms	Relations
Person Emotion Object	Person: angel Person: cherub Person: cupid Emotion: desire Emotion: love Object: harp Object: cloud Object: home …	inspires (Person, Emotion) strokes (Person, Object) composes (Object, Object) lives-in (Person, Object) …	inspires (cupid, desire) inspires (angel, love) strokes (cherub, harp) composes (cloud, home) lives-in (angel, cloud) …

FIGURE 3.7
A sketch of the epistemology for angels used in *The Girl with Skin of Haints and Seraphs* reveals subjective decisions of the system author.

The epistemology for "angels" is not meant to be an objective representation of canonical information defining angels culled from literary or religious texts. From this point of view, it would be incorrect to include constants such as "Cupid," which a human would interpret as referring to the god of desire in Roman mythology. Rather, the epistemology is a subjective representation of loosely related thematic information related to winged humans: emotions such as love and desire, mystical places such as clouds for homes, and more. The epistemology has been authored to evoke a range of associations that make allusions to literature, fantasy, culture, and religion[12]—the author's intended allusions for the interpretive purposes at hand. It must also be noted that the interpretation of the content of the epistemology is strictly a matter for human authors and users. The tokens themselves such as "love" or "cherub" do not mean anything to the system. It is therefore up to the authors to ensure that their meanings are consistent in some way with humanly interpretable cultural information.

Let us now look similarly at a sketch of an expressive epistemology for skin used by the polymorphic poem (see figure 3.8).

Just as with the epistemology for angels, the epistemology for skin is idiosyncratic and subjectively determined. For example, a type of personification takes place, in that skin is of type Person, which a human could interpret to mean that skin can stand in for an entire person under this worldview. Certain details about the everyday inconveniences of skin are included, such as the skin problems of eczema and dandruff. At the same time, more sweeping statements about skin are included, such as the relation that skin, considered as a whole person, causes hate (perhaps based in the worldview revealed by the Clark study [Clark 1947] discussed in chapter 1 in which a degree of self-hate could have been revealed in the cases of some participants) or that youth causes envy (based in a cultural worldview that values young people's skin).

Expressive Epistemology for Skin			
Data types	Constants	Axioms	Relations
Person Emotion Object	Person: girl Person: skin Person: youth Emotion: hate Emotion: envy Object: dandruff Object: balm Object: eczema ...	causes (Person, Emotion) soothes (Object, Object) uses (Person, Object) flakes-off (Person, Object) ...	causes (skin, hate) causes (youth, envy) soothes (balm, eczema) uses (girl, balm) flakes-off (skin, dandruff) ...

FIGURE 3.8
A sketch of the epistemology for skin used in *The Girl with Skin of Haints and Seraphs* also reveals subjective decisions of the system author.

During execution, epistemic spaces are drawn from these epistemologies in the form of subsets of their relations. For example, an epistemic space drawn from the angels epistemology might include only inspires (angel, love), composes (cloud, home), and lives-in (angel, cloud). An epistemic space drawn from the skin epistemology might include only causes (youth, envy) and flakes-off (skin, dandruff). In this case, a blended epistemic space output by Alloy might include inspires/causes (angel/youth, envy/desire) and flakes-off (angel/youth, dandruff), with the slashes representing combined concepts with characteristics of both.[13] A very simple English language mapping from this concept might be: "The angel youth inspires and creates envy and flakes-off dandruff." Minor syntactic and lexical transformations can produce somewhat less grammatically clunky realizations in English such as "The dandruffy young angel inspires envy and desire." Furthermore, though we have not implemented this extension yet, by checking a lexicon for synonymy (perhaps by utilizing another system such as WordNet), such a phrase could be rewritten in a way that reveals even less of the underlying logical structure, such as "The dandruff-headed cherub inspires jealousy." When the blend of epistemic spaces is represented in English and integrated with a phrase template, we can say that the result is a phantasm if the verbal imagery it creates is meaningful to a human interpreting it.

Taking a step back, we can say these two epistemologies for angels and skin are meant to lend themselves to prompting the phantasms that one might imagine when hearing the phrase "skin of angels." The phrase could mean skin with the qualities of angel skin, but it could also more literally mean skin composed of attributes associated with angels. This conception of the blend between concepts representing angels and skin is quite nontraditional and lends itself to a host of unlikely, and possibly uncanny, metaphors. Although it cannot be claimed that a phrase such as "The dandruffy young angel inspires envy and desire" has this effect for all readers (of course, even the most renowned poets cannot be assured of their works' effects upon readers), the authorial intention has been made clear here. Along with social values, such as those elicited from the Clark study, aesthetic values juxtaposing everyday information with fantastic information can be embedded in the choice of content. These are the types of characteristic that cause these epistemologies to be considered *expressive*. They were authored for the explicit purpose of creating uncanny metaphors that contrast greatly with more typical notions of skin and the social binary oppositions that they represent. They include typical stereotypes but also include specific everyday and fantastic details so as to render those stereotypes unfamiliar—with the hope of revealing the phantasms that cause the stereotypes to hold so much sway under some cultural worldviews.

The GRIOT Architecture

The GRIOT system can dynamically compose multimedia elements using a server to handle generating text as described previously, but with the added functionality of an algorithm to find analogical matches between the metadata (e.g., describing both visual and conceptual content of the asset) used to annotate multimedia files. Based on these matches, graphics, sounds, and other types of media can be composed. For each work built in GRIOT, a client must be developed that consists of a set of graphical assets, rules for displaying assets and sending messages to the server, and a graphical user interface (GUI) to allow users to interact with assets. I shall discuss an example of such a work later in the case of the *Living Liberia Fabric*. The complete GRIOT architecture is illustrated in figure 3.9. The GRIOT system's functionality can be summarized as follows:

1. Authoring with GRIOT: Initially, a narrative or poetic system designer inputs the following components, which are processed by the system in preparation for user input:

   a. a set of *Epistemologies* that provide information about a set of concepts (in "The Girl with Skin of Haints and Seraphs," the *Epistemologies* are: skin, angels, demons, Europe stereotypes, and Africa stereotypes, all composed of sets of axioms),

   b. a set of *Media Assets* (*Phrase Templates* in the case of text-based systems, which are phrases organized by the type of clause they can compose, with wildcards that will be replaced on each execution), and

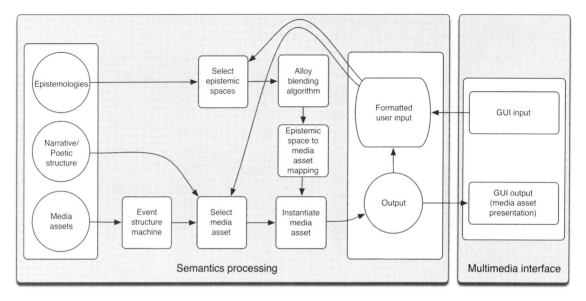

FIGURE 3.9
The GRIOT architecture supports building interactive multimedia narrative and poetic works as forms of phantasmal media.

    c. an *Event Structure Machine* that defines how clauses can be narratively or poetically composed (in *The Girl with Skin of Haints and Seraphs*, these are based on a model from sociolinguistics research, a formalization of William Labov's structure of narratives of personal experience; Labov 1972).

2. Using GRIOT: During the execution of GRIOT, user input determines one of the *Epistemologies* used and responses are produced as output to the GUI. This process occurs as follows:

    a. The system selects *Epistemic Spaces* from the selected *Epistemologies* based upon the user's input. These *Epistemic Spaces* constitute input that describes two concepts that will be combined along with the commonalities between them.

    b. The generative core of the work is a conceptual blending algorithm called *Alloy*. This component can be used to blend epistemic spaces to construct new ones. In some multimedia systems, this component is used to find analogies between *Epistemic Spaces* that act as metadata for *Media Assets* in order to select the most appropriate asset to display.

c. The blended output from *Alloy* is mapped to a media form using a *Media Mapping*; these mappings are rules describing how the logical representation should be mapped to a *Media Asset* (in the case of text-based works, these are often grammatical mappings from logical axioms to natural language).

d. The *Media Asset* determined by the *Media Mapping* is integrated with other assets as determined by the *Event Structure Machine* (in the case of text-based works, the *Phrase Template* is now said to be "instantiated" and is output).

3. User-System Input Loop: If the poem is not yet complete, the system awaits new user input. The poem's ending is determined by the *Event Structure Machine*.

We can now turn our attention to how GRIOT was used to develop a multimedia interactive narrative system. In order to express more clearly how human judgment, subjectivity, interaction, and expressive epistemologies play a role in design and implementation with GRIOT, I now turn our attention to a system called the *Living Liberia Fabric*.

GRIOT Case Analysis: The *Living Liberia Fabric*

The *Living Liberia Fabric*, created with GRIOT, is a computer-based memorial and an interactive narrative developed to support the goal of lasting peace after years of civil war in Liberia (1979–2003; Harrell et al. 2010). Because the goal of the *Living Liberia Fabric* is to serve as a memorial, understanding the tragic nature of the war and its related history with sensitivity and awareness is an important prerequisite to considering the system technically, both while the system was being developed and while discussing it now.

The Final Report of the Republic of Liberia Truth and Reconciliation Commission (TRC) describes the country of Liberia and its history of contestation as follows:

> Liberia is located on the Atlantic coast of West Africa and encompasses a territory of 43,000 square miles. The country shares borders with Sierra Leone to the northwest, Guinea to the northeast, and Côte d'Ivoire to the southeast. Liberia's 15 counties correspond to territories historically claimed by particular Liberian indigenous ethnic groups. English is the official language of Liberia, although more than 20 indigenous languages and a form of English known as Liberian English are also in daily use. . . .

> While Liberia has often been hailed as one of the only African nations never to be colonized, the historical facts are more complex. The settlements of repatriated Africans were in fact, governed by white American agents of the American Colonization Society for the first several years of their existence.
>
> Although the U.S. government funded much of the American Colonization Society's efforts, it was clear that the United States never intended to formally establish itself as a colonial power in Liberia. Liberia became a sovereign nation under Americo-Liberian rule in 1847. The indigenous inhabitants of the territory claimed for Liberia were largely antagonistic to the establishment of the Liberian nation. In fact, the American Colonization Society, and later the fledgling Liberian government, was at war with various indigenous tribes over territory and trade routes throughout the 1800s. Liberia's complex history created a "state of contestation" which remains today a major source of conflict and disunity. (Republic of Liberia Truth and Reconciliation Commission [TRC] 2009, 3–4)

This conflict and disunity led to numerous tensions that erupted beginning in the 1970s and led to a military coup in 1980. This conflict later escalated into two civil wars in Liberia between 1989 and 2003, initiated when Charles Taylor and his National Patriotic Front of Liberia invaded. Yet one must remember the context for the conflict in that the nature of Liberia's founding led to "lack of education and other opportunities for those of non-Americo-Liberian origin," and that "impunity for corruption and systematic human rights abuses were attributes of the Monrovia hegemony of a few families that controlled the wealth of the nation" (TRC 2009, 4–5).

The TRC identified ten root causes of the conflict: poverty, a weak judiciary, polarizing disparities between settlers and indigenous peoples, ethnic diversity, entrenched corrupt political social and military systems, discrimination against women, land disputes, misunderstandings of Liberian history, crises of identity and sense of nationhood, and the breakdown of the family and traditional values. During the war, brutal acts of atrocity took place that mere statistics could never begin to convey. However, it is important to state that around 250,000 people were killed and one-third of the population displaced. A host of violations including assault, forced labor, rape, torture, murder, and other heinous acts have been documented as occurring on a grand scale to women, men, and children alike, with men as the much higher percentage of perpetrators, though both women and men were victimized in more equal proportions.

It was a monumental challenge for the TRC in light of these events to develop recommendations for Liberia to rebuild social ties in light of persistent memories of war and violence. The TRC wrote:

> Collective memories built around war and violence play an important role in the process of rebuilding positive ties between the different segments of a society. *Particularly crucial in such a process are the public and private rituals and narratives that sustain collective and individual memories of the history, causes and course of mass crime, and allow the re-interpretation and re-assertion of the belief systems* [emphasis added]. However, while memorialization can be a bridge between past and future and contribute to reconciliation and healing projects, in many instances it further marginalizes women. Women's experiences, contributions, struggles for change, and campaigns for peace in Liberia must be mainstreamed into the memorialization practice to ensure that they serve as mechanisms for inspiration and motivation for current and future generations. This would also encourage civic engagement around women's experiences of conflict, breaking cultures of silences and shame, and furthering the course towards gender equality. (TRC 2009, 350–351)

It is in the context of these observations and recommendations regarding memorialization, and the role that narrative plays in it, that the *Living Liberia Fabric* was conceived. Initiating the project required an attempt to gain some comprehension of the nature of the civil war and its effects. Questions were raised by students and researchers regarding issues such as our qualifications as a non-Liberian team to engage the subject matter, our roles as outsiders or as stakeholders, sensitivity to the nature of the atrocities of war, and the degree to which the technologies at our disposal were relevant to Liberian people both in Liberia and the diaspora. We asked who the audience would be for any memorial we could create. We considered whether the memorial should reflect a particular view toward the civil war, such as that of a peace-museum or that of the TRC itself.

Some orientation was gained through engaging a concept emerging from another site of genocide that many of us were aware of, even if geographically far afield from Liberia. It was the notion of *survivance*, a term from Native American studies, which refers to people who have grappled with the threat of extinction of their cultures. Native American studies scholar Gerald Vizenor writes: "Survivance stories are renunciations of dominance, detractions, obtrusions, the unbearable sentiments of tragedy, and the legacy of victimry. Survivance is the heritable right of succession or reversion of an estate and, in the course of international declarations of human rights, is a native estate of native survivance" (Vizenor 2008, 1). The multiple genocides faced by Native Americans may seem far distanced from the context of Liberia with its multiplicity of peoples with long, enduring, and noble histories. Yet war in post-colonial settings has the shared characteristics of demeaning humanity, replacing kinship with brutality, tradition with loss of values, and history with a colonial legacy. Survivance emphasizes the importance of concepts such as liberation, dignity, and hopes for a future with cultural foundations, human rights, truth, and reconciliation. These themes provided some early orientation for the role of a memorial system.

Before engaging with any technology, we spent half a year talking to people. Our process encompassed historical background research, a review of peace museums and memorials (virtual and physical), user analysis, scenario-based design, needs assessment, stakeholder analysis, requirements assessment, and iterative design, prototyping, and development.[14] During our iterative research and development phase, two subgroups were assigned. Group I created a stakeholder analysis derived from the TRC report and an assessment of memorial narrative goals. Group II focused on understanding traditional Liberian cultural memorialization and assessing how to facilitate memorialization of events based on that understanding. As an outcome of this process, we saw ourselves as stakeholders, albeit not central ones, rather than outsiders. We decided that the project would be oriented toward giving voice to a diversity of Liberian perspectives and that we would make a GRIOT-based work that was web-accessible and capable of being used with a modest broadband connection. This design was a compromise, because it meant that a large number of people in Liberia might not be able to access it easily, but there were many benefits to the implementation that served the goals of the memorial, such as the ability to honor the subject matter with higher-quality content, as well as serving pedagogical and practical goals. Although diaspora Liberians might have a greater degree of technical access to the work than those in the country, through incorporating content collected by a colleague in the rural areas of Liberia, we could attempt to ground the work in the perspectives of people in the country itself. At the same time, we also tried to ground the project specifically in aspects of Liberian culture and stakeholder perspectives—for example, by better understanding how mourning and memorialization take place in the everyday lives of people in Liberia, then using those preexisting values and practices to guide development of our system. Recognizing that a memorial cannot be agenda-free, two key guides in developing the project were as follows:

• Survivance, which emphasizes traditional culture interfacing with contemporary empowerment. It emphasizes children as the future generation and the role of education in preparing that generation for self-determination. It emphasizes the dignity of people. It emphasizes the margins, not the elite.

• Reconciliation, which emphasizes the future. It must acknowledge that many people have lost an unknowable and irredeemable amount through tragedy. It must acknowledge the ambiguities of issues such as amnesty versus accountability. It must provide a space for exploration of emotion about these issues as well as political reasoning. Simultaneously, it can emphasize the potential for future peace, the dignity of survivors, and exemplars who have forged bonds across diverse lines.

I cannot say that these were the correct decisions, that all of our goals were met, or that we can engage the topic of war with appropriate sensitivity even now. However, I hope that I have conveyed our earlier perspectives and the nature of our attempt while highlighting the small scale of our intervention in light of the broader work of the TRC and the history and context of the war itself.

The *Living Liberia Fabric* is a dynamic document than can be explored at multiple levels. One can enter the space deeply, or meditate upon the surface as one does at a reflecting pool. It is an experimental project, as there is no off-the-shelf solution available to construct a digital system based in Liberia's culture, the specificities of the conflict, and the nuances of the needs: hence the necessity of a *cultural computing* perspective. We aimed to construct a computational system rooted in Liberian culture, to tell multiple Liberian stories, and to serve the more abstract need to counteract phantasms that enable subjugation, violence, and oppression without regard for human rights, dignity, or survivance. We would like the *Living Liberia Fabric* to be understood as an ongoing dialogue with the people of Liberia and the Liberian diaspora. Stakeholders may choose to reject its values, but the system must not attempt to be objective and values-neutral.

We can now begin to describe the system itself. The *Living Liberia Fabric* uses expressive epistemologies and represents the perspective on aims and methods regarding the design of expressive AI systems that I have termed "subjective AI." For example, the *Living Liberia Fabric* exhibits a degree of system intentionality because the program expresses value judgments regarding the real-world issue of civil war in the country of Liberia. It does not merely respond to user control and give users stories that they want. It exhibits a degree of animacy because it is based on a "living fabric" metaphor in which user input directs which multimedia assets are figuratively "dyed" into graphical fabric. Furthermore, it uses an expressive epistemology in order to generate stories from different perspectives and focused on different themes each time it is run.

The memorial resembles a traditional West African fabric. The system begins by displaying illustrated figures representing different stakeholder groups as the sound of the ocean plays in the background, creating a reflective space for mourning (see figure 3.10). Exploring the image interactively, by moving a cursor over a figure, causes ghostly figures related to that stakeholder to fade in around it.

Subsequently, it features a pattern composed of shapes such as flowers or diamonds. As shown in figure 3.11, these shapes act as frames for displaying assets such as video clips and archival photography.

FIGURE 3.10
A user encounters a variation of the initial screen shown here when interacting with the *Living Liberia Fabric*. The interface contains dynamically placed clickable images of stakeholders that aid in determining the narrative theme.

FIGURE 3.11
Subsequent fabric-inspired patterns in the *Living Liberia Fabric* contain videos, images, and related assets.

As the system runs, poetic captions frame a narrative that provides background information on the war, reflections by stakeholders, and ideas to support peace and reconciliation in the future. Figure 3.12 displays excerpts of the raw poetic text generated from two executions of the system before it has been integrated into the visual imagery.

1) Youth-focused poetic narrative	2) Woman-focused poetic narrative
one of 1.5 million displaced,	our lost mother reflecting
children of Liberia now tracing the tangled	not a story, a human
roots of the loss	the first Americo-Liberians acquired land
as Liberia began to establish itself as a	with arms
new nation, a small number of Americo-	there were positive stories of survival
Liberian families and their patronage	Margibi 3,394 victims
networks dominated all aspects of	that woman forgetting there
government	Rivercess 2,315 victims
individuals were affected; we need to	what can we do in the future?
remember more than statistics	regal, everyday women lead the way
Bong 12,546 victims	it is a process driven by the people
decolonizing boy remembering	the post-colonial often recaps the venom of
unknown 781 victims	the colony
what can we do in the future?	woman forgetting, we can be one
we are uplifted	we can love again
rising like a baobab	look toward ourselves
the post-colonial often recaps the venom of	possibility
the colony	
victim forgetting, child of the nation	
the government has a role to play, the	
people are the true answer	
we are moving to new horizons	
survivance is our nobility	

FIGURE 3.12
The text here consists of two excerpts of poetic narrative text generated while running the *Living Liberia Fabric*.

The user's input guides which stakeholder groups and other themes the story focuses on. At the same time as the users select aspects of the narrative's direction, a polymorphic poem implemented with GRIOT plays two roles: it generates the narrative text displayed as captions and ensures that the next assets to be displayed are coherent with the stakeholder group, theme, and visual qualities of the user's selection. The *Living Liberia Fabric* ensures these types of coherence by using aspects of expressive epistemologies described in the previous section. As such, the remainder of this section uses this aspect of the system to provide examples of the concepts of epistemologies, formats, epistemic semantics, epistemic algorithms, and epistemic design processes.

The *Living Liberia Fabric* features epistemologies. All of the assets are annotated with logical data structures. These are small sections of text describing the assets. This annotation describes the content of the assets at three different levels. The division of metadata into these levels is based on the insights regarding the relationship between visual structure and conceptual information argued for in Hiraga 2005 based on the influential ideas of Charles Saunders Peirce (1965). First, the assets are described at the visual, or *iconic*, level, which includes information such as the degree of saturation or dominant color of an image. Second, the assets are described at the structural, or *diagrammatic*, level, which provides information related to layout and conventions from related media such as film (e.g., the appropriate types of frame—whether it is a close-up, medium shot, or long shot). Third, the content, or *conceptual*, level provides information about the content of the tiles such as theme or relevant stakeholder group. The conceptual level may be the most important of the three because it connects assets to expressive epistemologies implemented by the system's developers based on our preliminary studies. The primary expressive epistemologies are related to overlapping stakeholder groups, such as "youth," "women," "survivors," or "combatants." They also represent subthemes that are more nuanced, such as "postwar," "atrocity," "education," or "hope." To arrive at these subthemes, we standardized the results of interviews conducted with survivors of the civil war and the final report of the TRC. Additionally, we conducted research into traditional memorialization practices in Liberia and media conventions established in previous work using the GRIOT system (Chow and Harrell 2009a; Harrell 2007a). The standardization of these highly subjective categories of information represents computer code that captures a particular set of ways of knowing the world. Hence this encoding resulted in epistemologies.

The *Living Liberia Fabric* also can be used to demonstrate the concept of an epistemic format. The metadata format was designed to be easily picked up by non-technical practitioners working on the project. Based on the three-level epistemologies discussed previously, we settled on a uniform set of descriptive labels (tags) to be used at each level. At the conceptual level, these tags emerged from a process that took into account a number of socially sensitive issues. For example, a video focused on the broad stakeholder group of "women" might include tags describing subthemes such as

```
<subtheme>
   <theme>activism</theme>
   <theme>empowerment</theme>
   <theme>social justice</theme>
</subtheme>
```

whereas another might focus on subthemes such as

```
<subtheme>
   <theme>activism</theme>
   <theme>nationalism</theme>
   <theme>daughter</theme>
   <theme>bravery</theme>
   <theme>survivor</theme>
</subtheme>.
```

Subthemes can be nested within one another. Furthermore, there is a partial ordering on the elements of a subtheme, with most important elements appearing earlier. The system takes this representation of conceptual information and renders a set of logical propositions constituting epistemologies such as those used in *The Girl with Skin of Haints and Seraphs*. Using a standardized format saved developers from having to engage directly with the mathematical representations required by the underlying AI system (programmed in LISP). We ensured that this format was simple to use, yet amenable to complex processing.

The *Living Liberia Fabric* also exhibits epistemic semantics algorithms. It uses the previously mentioned Alloy algorithm to blend epistemic spaces and an algorithm to find matches between epistemic spaces. As in *The Girl with Skin of Haints and Seraphs*, these blends are then mapped to natural language and then integrated into output text. For example, a line of text can be customized to refer to a "woman activist" rather than a "boy survivor" using this mechanism. The text is then narratively structured using the Event Structure Machine as discussed earlier. Additionally, the system employs an analogical matching algorithm that uses the epistemic spaces as metadata for assets and ranks the similarity between a given asset and all of the others. The system can prioritize either visual, media conventional, or conceptual coherence by changing the relative weighting between the iconic, diagrammatic, and conceptual levels. When the user clicks an asset, the next assets to be displayed will be selected from those ranked as most coherent with the user's selection. The combination of customized narratively structured text and visually/conceptually coherent assets results in an experience that is meaningfully different for users each time. Users do not directly select which videos they will see, yet they can guide the system in ways that will reveal multiple perspectives on the civil war and suggestions necessary to maintain peace in the future.

Finally, the *Living Liberia Fabric* exhibits an epistemic design process. For us, the most challenging part of the project was engaging with the human needs and values that we discussed earlier and that we tried to use as the foundation for the system. The project addressed a topic whose social and emotional impact cannot be overstated. The values that we sought to uphold are not mere technical determinations. These values include not prioritizing the perspective of any particular Liberian ethnic group, respectfully engaging with sensitive content because none of the system developers experienced the Liberian civil war directly, and making sure to place the needs of Liberian stakeholders first (including those who were not computationally or print literate). Our hope is that the structure of the expressive epistemologies constructed and the selection of media assets can begin to address these needs. We sought to ground the aesthetic sensibility of our project, including its model of interaction, in Liberian culture rather than just picking a currently popular interaction model. The specific fabric interface metaphor emerged from this aim, though it is clear that many conventional interface mechanisms such as pointing-and-clicking using a trackpad or mouse persist. In retrospect, I would say that the system is insufficiently oriented toward people in Liberia; perhaps a better implementation would (or could, for a future iteration) target smaller mobile devices, to which more Liberians have access. We cannot claim to have solved all of the problems we meant to address; however, what I hoped to convey here is a process of system development involving the central concepts of phantasmal media in constructive and engaged dialogue with serious real-world issues, meanings, and worldviews. The concept of expressive epistemologies is aimed at supporting design of such subjective systems.

Developing a system to address all of these subjective challenges requires a process driven by human values, not technical needs. In particular, the memorial's production of a different story each time it is used is based on the fact that there is no singular perspective on the war that we sought to promote. The technical approach of using epistemologies based on stakeholder perspectives was a response to this aim. The system's capacity to evoke and reveal phantasms through image spaces based in its specific media assets was similarly a response to this aim. The narrative structure implemented using the event structure engine is another example of a technical approach to a subjective issue. In this case, regarding thematic narrative content, the system presents narrative events in three stages. Initially, the system creates a space for reflection, grieving, and mourning. Key issues addressed include the scale of loss and diversity of the peoples involved in the civil war. The system also addresses the context of horrendous loss resulting from the war. For example, there were positive narratives, including often overlooked women's tales and everyday heroics. At the same time, there were atrocities at a grand scale and many unnamed victims. Finally, in terms of thematic content, the system is intended to raise ambiguities and complexities of war—it does not provide answers. The subjective choices made in the development of the expressive epistemologies were intended to balance concerns such as respect for traditional culture with awareness of situations in which traditional culture also may have oppressed people. They are intended to balance the need for perpetrators to be held accountable with the need for peace. A process for understanding how humans negotiate these tensions was necessary before our epistemologies could begin to encode these oppositional concerns.

The interaction in the work is another case in which the technical approach was an outcome of highly subjective aims. The user-driven nature of the memorial needed to allow users to see that their own self-identified affiliations were represented at the same time as the system represented a diversity of stakeholders. These different perspectives cannot be laid out explicitly due to tensions that remain between different stakeholder groups, yet they can be culturally and metaphorically implied. Again, our epistemologies needed to encode these differing perspectives, and our epistemic algorithms needed to be able to integrate them. Yet before any aspect of the expressive epistemologies could be implemented, we needed to increase our humanistic understanding of the war.

In order to achieve greater understanding of our aims, we undertook a process that in many respects was more social than technical. For example, I have described how the West African fabric-based GUI metaphor emerged from a combination of empirical fieldwork and research into cultural needs, values, histories, and aesthetics. Our design process encompassed historical background research and a review of peace museums and memorials (virtual and physical). Simultaneously, we also drew on approaches from computer science and design. All of these approaches, accompanied by healthy discussion of the disciplinary values informing each of these techniques, played a role in iterative design, prototyping, and development.

In the end, the *Living Liberia Fabric* is able to create quite variable, yet coherent narratives from different viewpoints. The system's output is successful only to the degree that it can effectively provoke, challenge, inspire, and transform users in light of diverse perspectives of the Liberian civil war and needs for sustainable peace. At the same time, I hope that the aims and perspectives taken in development of the system are useful for developers interested in producing subjective AI systems with related aims.

Reflections on GRIOT

With hindsight, certain strengths, characteristics, and limitations of GRIOT and Alloy have become clear. Aside from exemplifying the concepts of expressive epistemologies, epistemic formats, epistemic semantics algorithms, and epistemic design processes, the primary phantasmal media contribution presented here consists of a developing set of subjective AI methods. This work also contributes a new theoretical framework to ground those methods and a set of techniques for producing computational narratives grounded in cognitive science and empirical study of the social and cultural needs and values of stakeholders. The focus is on enabling the *subjective* construction of expressive epistemologies, creation of a GUI metaphor, and conducting of asset collection based upon the results of the empirically determined, culturally situated story content. The method that we undertook, and the computational approach exemplified by GRIOT, can generalize to a range of narrative forms not limited to those recognized as traditional Western narratives.

The second contribution relates to the cognitive linguistics foundation of the GRIOT system and its applicability to figurative meaning-making in computational media. As mentioned earlier, cognitive scientists interested in meaning-making processes have described the hallmarks of narrative imagining and poetic thinking—event stories, action stories, parable, metaphor, metonymy, force dynamics, and more (Fauconnier 1999; Fauconnier and Turner 2002; Lakoff and Turner 1989; Narayanan 1999;

Talmy 1988; Turner 1996, 2003)—modeling these building blocks for narrative and poetry has resulted in an extensible framework that has been used in a variety of projects ranging from interactive poetry games to the civil war in Liberia. This is a cognitive-computational substrate upon which specific cultural forms of narrative can be built. The theory of phantasmal media and the specific concept of expressive epistemologies, grounded in cognitive and computational approaches, provide appropriate terminology and structures for GRIOT's algorithms for composing and generating multimedia content within a narrative structured according to users' needs, interests, values, feelings, and more.

Regarding Alloy, for a conceptual blending algorithm to be effective, the input data has to come from somewhere. Ideally, there should be a way to say that one has the right data and that the data is structured in the right way, as well as a nuanced characterization of what counts as "right" in such circumstances. In the absence of knowledge that the data is correctly selected/authored and structured according to some explicitly defined criteria, any algorithm attempting to implement phenomena such as conceptual blending, analogy, or metaphor is really an exercise in what was called *epistemic fluency*, as discussed in this chapter. In other words, authors who know how the algorithm works (though it may be so complicated that the author cannot predict specific output) can create and structure data in ways that ensure the algorithm will produce output that people find compelling (in artistic settings) or convincing (in scientific or engineering settings). This outcome does not diminish what the algorithm does technically; it is only to say that producing effective artworks using GRIOT is not a purely technical endeavor.

In practice, poetry of the type output by *The Girl with Skin of Haints and Seraphs* could probably be created using simpler text-replacement rules lacking a complex underlying cognitive semantics system. However, using an algorithm like Alloy has several advantages. It ensures greater coherence of results because matches are based on concepts sharing the same logical structure, not just choosing text from a database or using a thesaurus. More important, what can be taken from GRIOT and Alloy is a way to think about the problem of generating meaningful variation in a story or computer artwork. The idea is to combine concepts according to a set of stylistic and/or ideological rules predefined by an author. Optimally, this process will take advantage of the latest cognitive science results on how humans manage to come up with new imaginative visions that are coherent enough to share with others. Only after concepts are combined does the system try to find the best way to represent these new concepts. In GRIOT, this process is still rudimentary. Yet GRIOT's ability to concatenate words from logical axioms and insert them into text or to match images based on similar metadata suggests a way to think about the challenge of computationally improvising *meaningfully different content each time the computing system is run.*

Finally, an interesting philosophical issue is raised by this program: human input might be considered cheating by traditional AI practitioners, as most AI text-generation projects are oriented toward total automation and Turing test competence. But my quite different goal has been to use the blending algorithm in a human designed system that generates poetry containing novel metaphors in real time. Just as with computer games, it is desirable and necessary for humans to provide rich content. For such projects, artistic freedom—along with human judgment and subjectivity—must take precedence over dogmatic Turing test reductionism.

Remarks on Evaluation

Artificial intelligence system design processes typically also include evaluation of how the systems function both formatively, as projects develop, and summatively, after projects are complete. Subjective AI and epistemic design processes must be no exception. In this light, we can ask how subjective AI systems such as GRIOT and works built with it such as the *Living Liberia Fabric* can be evaluated. There are existing methods for evaluating technical aspects of such systems. For example, we can make sure that the output of the Alloy algorithm is efficient and exhaustive with respect to its input. This matter can be determined mathematically by articulating the order of growth of the system's operation and proving that it produces all possible combinations of elements in the epistemologics under the optimality constraints given. Furthermore, there are well-known methods taught in HCI courses for ensuring that users can engage in clear interactions with a system's interface, ranging from simple questionnaire-based studies to ethnographic studies that utilize a range of techniques, including statistical analysis of quantitative responses, focus group interviews, eye tracking, biofeedback device monitoring, and more. More difficult to evaluate are questions regarding issues such as how users interpret subjective system output, the degree to which authorial intentions are evidenced by system operation (when authors themselves may even have aims of creating ambiguous meanings), the nature of phantasms prompted by systems, and the degree of uniformity of those phantasms under the interpretations of various users. Although objective measures of success are often useful, they may not be of primary importance in evaluating subjective media. In the case of creating artworks, success is a subjective prospect—and perhaps not even the goal.

To answer this question, we must realize that the call for empirical evaluation must be understood through the lenses of diverse disciplinary and social values. A divergence of values between fields in the arts or humanities on one hand and the sciences and engineering on the other has been oft articulated, perhaps most famously by C. P. Snow in his famous lecture "The Two Cultures" (Snow 1959). However, for subjective computing research and development, what is needed is not a recapitulation of stereotyped oppositions between fields, but rather clear understanding of practitioners' values and appropriate hybrid or new values. Doing so may entail revising conventional disciplinary assumptions.

To offer a highly simplified view of what this means, consider that in the arts it is not common (it might even be scoffed at) to do a quantitative or qualitative study to prove the success of a work. However, in cultural creations with more instrumental functions, as in persuasive advertising, such methods are more accepted. In some cases, methods could be adopted in the arts not as a compromise of ethics or capitulation toward an instrumental view of the artwork but rather as an additional tool with which to better articulate the ways that audiences engage with the work and the specific types of ambiguity the artist wishes to raise. For example, in *The Girl with Skin of Haints and Seraphs*, it is desirable for audiences to consider whether Europe or Africa are demonized or angelicized, but it is less desirable for audiences to consider whether the poem addresses issues of identity or is simply a coming-of-age story about a happy Greek girl. In the case of activist artwork or artwork aimed at empowerment, it may also be important in knowing whether conceptual or social change is effected. It is reasonable to ask whether the *Living Liberia Fabric* might engender peace-oriented phantasms that lead to lasting conceptual change.

At the same time, engineers must recognize that sometimes "evaluation" is not the correct term for assessing a work and that terms such as "critique" and "interpretation" might be more important. Such assessments in the arts are conveyed through reviews of exhibition and performances, awarding of prizes, media coverage, and journalism as well as through critical academic engagement with the work, including peer-reviewed articles, juried exhibitions affiliated with conferences, various assessments used to gauge academic progress through degree-granting programs, and more. For example, the GRIOT system and the systems built with it have been subjected to the standard double-blind peer reviews for numerous articles, conferences, books, and more. This process is analogous in some ways to critique in the arts. For specific works, we have used methods including social scientific qualitative approaches such as grounded theory techniques, cognitive linguistics–based approaches that track metaphor usage, questionnaire-based assessments, and critical assessments by experts in arts and humanities domains.

It is crucial finally to recall the nature of this book. This book urges designers of subjective computing systems to consider the central roles of content and meaning, particularly phantasmal meanings, in their systems. The examples illustrate what I see as promising avenues in subjective computing. This brief note on evaluation is meant to suggest the issues at stake in judging the effectiveness of subjective computing systems. I leave it to readers to assess the means and nature of evaluation of my systems and others' systems alike in the manner most appropriate to your own aims and values.

From Expressive Epistemologies to Polymorphic Poetics

This chapter has focused on how phantasms are represented computationally and how they can be deployed for subjective and expressive purposes. In contrast to approaches that focus on representing general insights, expressive epistemologies are useful for expressing the voices of those on the margins, those who are inclined toward the individual and the poetic, and those whose unique perspectives point society toward new and profound observations that might have otherwise have been left unstated. At the same time, the discussion has touched on issues such as interactivity, material-based intelligence, and user feedback loops. These all involve a negotiation of meanings between systems and users. Just as data representation has been considered here in relation to how it can be effectively deployed, the next chapter provides an expansive view of how computers represent and transform meanings in ways that can be used as expressive tools for computational media.

4

POLYMORPHIC POETICS

Analogy, metaphor, representation and user interface have much in common: each involves signs, meaning, one or more people, and some context, including culture; moreover each can be looked at dually from either a design or a use perspective. Recent research in several disciplines is converging on a general area that includes the four topics in the first sentence above; these disciplines include psychology, semiotics, and philosophy. Of these, semiotics takes perhaps the most general view, although much of the research in this area has been rather vague. A goal of the research reported here is to develop a mathematically precise theory of semiotics, called algebraic semiotics, that avoids the error of reification, that is, of identifying its abstractions with real world phenomena, making only the more modest claim of developing potentially useful models.

—Joseph Goguen, *An Introduction to Algebraic Semiotics*

Computational systems, as I have mentioned, can prompt humans to imagine. A computer-based work of art can prompt remembrance of the depravity of colonialism and the human capacity for peace, as in the *Living Liberia Fabric* memorial. In this case, a computational system prompts humans to conceptualize and interact with world events, emotional experiences, and/or social exchanges. The process of designing such a system involves having a concept one wishes to express and finding a computational means of expression. Of course, real-world events, emotional experiences, and social exchanges are incredibly complex, so expressing such concepts using a computer requires deciding what in all that complexity is important enough to represent on the computer and what can be left out. Designing such subjective computing systems also requires deciding on the *best way* to represent the concepts that are deemed important. This process requires that system designers first be aware of their own needs and values, the needs and values of users, and how to explicitly prioritize them. The system's design must then preserve these priorities.

This chapter provides a language useful for design and analysis of subjective computing systems. In other words, the chapter provides theoretical support for the problem of designing computing systems that reflect their developers' awarenesses about the way they express concepts and that can have an impact on human imagination and ideology through prompting and revealing phantasms, a problem that is a central aim of *subjective computing*. Another way to describe the intention of this chapter is to say that it gives us *a computationally oriented way to describe structures of signs, phantasms, the systems they come in, and how they convey meanings*. Serving this need, in this chapter I shall focus on an approach primarily developed by Joseph Goguen called *morphic semiotics*,[1] which provides a language I shall use for describing phantasms and sign systems more generally,[2] in a manner that is computationally amenable (Goguen 1998). Morphic semiotics as presented here is meant to be a less mathematical (and more generally accessible) articulation of Goguen's groundbreaking theory of *algebraic semiotics.* Morphic semiotics contributes insights from mathematics to issues of meaning representation pursued in the field of semiotics. Regarding the contribution from mathematics, Goguen wrote:

> One of the great insights of twentieth century mathematics with consequences that are still unfolding is that structure preserving morphisms are often at least as important as the structures themselves. . . .
>
> Semiotics has escaped this particular revolution probably in part due to its increasing alienation from formalization during the relevant period. (Goguen 1998, 4–5)

Because of its heritage from mathematics, morphic semiotics can allow us to precisely describe structures of signs[3], including signs used in expressive artworks such as those in memorial stories. This type of description can help make clear the insight that interface elements in computational media systems can be represented in any of a number of ways. In the *Living Liberia Fabric*, most stories are represented using elements such as clickable videos within patterns, yet they could instead have been represented using static hand-drawn images revealed by moving the mouse cursor over onscreen elements. Another way of saying this is that a representation specifying the content and structure of a system can be mapped onto any of a number of different interface representations, which is true for expressive systems like the *Living Liberia Fabric* as well as for more practical systems such as interfaces for online stores.

The aim of this chapter is to provide a language to describe how different ways of computationally representing conceptual structures of interest results in different meanings and values. Toward this end, the chapter introduces the concept of *polymorphic* poetics, which applies morphic semiotics to the analysis and design of subjective computing systems. The concept of the expressive epistemology, which we saw earlier, involves computational representations of imaginative concepts and real-world phenomena; these representations can be designed to evoke and reveal phantasms. Polymorphic poetics can help with the important task of precisely determining the nature of the relationship between such computational representations and phantasms. Polymorphic poetics is especially useful for articulating how phantasms are distributed onto, and prompted by, subjective computing systems. Polymorphic poetics uses morphic semiotics as a descriptive language for discussing how phantasms can be prompted and revealed effectively using a computer. In this regard, polymorphic poetics can help with both designing and understanding subjective computing systems. At the risk of oversimplifying matters, we could say that polymorphic poetics uses morphic semiotics to help describe how meaning "gets into" computing systems.

The next section continues with an example of an online marketplace and auction site used to provide an overview of the key ideas from morphic semiotics. This example is followed by detailed definitions of the two key concepts of morphic semiotics, *semiotic spaces* and *semiotic morphisms*, along with further examples. Then the central topic of *polymorphic poetics* is elaborated to describe how morphic semiotics can be used for the design and analysis of subjective computing systems focused on imaginative and expressive aims. The section's discussion is driven by detailed examples taken from traditional poetry and a subjective computing system about life, death, and remembrances of mortality. The chapter concludes with a brief reflective discussion on polymorphic poetics and the ways morphic semiotics can be used to describe how subjective systems function to make expressive statements about the real world.

Brawn at the Bazaar: An Example Illustrating Key Concepts in Morphic
Semiotics

Your name is Brawn. Entering the bazaar, you are prepared to haggle; you are prepared to buy. You have a method for deciding whether to make a purchase from any
given seller. You size up the seller using a set of criteria. You prefer buying from men,
because you can just plain trust a good man more than a woman—though you
cannot explain why and would balk at being called sexist. The seller should be clean
and well groomed, but not too well dressed (that would mean that he is doing too
well). You do cast some judgments based on facial hair; ideally, you would prefer to
buy from someone from your own clan. You want to see if others buying goods from
the same seller walk away with a smile. You want to be able to look the seller in his
eyes and trust him—you need to have a good gut feeling about him in order to buy
from him.

The previous paragraph is a fictitious description of a buyer named Brawn considering how to pick a seller from whom to buy goods. Brawn's decision involves a
number of subjective and cultural factors—that is his conception of the buying process, which relies upon epistemic spaces drawn from a particular epistemic domain.
We may not agree with the ideology influencing Brawn's purchasing decision, but
this is because we use different epistemic domains. People use their epistemic domains
as the bases for making decisions like this for all kinds of reasons, ranging from the
ethically sound to the morally dubious; indeed, what seems ethically sound to one
person may seem morally dubious to another when they are relying on different epistemic domains (as may be the case if we disagree with Brawn's prejudice against
women). Brawn's decision relies upon encountering a real person, face to face; it also
involves an image space. We can thus ask what would happen if Brawn were to
encounter a seller in the form shown in figure 4.1.

Brawn would find that this form, a profile on the commercial website called
eBay, is a highly limited representation of a seller, to say the least! It certainly provides no information about his concerns regarding gender and clan. The seller representation does provide some potentially useful information. Brawn could look at
positive, neutral, and negative feedback left by previous buyers, which he could liken
to his desire to see whether customers are walking away smiling. Seller ratings are
included that provide information about the items sent by the seller or the quality of
the seller's communication. Brawn may or may not realize that some information is
generated algorithmically (e.g., if a seller does not charge for shipping and handling,

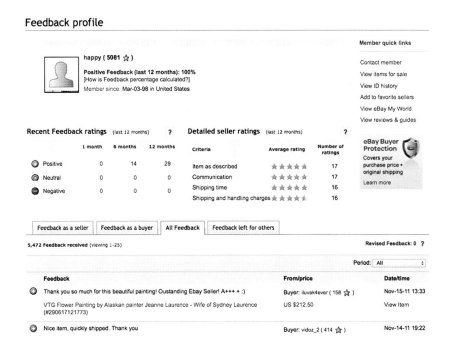

FIGURE 4.1
A seller's feedback profile on the eBay online marketplace website displayed on the screen consists of a number of elements.

the highest score is automatically recorded) and other information is provided by previous buyers (e.g., statements such as "Nice item. Quickly shipped. Thank you"). Although all of this information is available about the seller, many pages on the eBay site only provide a subset of this information to refer to sellers. In particular, three components of information from the feedback profile are often used to give potential buyers a quick impression of the seller. Let us imagine that Brawn pays attention to these simple components of the seller's feedback profile, as shown in figure 4.2.

happy (5081 ☆)

FIGURE 4.2
One component of a seller's graphical representation on the eBay online marketplace website consists of the elements shown here.

Brawn would have a hard time using his criteria to decide whether to buy from this seller. Here, this seller[4] is represented using only three elements. The seller representation is composed of the name "happy," and a number and green star enclosed in parentheses. The name "happy" is not strongly gender-identified and therefore provides little information that would allow Brawn's gender preference to influence the decision. Additionally, hygiene, fashion, and grooming are not represented, nor is clan affiliation. The experiences of other buyers *are* represented: the number and green star summarize the ratings that buyers have given the seller and the rough number of buyers who have purchased from the seller. Still, Brawn cannot tell from the number and star whether those buyers walked away with smiles, smirks, or contented mouths with corners turned neither up nor down. Brawn might balk at the simple eBay seller representation component because it is so reduced from his normal purchasing experiences with real-world sellers that he cannot apply the criteria he would normally use to make a decision.

Let us consider in more detail how the eBay seller representation component models a seller. We could say that it consists of three elements: a name, a feedback score, and a star. Each of these elements has a data type determining which sort of information it is. The name is a string, the feedback score is an integer, and the star is a GIF (Graphics Interchange Format) image. These three elements constitute a structure for representing sellers that is summarized in figure 4.3.

The elements of the simple seller representation refer to classes of things, not things themselves. In other words, they provide the syntax used to describe a seller. We could have called the three elements "member," "value," and "rating image" (or anything else) without changing anything about how they are used.

Notice that the structure shown in figure 4.3 could be displayed differently (such as shown in figure 4.4).

Simple Seller Representation	
Interface element	Sort of element
Name	A string
Feedback score	An integer
Star	A GIF image file

FIGURE 4.3
The structure of a component of a seller representation can be described using three elements as is shown here.

happy **5081**

FIGURE 4.4
Another graphical representation a component of a seller representation similar to the one on the eBay website is shown here.

The version shown in figure 4.4 is a graphical depiction of the results of a mapping from the same simple seller representation to a differently structured representation. Following the terminology introduced by Goguen, I shall call precise descriptions of the structures of signs, like the simple seller representation, *semiotic spaces* (Goguen 1998).[5] I shall call mappings from one semiotic space to another *semiotic morphisms* (Goguen 1998).[6] The terms "semiotic space" and "semiotic morphism" shall be defined in detail in later sections, but for now they are introduced to help provide intuitive senses of the concepts. Figure 4.5 graphically depicts the results of two different semiotic morphisms.

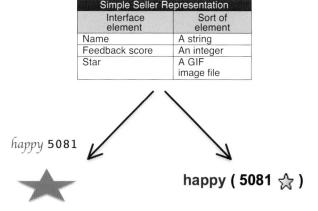

FIGURE 4.5
The black arrows in this diagram represent two semiotic morphisms from the simple seller representation to two different representations (interpreted graphically).

Simple Seller Representation 2	
Interface element	Sort of element
Name	Matrix of N x M pixels
Feedback score	Matrix of O x M pixels
Star	Matrix of P x M pixels

FIGURE 4.6
A different representation of the structure of a component of a computational representation of a seller used in eBay is shown here.

There are some notable differences between the two graphical representations, even though both are composed of the same three elements. The green star in the new version is centered and larger than in the earlier graphical representation. This change might seem to give it more prominence. The parentheses are missing; instead, a change of typeface distinguishes the name from the feedback score. These changes are specified by the different semiotic morphisms. Humans may have reasons for preferring one or the other, which is a matter of values, but the semiotic morphism itself does not make any determination of human values.

Changing the simple graphical representation of the seller is not the only type of change we can envision. There are different ways in which the same elements of a seller representation could be described for different aims. When the aim is specifying how to display the simple seller elements to a computer monitor, perhaps a representation such as that shown in figure 4.6 would work better.

Simple Seller Representation 2 (shown in figure 4.6) depicts a different semiotic space because it uses different sorts. There are slight, but significant, differences between the semiotic spaces shown in figure 4.3 and figure 4.6. Consider the functions that would be needed to decide which of two sellers has a higher score. Although a simple > (greater than) comparison would work on integers, it would not work directly on a matrix of pixels. One way that a > function could work equivalently on matrices of pixels would be to deploy a subroutine that first would convert the pixel representation into an integer value, rejecting all matrices that do not correspond to an image of an integer. The > comparison is easier using an integer representation than graphic representations. At the same time, one could more easily specify that the feedback score should be depicted in a specific typeface using the matrix of pixels representation. The integer representation alone is not capable of providing this information. This example begins to illustrate how the same content could be described by two different structures.

Brawn's Seller Representation	
Interface element	Sort of element
Maleness Indicator	Boolean value {'True' or 'False'}
Hygiene rating	An integer from 1 to 10
Facial hair style descriptor	A string describing facial hair style
Previous buyer portraits	An array of image files showing the faces of previous buyers immediately after a purchase
Video chat window	A rectangular window that enables real-time communication with the seller

FIGURE 4.7
A description of a structure for representing sellers for a fictitious online marketplace is shown here.

Sellers could also be described using an extremely different semiotic space. Let us imagine an online marketplace site designed just for the character Brawn. We can call this the "Brawn's Seller Representation." Brawn's Seller Representation might require the elements shown in figure 4.7.

Brawn's Seller Representation describes a class of structures called "sellers." When we contrast Brawn's Seller Representation with the eBay Simple Seller Representation, we can clearly see how the choice of an underlying structure is both determined by, and revealing of, the values of the person (in this case, Brawn) who created the system. A structure that includes a "maleness indicator" and "facial hair descriptor" enables Brawn to make decisions based on his gender bias in a way that a "feedback score" does not. The Simple Seller Representation does not support appearance-based discrimination between sellers, nor does it support many of the subjective criteria that Brawn—or any other buyer in the real world—would often use, including body language, fashion, or the emotional inflection of a seller's voice. We can begin to see that the choice of underlying representation can have real-world effects. When confronted with the eBay site, a buyer like Brawn might change his method for choosing sellers or just fail to use the site altogether. But if eBay were to use Brawn's Seller Representation, other buyers might also be more inclined to invoke sexist discriminatory criteria when using the site or might just reject the site altogether. Designing a system such as eBay's interface requires deciding on a set of underlying needs and values, such as the fictitious ones of Brawn's or the real ones of eBay, and ensuring that their structures and priorities are preserved in the design. Note that explicit and precise descriptions of values are also useful for analysis and decision making regarding preexisting systems. Reversing the design process, we can analyze systems such as interfaces, constructing a precise description of values based on the structure of the interface, and we can clearly reject those values if we disagree with them (such as we may with Brawn's).

The example of the Simple Seller Representation versus Brawn's Seller Representation highlights many of the definitions and issues to be elaborated upon in this chapter. Both are composed of a graphical image (the image space) that has been combined with an epistemic space representing how a user interprets the technical structure and values of the system; as such, both prompt phantasms. The example illustrates key concepts from morphic semiotics that can be used to represent phantasms and the systems that prompt and reveal them. The seller representation examples help illustrate the idea of the semiotic space. The examples set the stage for a detailed definition of a semiotic space in the next section. The mappings from one semiotic space to a different semiotic space illustrate the basic idea of the semiotic morphism, discussed in the section after that.

We have also seen that semiotic spaces and semiotic morphisms can help reveal the values embedded within systems. Examining the ways in which values are embedded in computational systems is a crucial aspect of subjective computing. Morphic semiotics can also help with designing computational systems with particular desired values of developers and users embedded within them. The design of systems to evoke and reveal phantasms and the associated values they impose is another aspect of subjective computing. This chapter proposes morphic semiotics as a useful tool for the design of subjective computing systems. Toward doing so, let us first review a few of the basic concepts from semiotics more generally.

Basic Semiotic Concepts

Some readers may find it useful to review a few of the basic concepts from semiotics more generally. Semiotics is the study of signs; it is the investigation of how representations in the world convey meaning.[7] The central idea in any semiotic theory is the relationship between two terms—one that represents and another that is represented (Barthes 1972). In Saussure's terminology (Saussure 1959), these are called the "signifier" and the "signified," respectively. The combination of these two terms is a "sign." Let us consider an example outside of computing that has broad social salience. For people of the Jain religion from India, the swastika symbol represents the Tirthankara (a person who has achieved enlightenment) named Suparshvanath (Jainism Global Resource Center 2006; Unknown n.d.). In figure 4.8, we see the

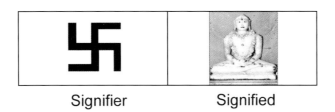

Signifier   Signified

FIGURE 4.8
The sign for the Tirthankara Suparshvanath is a swastika.

right-facing swastika, which acts as a signifier for the concept of the Tirthankara
Suparshvanath (i.e., the image in the rectangle on the right represents the idea of the
Tirthankara, as opposed to the image on the right itself, which is a graphical image
of the Tirthankara (Unknown n.d.).

The sign in one system, however, can become the signifier in another system. For
example, a website for a group called Youth Against Racism in Europe (Youth Against
Racism in Europe 2006) contains the sign in figure 4.9, which depicts a swastika
being tossed into a wastebasket.[8]

Though it may seem to be the case, the swastika in figure 4.9 is *not* used to represent the German Nazi party of the 1930s and 1940s. Rather, this swastika represents
the more generalized concepts of racist fascism, neo-Nazism, and the related ways
that contemporary racist movements have reappropriated the swastika. The sign presented in figure 4.9 is now a second-level signifier, because the signifier contains the
meaning of the Nazi political party only at one level removed; now, instead of directly
signifying the Nazi party of early- to mid-twentieth-century Germany, it signifies

FIGURE 4.9
A sign from the Youth Against Racism in Europe website shows a swastika being put into a wastebasket.

contemporary groups, policies, and attitudes that either sympathize with or echo those of Adolf Hitler's Nazi party. Showing figure 4.9 in a context where the Jain interpretation of the sign prevails would result in quite a different interpretation. In such a situation, due to the multilayered meaning of the sign, alternate meanings would be constructed—perhaps it would be interpreted as a critique against recent Eurocentric interpretations of the ancient religious symbol. Or perhaps it would seem to be an anti-Jain sign. The core concept here, however, is that signs come in systems: signs become signifiers in new systems and are incorporated within other signifiers. In other words, the differences in meaning of the signs reveals phantasms—each meaning involves shared epistemic and image spaces and each meaning can be revealed by contrasting different phantasms.

Peirce's approach to semiotics expands the relationship between the signifier and signified into a triad, by adding a third element called the "interpretant" as depicted in figure 4.10 (Peirce 1965). In his terminology, the signifier is a "representamen," the signified is an "object," and the relation that holds between the two for some individual is the "interpretant." The interpretant reflects the idea that a particular observer in a particular situation may interpret the relationship between the representamen and object in an unlimited number of ways. Peirce referred to this notion of innumerable possible interpretants as "unlimited semiosis."

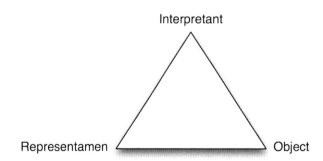

FIGURE 4.10
Peirce's semiotic triad can be illustrated as shown here.

FIGURE 4.11
These three signs warn of the danger of a child crossing the road in different ways.

Peirce also classified signs by type, with the basic triad of sign types being icons, indexes, and symbols (Peirce 1965). An icon is a sign in which the representamen holds similar qualities as the object that it represents. An index is a sign in which the representamen directly connects to the object via a physical or causal relationship. For example, the presence of the representamen could indicate that there is usually an instance of the object (Lechte 1994). A symbol is a sign in which the relationship between the representamen and the object is attributable to arbitrary social convention, such as most signs used in speech and language. For example, figure 4.11 depicts three road signs bearing representamens signifying the following object: the danger of a child crossing the road in the path of an oncoming vehicle.

The iconic sign depicts an actual child crossing the road in silhouette. This sign is iconic because it bears a clear similarity to the real image of a child crossing the road. The fact that an older escort accompanies the child only adds to the sign's iconicity. Because most commonly a child would not cross the road alone, the sign bears a strong similarity to a likely real-world scenario. The indexical sign depicts a scenario in which a ball has bounced into the path of an oncoming vehicle. The scenario illustrated by this representamen exists in a type of causal relationship with the object. The scenario indicates a strong possibility that a child will soon cross the road in front of the vehicle to chase after the ball; that is, the presence of the ball in the scenario indicates a strong possibility that the sign's object (a child crossing the street) will occur. The symbolic sign bears no physical resemblance to its object. The letters and words used in the English language sign gain their meaning only through conventional use. The core idea here in presenting Peirce's semiotic triad and his three basic sign types is to emphasize his observations about how the relations in a given sign are necessarily interpreted in a particular context, by a particular individual. Without this context, the signs fail to convey meaning.

Morphic Semiotics

Before discussing morphic semiotics in depth, it is important to be clear about the philosophical orientation here (Goguen and Harrell 2009).[9] The reason for this special care is that within the hegemonic construct called Western culture,[10] mathematical formalisms are often given a status beyond what they deserve. For example, Euclid wrote, "The laws of nature are but the mathematical thoughts of God." Similarly, in the situation semantics of Barwise and Perry, "situations," which are similar to semiotic spaces (but more sophisticated), are considered to be actually existing, ideal Platonic entities (Barwise and Perry 1983). Somewhat less grandly, other researchers might consider semiotic spaces to be directly instantiated in the human brain. The point of view taken here is different: all such formalisms are constructed by human researchers in the course of particular investigations, having the heuristic purpose of facilitating consideration of certain issues in those investigations. Reinforcing this point of view, Goguen wrote:

> We do not seek to formalize actual living meanings, but rather to express our partial understandings more exactly. Precision is also needed to build computer programs that use the theory. I do not believe that meaning in the human sense can be captured by formal sign systems; however, human analysts can note the extent to which the meanings that they see in some sign system are preserved by different representations. Thus we seek to formalize particular understandings of analysts, without claiming that such understandings are necessarily correct, or have some kind of ideal Platonic existence. (Goguen 1998, 6)

Under this view, all theories are situated social entities—mathematical theories no less than others. Of course, this concept does not prevent such theories from being useful representations for describing reality.

Morphic semiotics can be used to describe the structure of signs, including computational media signs. Describing the structure of signs is important in understanding diverse types of media. It can help us understand, for example, how a particular rhythm combines with a set of lyrics in music, or how a videogame character's capacity for movement is constrained by elements on the screen such as mountains and trees. Yet it is important not to use structural approaches to explain away subjectivity and culture.[11] Overly structural approaches often ignore that cognition is situated and that given representations can always be interpreted in an unlimited number of ways. Human interpretation is always necessary for subjective and cultural representations and human interpretation cannot be accounted for in purely structural terms.

Morphic semiotics is a mathematical approach to meaning representation that captures insights of both Saussure and Peirce (Saussure 1959; Peirce 1965). Saussure emphasized (among other things) that signs come in systems. Peirce emphasized (among other things) that the relation between a given token and its object is not just a function, but a *situated* relation that depends on the context in which the token is interpreted. Goguen's concept of semiotic spaces captures Saussure's insight; his concept of semiotic morphisms can be used to capture (and extend) Peirce's insight. Because the focus here is not on individual signs but the broader systems that they come in (e.g., entire subjective computing systems rather than single images in such systems), morphic semiotics provides a *relational* rather than a *denotational* means for describing meanings (Goguen 1998). Therefore, in morphic semiotics, much or all of the meaning captured in the representation is implicit in the relational structure of the sign system. Inferring meaning beyond that relational structure requires human judgment. To better express what is meant by the relational structure of signs consider the following: I can say that the word "lion" is a sign that is composed of four letters, which is a structural observation. I could also say that "lion" is a word that describes the *sort* of thing it is—another structural observation. I could even say that "lion" is of data type String in a computational setting, which is a more technical structural observation about the sort of thing that it is. These are all structural observations about the sign "lion." We could also have said that they are structural observations about the signifier "lion" (to use Saussure's term), yet just attending to the signifier does not mean that "lion" is not still a sign that is given meaning by someone in a particular context. For this reason, in the discussion of morphic semiotics to follow, the term "sign" will be used even at times when we are focusing on structural aspects of such graphical layout.

Furthermore, morphic semiotics is incredibly flexible in that it is not restricted to focusing on the structures of signs in terms of their signifiers. Morphic semiotics can also be used to describe the structure of the signified, as well. Morphic semiotics has been used to describe the structures of mental/conceptual spaces such as proposed by cognitive science researchers including Lakoff, Fauconnier, and Turner. Their theories, discussed earlier, enable us to describe a concept such as "lion" in terms of relations for some given purpose in a particular context; for example, the concept "lion" as explained to a child might be described by the following relations: has-claws (lion), has-mane (lion), roars (lion), and eats (lion, gazelles). Their notations, used to represent concepts such as mental spaces and conceptual blending diagrams, provide models to discuss meaning that roughly correspond to Saussure's "signified." Morphic semiotics can also be used as a precise language to provide another (mathematical) way to describe such conceptual meanings.

Providing even greater expressivity still, morphic semiotics can also represent sign systems, in the Saussurean sense, by showing mappings from conceptual spaces to specific structural representations. These representations can then be mapped onto other representations, just as a Saussurean sign can become a signifier in another sign. For example, a design concept (e.g., the animal called a "lion" that I imagine) can be mapped to a design specification (e.g., "a sprite animation of a lion"), which can then be mapped onto an actual interface design (e.g., a specific 10 × 10-pixel lion sprite animated in 16 frames). Morphic semiotics is a language for describing sign systems in terms of the relationships formed by semiotic morphisms between semiotic spaces. A good place to start in understanding morphic semiotics more deeply is with a detailed discussion of semiotic spaces. Some of our initial examples will be relatively simple to start; it will be useful to readers, however, to bear in mind the flexibility of morphic semiotics and that much of its power derives from its ability to represent the structures of meanings ranging from the very abstract (e.g., concepts) to the very concrete (e.g., specific user interfaces).

Semiotic Spaces

Semiotic spaces, also called "sign systems," can describe the kinds of things we might typically think of as signs, such as numerals, words, road signs, or graphical images. Therefore, semiotic spaces can describe image spaces. However, they can also describe things that are more abstract, such as epistemic spaces—a key reason for their utility here. Semiotic spaces can even describe very abstract systematic notions such as time. For example, a semiotic space can express time in terms of the Gregorian (sometimes called "Western") calendar. This semiotic space has a basic unit that is an integer, called a day, with an initial value of "1" and an operation that is a successor function indicating the next day. Such a semiotic space would also have rules indicating that the value of the day restarts each month and other constraints of the calendar year system, such as differences in month lengths and leap years.[12]

Furthermore, semiotic spaces can describe complex concrete signs such as computer interfaces, which can be considered to be single signs despite being built from multiple components. The fact that semiotic spaces can describe image spaces, epistemic spaces, and computer interfaces alike makes them especially useful for analyzing computing systems that prompt or reveal phantasms.

Components of Semiotic Spaces

We can now define semiotic spaces more precisely. Semiotic spaces primarily consist of four components (Goguen 1998). The first is a set of elements called "sorts." Sorts describe the *types* of things one might find in a sign system. In a computer application, sorts might include elements such as windows, menu bars, icons, characters, and a cursor. On the initial page of an online journal, sorts might include elements such as a title, subtitle, editor's name, cover image, list of authors, volume number, and issue number. Notice that the sorts do not refer to the content of the elements such as a specific title or editor name; they only provide a set of types of things that such elements can be. In short, sorts are just the labels of groupings of elements that have similar qualities as one another, such as journal titles, personal names, integers, days of the week, canines, or conifers. A more restricted type of sort, called a "data sort," provides information about signs. For example, data sorts provide information about images such as x and y coordinates, color, size, or other related attributes. The values that instances of data sorts can take are called "data."

The second component of a semiotic space is a set of elements called "sign constructors" or just "constructors. As discussed in the example of the swastika, signs can be composed of other signs. Constructors are rules that show how signs are built up from other signs with data sorts as parameters.[13] For example, consider a window in a computer system as a sign. A window in a computer system may be the result of combining other signs, such as a menu bar, a scroll bar, and an input/output area, along with parameters consisting of data sorts for location and size. A circle might be built from a name and a radius, along with data sorts for an x coordinate, y coordinate, and color. As these examples show, a constructor takes a group of sorts and data sorts and produces a new sort. In this manner, constructors capture the idea that signs come in systems, because most signs we encounter are composed of other signs. In the few cases in which a sign is not built up from other signs, a special simple type of constructor is used. This simple type of constructor is called a "constant." Constants are not made from other signs and take no data sorts as parameters. Constants are useful for building signs that are considered not to be decomposable for the purposes at hand. An example of a constant is a road sign that is standardized in terms of size, colors, materials, and graphic design.

The third component of a semiotic space is a set of elements called "functions." Functions can be defined to take in signs of a given sort in order to return information such as the size or position of the sign. In this regard, functions provide the attributes for sorts. For example, a function could be defined on a sort called "two-dimensional videogame character" that would return its height attribute. As another example, a function could be defined on a sort called "merchandise" that returns the cost attribute of the particular item.

The fourth component of a semiotic space is a set of elements called "axioms." Axioms are used to constrain the signs that the semiotic space can be used to describe. For example, consider the case of computer windows on a particular computer. A monitor has a maximum resolution at which it can display content. In a semiotic space describing windows on a particular computer, an axiom could be provided that constrains all windows to be of dimensions less than or equal to 1366 × 768 pixels. As another example, consider a semiotic space describing the integers. The sorts might include digits between 0 and 9. A constructor could take digits and produce concatenations of those digits. However, we would not want to consider "0000045" to be an integer because the leading zeros are unnecessary. The semiotic space might then constrain integers other than 0 itself to begin with digits other than 0. In practice, axioms should be precisely stated so that they can constrain the set of possible signs without ambiguity.[14]

The Structure of Semiotic Spaces

Aside from the four components defined previously, a semiotic space also accounts for the way that those components are structured relative to one another. Sorts can be arranged in hierarchical relationships with one another. That is, there can be a *subsort* relationship between sorts such that some sorts are "children" that "inherit" the characteristics of others. For example, a triangle and a parallelogram are both subsorts of the type of shape called a "polygon." Sorts can have multiple subsorts. However, a sort does not have to be a subsort of another sort.[15] The sorts in a semiotic space can also be arranged in similar hierarchy to indicate part-whole relationships. Each tier of importance we can call a *level* (sorts do not have to be in a level relationship with other sorts). For example, the menu bar, scroll bar, and input/output area are at the same level as each other but are at a lower level than a window because they are parts of a window. If the window is the maximal element in a semiotic space, we would say that it is the "topmost sort." All sorts are considered to be at higher levels than data sorts. As I have discussed, sorts need not all be related to one another hierarchically, in which case we would say that the sorts are not comparable to each other.

Constructors can also be arranged in a similarly structured hierarchical relationship. There can be a *priority* relationship between constructors, indicating the relative importance of the signs built by the constructors. The designation of importance is a matter of human interpretation, specified by the author of the semiotic space. It is not intrinsic to the constructors themselves. For example, a semiotic space for a videogame character in a first-person shooter[16] game might have assigned the constructor for the gun the highest priority. In contrast, the semiotic space for a videogame character in a Japanese role-playing game from the 1980s or early 1990s might have assigned the character's head as the highest priority since the character style preferred at the time, now called the "super deformed" style, featured tiny bodies with large heads as the primary visual distinguishing features between characters. Figure 4.12 depicts images from the games *Fallout 3* (a computer role-playing game with first-person shooter elements) and *Final Fantasy III* (a classic Japanese computer role-playing game), illustrating graphical styles that represent the signs created by constructors with these priorities, respectively.

FIGURE 4.12
Characters from *Fallout 3* (left) and *Final Fantasy 3* (right) reveal different priorities. Images (left) © Bethesda Softworks, (right) © 1990 SQUARE ENIX CO., LTD. All rights reserved. Illustration/© 1990 YOSHITAKA AMANO.

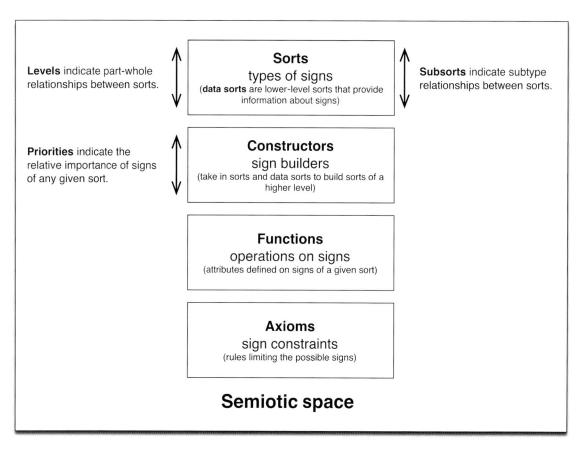

FIGURE 4.13
The elements and structure of a semiotic space constitute a formal description of a sign system.

All of the elements of a semiotic space, along with the hierarchal relationships that structure their elements, are illustrated in figure 4.13.

Analyzing the elements in a semiotic space can help reveal how phantasms are expressed by computing systems. The decision of which components should be included within a semiotic space is a way of representing the structure of a computing system that prompts a phantasm. That is, the semiotic space can describe a computer interface and the meanings that it is intended to represent for different people, under different worldviews. For example, the semiotic space describing the interpretation of a sign by an experienced user versus a semiotic space describing that of a novice user might be different based on the amount of knowledge each possesses and what is important to each. The example of two overlapping windows in a GUI can be used to help make this point clear. Figure 4.14 shows two windows with one overlapping the other. The larger window in the background is called an "example window" and the smaller window is called a "nested example window."

These windows each reveal the content of a file folder in the operating system. Experienced users of the operating system will realize that just because one window is completely enclosed within the perimeter of the other window does not mean that the smaller window is a subwindow contained within the larger window. Similarly,

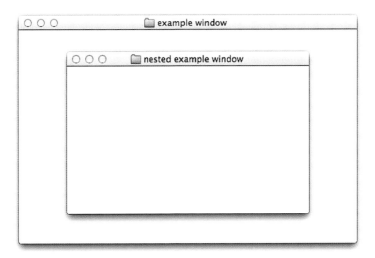

FIGURE 4.14
An image of two windows, with one overlapping the other, is shown here.

the fact that the smaller window represents a folder called "nested example window" does not mean that it represents a subfolder of the "example window." It could just be misleadingly named. A novice user, in contrast, might be confused by the example and think that the "nested example window" is *contained within* the "example window" rather than merely being shown on top of the other window.

Let us now explore how we could use different semiotic spaces to describe the interpretation held by a novice user who has experienced the image in figure 4.14 only one time as compared to the interpretation of an expert who has manipulated windows on a computer screen many times. We could describe the difference between novice and expert users' interpretations by articulating the different epistemic domains they draw from and realizing this difference in the semiotic spaces used to represent their interpretations. The novice might see the smaller window as being of a lower-level sort than the larger window. For the novice user, the "small window" might even be represented as a subsort of the larger window, resulting in a nested window being interpreted as a subtype of a standard window. Furthermore, the novice might omit axioms describing overlapping in favor of ones describing containment. Because the actual implementation represents the structure that I attributed to the expert user, we would say that the system supports the needs and values of an expert user in its structure. A novice user's expectations for system behavior will be thwarted because the system's structure does not capture the structure of the novice's conception. All of this information begins to show that different degrees of user knowledge result in different semiotic spaces for describing signs. This information also begins to show that designing systems based on these semiotic spaces requires an understanding of how the structures of signs affect a system's ability to be used by diverse groups of users.

Priority relationships are especially important to attend to when discussing phantasms. The decision of what is more important in a given sign system is a value judgment. It is a matter of human interpretation. Analyzing the structure of a semiotic space can also be a means of revealing what is important within system designers' or users' epistemic domains. Returning to the example of Brawn's Seller Representation, imagine how an online marketplace could be designed so that the gender ("maleness" in this case) is given the most importance and video chat with the seller is given the least importance. This difference of prioritization may be implicitly captured in the structure of semiotic spaces. In a semiotic space for an actual GUI for Brawn's Seller Representation, this might mean that the high priority for maleness is represented by using large, strikingly colored icons for all male sellers while using smaller, subtler icons for female sellers. In such an interface, Brawn's personal values are implicit in how the different elements that make up the signs are related to each other. The video chat window might be represented by only a small button that can be clicked to bring up a tiny window. In this case, the priority of the constructors for the interface elements of the semiotic space express values that will affect how all users—not just Brawn—view and interact with sellers. The ways in which semiotic spaces are depicted based in a particular epistemic domain, such as the actual GUI in the Brawn's Seller Representation example, reflect shared values imposed by the structure of the semiotic space.

Finally, we must be clear about the nature of the signs that are used to express the structure described by a semiotic space. Semiotic spaces describe the structure of signs. One way to think of this distinction would be to say that semiotic spaces provide syntax, whereas human imaginative cognition processes are required to provide interpretations of content. Another way to say this is that human interpretations of actual signs provide epistemic spaces that can instantiate the structures described by semiotics spaces.

We have seen that semiotic spaces are basic elements in a language for describing the structure of computing systems. Signs (as interpreted by humans) are the models that constitute actual content, including graphical imagery. Let us turn our attention now to an example of a subjective computing system. The structure of the image space of the videogame *Superman* for the Atari 2600 (also known as the Atari VCS[17]) videogaming console could be described by a semiotic space. The semiotic space representing the *Superman* game image space has a relatively small number of sorts such as location areas, a playing area on the screen, background images, a player character (Superman), enemies, an information area, a line dividing the screen between the playing area and information, a score, and remaining enemy counters. The location area, which represents the gameplay area shown on the screen, would be the topmost sort. It is composed of all of the other lower level sorts, including the background image and characters such as Superman and his enemies. The information area has the score and the counters for remaining enemies as subsorts and so on. Figure 4.15 shows a screenshot containing a single location screen, the player character Superman (the pink, red, and blue roughly human-shaped group of pixels), enemy counters (slim rectangles in the upper-left corner represent remaining enemies; the square represents the main enemy called "Lex Luthor"), a score (upper right), a dividing line between information area (containing counters and scores) and the play area, and

FIGURE 4.15
This screenshot from the game *Superman* for the Atari 2600 videogame console shows
Superman flying past two buildings.

background image (turquoise and pale-gray underlying image). We could describe
the signs and their given sorts as shown in figure 4.16.

The interface element of sort "player character" (called "Superman") could be
represented using a variety of images. It could be represented using a highly pixelated
humanoid figure or richer hand-made image as shown in figure 4.17. Similarly, the
city structure could be represented using a pixelated image or an altered photographic
image such as the depiction of the Petronas Towers in Kuala Lumpur, Malaysia, also
shown in figure 4.17. Regardless of whether the actual images used are those of figure
4.15 or figure 4.17, the structure of the semiotic space is maintained (Comic Vine
2011; Someformofhuman 2008).

It is worth noting (without going into depth here) that although we have been
discussing semiotic spaces describing static image spaces in the examples thus far,
morphic semiotics can also be extended to address dynamic image spaces such as we
often associate with computing systems. One advantage of morphic semiotics is that
its constructs have roots in algebraic semantics, an area of computer science that
mathematically describes the functional meanings of computer programs (Goguen
and Malcolm 1996). A discussion of how morphic semiotics can provide accounts of
dynamic computing systems is important because, as Espen Aarseth (1997) has

Elements of a *Superman* Screenshot Semiotic Space	
Constructor name	Sort of element
Current screen (level 0)	Location area
Superman (level 1a)	Player character
City structure (level 2a)	Background image
Sky (level 2a)	Background image
Current statistics (level 1b)	Information area
0030 (level 2b)	Score
Square Lex Luthor token (level 2b)	Enemy counter
5 rectangular thug tokens (level 2b)	Enemy counters
Red and black divider (level 1c)	Dividing line

FIGURE 4.16

Elements of a semiotic space describing the Atari 2600 game *Superman* are shown here; row shades are used to group sorts by levels indicating part-whole relationships; the lettered levels (a, b, and c) are not comparable with one another (e.g., level 1a is neither above nor below level 1b or 1c).

FIGURE 4.17

The *Superman* game can be illustrated by another graphical interpretation of the semiotic space. For example, it is illustrated here by a composition made using found images.

noted,[18] it is not straightforward to apply semiotics to computer programs. The simple way to extend morphic semiotics to represent dynamic systems is to add information describing the sign systems at various states of operations, along with rules for changing state. Doing so means looking at a dynamic system as a series of static signs. However, although this approach may work for rudimentary systems (for example, selecting from a small selection of background colors of a screen), it is not satisfying for highly dynamic computational media such as videogames. In these cases, we might extend morphic semiotics in another way. Sorts could also be used to refer to discrete *interactions* that have starting and stopping points, such as pressing a button or swiping a finger across a touch-sensitive pad. Axioms could then be used to capture the rules describing the system's functionality in response to those interactions. Furthermore, where added precision is needed, semiotic spaces could be expanded to include information about the current state of a system and function for moving to new states. The extensions to morphic semiotics offered briefly earlier are not sufficient for describing dynamic systems entirely. However, these extensions could certainly be applied informally (which should be sufficient for many design problems).

To conclude our discussion of semiotic spaces for now, we can focus our attention on how the example of *Superman* illustrates how semiotic spaces can describe the signs that can be realized in a number of possible ways. It is now worth considering how designers choose a particular way to represent a semiotic space. In terms of the previous example, this means considering how the actual game structure described by the *Superman* semiotic space came to be designed.[19] The concept of the semiotic morphism, introduced in the next section, can help answer this question.

Semiotic Morphisms

Semiotic morphisms, it was claimed earlier, are useful for supporting the design of computing systems. Toward addressing this type of design problem, Joseph Goguen described the concept of the semiotic morphism as follows:

> A user interface for a computer system can be seen as a semiotic morphism from (the theory of) the underlying abstract machine (what the system does) to a sign system for windows, buttons, menus, etc. A web browser can be seen as a map from HTML (plus JavaScript, etc.) into the capabilities of a particular computer on which it is running. Metaphors can be seen as semiotic morphisms from one system of concepts to another. A given text (spoken utterance, etc.) can be seen as the image under a morphism from some (usually unknown) structure into the sign system of written English (or spoken English, or whatever). (Goguen 1998, 5)[20]

We can see how this approach to design is useful by continuing the example of the game *Superman*. Clearly John Dunn, the programmer of *Superman*, did not actually use a semiotic space such as specifically described in figure 4.16 to inform development of his design for the game. At the same time, he did need something like it as a plan to structure his game design concepts in such a way that they could be implemented on the Atari VCS. In the following discussion, I shall create a rational reconstruction of a plan for *Superman's* design using a semiotic space with a set of sorts closer to those required by the actual implementation. In order to do so, we first need to discuss a little bit about how games are implemented in the Atari VCS console.

The Atari VCS used a computer chip called a Television Interface Adaptor (Montfort and Bogost 2009). This chip was capable of representing a static graphical object called the playfield (background) and five types of movable graphical objects consisting of two players, two missiles, and a ball. We can see now that part of the process of designing *Superman* involved mapping Dunn's design concepts onto these six graphical objects. Figure 4.18 describes some of the elements of such a semiotic space (focusing just on the background image and player character while eliding the rest).[21]

In short, the game development task could be seen as a morphic semiotics design problem.[22] Dunn needed to come up with a mapping from an early game design concept to an implementable game specification, taking into account the constraints of the Atari VCS. This mapping is an example of what I earlier called a semiotic morphism. For example, Dunn might have envisioned any number of background images, but when programming for the Atari VCS, he was required to use the playfield, which could be used only to create symmetrical background images (images in

Elements of an Atari VCS Implementation-Oriented *Superman* Screenshot Semiotic space	
Constructor name	Sort of element
Current screen (level 0)	Playfield (mirrored or duplicated)
Superman player character (level 1a)	Player
Superman graphical component 1 (level 2a)	8-pixel horizontal line
Superman graphical component 2 (level 2a)	8-pixel horizontal line
...	...
Superman color 1, red [$40+8] (data level 1)	NTSC color (data sort)
Superman color 2, pink [$30+6] (data level 1)	NTSC color (data sort)
Superman color 3, blue [$80+6] (data level 1)	NTSC color (data sort)
...	...

FIGURE 4.18

The elements of an implementation-oriented semiotic space are used to describe the Atari 2600 game *Superman*.

which one half of the screen was a reflection of the other half). Dunn needed a semiotic morphism from a semiotic space describing a background image to a semiotic space describing the playfield and its duplicated or mirrored image.

A semiotic morphism from an early *Superman* game design concept to an implementable game specification would also have had to take into account other constraints based on real-world values and preferences. The semiotic morphism would reflect constraints such as a tight production timeline along with budgetary and creative restrictions imposed by Warner Communications, the owner of Atari at the time, which wanted the game to be developed as a commercial tie-in with a Superman film that was released in 1978 (Ball 2000). Based on both the content of the film and time limitations on implementation, there were restrictions on the number of enemies in the game. There were also restrictions on the name of the main villain based on the villain who was featured in the film (Lex Luthor). Dunn also was constrained by the lore of the Superman comic upon which both the game and film were based (e.g., the game's lead character, Superman, had to resemble the figure in the comic books and the movie).

The structure of *Superman*'s implementation needed to satisfy all of these constraints. Describing the game's structure using semiotic morphisms from an early design concept to a more precise design specification helps clarify the task of designing the game to satisfy these constraints. Regardless of whether such constraints were determined by logistical needs, technical limitations, or user analyses, they represent values that guide the design. Morphic semiotics does not help determine what those values are, but it does help make sure that they are represented in the design's structure. Morphic semiotics helps by enabling a designer to choose a semiotic morphism that *preserves* the values implicit in the structure of the source space. For example, assigning the Superman player character a high priority in the game by giving the image prominent and recognizable colors clearly supports the commercial values of the company that produced that game.

Having illustrated the utility of semiotic morphisms for design using the *Superman* game as an example, we are now in a position to define the elements of a semiotic morphism more precisely. A semiotic morphism is a mapping from one semiotic space, called the *source* space, to another semiotic space, called a *target space*. A way to think about this process is as "translating from the *language* of one sign system to the language of another" (Goguen 1998, 11). Semiotic morphisms perform these mappings in such a way that they preserve some of the structure of the original concept. The idea is that typically we want to preserve as much as possible, but we may not always be able to preserve all of the elements and/or structure of the source space in the target space. This process may all seem somewhat abstract. But remember the aim stated in the first paragraph of the chapter: real-world events, emotional experiences, and social exchanges are incredibly complex. Designing a socially engaged computing system requires a designer to decide what from all of that complexity is important to represent on the computer and what is worth leaving out. Designing such systems also requires deciding the best way to represent those aspects of the concept that are deemed important. Semiotic morphisms provide a language for doing so.

Semiotic morphisms consist of three kinds of components. These components are partial mappings ("partial" in the sense that not every element has to be mapped): (1) from the sorts of the source space to the sorts of the target space, (2) from the constructors of the source space to the constructors of the target space, and (3) from the functions of the source space to the functions of the target space. For example, imagine a semiotic morphism that maps a semiotic space describing a 3D image of a sphere to a semiotic space describing a 2D image of a circle, such as shown in figure 4.19. Although this example may seem somewhat mathematical, it is illustrative because it conveys the concept of a semiotic morphism from a complex space (a 3D world) to a simpler one (a 2D world).

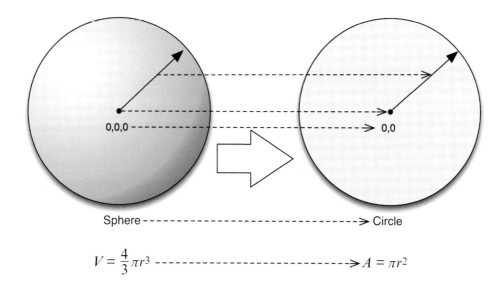

FIGURE 4.19

A semiotic morphism from a sphere to a circle; the large arrow represents the semiotic morphism, and the smaller arrows are individual mappings that constitute the semiotic morphism.

The topmost sort in the sphere source space, which is called "sphere," would be mapped to "circle." Yet the sort "x, y, z coordinate" in the source space would be mapped to a sort called "x, y coordinate" in the target space, reflecting the reduced dimensionality. The lower-level sorts "center" and "radius" would be mapped to sorts of the same name. Because the center in the source space is a subsort of "x, y, z coordinate," the center in the target space will be a subsort of "x, y coordinate." The constructor for circle would be mapped to the constructor for "sphere." Yet because the source space constructor builds a "sphere" from a "radius" and a "center" (a subsort of "x, y, z coordinate"), the analogous target space constructor would build a "circle" from a "radius" and a slightly different "center" (a subsort of "x, y coordinate"). Any functions would be mapped to analogous functions, such as a function describing how to compute the volume of a "sphere" being mapped to a function describing how to compute the area of a "circle."

Semiotic morphisms also describe how mappings preserve the elements and structure of the source space in the target. For this purpose, there are four rules that constrain the mappings described by a semiotic morphism. The first rule states that if a sort in the source space is a subsort of another sort, that subsort relationship holds for the analogous sorts in the target space, as seen in the earlier example. The sort "center" in the "sphere" space was a subsort of "x, y, z coordinate." Because "x, y, z coordinate" was mapped to "x, y coordinate," the sort "center" in the target space was a subsort of "x, y coordinate." The second rule states that if a constructor builds a sign from some set of sorts in the source space, then the analogous constructor in the target space builds an analogous sign from the analogous sorts in the target space. For example, the "circle" constructor builds a sphere from the analogous (to those in the sphere source space) sorts of "radius" and "center" (remembering that in translating "center" from the sphere to the circle, it is reduced to a 2D sort). The third rule is analogous to the rule for constructors but holds for functions. We have already seen this in the case of the mapping from the function for volume to the function for area. The fourth rule is simple: the data sorts and axioms from the source space should stay the same if they appear in the target space.

It is worth noting that in practice, system designers and developers do not just develop plans and then steadfastly build systems exactly according to plan. In practice, designers and developers tend to iteratively refine the systems that they work on. Furthermore, they often repurpose old designs, mixing and matching elements as needed. Indeed, Dunn has described how animated elements in the design of *Superman* may have been exchanged with another Atari game called *Adventure* (Ball 2000).

Semiotic morphisms can be composed with one another as a way of describing both iterative refinement during design and the combining of elements from more than one source space in a single target space. For example, Dunn could have first applied a semiotic morphism from his early design concept to a semiotic space useful for planning, like the one in figure 4.16, which contained sorts useful for visual design like "background image" and "player character." As he progressed from a design stage to an implementation stage in the game's development, he could have then used another semiotic morphism from that space to one more geared toward implementation, such as in figure 4.18, which uses sorts that describe how the game would need to be programmed for a particular chip.

The combining of elements from different semiotic spaces using more than one semiotic morphism is something we have already seen. The polymorphic poem *The Girl with Skin of Haints and Seraphs* in chapter 3 features metaphors generated from semiotic morphisms from two source spaces such as "angels" and "skin" in a single target space with elements of both sources. We call this target space a *blended space*, because it blends elements from multiple source spaces (sometimes called "input" spaces). In fact, *The Girl with Skin of Haints and Seraphs* functions, and provides its social commentary on the limitations of racial binaries, by actually representing epistemologies mathematically as semiotic spaces. The Alloy algorithm used in GRIOT constructs blends of semiotic spaces using semiotic morphisms from multiple semiotic spaces to generate a single blended semiotic space. One of the reasons that different instances of the poem are consistent in style is because aspects of the structure of the sorts, constructors, and axioms from the source spaces are preserved in the target space. One example of this preservation property is that elements never switch sort; for example, in a line such as the following:

```
she worked raising ashy-skin wintery-skin children of her own
```

`ashy-skin` and `wintery-skin` can be combined because they are of the same sort ('Person'), but neither could be combined with a `yam` from the Africa semiotic space because it is a different sort ('Object').[23] It makes sense that the poem's protagonist could have `ashy-skin wintery-skin`, but it would not make nearly as much sense for her to have `ashy-skin yam`. In works such as this and others, we have found that *blending* semiotic spaces by composing multiple semiotic morphisms (what Goguen and I have called *structural blending*[24]) can be a powerful tool for generating system content as well as designs (Goguen and Harrell 2009).

Quality of Semiotic Morphisms

All of the terminology in the discussion of semiotic morphisms thus far has been introduced to help with the problem of designing subjective computing systems. In particular, it can help with the task of judging the quality of a particular design. Quality can be assessed by looking at what the semiotic morphism preserves from the source space in the target space. More specifically, we can assess the degree to which a given semiotic morphism is *level preserving, constructor preserving, priority preserving, function preserving*, and *axiom preserving*. The meaning of each of these terms is relatively straightforward: they describe how much of the elements and structure from the source space are retained in the target space. For example, consider the case of a computer's file hierarchy (Goguen and Harrell 2004). As shown in figure 4.20, there are multiple ways that this hierarchy can be represented on a computer. Figure 4.20 sketches a semiotic space for a file hierarchy, along with two semiotic morphisms for visualizing it two different ways in a graphical user interface.

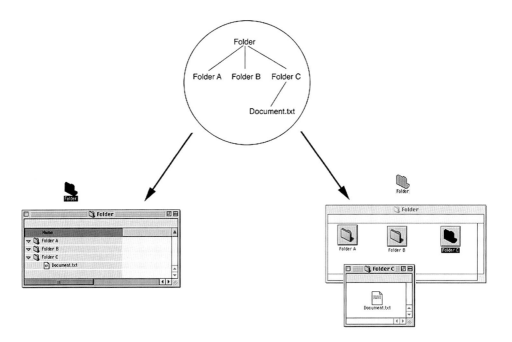

FIGURE 4.20
Two semiotic morphisms from a file hierarchy to graphical user interfaces are shown here.

The source space is a rational reconstruction of a specification for the file system; in computer science terms, it is an ordered, labeled, finite tree. When Folder C is opened in the icon-based representation on the right, the location of file Document.txt is represented textually in the small area at the top of its window, whereas in the column-based representation on the left, its location has a visual representation, based on position, including indentation. All things being equal, the left semiotic morphism produces a visualization of higher quality. This is because it preserves more of the source space structure in the image space (visual form) and also provides more browsing affordances in the image space. Clicking on Folder C in the column-based representation reveals that the file Document.txt is in Folder C and simultaneously that Folder C is at the same level in the file hierarchy as Folders A and B; in contrast, clicking on Folder C in the icon-based representation opens up a new window for Folder C that does not reveal its relationship in the file hierarchy to Folders A and B. The column-based representation preserves more information about the file system's structure than the icon-based representation. If we consider there to be a part-whole relationship between folders and subfolders, we could say that the left semiotic morphism is *level preserving* because it visually retains those part-whole relationships. Folders that are at a lower level than other folders are indented. In the example on the right, the window for Folder C could have instead referred to a different folder altogether that happened to have the same name.

Both morphisms are *constructor preserving* in that they contain all of the same elements as each other. Stating which of the semiotic morphisms is more *priority preserving* requires us to first decide what our values are because priorities represent the relative importance of elements according to a designer. One design adage promoted by Goguen is the "Principle of F/C," which suggests that it is generally better to preserve form over content (Goguen and Harrell 2004; Goguen and Malcolm 1996). The left morphism preserves more of the file hierarchy's structure, whereas the right semiotic morphism highlights the files themselves to a greater degree. If visibility of the files is the most important value of a designer, the right semiotic morphism is more *priority preserving.* Let us assume that the same functions on files (such as checking size, when it was last modified, and when it was created) are available in both target spaces. Given the assumption that all of these functions are present in both spaces, we would say that both semiotic morphisms are *function preserving.* Finally, both semiotic morphisms are *axiom preserving* if we assume that they both maintain the same rules, such as those for file creation, deletion, opening, and closing (e.g., in the left semiotic morphism, a small triangle to the left of each folder indicates whether it is open or closed; in the right semiotic morphism, the image of the file and its name are highlighted).

As a final note on the quality of semiotic morphisms for now, it may not always be the case that we want to design systems for clear, commonsense interpretation and use. In such cases, we might assess the quality of semiotic morphisms by valuing different properties other than how much structure they preserve, perhaps even seeking morphisms that fail to preserve aspects of the source space's structure. This type of approach may initially seem surprising; however, there may be good reasons for it. Semiotic morphisms that fail to preserve properties of a source space may be useful, such as when the experience of using an interface itself is the primary vehicle providing social commentary (Johnson 1999). For example, in the case of a game that conveys a character's confusion using a blurred screen and difficult-to-operate controls, the challenging interface communicates information about the character's state. This type of interface can be seen in works such as Ian Bogost's persuasive games (further discussed in chapter 7) such as *Disaffected!* and *Airport Insecurity*, which engage in agency play via difficult interfaces to reflect difficult life situations (e.g., backward control schemes to represent confusion).

Perhaps more profoundly, we can say that intentional failure to preserve properties can be desirable when creating works of art. Indeed, Goguen writes the following regarding the use of semiotic morphisms for design: "Notice that we are not addressing art in this note, but rather design, in the sense of craft. Art is even more inherently demanding, difficult, and creative than design; for example, it often involves deliberate transgression of preservation properties (among other things)" (Goguen 2004).

We can see an example of this usage in poetry. When composing poetry, sometimes a poet may select to deploy what we might call "dis-optimal" semiotic morphisms (Goguen and Harrell 2009). Let us examine the example of the poem "Walking Around" by Pablo Neruda (1947). Its first stanza introduces the protagonist, the place, and the time (the latter two in a condensed poetic form); the location is perhaps a small city in Chile. Subsequent stanzas explore aspects of some area within that city using metaphors (which are types of mappings that can be described using a semiotic morphism) that are often quite striking. The general theme of the poem is weariness induced by consumerism. Here are its first two stanzas (out of ten):

It so happens that I am tired of being a man.
It so happens, going into tailorshops and movies,

I am withered, impervious, like a swan of felt
navigating a water of beginning and ashes.

The smell of barbershops makes me weep aloud.
All I want is a rest from stones or wool,
all I want is to see no establishments or gardens,
no merchandise or goggles or elevators.
(Neruda 1947, 311)

Neruda's verbal imagery and objects in the phantasms evoked by the poem can be described using semiotic spaces. Objects such as a tailor shop, movie theater, or barbershop could all be defined to be of sort "town-location." Objects such as goggles, elevators, wool, and stones could all be defined to be of sort "town-artifact." The data sorts used to describe felt and wool might be "weight" (which could have values such as "light" or "heavy") and "fabric-characteristics" (which could have values such as "impervious" or "absorbent"). In order to describe the poem in morphic semiotics terms, we can think of the poem's different metaphors as constructing mappings from semiotic spaces describing some concepts onto others. Neruda's metaphors often blend concepts in unconventional ways. For example, the phrase "water of beginning and ashes" could be described using mappings from source spaces including the constants "beginning" and "ashes" to a target space including a constant representing "water" being navigated. These semiotic morphisms are not very good at preserving levels, constructors, priorities, and/or axioms. The reason is that the semiotic morphisms describe mappings between things of enormously different sorts and with very different structures (beginnings and ashes are not typically thought of as either sorts of liquids or navigable areas). A less drastic example in the same text is "swan of felt." In cases like these, we could say that Neruda intentionally chose semiotic morphisms that are of a lower quality from the point of view of clarity and common sense (i.e., one should not read his metaphors in a literal, commonsense way) but that result in novel, surprising, and poignant metaphors. Alternatively, we could say that he chose priorities in his source spaces that are unconventional and chose to preserve these unconventional priorities in his mappings. Regardless, from this example we can see that morphic semiotics provides a language with which one can describe expressive strategies for prompting phantasms that are both straightforward (with strong preservations properties) that rely upon more exaggerated imaginative associations between ideas (with more idiosyncratic, but still possibly systematic, preservation properties).

Constructing Imaginative Worlds and Poetic Phantasms Using Morphic Semiotics–Based Design

This chapter began by claiming that computers can prompt people to imagine and that they can prompt and reveal phantasms. This book began by stating that the computer can be used to express experiences of the human condition, just as other media for the arts can. In chapter 3, we focused on expression of the human condition by means of imaginative world building and poetic phantasm construction. This section elaborates upon the concept of *polymorphic poetics*, a morphic semiotics–based approach to the design and analysis of subjective computing systems with imaginative and expressive aims. Polymorphic poetics describes how the choice of a semiotic morphism (or multiple semiotic morphisms, as in the case of blending) affects the expressive effectiveness of a work. The polymorphic poetics approach uses the structured language of morphic semiotics as a lens through which to see how values are built into systems and as a formal foundation for representations that are implemented on a computer. It also provides a lens to aid in seeing how imaginative worlds can be built out of metaphor and the blending of concepts. To illustrate the power of these lenses, what better example of an engaging subjective aspect of the real world and the human condition is there than probing reflections on life and death? In considering this issue, I shall begin with a cognitive science account of examples from poetry as a prelude to looking in depth at how reflection upon mortality has been poetically designed in a poignant, five-minute-long computer game.

In their book *More than Cool Reason*, George Lakoff and Mark Turner describe how conceptual metaphors serve to structure poetic imagination about death (Lakoff and Turner 1989). Citing works including Emily Dickinson's "Because I could not stop for Death" and Robert Frost's "The Road Not Taken,"[25] Lakoff and Turner write:

> Life and death are such all-encompassing matters that there can be no single conceptual metaphor that will enable us to comprehend them. There is a multiplicity of metaphors for life and death, and a number of the most common ones show up in the Dickinson poem. To begin to sort them out, let us return to the line "Because I could not stop for Death—." We understand here that what the speaker cannot stop are her purposeful activities. A purposeful life has goals, and one searches for means toward those goals. We conceive metaphorically of purposes as destinations and of the means to those destinations as paths. We speak

of "going ahead with our plans," "getting sidetracked," "doing things in a round-about way," and "working our way around obstacles." Thus there is a common metaphor PURPOSES ARE DESTINATIONS, and such expressions are instances of it. (Lakoff and Turner 1989, 2–3)

In this quotation, Lakoff and Turner argue that there is a structure to metaphors about death. By "metaphor," Lakoff and Turner do not mean just a literary device; they are talking about the basic cognitive capacity to map one idea onto another (discussed in chapter 2). In this case, the cognitive capacity is applied to literature, but the same capacity is also evident in everyday life as revealed by such basic statements as "I feel close to her" (mapping proximity onto affection) or "Wake Up!" (mapping upward directionality onto emerging from sleep). In the case of Dickinson's poem, some of the structure comes from mapping concepts about destinations onto concepts about purposes. Life becomes a poetic phantasm combining image spaces and epistemic spaces regarding mortality via metaphor.

Such metaphors have an embodied basis. As mentioned in chapter 2, George Lakoff and Mark Johnson have argued that the structures of most conceptual metaphors are ultimately rooted in our embodied experiences of the world (Lakoff and Johnson 1980). Patterns of early motor-sensory experiences, they argue, provide the rudimentary conceptual structures called *image schemas* used to understand more complex experiences. For example, phrases such as "getting ahead in life" are structured by an image schema cognitive scientists call MOTION ALONG A PATH (Lakoff and Johnson 1980; Lakoff and Núñez 2000). The MOTION ALONG A PATH image schema provides the structure for one of the most ubiquitous conceptual metaphors regarding life and death called LIFE IS A JOURNEY. This metaphor can encompass the PURPOSES ARE DESTINATIONS conceptual metaphor and more.

In discussing Robert Frost's poem "The Road Not Taken," Lakoff and Turner draw upon this fundamental conceptual metaphor in their analysis. They observe that the poem is typically read as "discussing options for how to live life, and as claiming that he chose to do things differently than most other people do," (Lakoff and Turner 1989, 3) and then go on to discuss the origin of this reading of the poem as follows:

This reading comes from our implicit knowledge of the structure of the LIFE IS A JOURNEY metaphor. Knowing the structure of this metaphor means knowing a number of correspondences between the two conceptual domains of life and journeys, such as these:

—The person leading a life is a traveler.

—His purposes are destinations.

—The means for achieving purposes are routes.

—Difficulties in life are impediments to travel.

—Counselors are guides.

—Progress is the distance traveled.

—Things you gauge your progress by are landmarks.

—Choices in life are crossroads.

—Material resources and talents are provisions.

We will speak of such a set of correspondences as a "mapping" between two conceptual domains. (Lakoff and Turner 1989, 3–4)

In each of these cases, a source space that is more familiar is mapped onto a target space that is more abstract (Turner 1996). For example, difficulties in life and choices in life are both abstract and challenging concepts. Impediments to travel and crossroads are much more sundry and everyday. The ability to relate to an abstract concept in everyday terms is part of the value of metaphor. To relate these types of metaphors back to morphic semiotics, let us now draw upon Goguen's words regarding semiotic mappings: "The essential idea is that interfaces, representations, metaphors, interpretations, etc. are morphisms from one sign system to another" (Goguen 1998, 5). Morphic semiotics, we have seen, provides a language for expressing just the type of structure as the mappings that Lakoff, Turner, Johnson and other cognitive scientists discuss.

In addition to the problem of analysis such as tackled by Lakoff and Turner with regard to mappings in poetry, we have seen that morphic semiotics can also be useful for design, including using mappings (semiotic morphisms) to guide design of user interfaces for subjective computing systems. For example, semiotic morphisms could represent metaphors such as LIFE IS A JOURNEY in the form of a computer game rather than as written text. Building upon this observation, I shall use morphic semiotics to consider how independent game developer Jason Rohrer did just that. Rohrer constructed an imaginative world and poetic phantasms based on his reflective moments about mortality in the form of a brief, powerful computer game called *Passage*. The game involves the LIFE IS A JOURNEY metaphor in addition to a number of constraints that are resolved by choosing a quality preserving semiotic morphism.

Rohrer's creator's statement about his game *Passage* begins: "A tiny bit of background about me: I turn 30 tomorrow. A close friend from our neighborhood died last month. Yep, I've been thinking about life and death a lot lately. This game is an expression of my recent thoughts and feelings. *Passage* is meant to be a memento mori game" (Rohrer 2007). The concept of a *memento mori*, or a reminder of mortality, is well known in the arts; you probably have seen a memento mori artwork in the form of a still life featuring a lush flower arrangement next to an inert skull. Even the Mexican holiday called the Day of the Dead (*Día de los Muertos)* that inspired the computer game *Grim Fandango* (chapter 3) can be called a memento mori holiday. In each of these cases, skeletal imagery and the associations that they evoke constitute a memento mori that acts as a phantasm that reinforces a shared conception of mortality within society.

Just as the Dickinson and Frost poems discussed by Lakoff and Turner take a specific focus, a computer game about life and death must focus only on certain aspects of life, death, and mortality (neither poem nor game can represent every conception of death). *Passage* does not directly address all of the death-related issues that inspired Rohrer to create it. For example, it does not explicitly explore issues such as the loss of a friend or reaching the particular age of thirty. Yet it does touch upon more general themes of young adulthood, aging, marriage, journeying through life, and death.

We can begin our analysis by creating a rational reconstruction of the semiotic space that Rohrer used to develop his concept for the game. We are engaging in the analysis problem here, but it should be clear that Rohrer's process of taking abstract concepts about life and death could be described as *the design problem of taking a complex real-world phenomenon and deciding what from all of that complexity to represent*. Recall that we can describe this problem using morphic semiotics. In this case, we would describe the problem using a semiotic morphism from a semiotic space describing the structure of a real phenomenon (the journey of life and death) to a semiotic space describing the structure of computational model of the phenomenon (the specification for a game about life and death). This design problem is usually pursued informally, based on an artist's introspection, though other means can be used. Note that "informally" here means that an artist might not use a precise mathematical description; however, the process may still be rigorous, well planned, and based on any of a number of theoretical or practical approaches. Let us call this the *planning design problem.*

After the planning design problem, in game development there is a second design problem. It is the problem of creating a semiotic morphism from the abstract specification of the computational model (gameplay) to a concrete interface and implementation.

Let us call this the *implementation design problem.* I shall discuss *Passage* using morphic semiotics by first scrutinizing Rohrer's own description of the game's meaning to gain a sense of the semiotic morphism involved in the planning design problem. Then, I shall use the language of morphic semiotics to discuss Rohrer's solutions to the implementation design problem.

Rohrer's *Passage* employs an abstracted retro graphics style as can be seen in figure 4.21.[26] The gameplay of *Passage* expresses the conventional LIFE IS A JOURNEY metaphor mentioned earlier. In this game, the blond, male player character transitions from being statically located on the left side of the narrow screen to the right side while exploring an abstracted and pixilated space. He accumulates meaningless treasures, and perhaps a life partner, and eventually grows bald, old, loses his partner, and dies.

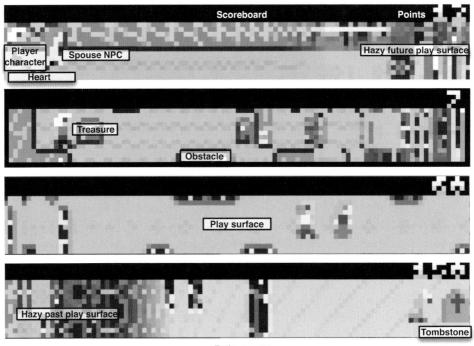

Entire screen

FIGURE 4.21
Four screenshots taken at different stages of life in *Passage* are shown one on top of the other here. Individual screen elements are labeled. The second screenshot illustrates a different play session than the others to depict an unmarried player character.

In Rohrer's own words:

[The game] presents an entire life, from young adulthood through old age and death, in the span of five minutes. . . .

The world in *Passage* is infinite. As you head east, you'll find an endless expanse of constantly-changing landscape, and you are rewarded for your exploration. However, even if you spent your entire lifetime exploring, you'd never have a chance to see everything that there is to see. If you spend your time plumbing the depths of the maze, however, you will only see a tiny fraction of the scenery. (Rohrer 2007)

As we can see from Rohrer's description, concepts about a journey through space amid rich rewards and mazelike barriers are mapped onto the more abstract ideas of life and death.

Rohrer, like Frost and Dickinson, deploys a number of metaphorical mappings in his game design. We can start describing the game by saying that an abstract semiotic space for JOURNEY, consisting of sorts for a start, middle, and end, has been blended with an abstract semiotic space for GAME, consisting of the same sorts with the addition of a sort for points. This blended JOURNEY/GAME is then blended with a semiotic space for LIFE that consists of the same sorts along with additional sorts for things such as age, obstacles, a partner, and more, along with life-related axioms for things such as aging, getting married, and so on. Let us consider in more detail how the actual game implements this blend. Just as the LIFE IS A JOURNEY metaphor explains something abstract (a lifetime) in terms of something more familiar (a journey), these other metaphors explore other aspects of life in more familiar terms. Interestingly, in some cases these more familiar terms consist of gaming tropes such as scoring points, accumulating treasure chests, or a tombstone icon representing a dead player character. Some metaphors are also subcomponents of other metaphors; for example, Lakoff and Turner (1989) showed how the PROGRESS IS THE DISTANCE TRAVELED metaphor is a subcomponent of LIFE IS A JOURNEY. Figure 4.22 is a table that shows some of the important metaphors and their subcomponent metaphors from *Passage*. The left column shows the name of the metaphor and the right column shows quotations from Rohrer's own creator's statement from which these metaphors are extrapolated. Most of the relationships between the quotations and the metaphors are self-explanatory. Bold text indicates the relevant part of the quotation. To provide one example of the way in which the quotations are used to reveal the metaphors, consider the case of PLAYER CHARACTER IS PLAYER.

In the quotation, the second-person pronoun "you" is in bold to reveal that Rohrer is referring to the player, not just the character on the screen. In other cases, the bold text indicates terms in the metaphor itself, clearly related terms (e.g., old age is clearly related to life), or specific information (e.g., Rohrer's discussion of his favorite outfits clearly refers to his real self). The table helps reveal how Rohrer approached the planning design problem. In the table, metaphors are grouped with their subcomponent metaphors.

Rohrer's statement is a mixture of descriptions of game mechanics and reflective ponderings about the real world. He combines discussion of the game's interface with ruminations on mortality, memory, and even an allusion to another video game (*Crypts of Despair*). In order to actually implement *Passage*, however, he needed to make some decisions about the best way to realize his vision as a subjective computing system. In other words, he needed to tackle the planning problem. To illustrate a polymorphic poetics approach to the planning problem, I shall use a semiotic space to sketch some game design concepts that Rohrer would need to map into an implementation. This semiotic space was developed from the metaphors in figure 4.22 and is presented in figure 4.23. This semiotic space was created by listing a set of broad concepts taken from elements of both the source and target spaces of the metaphors in figure 4.22. The semiotic space is somewhat informal, especially in its articulation of game mechanics using axioms. It is also not exhaustive because some specific aspects of the game may be omitted. It is, however, suitable for planning purposes.

The terms in the "Broad Concepts" column of figure 4.23 are not technically a part of the semiotic space. They are included for reference to help human readers keep in mind the conceptual metaphors that inform the design plan. Regarding those conceptual metaphors, the terms used in the "Broad Concepts" column tend to focus attention on the metaphors' source spaces. The reason for this focus is that Rohrer's game design task required him to decide upon a design plan resulting in an interface metaphor that best reflects the abstract themes of life, death, and mortality. For example, the LIFE IS A JOURNEY metaphor provides the idea in the design plan that life can be represented using a game character's iconic journey across a space on the monitor. In this design plan, the journey must not appear to be only a character walking. It must also reflect passage through life in some way, such as depicting the player character aging as he moves along.

To evoke the game designer's intended themes, the design plan should strongly match the structure of the metaphors that inform it. We saw an example of this earlier in Lakoff and Turner's list of metaphorical correspondences underlying Frost's

Metaphor	Quotation from the *Passage* Creator's Statement (Rohrer 2007)
LIFE IS A JOURNEY	• The game presents an entire **life**, from **young adulthood** through **old age** and **death**, in the **span** of five minutes. • At its **midpoint**, **life** is really about both the **future** … and the **past** • **Toward the end** of **life**, there really is no **future** left, so **life** is more about the **past,** …
A LIFETIME IS SPACE	• You can see quite a distance out **in front of you** (and, later **in life**, **behind you**), • At start, you can see your **entire life** out **in front of you**, • As you **approach middle age**, you can still see quite a bit out **in front of** you, • …but you can also see what you've **left behind**. • **Toward** the **end of life**, there really is no **future** left, so **life** is more about the **past** • As you grow **older**, your view of the **territory in front of you** shrinks, …
LIFE CHALLENGES ARE A MAZE	• *Passage* represents **life's challenges** with a **maze**. • …deeper into the **maze** …, the **path becomes more convoluted**, • …and **navigating new areas** in life's **maze** • Some rewards deep in the **maze** …
LIFE'S JOURNEY IS MOTION RIGHTWARD ON SCREEN	• The "long" **screen**, of course, represents a **lifetime**. • As you **age** in the game, your character **moves** closer and closer to the **right edge** of the screen. • Upon reaching that **edge**, your character **dies**.
EXPLORATION IS EAST	• …the scenery that unfolds before you to the east • As you head **east**, you'll find an **endless expanse** of **constantly changing landscape.**
DIFFICULT IS SOUTH	• … to the south, the path becomes **more convoluted**, …
EASY IS NORTH	• … though an **obstacle-free** route is always available to the north.
MEMORY IS VISIBILITY	• At the beginning of the game, **you can see** your entire life out in front of you, • but **you can't see anything** that's behind you, because you have no past to speak of. • … but you can also **see** what you've left behind—a kind of store of **memories** that builds up. • …and you can **see** a lifetime of **memories behind you**.
PAST IS VISIBLE SPACE	• …and you can **see** a **lifetime of memories**…
PLAYER IS PLAYER CHARACTER	• …*you* can see your entire life out in front of *you*… • As *you* age in the game, your character moves • So what can **you** do with *your* life?
ROHRER IS PLAYER CHARACTER	• That's **me … in there**, distilled down to **8x8 pixels** … • And if you're wondering, I do have **light hair** and **blue eyes**… • When **I** was younger, I wore a **green shirt**, **blue pants**, and **black shoes**. Now **my favorite outfit** involves **white shoes**, **brown pants**, and a **black shirt**. • And yes, **my hair line** is starting to creep back.

Metaphor	Quotation from the *Passage* Creator's Statement (Rohrer 2007)
MORTALITY IS GAME DEATH	• This treatment of **character death** stands in stark contrast with the way **death** is commonly used in **video games** (where you **die** countless times during a given game and emerge victorious—and still **alive**—in **the end**). • *Passage* is a game in which you **die only once**, at **the very end**, and you are **powerless** to stave off this **inevitable loss**.
DEAD PERSON IS TOMBSTONE ICON	• Speaking of that little, pixelated **tombstone** • … I played a fair bit of … *Crypts Of Despair.* I was struck by the little **tombstone** that appears when your **character dies**… • It's so shocking when it happens—snap!—**you** instantly turn into a **tombstone**.
PLAYER'S (FEMALE) SPOUSE IS NPC	• **You** have the option of joining up with a **spouse** on **your journey** (if you missed **her**, **she's** in the far north near your original starting point). • …if **you're** with **your spouse**.
ROHRER'S SPOUSE IS NPC	• **My spouse** used to have a **light-green dress** that was **her favorite**. That's … **my spouse** in there, distilled down to **8x8 pixels** • …and **my spouse** does have **red hair** and **green eyes**.
SPOUSE IS DIFFICULTY JOURNEY	• Once you **team up with her**, however, you must **travel together**, and **you are not as agile** as you were when you were single. • Some **rewards** deep in the maze will **no longer be reachable** … **with your spouse**. • You simply **cannot fit** through narrow paths when you are **walking side-by-side**. • In fact, you will sometimes find yourself **standing right next to a treasure chest**, yet **unable to open it**, and the **only thing standing in your way will be your spouse**. • When **she dies**, though, **your grief will slow you down** considerably.
SPOUSE IS ENRICHED JOURNEY	• …**exploring the world** is **more enjoyable** with a **companion**, • …and you'll reap a **larger reward** from **exploration** if **she's along**. • …**exploration**, which **gives double points** if you walk **with your spouse**.
REWARDING EXPERIENCES ARE TREASURES	• During your **lifetime**, you can learn to read the seeming **treasures** and only spend your **precious time** opening worthwhile **treasure chests**.
LIKELY REWARDING EXPERIENCES ARE DIFFICULT TO REACH TREASURES	• However, **treasure chests** are **more and more common** as you go **deeper into the maze**. • You can spend your time in pursuit of these **hard-to-reach rewards**. You may see a **reward up ahead** but **not be able to see a clear path** to it. • … seemingly nearby **reward** is in fact **unreachable**.
MEANINGLESS ENDEAVORS ARE POINTS	• Yes, you could spend your five minutes trying to **accumulate as many points as possible**, but in **the end**, **death** is still coming for you. Your score looks pretty **meaningless** hovering there above your little tombstone.

FIGURE 4.22

Selected metaphors underlying *Passage* can be considered the result of the planning design problem.

Planning Semiotic Space for *Passage*		
Broad concepts (for reference)	Constructors and axioms (grouped according to level hierarchy)	Priority
Life journey	Space	0 (top)
	Maze	4
Past, present, and future	Visible past	2
	Visible exploration space	2
	Visible future	2
Characters	Rohrer player character	1
	Spouse NPC	3
	Tombstone icon	1
Exploration and treasure points	Treasure chests	4
	Points	5
Axioms	Axiom: Time passage as journey	
	Axiom: Future visibility rules	
	Axiom: Past visibility rules	
	Axiom: Player character movement rules	
	Axiom: Player character death	
	Axiom: NPC movement rules	
	Axiom: NPC death	
	Axiom: Marriage rules	
	Axiom: Treasure point value rules	
	Axiom: Exploration point value rules	

FIGURE 4.23

This semiotic space for *Passage* describes the results of the planning design problem.

poem "The Road Not Taken." Rohrer's design, like Frost's poem, is effective because of the appropriateness of the detailed correspondences entailed by the metaphor it invokes to make the content of the target spaces salient for players. The constructors represent the elements that should appear in the design. They are grouped in levels to indicate part-whole relationships. The axioms represent the rule system that should constrain the elements in the design. Because this diagram uses a semiotic space as an informal sketch, it also uses axioms to loosely describe the design's dynamic rules. Finally, the relative importance of the constructors is indicated by priority. For example, the entire space itself is given top priority because it contains everything in the design. After the entire space, the player character (Rohrer's self-portrait) and the tombstone that represents him when he dies are assigned the next highest priority because the game design values the player's (and Rohrer's) personal reflection upon death.

Rohrer did not actually use morphic semiotics to plan the implementation of *Passage*, but, as with the discussion of Dunn's process of designing *Superman*, it is again useful to employ a semiotic space to describe the actual game and to rationally reconstruct some of the decisions he made in its creation. The benefit of doing so is twofold. First, such a description can help illustrate how a designer can use morphic semiotics to help guide the design process. Second, a morphic semiotics description of the game can help reveal how certain values are embedded in the game's structure. Figure 4.24 presents a semiotic space describing *Passage.* The semiotic space is not meant to be definitive; the game's structure could have been described using any number of slightly different semiotic spaces. Nor is the semiotic space meant to be exhaustive; rather, it is meant to capture just the primary aspects of the game's structure and mechanics. In this semiotic space, axioms shall again be described informally in natural English language.[27] Additionally, note that some constructors do not take data sorts as parameters because they contain their own display information (e.g., the play area, player and nonplayer characters (NPCs), and obstacles contain information about their colors and shapes). Finally, nonessential functions are omitted from the semiotic space.

We can now assess the effectiveness of this semiotic space as the specification for a game design. Its effectiveness should be assessed according to Rohrer's design goals. Based on our earlier definition of quality of semiotic morphisms, we can make this assessment of effectiveness based on analyzing what the semiotic space in figure 4.24 preserves from the design plan in figure 4.23. In other words, figure 4.25 depicts how we can scrutinize to what degree the semiotic morphism shown in figure 4.24 constructs a phantasm for mortality in the form of a computer game by using mappings that are *level preserving, constructor preserving, priority preserving, function preserving,* and *axiom preserving.*

We can see that levels have mostly been preserved by the semiotic morphism, with a few exceptions. The maze has been mapped to obstacles on the screen, rather than the entire space being conceived of as a maze. This shift of perspective on the nature of the maze has caused it to be at a lower level; the maze is part of the space rather than the whole space. Thus the maze is now at the same level as other objects that constitute the screen, such as characters. Treasure chests and points are now also at the same level as characters as they are all just considered to be parts of the screen (though treasure chests are part of the play surface, whereas points are part of the scoreboard). The past and future spaces are lower levels because they are now considered parts of the play space rather than separate entities—the elements representing the past, present, and future have been mapped onto the elements representing the screen. The elements are now parts of the play surface area of the screen.

Elements of the *Passage* Implementation Semiotic Space			
Constructor	Sort of element	Level	Priority
Entire screen	100x16 pixel image	0 (top)	0 (top)
Title screen	100x16 pixel image	1	1
Play surface	100x12 pixel image	1	2
Scoreboard	100x4 pixel image	1	2
Hazy past play surface	Variable-size pixel image	2	2
Hazy future play surface	Variable-size pixel image	2	2
Player character	8x8 pixel image	3	1
Spouse NPC	8x8 pixel image	3	3
Obstacles/Walls	Variable-size pixel image	3	4
Points	Integer	3	5
Treasure	6x6 pixel image	3	4
Heart	Variable-size pixel image	3	5
Tombstone	8x8 pixel image	3	1
Treasure value	Integer data sort (parameter of treasure)	data	n/a
Screen position value	Integer pair data sort (parameter of all other sorts except entire screen)	data	n/a

Axioms: Movement and control function as follows (Rohrer 2007):
- Press any button (or key) to start the game.
- Use left analog stick (or arrow keys) to move character (up, down, left, right).
- F (on keyboard) to toggle fullscreen mode.
- B (on keyboard) to adjust screen blow-up factor.
- Q or ESC (on keyboard) to quit.

Axiom: Award treasure points (points are given based on type of treasure chest)

Axiom: Award exploration points (points are given based on eastward movement over time; double points are given if player character and spouse NPC are traveling together)

Axiom: Age character (change character appearance; move character right on play surface)

Axiom: Compress past area (play surface becomes hazy past area)

Axiom: Expand future area (hazy future area becomes play surface)

Axiom: Fall in love (display heart; set player character and spouse NPC to travel together)

Axiom: Travel together (player character and spouse NPC move in unison)

Axiom: Spouse dies (replace with static tombstone icon)

Axiom: Player character dies (replace with static tombstone icon)

Axiom: Game over (game ends)

FIGURE 4.24

This semiotic space for *Passage* describes the game's implementation.

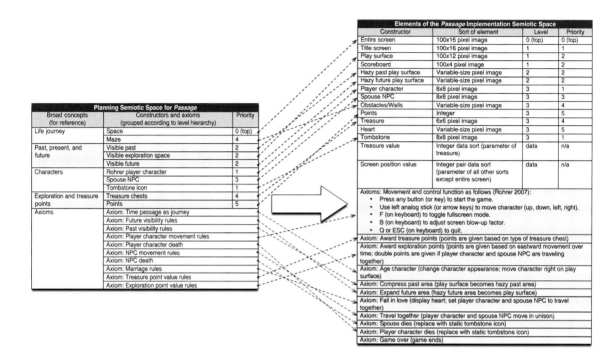

FIGURE 4.25
Analyzing this semiotic morphism from a design-plan semiotic space describing *Passage* to an
implementation-specification semiotic space helps reveal the quality of the semiotic morphism.

The constructors are all preserved by the semiotic morphism. However, some constructors have been introduced that were not in the design-plan semiotic space. These represent elements that were either conceived of later or are specific to the implementation, most likely because the plan focused on the game's construction of an imaginary world rather than its display of gaming conventions such as a title screen (which appears before gameplay starts and the play surface appears) or a scoreboard for displaying points separately from the play surface. Because these elements are not a part of the imaginative world of the game, it makes sense for them to have been introduced when developing final specifications for the implementation. One exception, which is a part of the imaginative work that the design-plan semiotic space did not include, is a heart image that appears when the characters get married—most likely because it is a fleeting flourish (and cliché), rather than an aspect of the game's central metaphors.

All of the priorities are preserved. This preservation property is important, because in this way the values regarding what is important in the source space are maintained in the implementation. The most important element of the implementation according to the priority preservation of the semiotic morphism is the entire screen. This is obvious because without being able to see the entire screen, the user's actions and the expressive power of the game would be severely limited. Of next greatest importance are the player character and the tombstone that replaces him (and his spouse). The priorities of both are preserved. The player character and tombstone that replaces him are of extreme importance in the source and target spaces because the reflection upon oneself and one's eventual death are the primary aspects of a memento mori. In both the source and target spaces, the passage of time and concepts of past, present, and future are the next most important elements. Marrying the spouse NPC is optional, so she is of less importance, but she is still more important than walls, treasure chests, points, and the heart that briefly appears to symbolize the characters' marriage.

Because the source and target semiotic spaces are not presented exhaustively, we have not identified specific functions in our analysis. Analyzing the attributes of the signs in the system is not crucial to the argument here. Hence we can say that the semiotic morphism is (trivially) function preserving. In practice, functions would be important in actually implementing the various axioms in the semiotic spaces and providing information about signs. Even if we had represented them, we likely would have preserved them in the design plan and introduced new ones as necessary for the implementation.

Finally, axioms are all preserved. A single new axiom has been introduced to specify the constraints indicating when the game is over. We could explain the introduction of this axiom by assuming that the death of the player character was planned to be the end of the game in the source space; however, during implementation a decision was made that the end of the game should come slightly after the character's death to allow for a reflective pause and more dramatic ending.

We can now reflect on the meaning of these various types of preservation. The semiotic morphism to the implementation semiotic space expresses all of the conceptual metaphors underlying *Passage* described in figure 4.22. For example, the player character simultaneously represents the player and Rohrer alike as a player character. This blend integrates the player's agency in the virtual world with a highly pixelated self-portrait of Rohrer himself as a video game character. The player character can be visually distinguished as the most important because movement is represented by scrolling of the play area, not by the player character's movement. The fixed position of the player character (aside from its translation from left to right, or west to east, across the screen as it ages) gives it a special status to distinguish it from the background image. The priorities of other elements are likewise indicated visually; for example, the less important treasure chests and the marriage heart appear on the screen much more briefly than the player character or hazy future and past areas. Points are relegated to a corner of the screen. All of these choices reveal that the actual signs used in the game express the elements, priorities, and structure of the semiotic space we use to describe the game. Thus the game represents the values that the semiotic space entails. The signs used in the game combine to create a rich combination of image spaces and highly structured epistemic spaces about mortality. In this sense, *Passage* prompts players to engage in constructing a memento mori phantasm, a rich combination of mental imagery and ideology regarding the nature of our human lives.

This analysis, from the rational reconstructions of the source and target space used in planning *Passage* to the semiotic space used to illustrate the implementation of the game itself, has revealed several subjective computing concepts. We have seen a description of the structures of *Passage*'s signs, the systems they come in, and how they convey meanings. We have seen detailed descriptions of the problems of designing and implementing computing systems using profound concepts of life, death, and mortality as examples. The descriptions of the design and implementation problems are intended to exhibit social and cultural awareness about the way they express imaginative concepts.

Passage is a critically acclaimed game. A major reason for its very positive reception, I contend, is largely the strong quality of the semiotic morphisms from its underlying metaphors all the way through the way that they implement a particular phantasm about mortality. Every element and action in the game reflects an underlying metaphor involving abstract ideas about the passage of time and one's (both Rohrer's and the player's) eventual death. We must also acknowledge the intangible artistry Rohrer exhibited in making the game. This artistry rendered his conception of mortality into an effective phantasm. Design decisions such as his choices of color, music, style, and related aesthetic attributes also reflect the structure of Rohrer's priorities. In practice, however, designers like Rohrer make many of these choices intuitively. By "intuition" here I do not mean something magical and fuzzy. I really mean that factors such as his experience in playing and building games and being immersed in a culture informed his embodied senses of "rightness" when making design decisions. This embodied sense, along with his understanding of the pensive and somber emotions evoked by the game's theme, allowed Rohrer to identify when his design was emotionally moving. The hope here is that morphic semiotics can help demystify and aid this process without impinging upon the creativity of developers, designers, and artists, despite its structured approach.

Reflections on Polymorphic Poetics, Interface Metaphor, and Social Engagement

Having now looked at the game *Passage* in detail, we can observe that Rohrer connected concepts of life and death to real-world experience, in part by mapping aspects of his own experience and even self-image into the game. In this regard, the previous discussion regarding *Passage* provides an example of polymorphic poetics.

The importance of polymorphic poetics is that we can judge the quality of, and values embedded within, subjective computing systems based on the choices of semiotic morphisms involved in designing and implementing them. There are many possible choices of a semiotic morphism, and this choice results in expressive differences in the system. Our polymorphic poetics account of *Passage* has shown how the game is a subjective computing system that provides commentary on the real world. Polymorphic poetics is not limited to addressing poetic reflection on abstract aspects of the human condition. Systems based on a polymorphic poetics approach could also interrogate life and death in the broader context of natural, social, political, cultural, and economic factors. In other words, polymorphic poetics can help guide development of subjective computing systems used to analyze—and even attempt to change—social order. In deploying such a semiotic morphism, a design must preserve the right kind of structure and content. Most important, the design must preserve the right kind of values, which are expressed through the priorities inherent in the structure and content. The morphic semiotics approach, in particular, analyzing the nature and quality of a semiotic morphism, can help in doing so. The quality of metaphors determines how useful they are as explanatory or rhetorical tools. Semiotic morphisms can catalyze cultural reflection, conceptual change, and even social action. This is the case whether they are used for thinking about the nature of mortality or about how life and death are intertwined with broader relationships between socioeconomic policies, race, history, and more. These themes are taken up in depth later (in part IV of this book).

Morphic semiotics can also be used as a tool for expression and social awareness when engaging in the use of everyday computing systems, as seen in the example of the online marketplace at the start of this chapter. It is for this reason that the chapter has interspersed examples from creative works such as games with utilitarian examples such as desktop windows and file hierarchies in an operating system. Values are built into the structure of all computing systems, but there is as of yet no well-known systematic approach to help reveal and/or design them. Morphic semiotics is a useful tool for *a subjective computing application* of what I have called polymorphic poetics. That is, polymorphic poetics provides an approach useful for *describing and mapping values and imaginative visions into expressive computing systems.*

Goguen's work in morphic semiotics offers groundbreaking potential to bridge the expressively, socially, and culturally engaged worlds of the humanities and social sciences with expressive design of computing systems using the language of mathematics. One of this chapter's goals has been to pay to tribute to his work with an attempt to convince readers from a range of backgrounds of his work's implications for subjective computing and phantasmal media. I hope that elaborating his work using the new framing concept of polymorphic poetics is a step in that direction.

CULTURAL COMPUTING

We have seen that computing systems, which are typically seen as objective, can be used for subjective purposes such as prompting phantasms. For example, mathematics is typically considered to be an objective language. For objectivist[1] thinkers, mathematical constructs such as numbers, functions, and sets are seen as simultaneously real and ideal. Such thinkers view mathematical constructs as objective and unadulterated by human beliefs, values, societies, and cultures. Computing, with its heritage from mathematics, is also sometimes not only thought of as objective, but also as acultural. Yet not only can computing systems be used for subjective purposes, their very foundations depend on cultural phantasms shared among people.

Computational systems are cultural systems. There are many important reasons for paying attention to the cultural foundations of computing systems. To give one, people participate in cultural groups that use particular computing platforms. These groups can share preferences that weave together elements such as senses of style (e.g., participation in fan culture around hardware, simply wearing corporate logos, or even programming style), politics (e.g., preference for commercial, open source, or free systems), and computing needs (e.g., choice of operating systems or software applications). Style, for instance, is based on adherence to a set of conventions valued by particular cultural groups. Programming styles alone can include or exclude programmers from using, altering, hacking, or admiring programs based upon their familiarity with the values that the style is based in. Going further than just the example of style, in part III I shall discuss how it is even a matter of debate whether different cultures even participate in mathematics practices differently. Participation in one of these cultures may have practical effects; for example, applications that are fully functional and easily used on a platform used by members of a given group may take tremendous effort to use on another platform (if possible at all). Accounting for the cultural foundations of computing can have profound implications. Critics of AI from computer science and philosophy have argued that flawed underlying assumptions render the goals of classic AI practitioners unattainable (Agre 1997; Dreyfus 1992; Winograd and Flores 1986).

Culture is composed of groups with multiple value systems, aesthetic and practical necessities, histories, and artifacts. Computational artifacts are not somehow outside of this cultural milieu. I have already presented a number of examples such as *The Girl with Skin of Haints and Seraphs*, the *Living Liberia Fabric*, and Brawn's Seller Representation that have begun to illustrate ways culture plays a role in designing, implementing, and using computing systems. For the purposes of this book, *cultural computing systems* are subjective computing systems, like those discussed in part II, that are built with awareness of their cultural foundations. In particular, part III further expands the notion that computing systems can be used to build effective forms of poetic culture. Toward articulating the concept of cultural computing, part III of this book consists of two chapters.

Chapter 5 addresses how phantasms are shared within societies and cultures. The chapter goes beyond describing how phantasms are prompted for individuals by subjective computing systems to address how phantasms become culturally widespread. As in the previous chapter, there is a focus on both practical computing applications ranging from online shopping to computer-based artwork. Chapter 5, however, also pays close attention to revealing the phantasms that system developers inherit from their cultures, which in turn shapes the systems the developers build. Toward these ends, the chapter introduces the concept of the *cultural phantasm*. The discussion is ultimately aimed at exposing how socially and culturally shared phantasms are built into and constructed by computing systems.

Chapter 6 describes the challenges and benefits of the grounding of computing practices in cultural systems and the virtues of making this cultural grounding explicit. Secondarily, chapter 6 also advocates the grounding of computing practice in a wider range of cultural practices and values than those that are privileged in computer science and engineering currently (which are often driven by "Western" materialistic, symbolic language–focused, and production-oriented modes of thought). The term *integrative cultural system* is introduced to describe how cultural values, knowledge, and representations are distributed onto material and conceptual artifacts—with a focus on computational artifacts. Diverse cultural phantasms are shown to have enabled new expressive forms of phantasmal media that have been well received in both humanistic and computing venues, and with implications for many broader forms of generating content computationally (such as educational technology and gaming).

The idea of cultural computing represents an important nexus of cultural grounding, social values, and expression of ideas within society. It is important because ignoring the role of culture in system design is a major cause of failure of computing systems. Even more significantly, it is important because for cultural computing systems to be used effectively, for them to have transformational effects upon minds and societies, and for them to be phantasmal media systems, they need to be addressed with the same cultural nuance exhibited by the best of humanities researchers and artists in exploring and creating other media. At the same time, these nuanced analysis and design principles need to be based on an understanding of the uniquely computational aspects of their media. The constructs of cultural phantasms and integrative cultural systems are steps in this direction.

5

CULTURAL PHANTASMS

Current thinking about computers and their impact on society has been shaped by a rationalistic tradition that needs to be re-examined and challenged as a source of understanding. As a first step we shall characterize the tradition of rationalism and logical empiricism that can be traced back at least to Plato. This tradition has been the mainspring of Western science and technology, and has demonstrated its effectiveness most clearly in the "hard sciences"—those that explain the operation of deterministic mechanisms whose principles can be captured in formal systems.

—Terry Winograd and Fernando Flores, *Understanding Computers and Cognition: A New Foundation for Design*

If anything my desire here has been to demystify the curious notion that theory is the province of the Western tradition, something alien or removed from the so-called noncanonical tradition such as that of the Afro-American.

—Henry Louis Gates Jr., *The Signifying Monkey: A Theory of African-American Literary Criticism*

Phantasms do not exist only in the minds of individuals; they are often shared within groups. The worldviews in which such phantasms are based encompass aspects such as culturally shared knowledge and beliefs, including specific preferences, norms, and values. Accounting for the roles of phantasms in a group is a complex endeavor. Even just stating what culture is in clear terms is a challenge. In thinking about what culture is, one quickly realizes the importance of considering issues such as the nature of participation, competency, membership, aesthetics, and authenticity. It is important to address how groups reinforce many types of relationships between people. It is important to address issues such as the fact that central members of groups negotiate membership differently than those on the margins. It is also important to recognize that discrepancies in power often necessitate different ways of participating in groups. In short, it is important to address a myriad of issues of culture. Up to this point, I have discussed what phantasms are; however, I have not yet attempted to explain what a culture is or how phantasms can be shared within a cultural group. Still, there are a few immediate observations I can make.

Toward addressing complexities of culture, many researchers develop conceptual frameworks to highlight key concepts that can help provide entry points to better understanding culture and phantasms that are shared across groups—cultural phantasms.

Later in this chapter, in order to better explain the word "cultural" in the term "cultural phantasm," I shall present a series of definitions and scholarly impressions of culture to gain a sense of how diverse concepts of culture, with a focus on ideas and images (phantasms), relate to computing practices. I shall also analyze specific computational cultural phantasms in some depth, with some degree of focus on the cultural phantasms that influence developers of systems. First, however, let me illustrate some of the issues related to computational cultural phantasms using an example.

An Example of a Computational Cultural Phantasm

Culture plays a pervasive role in the design of even the most practical of computer systems. It is important to consider the potential influence of the culture a system is built within or used by when analyzing or making computer systems. I have described some issues of this sort already when looking at the Brawn's Seller Representation in chapter 4, for example, if one considers the fact that many of Brawn's sexist and other preferences would likely be inherited from aspects of his culture. Brawn's preferences, and systems built based on them, would also contribute to the ongoing transmission and maintenance of such preferences within his culture. This embedding of cultural values in a system is true of the real eBay interface as well (although eBay likely intentionally avoided implementing the more onerous preferences in the fictitious example of Brawn). Continuing the discussion of online shopping, consider also the example of systems designed to capture and share people's preferences: recommender systems. Recommender systems have been used on many commercial retail websites to suggest potentially desirable purchases to users. Recommender systems are an example of a technology based on the notion of collective intelligence. Technologies based on this concept solve problems (show "intelligence") by using the aggregate data of a large number of people (a "collective"). The particular collective intelligence technologies that are commonly used may change in the future, and there may come a time when other approaches supersede collective intelligence. However, recommender systems are worthwhile to consider here as a historical snapshot to illustrate a process by which software influences aspects of culture as discussed at the start of the chapter.

Consider the case of a recommender system on a site for buying music and books coming up with recommendations for a user, as depicted in figure 5.1.

Imagine that this user's previous purchases include a documentary on a punk rock band and a textbook for an AI course. The system might suggest purchasing both a punk rock album for download and another book on LISP. Now let us consider how and why the computer came up with that recommendation. Describing computational recommender systems, computer scientists Xiaoyuan Su and Taghi M. Khoshgoftaar write, "In everyday life, people rely on recommendations from other people by spoken words, reference letters, news reports from news media, general surveys, travel guides, and so forth. Recommender systems assist and augment this natural social process to help people sift through available books, articles, webpages, movies, music, restaurants, jokes, grocery products, and so forth to find the most interesting and valuable information for them" (Su and Khoshgoftaar 2009, 1). "Spoken words, reference letters, news reports" and the other "natural social processes" described in the quotation enable the aspects of culture we have seen so far (knowledge, beliefs, preferences, norms, and values) to be perpetuated. Shared preferences and values are aspects of culture; the social process of a group's coming to share the same preferences and values is a process of culture maintenance and building. Yet notice the differences between the natural social processes described earlier and the process of collaborative filtering. Recommender systems capture and share preferences and values using algorithmic processes. This process happens without users clearly knowing whose preferences the system's recommendations are based on. An algorithmically generated measure of the shared preferences and values of a group of

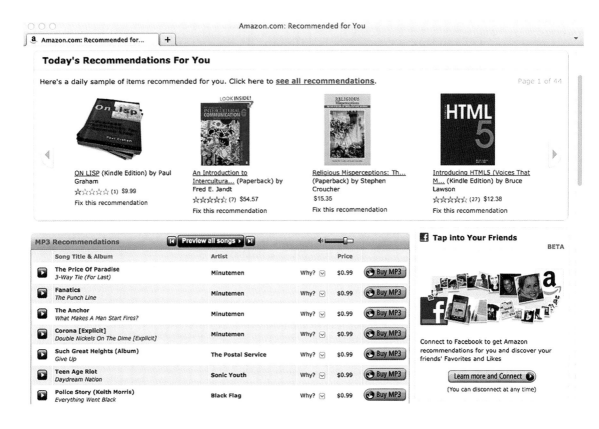

FIGURE 5.1

Recommendations from a commercial website produced by indicating preferences for music and books are presented to users as shown here. Such recommendations can be integrated with a social network using a tool on the bottom right.

users is still an expression of a process of building culture, as I describe it here. It is a process of culture building because shared values and preferences reinforce the membership of individuals in a cultural group. Yet the computer plays a crucial and partially unseen role in that process.

In the example of recommender systems, a process of culture building is at work that is mediated by both data structures and algorithms. I shall now more precisely elaborate this assertion of culture building by presenting an overview of how many recommender systems work. Recommender systems usually consider their domain of operation to be a matrix of users and items. Each cell in the matrix represents some type of user rating of the object, ranging from an indicator of whether the user has purchased the object, a binary choice of "likes" or "dislikes," or some other rating such as a number of stars ranging from one to four. For example, imagine an online store that sells books and music albums. Focus on just five of their items: a book on the LISP programming language, a book on media communication, a punk rock music album, a book on religion, and a jazz music album. Imagine five users of the system, named Leila, Thelonious, Shikha, Sakura, and Jimmy. Imagine also knowing the following information about the users: Leila likes the jazz album, Thelonious likes the book on religion and dislikes the punk rock album, Shikha likes the book on media communication, Sakura likes the LISP book, and Jimmy dislikes everything. Figure 5.2 summarizes this information as a "user ratings matrix."

As can be seen even in the simple case of figure 5.2, a user ratings matrix is usually sparse because most people have not rated most objects. A recommender system's job is to predict how a user would rate a currently unrated item and to recommend items that it predicts would have a high rating. Collaborative filtering algorithms, which represent a major approach to addressing this problem, look at the collective past ratings of items by users to generate recommendations. Content-based recommending is

A User Ratings Matrix for a Small Store					
	Lisp book	Media book	Punk album	Religion book	Jazz album
Leila					Likes
Thelonious			Dislikes	Likes	
Shikha		Likes			
Sakura	Likes				
Jimmy	Dislikes	Dislikes	Dislikes	Dislikes	Dislikes

FIGURE 5.2
An example of a small *user ratings matrix* illustrates the common case in which many cells do not contain entries.

another approach to the problem, which is based on looking at attributes of items that a user has previously ranked highly and other attributes of the user's profile (Melville and Sindhwani 2010). In either approach, the user ratings matrix can be considered to be an epistemology because it represents a formalized description of an epistemic domain—namely, it is a specification of which items are known, or believed, to be preferred by users.

To give a concrete example of how this epistemology can be used algorithmically to make predictions about subjective preferences, let us consider just one collaborative filtering approach: memory-based collaborative filtering algorithms. These algorithms group users according to their interests. Users in these groups are organized based upon similarities between their vectors of ratings (rows in figure 5.2). Users with highly similar vectors are considered to be "neighbors." Predictions are then created based on the assumption that a user's preferences resemble those of his or her neighbors.[2] These predictions can be characterized as the results of an algorithmic notion of a "neighborhood" of likes operating on an epistemic domain for shared preferences derived from the user ratings matrix epistemology. When these predictions are combined with an image space, such as that in illustrated in figure 5.1, in which images of certain items fall under a header boldly stating "Today's Recommendations for You," *these predictions become phantasms for many users.* That is, some users will view these as personally customized suggestions for purchases similar to recommendations by other people (or they may even see the recommender system as *more* authoritative than other people) and may be more inclined to purchase items based upon them. In fact, the recommender system has standardized the way the recommendations are presented. This standardized form of recommendation and the similar recommendations it gives to algorithmic neighbors constitute shared phantasms.

In other words, data-structural and algorithmic mediation of social processes can result in the semivisible shaping of people's shared phantasms, also affecting patterns of behavior. The process is semivisible in the sense that some will accept it without notice, particularly if it is based in epistemic domains in which the user's knowledge and beliefs are also based (e.g., an unaware consumerist epistemic domain), and others will see it as a system attempting to shape their behavior, particularly if they draw information from a contrasting epistemic domain (e.g., an epistemic domain that includes knowledge of the computational approach used to create the recommendation). This culture-building process is an example of constructing *cultural phantasms* on a computer.[3] Su and Khoshgoftaar, in the quotation presented earlier, even claim that recommender systems "assist and *augment*" the non-computer-based "natural social process" people use to share recommendations (Su and Khoshgoftaar 2009, 1; emphasis added). This is a telling claim because it reveals a cultural phantasm in which the paper's authors value automation over interaction between humans. This discussion of recommender systems begins to suggest that development and use of computing systems can be a means of building culture and constructing cultural phantasms. At this point, it is useful to pin down these terms in order to more precisely account for these phenomena in computational systems more generally.

Cultural Phantasms

It is possible to now say more precisely that a *cultural phantasm* is a phantasm that is shared within a group that can be described according to a cultural model. This definition of the term requires, in turn, a definition of "cultural model," a phrase that has many different meanings for researchers analyzing cultural ideas and images. For some, a cultural model is a conceptual framework for comparing cultures to one another. I shall call this a *comparative cultural model*. For others, a cultural model is a conceptual framework that tries to capture a set of features of the complex milieu of everyday social life that people often call culture. This second type of cultural model[4] is an abstraction from reality that is meant to be descriptively or predictively useful. I shall call this a *descriptive cultural model*.[5] In the social sciences and humanities, it is clear that such models are just analytical tools, not real objects out there in the wild to be studied. When a single descriptive cultural model is used to describe the differences between multiple cultures by comparing them using the set of features across different cultures, it becomes a comparative cultural model.

In computing, programmers implement models algorithmically and data-structurally, giving them a kind of reality. Computational models of real-world subjective phenomena are reductions from phenomena that require humans to make sense of them in order to be formally represented so that a computer can execute them. Hence, computer scientists might introduce a third meaning of the term "cultural model" to mean a computational simulation of some set of phenomena exhibited by humans in a society. I shall call this a *computational cultural model*. Given all of these different senses in which the term cultural model is used, it is important to clarify the sense of the term used in this book. "Cultural model" here generally shall refer to a descriptive cultural model, but none of these senses of the term are intended to be universal definitions. Rather, they are merely different aspects of a complex conceptual category appropriate for use in different contexts; in this case, the context is our focus upon cultural ideas and images. These notions of cultural model will help us move toward an understanding of cultural phantasms that adds detail to the definition given at the beginning of this section.

The phantasmal media approach here emphasizes that cultural ideas and images are subjective, and often both mysterious and only semivisible. A challenge, then, is to come up with terminology that allows discussion of the subjective nature of the ideas and images composing particular cultural models in parallel with definitions of culture from different disciplines and practices. The term *cultural phantasm* is intended to address this challenge. Like phantasms more generally, which may be individual or shared, cultural phantasms are embodied, distributed, and situated. Let us first attend to these characteristics of cultural phantasms in turn.

To start, the embodied nature of phantasms means that "we create them on the basis of our concrete experiences and under the constraints imposed by our bodies" (Ibarretxe-Antuñano 2004, 7). The embodied nature of phantasms is important to remember when considering cultural phantasms because they involve much more than shared facts and propositions about the world. Cultural phantasms rely on the shared nature of our experiences as embodied human beings. An embodied cognition perspective requires us to also "look at the felt qualities, images, feelings, and emotions that ground our more abstract structures of meaning" (Johnson 2007, 17). When many members of a group uniformly experience a computer game in a similar way—for example, if they tend to feel an intense sense of melancholic reflection after playing *Passage*—the embodied response reveals that a cultural phantasm that exists for the group.

The distributed nature of phantasms is likewise important. In particular, media artifacts often play strong roles in helping phantasms become culturally widespread because they act as prompts "for the construction of meaning in particular contexts with particular cultural models and cognitive resources" (Fauconnier 2004, 658). Remember also that phantasms may be distributed across members of a social group, external artifacts, and time. Subjective computing systems such as interactive computer animation often provide such phantasmal anchors for the imagination. An example of this is a character in a videogame onto which the user projects aspects of his or her real-world identity (Gee 2007), such as the proclivity to move a certain direction or desire to explore strange locales. When players uniformly see themselves as a character in a game, such as Nintendo's Mario, those hybrid characters/selves are cultural phantasms.

Finally, remember that phantasms are always situated in particular social and cultural contexts (Lave and Wenger 1991); the use of recommendations from a recommender system to buy something provides an example in which the context helps shape the development of cultural phantasms. The culturally situated nature of phantasms is the focus of this chapter. The concept of the cultural phantasm examines the ways in which phantasms are shared by being situated within cultures. This point can be elaborated using the example of a phantasm just mentioned, the hybrid character/self that players control in videogames. When a female gamer in a sexist culture plays a game featuring only male player characters, her particular contextual situation (being female, distributing her identity onto a male character) will result in a conceptual clash if she does not identify at all as male. Given that empirical research has shown that her real-world behavior may change (e.g., her sense of confidence or interpersonal comfort with others) as a result of her digital representation in the game (Yee and Bailenson 2007), this is an important point. The female gamer might feel tension in elaborating an imaginative game-world self-image and self-conception because her embodied experiences as a female make it hard to identify with a male player character; this tension may have an impact on her behavior. At the same time, because of gender bias in her cultural context, she may in fact be accustomed to distributing her identity onto male characters (such as Mario, mentioned earlier). In such cases, the situated nature of the cultural phantasm at hand (her imagined self as a character capable of acting in an imaginative game world) enables the player character to act as a prompt for her cognitive processes involved in being immersed in gameplay. She may even alter her behavior to express a type of male privilege and entitlement. Regardless, the phantasm is not prompted only by her individual imagining; her experience of the phantasm is structured by the culturally shared concepts about gender that have been encoded in the game.

Perspectives on Defining Culture

When claiming that people share phenomena that are rooted in cognition, it becomes important to describe the nature of this sharing. It is important because I want to be clear that this is not a discussion of a mystical and unknowable process. Cultural phantasms are not some form of mystical collective unconscious. Cultural phantasms are not ideals that exist in some abstract transcendental reality. At the same time, they are also not real in the same sense that observable physical objects are real. I have defined them as the results of processes of embodied, distributed, and situated cognition. They are developed through the interaction of social practices with individual cognitive processes, along with phenomena such as tool use, social behaviors, and distribution of ideas using communication media. Cultural phantasms are created, sustained, dismantled, and reconfigured through human practices and experiences. They can change dynamically and continuously. Their degree of "reality," in terms of impact on people's minds and lives, depends upon people subscribing to them.

Cultural phantasms are "conceptual artifacts," as real as any concept is. They are also only as intrinsically natural as any other human-made artifact. Consider the example of social class as an epistemic domain. Certainly, differences of cultural prestige, wealth, and other aspects of class are found within many societies. However, the formulation of class as consisting of the three categories familiar in the United States—namely, "working," "middle," and "upper" classes—has been traced back to statistician T. H. C. Stevenson's work in *The Registrar General's Annual Report for 1911* (Rose 1995).[6] This three-tiered concept of class has become so pervasive (sometimes with variations of terminology or further subdivisions) that it has entered into common parlance. Many people even define their behaviors and affiliations based upon notions of shared membership in these social classes. This conception of class has had real social impact upon people's lives, yet it is a conceptual artifact that can be traced back to a single inventor. The function of these class labels may be invisible for those who are based in the same epistemic domains, but quite visible to others, such as Marxists. For example, when politicians speak of aiding the middle class, listeners must decide whether they are the ones being referred to based upon their own epistemic domains for class.

To define cultural phantasms in a more nuanced way, it is important to undertake the task of addressing what culture is, which is no simple task; as anthropologist Hervé Varenne reminds us (Varenne 2002), there are different cultures of understanding culture! To emphasize this point, recall that anthropologists Alfred Kroeber and Clyde Kluckhohn (Kroeber and Kluckhohn 1952) famously listed 164 definitions of culture. This variation illustrates how, when exploring existing definitions of culture, researchers are bound to encounter an abundance of different academic definitions, vernacular uses, dictionary definitions, and more.

One way to begin understanding this matrix of definitions of culture is to provide examples of discussions and definitions of "culture." A good place to start is Raymond Williams's 1958 essay, which reminds us that "Culture is Ordinary." Williams writes, "A culture has two aspects: the known meanings and directions, which its members are trained to; the new observations and meanings, which are offered and tested. These are the ordinary processes of human society and minds, and we see through them the nature of a culture: that it is always both traditional and creative; that it is both the most ordinary common meanings and the finest individual meanings" (Williams [1958] 1989, 4). His perspective on culture is extremely relevant to the idea of the cultural phantasm because of its focus on both the individual mind and broader society. This focus is in line with the cognitive science approach in this book, which sees imaginative thought as being embodied, situated, and most important in the present context, *distributed across individuals and artifacts*. The idea of an "entrenched metaphor" in cognitive science arises from the observation that the results of conceptual feats eventually can become socially shared and widespread. A good example of this is George Lakoff and Rafael Núñez's discussion of the mathematical invention of imaginary numbers, building upon earlier concepts like the basic ability to recognize the number of things in a group and the number line, and how the nontrivial mathematical notion of imaginary numbers have now entered into the everyday elementary mathematics even taught in elementary schools around world (Lakoff and Núñez 2000).

Another parallel exists between the cognitive science arguments regarding entrenched metaphors and Williams's reflections on culture. Recall Gilles Fauconnier's discussion of the "operational uniformity" of conceptual cognitive processes mentioned in the introduction to this book (Fauconnier 1999). Just as Williams emphasizes the commonality between "the most ordinary common meanings and the finest individual meanings," Fauconnier, like Lakoff and Turner (Lakoff and Turner 1989), emphasizes that the same cognitive processes in everyday conceptualization are also at play in high-level artistic and literary conceptualization. The cognitive science based concepts of epistemic domains and spaces, image spaces, phantasms, and cultural phantasms here provide descriptive models for the type of creation and sharing of concepts within culture identified by predecessors such as Williams.

It useful to distinguish a common meaning of culture from an academic meaning, such as done by anthropologist Geert Hofstede: "The first, most common, meaning is "civilization," including education, manners, arts and crafts and their products. It is the domain of a "ministry of culture.". . . The second meaning derives from social anthropology, but in the past decades it has entered common parlance. It refers to the way people think, feel, and act" (Hofstede 2011). Hofstede's first meaning provides a vernacular, and often elitist, definition of culture that typically excludes all but the most privileged members of a society. Indeed, the first meaning of culture described by Hofstede is itself a cultural phantasm, operating invisibly for those who are considered to be civilized and cultured, but often oppressing those who are not (typically people who are marginalized in some way). His second meaning is the focus here. Regarding this second type of definition, influential anthropologist Clifford Geertz wrote that "culture" "denotes an historically transmitted pattern of meanings embodied in symbols, a system of inherited conceptions expressed in symbolic forms by means of which men communicate, perpetuate, and develop their knowledge about and attitudes toward life" (Geertz 1973, 89). Proposing a more elaborate version of this type of definition, Kroeber and Kluckhohn have developed what Hofstede calls an "anthropological consensus definition," which reads: "Culture consists in patterned ways of thinking, feeling and reacting, acquired and transmitted mainly by symbols, constituting the distinctive achievements of human groups, including their embodiments in artifacts; the essential core of culture consists of traditional (i.e., historically derived and selected) ideas and especially their attached values" (Hofstede 2001, 9; Kluckhohn and Kluckhohn 1952). Hofstede himself has defined culture as "the collective programming of the mind that distinguishes the members of one group or category of people from another." For Hofstede, the term "category" can refer to "nations, regions within or across nations, ethnicities, religions, occupations, organizations, or the genders" (Hofstede 2011). Jointly, this set of definitions captures an anthropological perspective on culture.

Each of these definitions overlaps quite a bit with the others, but they differ in their emphases and degrees of specificity. Though these anthropological views offer a fair starting point, they fail to highlight some of the distinctions made by diverse thinkers about culture. Varenne's discussion in "the culture of CULTURE" cites a number of quotations from thinkers including Claude Lévi-Strauss, Michel Foucault, and Bruno Latour, along with many others (Varenne 2002). Varenne calls to mind a diverse set of issues involved in defining culture, ranging from the fine-grained to the abstract. At a fine-grained level, his list of definitions addresses the role of individually learned behavior in culture. At a medium-grained level, the definitions address socially shared systems of art, economics, and law. At a large-grained level, these definitions address overarching systems of power and hegemonic systems of exclusion such as those described by Michel Foucault (Foucault 1971). Also toward the abstract end of the spectrum is the notion that culture is both an oppositional concept to "nature" (as in nature versus nurture debates) and a transmutation of nature.

For our purpose of defining cultural phantasm, three emphases stand out. These are the subjectivity, mystery, and invisibility of culture. Although they are not absent from the anthropological definitions (indeed, Hofstede stressed the invisibility of cultural values), several quotations highlight these aspects of culture in ways that are illuminating. Literary artist James Baldwin emphasizes circumstance and subjectivity: "a culture [is] not a community basket weaving project, nor yet an act of God; [it is] something neither desirable nor undesirable in itself, being inevitable, being nothing more or less than the recorded effects on a body of people of the vicissitudes with which they had been forced to deal" (Baldwin 1955, 140). Baldwin's viewpoint helps emphasize the experiences of the marginalized or the oppressed in a way that the anthropological definitions discussed previously have not. A complementary perspective is offered by literary critic Lionel Trilling and his emphasis on mystery:

> When we look at a people in the degree of abstraction which the idea of culture implies, we cannot but be touched and impressed by what we see, we cannot help being awed by something mysterious at work, some creative power which seems to transcend any particular act or habit or quality that may be observed. To make a coherent life, to confront the terrors of the outer and the inner world, to establish the ritual and art, the pieties and duties which make possible the life of the group and the individual—these are culture, and to contemplate these various enterprises which constitute a culture is inevitably moving. (Trilling 1978, 91–92)

Trilling's emphasis on mystery and the creative act is revealing. It describes a perspective on how an artist such as Baldwin might become a poignant voice to both represent and decry culture. A telling perspective also comes from Bruno Latour, who highlights culture's invisibility, stressing the fact that it involves "a set of elements that appear to be tied together" until disrupted (Latour 1988, 201). Considering that Baldwin's quotation was composed after having been mistakenly arrested and cast into a Parisian jail, Latour's idea that cultures are revealed by disruptive acts seems quite apropos. In light of Baldwin's celebrated artistry, Trilling's sense of how creative power makes the terrors of life coherent also gains increased salience. In integrating the concerns of Baldwin, Trilling, and Latour, the trio of subjectivity, mystery, and invisibility comes to the fore. Subjectivity, mystery, and invisibility are crucial aspects of constructing the mental images and ideologies associated with culture, and thus our notion of a cultural phantasm depends on them.

Cultural phantasms are inherently mysterious. People cannot pin down precisely how they came to be possessed by a particular phantasm. People cannot truly feel that they know many cultural phantasms deeply. The phantasms of others often seem only partially knowable (these can be called "phantasms of the exotic"). This mysteriousness is often used to support justifications or explanations of behavior: "Her proclivity to touch others is because she is from an outgoing culture." "You won't really understand the meaning of my prayer because you are from a different culture." By another token, phantasms can be demystified: "I thought all of you people acted one way, but I see now that there is just as much variety as there is in my own people!" Although shared, individuals also uniquely make sense of cultural phantasms as intermixed with a plethora of felt emotions, subtle urges, daydreams, fantasies, dreams, aspirations, and personal circumstances. In fact, this is why the arts hold a unique descriptive power for thinking about cultural phantasms. The arts are capable of expressing these subjective aspects of cultural phantasms.

Given the subjective qualities that make cultural phantasms challenging to pin down, making sense of them requires new conceptual tools. There are many perspectives on the subjectivity of meaning that focus on meaning as the result of processes of negotiation between people and with objects. Such ideas include the dialogic construction of meaning put forward by literary theorist Mikhail Bakhtin, meaning construction through the lens of symbolic interactionism as argued for by sociologists George Mead and his student Herbert Blumer, and the production of meaning via discourse as articulated by philosopher Michel Foucault (Bakhtin 1982; Blumer 1986; Foucault 1982). Without going into detail, let it suffice to say that these venerable ideas all inform the idea of the cultural phantasm. The construct of the cultural phantasm enables the weaving together of different registers and disciplines in order to highlight the aspects of culture revealed by each. Understanding the ways in which cultural phantasms function and help structure people's behaviors and societies can be a stepping stone toward identifying phenomena detrimental to the human condition and advancing phenomena and ways of knowing that can improve it.

The Nature of Cultural Phantasms

Given the aforementioned views of culture and the idea of entrenched metaphors, It is possible now to supplement the earlier definition of cultural phantasms by saying that they are *phantasms that are culturally entrenched*. We shall especially attend now to the natures of cultural phantasms as shared systems of integrated:

• Knowledge and beliefs (epistemic domains including preferences, norms, and values along with social practices and embodied knowledge such as behaviors)

• Representations (image spaces including artifacts, verbal images, mental images, etc.)

Furthermore, like phantasms in general, cultural phantasms are revealed only through perspectives grounded in multiple epistemic domains and image spaces. That is, cultural phantasms operate invisibly for some group members; for others, they operate in plain sight. In this manner, cultural phantasms provide the underlying epistemological, cognitive, and cultural forces informing entrenched, integrated concepts and images, as well as being integrated concepts and images themselves.

This second notion of associated concepts and images relates to the idea of the semiotic *myth* introduced by Roland Barthes (Barthes [1957] 1972). For Barthes, a myth is "the associative total of a concept and an image" (a *sign*), but it is a "second-order" sign in which underlying assumptions about its components are not questioned. A cultural phantasm differs from a myth in important ways. A cultural phantasm can include a second order sign, but it goes further, explicitly accounting for worldview and also articulating a range of cognitive images—from sensory to mental, from immediate to remembered or imagined—that are components of signs. Furthermore, the cultural phantasm is based in an embodied, distributed, situated cognition perspective. Despite these distinctions, it is useful to engage Barthes's useful notion of a second-level sign. Barthes's classic example of a myth is an image of a (then-called) "Negro solider" saluting a French flag. Superficially, the image seems to signify "that France is a great Empire, that all her sons, without any color discrimination, faithfully serve under her flag" (Barthes [1957] 1972, 116). At the same time, Barthes argues that, when presented uncritically, the image fails to question "the contingent, historical, in one word: fabricated, quality of colonialism" (143). The image's meaning is invisible for unwitting people seeing it.[7] Because signs come in systems, failing to look at the meanings of their components renders them invisible while they are in plain sight. In this book, our approach is not to read society and culture as texts, as has been done by semiologists such as Barthes. Yet although our approach differs from that of Barthes, it shares his emphasis on the semivisibility of shared meanings and images.

There are innumerable examples of the invisibility of cultural phantasms and the ways that multiple perspectives can reveal them. Let us return to the example of gendered characters in games. The game *Brink* has been noted for its lack of female character options (Gallaway 2010). When a computer game player perceives an image space composed of this set of options that has been integrated with a widespread epistemic space containing the belief that those options should accommodate most gamers preference, that perception of the game's character options is a cultural phantasm. Like Barthes's example of the "Negro" soldier, the male player character is a seemingly innocent sign that appears to be only a proxy for playing the game. The male game player's unquestioning selection and use of the character reveals knowledge, beliefs, and representations that operate invisibly in some gaming subcultures. A gamer seeking female representations might see the game differently. Cultural phantasms can also operate invisibly and visibly for the same person, shimmering in and out of view. That male gamer might see the game differently when he invites his sister to play the game and even remark that "there aren't any female characters in this game," yet quickly forget her moment of hesitation over character selection when he goes back to solo play.

The multiple epistemic domains and image spaces needed to reveal phantasms need not be based upon having different social identities such as gender categories. The shared experience of laboring at unfulfilling jobs without a sense of meaning in one's life is another example of a cultural phantasm. Consider Gregor Samsa's thought when he awakens transformed into an insect in Franz Kafka's famous story "The Metamorphosis":

> What about if he reported sick? But that would be extremely strained and suspicious as in fifteen years of service Gregor had never once yet been ill. His boss would certainly come round with the doctor from the medical insurance company, accuse his parents of having a lazy son, and accept the doctor's recommendation not to make any claim as the doctor believed that no-one was ever ill but that many were workshy. And what's more, would he have been entirely wrong in this case? Gregor did in fact, apart from excessive sleepiness after sleeping for so long, feel completely well and even felt much hungrier than usual. (Kafka [1915] 2002)

Consider the following rhetorical question: "Who does not know Gregor's anxieties about his boss, his doctor, and his insurance company?" These are familiar issues to the kind of people who read books like this one. But, in fact, many people do not know such anxieties! Some rural farm workers, people who have not experienced life in industrial or postindustrial societies, and even office workers who have not interrogated their own situations and insurance statuses might all perceive of their lives in ways that do not match Kafka's vision. Kafka's evocation of an office worker's anxiety is a cultural phantasm for those people who take Gregor's feelings to be universal. Kafka's artistry, however, enables him to evoke the phantasm of the banal and repetitive urban worker's life so that even those who have not experienced that life can begin to envision it through his tale, at the same time as he reveals it as a phantasm by using the metaphor of grotesque transformation, which in turn enables the reader to understand life through new imagery and a new conceptualization. As Kafka's work demonstrates, because the story has entered the canon of world literature, art forms such as literature can enable people to take perspectives outside of their own in order to prompt and reveal cultural phantasms.

The concept of the cultural phantasm can be illustrated with even more nuance by further dividing the aspects of cultural phantasms I am focusing on here (shared knowledge, beliefs, and representations). Each aspect can be split into elements that are consciously shared and those that are tacitly shared. For example, a distinction might be drawn between knowledge in the form of self-conscious cultural performances (e.g., overtly trying to "act like a man") and routine behaviors (e.g., eating with utensils customary to that culture). Another way to add nuance to our analysis is to focus upon *differences* of knowledge, beliefs, and representations between subgroups rather than just on what is shared. Indeed, many groups (such as neo-Nazis, anti-integrationists, and other reactionaries) define their identities in terms of differences from, or opposition to, other groups.

It is useful to consider the ways that cultural phantasms can be built by integrating new epistemic spaces with preexisting phantasms. For example, the shared aesthetic sensibilities of artistic movements are often such cultural phantasms. In these cases, the cultural phantasms associated with the movement result from integrating shared beliefs (in the form of values) with the representations that artists within the movement create, which may themselves prompt phantasms. For example, the art movement of surrealism can be considered to be a cultural phantasm when the term evokes a pantheon of canonical works by artists such as Salvador Dalí and Joan Miró, accompanied by values supporting ideas such as externalizing subconscious thought along with a revolutionary social disposition. At the same time, the works of Dalí and Miró already prompt phantasms themselves through painted images and their associated meanings. Another example of this type of double-level cultural phantasm is the belief that great works of literature are those that most closely resemble a set of canonical European texts, which in turn prompt and reveal their own sets of phantasms. This belief involves a double level of shared values, as many members of society assign high prestige and mental imagery to such texts by, for example, citing the names of a novel such as *War and Peace* or *Finnegan's Wake* as signifiers for "great books" without actually possessing much knowledge of the content of those novels.

There are certainly other possible foci we could take in exploring *cultural phantasms*—for example, further highlighting the distinction between practical and expressive artifacts. Yet, for the purposes here, the focus on shared knowledge, beliefs, and representations that can be revealed through multiple perspectives and images is more than sufficient for a fruitful discussion that highlights the strengths of the anthropological definitions of culture, while also admitting other approaches from literature or the arts. The aim is not to develop a new consensus definition or comprehensive account of all things cultural. Rather, the term "cultural phantasm" helps support creation and analysis of shared subjective meanings and their often mysterious and invisible natures, with a specific focus on supporting development of cultural computing systems.

Different artistic and academic pursuits utilize their varied analytical frameworks as cultural models in different ways. Literary theorists might talk about cultural narratives, anthropologists might talk about patterns of behavior along a set of dimensions, fiction writers might use elaborate metaphors and imaginative worlds, and quantitative sociologists might cite statistics about social phenomena or demographics, and so on. In this sense, comparative and descriptive cultural models can be seen as a means for respectively distinguishing and providing descriptions of particular cultures based upon which cultural phantasms seem to be most pertinent to the current analysis.

A good example of a comparative cultural model in anthropology would be Geert Hofstede's set of values for distinguishing countries from one another culturally. For Hofstede, one result of his statistical data about national values was four distinguishing "anthropological problem areas that different national societies handle differently" (Hofstede 2011). These are: "ways of coping with inequality, ways of coping with uncertainty, the relationship of the individual with her or his primary group, and the emotional implications of having been born as a girl or as a boy" (Hofstede 2011). Instantiations of each of these dimensions of national culture is a cultural phantasm. Hofstede uses quantitative and qualitative data to compare cultures along these dimensions; for example, in a study conducted for IBM, he collected "more than 116,000 questionnaires from 72 countries in 20 languages" (Hofstede 2001, 41). Under different criteria and with different ideological commitments, researchers might choose different cultural phantasms from which to establish a comparative cultural model. A noted believer that different races are not equal, Clyde Kluckhohn, and his wife, along with other colleagues, developed a theory based on the cultural phantasms of: *relationship with nature*; *relationship with people*; *human activities*; *relationship with time*; and *human nature* in order to compare cultures to one another (Kluckhohn and Strodtbeck 1961).

As an example of a set of cultural phantasms outside of anthropology, recall the examples of Jean Toomer's and Samuel Delany's stories given in chapter 1. Among many other feats of imaginative world building, those authors invoked descriptive cultural models built up from cultural phantasms based in epistemic domains emphasizing differences of race, class, discourse style, social capital, and civilization using poetic verbal imagery (Toomer [1923] 1969; Delany [1979] 1993). The point is not to argue whether the anthropologist's approach or the fiction writer's approach is more powerful. Rather, the point is that the concept of the cultural phantasm helps in understanding construction of culture in quite different endeavors of knowledge building, including anthropology research, writing, and the creation of cultural computing systems. Furthermore, the concept of the cultural phantasm emphasizes the roots of culture in the human imagination.

Computational Cultural Phantasms

It should now be clear that computationally prompting and revealing cultural phantasms clearly does not mean simulating entire cultures on a computer or anything like it. *Media cultural phantasms* are cultural phantasms transmitted, reinforced, sustained, and deconstructed through media. *Computational cultural phantasms* are a specific type of media cultural phantasm. Computational cultural phantasms play a role in media ecologies that create *shared knowledge, beliefs, and representations* through the development and use of computing systems. To revisit the example of recommender systems, at a general level, values such as consumerism and technological utopianism may be reinforced computationally by phantasms such as the ones created by granting authority to algorithmically generated recommendations through the ways they are presented to users. Collaborative filtering algorithms can suggest purchases a user is likely to desire but might not otherwise have thought to buy. At a more specific level, collaborative filtering algorithms in commercial settings instill values and preferences in consumers by developing recommendations that are often taken up, with those new preferences fed back into the user preference matrix, informing the recommendations made to other users. When effective in influencing users' purchasing patterns, recommender systems cyclically influence user preferences. In such commercial settings, collaborative filtering algorithms support the generation of shared values that encourage optimizing and maximizing the processes by which users purchase products.

The generation of shared values by computing systems can pose problems for some groups of users—although some system designers think about these problems the other way around and hold that it is those users who are troublesome. For example, in the research literature about collaborative filtering algorithms, sometimes users on the margins are seen as "problems." Indeed, such literature describes users with the terms "gray sheep" and "black sheep" to focus attention on two types of users that often prove challenging for collaborative filtering algorithms to handle appropriately (Su and Khoshgoftaar 2009). In particular, these challenging users are described as being difficult to provide appropriate recommendations for, or to use, as a basis for developing recommendations for others. Su and Khoshgoftaar write: "*Gray sheep* refers to the users whose opinions do not consistently agree or disagree with any group of people and thus do not benefit from collaborative filtering. *Black sheep* are the opposite group whose idiosyncratic tastes make recommendations nearly impossible. Although this is a failure of the recommender system, non-electronic recommenders also have great problems in these cases, so *black sheep* is an acceptable failure" (4). The aim here is to argue that recommender systems prompt cultural phantasms based on the idea that ideal users share group preferences and norms.[8] Under this assumption, users on the margins are seen as problematic. This understanding of users can have detrimental effects. On a commercial site using a recommender system, a cultural phantasm of bias against marginalized groups (i.e., people with unusual tastes with respect to the majority of users) may end up being built in to the system. Although such biases are common cultural phenomena, often involved in oppression, the point here is that those biases described here are not merely everyday individual interpersonal interactions. Rather, they are built into the structure of a computing system and affect all users of the system. To state the situation more precisely: the cultural phantasm is implemented through the use of a self-reinforcing expressive epistemology that is deployed by a collaborative filtering algorithm and presented as an authoritative recommendation by the system's interface. When this cultural phantasm is presented to marginalized users, the system is enacting a bias in favor of the mainstream.

Analyzing Computational Cultural Phantasms

I shall now analyze several examples of cultural phantasms in more depth. The aim, as with the case of recommender systems mentioned earlier, is not to demonize all systems that prompt phantasms. Rather, it is to expose the nature of cultural phantasms and the mechanisms by which cultural phantasms operate. These analyses will focus on the shared knowledge, beliefs, preferences, norms, values, practices, and behaviors that constitute epistemic domains and the shared artifacts and sensory images that constitute image spaces in specific computational cultural phantasms.

Phantasms in Operating Systems

Cultural phantasms are invoked by even the most fundamental computing systems. Computing systems are developed within particular histories, communities of practice, conceptual metaphorical bases, and other dimensions of specific contexts. Consider the example of the "von Neumann architecture," which refers to the type of stored-program architecture (depicted in figure 5.3) detailed by John von Neumann in his seminal work (von Neumann 1945).[9] Most contemporary engineering references to this type of architecture elide its historical, material, and metaphorical origins. Von Neumann's work was a profoundly mature articulation of an architecture type that persists in use to this day, but of course it arose in the context of its time. This context can be seen easily by its initial proposed reliance upon the technological

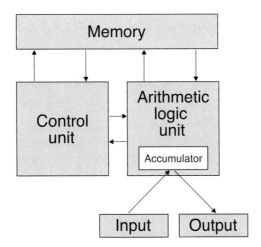

FIGURE 5.3
The von Neumann architecture is illustrated in this diagram (Von Neumann architecture.svg 2006).

resources of its times. Von Neumann wrote, "It is clear that a very high speed computing device should ideally have vacuum tube elements" (13). This shared value, a preference for using the particular high-speed enabling elements of the time, begins to help reveal that a cultural phantasm is at play that informed the reception of the von Neumann architecture by von Neumann's contemporaries.

Toward better describing the cultural phantasms at play here, consider that von Neumann's metaphors have an unfamiliar ring to contemporary readers. Of the "central control part" of a computer, von Neumann wrote "the logical control of the device . . . can be most efficiently carried out by a central control organ" (von Neumann 1945, 3). This usage of the biological term "organ" was not an isolated case of an incidental metaphor. In the parlance of his times, von Neumann wrote also of "memory organs," of "input and output organs," and of information produced by "human actions being sensed by human organs." The metaphorical mapping of a computer's subunits to "organs" has largely not persisted to this day. The metaphor is also an example of a cultural phantasm. The idea of computer organs depends on a biologically based mental image. It provides a shared representation that helped ensure mutual understanding of the operating system's components by researchers at the time. Making sense of the metaphor requires shared knowledge; clearly, some aspects of the biological organ are mapped onto the computer's subunits (e.g., the fact that they each have a particular function) and others are not (e.g., the computer's subunits are not composed of elements akin to biological cells). Von Neumann also claimed that "neurons of higher animals" are definitely "elements" such as those found in computing devices. The fact that some of this terminology seems anachronistic today illustrates that the cultural phantasm can be revealed by contrasting it to alternative perspectives, in this case to a historical and a contemporary interpretation of the metaphor.

For von Neumann, the analogy between computers and brains was a very literal analogy, as he stated that the central arithmetical part, the central control part, and the memory part each "correspond to the associative neurons of the human nervous system" and later he discussed them as "equivalents" to the sensory and motor neurons (von Neumann 1945, 6). Contemporary cognitive science has passed by the early McCulloch and Pitts model of the neuron (indeed, the cognitive linguistics enterprise within cognitive science has passed by the "computer is a brain" metaphor) that von Neumann refers to, which at one time was seen as potentially powerful enough to model human neural functioning (McCulloch and Pitts 1943).

The point of this discussion of von Neumann's work is that even ubiquitous hardware innovations are historically grounded in cultural phantasms such as that associating an epistemic space for an operating system with an image space of a biological body. The idea that the ideal computer should be made of vacuum tube elements is based on shared values exhibiting a preference for efficient and cost-effective operation. These shared values are informed by shared knowledge of the state-of-the-art technologies at the time, along with shared representations of what constituted a computer. The metaphor in which biological brain elements (the source domain) are mapped onto the computer (the target domain) represents a culturally prevalent view of computing machines: in short, a phantasm. The metaphor represents shared values in the form of norms that viewed computing machines as performing tasks reminiscent of human intelligent behavior. The knowledge of the types of biological processes enabled by human organs is necessary for the metaphor to have any explanatory use. Furthermore, the McCulloch and Pitts model of the neuron is a shared representation that had long-term impact on the strand of artificial intelligence research known as connectionist AI, which focused on a type of modeling inspired by human neural anatomy rather than planning and other problem-solving behaviors. All of this discussion of von Neumann and McCulloch and Pitts suggests shared cultural phantasms that influenced computing practices in von Neumann's time, many of which persist to this day. This influence does not mean that the views of the time were naïve; in fact they represented a self-conscious attempt to develop a nascent, sophisticated cybernetical discourse integrating the mechanical and biological. However, with the additional perspective enabled by the passage of time, contemporary thinkers can now clearly see the shared assumptions that undergirded the work of von Neumann and his contemporaries.

Most often, computational technologies are discussed in terms of functionality. Their historical origins and underlying cultural assumptions are often not articulated explicitly within technical or popular discourses. When technical work is conflated with philosophy, sciences studying the mind/brain complex, human languages, or related areas, the tangle of implicit cultural phantasm bases only becomes more challenging to precisely locate.

Phantasms in Foundations of Artificial Intelligence

Cultural phantasms, in the form of strange aspirational dreams and critical hypothetical scenarios, are a hallmark of artificial intelligence philosophy and research.

Early work in computer science and philosophy of AI prefigures many of them. Consider now one such cultural phantasm: the dream of an automaton that can imitate human discourse and behavior. Start by considering when, in 1950, Alan Turing famously chose to address the question "Can machines think?" Because of the difficulty in defining what thinking is, Turing posed a related question as a provocative substitute. He described a scenario consisting of

> a man (A), a woman (B), and an interrogator (C) who may be of either sex. The interrogator stays in a room apart from the other two. The object of the game for the interrogator is to determine which of the other two is the man and which is the woman. He knows them by labels X and Y, and at the end of the game he says either "X is A and Y is B" or "X is B and Y is A." The interrogator is allowed to put questions to A and B thus:

> C: Will X please tell me the length of his or her hair? . . .
>   His answer might therefore be:
>   "My hair is shingled, and the longest strands are about nine inches long."
> (Turing 1950, 433–434)

This scenario is the original formulation of the now famous Turing test. The key point of scenario is whether a computer could successfully take on the role of A (the man posing as a woman). This subjective question integrates an image space prompted by the imagined scenario of the test and epistemic spaces drawn from a host of epistemic domains outside of engineering research such as those representing social construction of femininity and masculinity, concessions to using a behavior-based approach as a surrogate for intelligence, and even understanding of the social relevance of games. This original formulation is not a widespread cultural phantasm, though it is a phantasm in its combination of concepts regarding machine intelligence and the verbal imagery in Turing's scenario. It is not a *cultural* phantasm both because it is not widely entrenched within a culture and because it draws upon so many epistemic domains that its idiosyncratic nature is automatically revealed (it does not operate invisibly under worldviews that are normative and privileged in AI research).

Most authors eschew the original formulation of the Turing test in favor of an informal formulation that reads: "Could a computer fool people into thinking it is human?" This reformulation does constitute a cultural phantasm because it replaces Turing's host of epistemic domains for gender, intelligence, and gaming with the normative and privileged epistemic domain within AI research of computer "intelligence." Literary scholar Tyler Stevens has neatly summarized the ways that this cultural phantasm operates invisibly under normative worldviews as follows (using the term "epistemology" in its cultural studies sense): "The critical claims for the epistemology of 'intelligence' have built into it, by gesturing to 'biography,' 'history,' . . . an assumption of normative gender roles, and an assumption by the computer of a normative gender role: or to put the claim in its strongest form, that 'intelligence' and 'humanity' can't be defined outside of sexual difference and the phenomenology of the sex-gender system" (Stevens 1996, 427). Though the reformulated version of Turing's test captures something of the essence of the original, it also loses some of the aspects of identity and play that shape the original by rendering its issues of gender tacit and inert, issues often seen outside the realm of computer science.

It is illuminating to ask, in contrast to the reformulated version deployed in computer science, what it would take to try to engineer a system responding to Turing's original provocation. To answer this question, interpretive and humanistic insight into the nature of gender would be required. This approach is no mere stand-in for intelligence or the whole of human behavior, but rather an area of inquiry long addressed (without definitive resolution) in the social sciences and humanities. The point is not to valorize the original Turing test over its popular reformulation—the argument here is not that AI should hold proper modeling of gender construction and politics as an aim! The seeming strangeness of the original Turing test can reveal an absence in common goals of computer science research and practice: expressing and better understanding subjective human experience (such as navigating gender norms) through computational means. The semivisibility of the subjective issues of gender raised by the Turing test begins to reveal it as a cultural phantasm. There has been much speculation about the relationship between the original formulation of the test and Turing's particular biography and history. For example, cultural and gender studies scholar Judith Halberstam describes an epistemic domain for gender in relationship to Turing's personal history, writing:

> Gender, we might argue, like computer intelligence, is a learned, imitative behavior that can be processed so well that it comes to look natural. Indeed, the work of culture in the former and of science in the latter is perhaps to transform the artificial into a function so smooth that it seems organic. In other words, gender, like intelligence, has a technology. There is an irony to Turing's careful analogical comparisons between bodies and machines. Two years after he published his

paper, in 1952, Turing was arrested and charged with "gross indecency," or homosexual activity. Faced with a choice between a jail sentence or hormone treatments, Turing opted for the hormones. (Halberstam 1991, 443)

In this manner, she suggests that Turing's vexed sexuality played a role in the epistemic domain of gender contributing to his formulation of the original test. Indeed the laws and social values of that time, and their repercussions, are evident in Turing's later being tried for homosexuality and subsequent chemical castration and accompanying physiological side effects from an enforced regimen of a synthesized form of the female hormone estrogen called diethylstilbestrol (Hodges 2012). Turing's tragic biography illustrates the type of severe social reception that Turing faced regarding his sexuality; it is highly likely that such a context played a role in influencing his original formulation of the test.

The notion that issues drawn from epistemic domains such as gender identity should be invisibly subsumed within epistemic domains for a general problem of modeling intellect and behavior reflects engineering values biased toward generalizable results and reductive modeling. Indeed, those biases are necessarily central to technical or scientific research and practice and, more generally, to the notions of objective truth and objective rationality. However, when illuminated by image spaces such as those prompted by Turing's original, gendered formulation of his test, the cultural phantasm of the Turing test is revealed as strangely divorced from the cultural context in which it was conceived to those outside of the AI philosophy and research traditions in which it is most often encountered.

To give an example of just such a strange issue, decades later in the midst of academic debate, philosopher John Searle cited and disputed a quotation he saw as illustrative of computer scientist John McCarthy's views, stating:

McCarthy, for example, writes: "Machines as simple as thermostats can be said to have beliefs, and having beliefs seems to be a characteristic of most machines capable of problem solving performance" (McCarthy 1979). . . . Think hard for one minute about what would be necessary to establish that that hunk of metal on the wall over there had real beliefs, beliefs with direction of fit, propositional content, and conditions of satisfaction; beliefs that had the possibility of being strong beliefs or weak beliefs; nervous, anxious, or secure beliefs; dogmatic, rational, or superstitious beliefs; blind faiths or hesitant cogitations; any kind of beliefs. The thermostat is not a candidate. Neither is stomach, liver, adding machine, or telephone. (Searle 1980, 420)

The phantasm of a thermostat with beliefs and Searle's disagreement with that concept is strikingly strange in its rhetorical use of a banal object whose function is mechanically well understood in a way that human thought is not. The use of a surrogate for human thought because of the difficulty of apprehending the notion directly parallels Turing's use of an imitation game as a surrogate for thought. Indeed, computer science and AI are rife with contentious, idiosyncratic debates about issues of what I have called epistemic domains that ultimately seem, paradoxically, to be subjective matters addressed by building and theorizing technical systems. Such quirky conversations, strange dreams, and cultural phantasms can be said to reveal where the deep challenges for harnessing computing for richer expression of the human condition lie.

Influential cultural phantasms for AI also have been argued to arise from much earlier bases. The philosopher René Descartes addressed whether systems described as "different automata, or moving machines fabricated by human industry" could produce intelligent discourse (Descartes [1637] 2008). He also addressed the notion accepted by many AI researchers that the human body is, in fact, a quite complex machine—a step for such researchers toward the argument that they should be able to create a machine that can emulate human intelligence because they can create machines the emulate other human behaviors. Philosopher of cognitive science and computer science Ronald Chrisley describes Descartes's argument as follows:

> Descartes offers two behavioural limitations of automata: (1) an automaton would be unable to produce different arrangements of words that are meaningful and appropriate; and (2) an automaton would only be able to imitate our behaviour in a fixed number of ways, since our reason is a "universal instrument" while an automaton must have a different organ for each purpose. Although Descartes relied on the implication of the form: "failure to match human behaviour means an automaton is not intelligent" (lacks reason), it is not unfair to suppose that the same reasoning would have led him to assent to the converse: "if something is behaviourally equivalent to a human, it must possess reason." Although Descartes was not restricting his attention to linguistic behaviour, his emphasis on language as being a stumbling block for mechanised reason makes it reasonable to see the Turing Test, which does restrict its attention to linguistic behaviour, as a descendant of Descartes's thinking. (Chrisley 2000, 11)

Chrisley does not limit his estimation of the role of Descartes's thought to its relationship to the Turing test. Going further, Chrisley attributes to Descartes a fundamental role in framing the conception of artificial intelligence itself. Noting that Descartes's second proposed behavioral limitation of automata could be considered incorrect on the bases of the Church-Turing thesis ("that for any effective procedure there is a Turing machine which can compute it"), he writes:

> Although these foundational notions in artificial intelligence contradict Descartes' [sic] conclusions, they give his work a fundamental role by accepting his framing of the issues—in particular, the idea that the essence of reason is seen only in diverse linguistic behaviour. This assumption, and the questioning of it, is a dichotomy which would go on to generate many of the branches in the concept of, and work in, artificial intelligence. (Chrisley 2000, 12)

This frame provided by Descartes is a cultural phantasm. It draws upon epistemic domains about the potentially similar natures of bodies and machines. It also draws upon image spaces regarding bodies and machines prompted by verbal imagery such as "great multitude of bones, muscles, nerves, arteries, veins, and other parts" and "machines bearing the image of our bodies," respectively (Descartes [1637] 2008). These combine to construct a phantom of a humanlike automaton, which Descartes disputes the possibility of, but that AI researchers have strived to build.

Chrisley is not alone in articulating the work of Descartes as foundational for AI. The origins of AI rest in an intellectual commitment to the "brain is a computer" metaphor, a related cultural phantasm that has become pervasive within engineering practice and scientific experimentation. However, this cultural phantasm has been criticized by Searle (1980) as being rooted in a particular tradition of thought, an important constituent of which is an interpretation of the philosophy of René Descartes. Describing the relationship between Cartesianism and computing in AI, Philip Agre writes:

> A powerful dynamic of mutual reinforcement took hold between the technology of computation and a Cartesian view of human nature, with computational processes inside computers corresponding to thought processes inside minds. But the founders of computational psychology, while mostly avowed Cartesians, actually transformed Descartes's ideas in a complex and original way. . . . Their innovation lay in a subversive reinterpretation of Descartes's original dualism. In *The Passions of the Soul*, Descartes had described the mind as an expressionless res cogitans [thinking thing] that simultaneously participated in and transcended physical reality. . . . Sequestered in this nether region with its problematic relationship to the physical world, the mind's privileged object of contemplation was mathematics. (Agre 1997, 2)

Agre concludes his argument: "The founders of computational psychology nonetheless consciously adopted and reworked the broader framework of Descartes's theory, starting with a single brilliant stroke. The mind does not simply contemplate mathematics, they asserted; the mind is itself mathematical, and the mathematics of the mind is precisely a technical specification for the causally explicable operation of the brain" (3). In other words, the acceptance of the mind as being computational relies upon a set of assumptions that are based on a cultural phantasm involving an epistemic domain of mathematics (including computing) and an image space composed of the metaphor of the mathematical mind. As with Chrisley's argument, mentioned previously, Descartes's philosophy has provided a fundamental frame for artificial intelligence (and cognitive science) in the form of a cultural phantasm.

We can now explore what some of the implications of that foundational role played by Descartes's framing ideas are. Before stating such implications, it is important to note that Descartes's writing does not describe the idea of the human body as a machine in the manner that contemporary science texts would. Rather, Descartes involves religion in his discussion. In fact, to describe people who consider there to be similarities between the human body and machines, Descartes writes: "Such persons will look upon this body as a machine made by the hands of God, which is incomparably better arranged, and adequate to movements more admirable than is any machine of human invention" (Descartes [1637] 2008). The invocation of a higher power in Descartes's statement is no mere idiomatic usage. For Descartes, theology and philosophy are intertwined. In his *Meditations on First Philosophy* (a diagram from which is shown in figure 5.4), for example, Descartes offers several philosophically based proofs of the existence of God (primarily in Meditations III and V; Descartes [1641] 1996).

Although some philosophers—such as Edmund Husserl, an influential founder of phenomenology—argue for the value of some of Descartes's work while dismissing the contemporary importance of his other work, including these theological proofs, it is a revisionist perspective to look at Descartes's work in such a fragmented way (Smith 2003). When considering Descartes's writing in a more holistic way, and in the spirit in which it was written, it is not a far stretch to see the aspects of Descartes's foundational framings most relevant to AI as a part-*theological* cultural phantasm—an idea that would be surprising or disconcerting to many empiricism-driven scientists and engineers. I make this stretch here to emphasize the point that implicit cultural beliefs, rooted in cultural phantasms, inform all of our technical practices. This argument says nothing about the utility of AI approaches or the possibility of

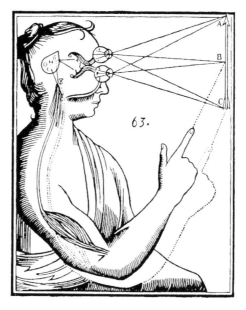

FIGURE 5.4
A diagram from *Meditations on First Philosophy*
indicates Descartes's conception of the interaction
between the material and immaterial [spirit].

achieving computers that act like humans, much less that all computer scientists researching AI share Descartes's beliefs. Yet it is worthwhile to consider the nature of these historical phantasms, as some may provide better bases for technical practices than others. Hence it is important to consider their roles in the development of computing systems.

In other words, cultural phantasms for AI, such as prompted by Turing and Descartes's arguments, operate invisibly for some AI practitioners; the origins of that framing are often not interrogated. Completing the portrait of the role of cultural phantasms in this type of AI practice, shared values must also be considered. Similar to Agre's critique, in earlier work, Terry Winograd and Fernando Flores critiqued the shared value consisting of a type of rationalism held to be "the mainspring of Western science and technology" (Winograd and Flores 1986, 14). Their critique of the rationalist tradition does not pit rationality against irrationality but rather addresses a tradition that focuses on systematic and precise formulations of how valid reasoning is constituted. They argue that scientists often feel that the only alternative to a narrow rationalistic approach is "mysticism, religion, or fuzzy thinking that is a throwback to earlier stages of civilization" (16). This argument draws upon an epistemic domain of rationalism that is problematic in that it omits any critique of its own implicit cultural origins, such as in the case of the Cartesian strand within artificial intelligence described previously (Winograd and Flores 1986). The earlier discussion of collaborative filtering provided an example of the limits of a rationalistic approach. The challenge of trying to universally capture and predict users' preferences using a data-structural and algorithmic approach revealed the subjective and, at times, seemingly biased formulation of the problem (toward uniformity of consumerist preferences in the cases of so-called gray and black sheep in commercial recommender systems). It might be the case that more nuanced analyses of the computational cultural phantasms involved and the natures of the preference of marginalized users might help yield a more effective solution to the problems of "gray sheep" and "black sheep." Better yet, more carefully chosen computational cultural phantasms might help in reframing such users as *sources of knowledge* rather than as problems.

Phantasms in Computer-Based Art

The implications and complexities of cultural phantasms in computing practices can be further exemplified by work in the arts. Indeed, some artists have relationships with the types of cultural phantasms associated with "mysticism" or "fuzzy thinking" that some scientists see as anathema to computing practice. The practice of developing computing systems for the arts is different from developing computing systems for science and engineering purposes. As already shown in examples including *The Girl with Skin of Haints and Seraphs* and the *Living Liberia Fabric*, computer-based artworks can be developed with the aims of prompting and/or revealing phantasms that affect users. Whether the phantasms that affect the designer can be understood, and whether that knowledge can be used to more effectively develop systems, are separate questions that I shall address now. The artist Guillermo Gómez-Peña uses a cultural computing perspective as the basis for implementing a great deal of his artwork. Gómez-Peña has written about a mythological version of a stereotypical cultural model, describing groups such as Latinos as a holistic entity: "The mythology goes like this. Mexicans (and by extension other Latinos) can't handle high technology. Caught between a preindustrial past and an imposed modernity, we continue to be manual beings; homo fabers per [sic] excellence; imaginative artisans (not technicians); and our understanding of the world is strictly political, poetical or metaphysical at best, but certainly not scientific" (Gómez-Peña 1998). Gómez-Peña continues by describing roles that people have in conceptualization of their own cultures:

> We, Latinos, often feed this mythology, by overstating our "romantic nature" and humanistic stances; and/or by assuming the role of colonial victims of technology. We are always ready to point out the fact that social and personal relations in the US, the land of the future, are totally mediated by faxes, phones, computers, and other technologies we are not even aware of; and that the overabundance of information technology in everyday life is responsible for America's social handicaps and cultural crisis. . . . This simplistic and extremely problematic binary world view portrays Mexico and Mexicans, as technologically underdeveloped, yet culturally and spiritually superior; and the US as exactly the opposite. (Gómez-Peña 1998)

In his own work, which I shall call a cultural computing practice, he uses the computer as a means to capture his complex view of culture as rife with contradictions, power inequalities, resonating representations (e.g., describing how his "low rider" laptop is decorated with a 3D decal of the Virgin of Guadalupe). By grounding his practice in a sophisticated model based in a complex epistemic domain for Latino culture, he exemplifies a cultural computing practice. Gómez-Peña states, "I sarcastically baptized my aesthetic practice, 'Aztec high-tech art,' and when I teamed with Cyber Vato Roberto Sifuentes, we decided that what we were doing was 'techno-razcuache art.' In a glossary which dates back to 94, we defined it as 'a new aesthetic that fuses performance art, epic rap poetry, interactive television, experimental radio and computer art; but with a Chicanocentric perspective and an [sic] sleazoide bent'" (Gómez-Peña 1998). In work critical of ethnic profiling such as the *Chica-Iranian Project* (developed by Gómez-Peña and Ali Dagar and involving others; shown in figure 5.5), Gómez-Peña and his collaborators' primary way of addressing social issues using the computer is through use of existing applications and technologies, as opposed to programming or building new technologies (Gómez-Peña and Dadgar 2011).[10] Their aims do not celebrate using complex technologies for their own sakes; rather, the work serves to develop "a multi centric theoretical understanding of the cultural, political and aesthetic possibilities of new technologies; to exchange a different sort of information (mytho poetical, activist, performative, imagistic); and to hopefully do all this with humor and intelligence" (Gómez-Peña 1998).

FIGURE 5.5
The collaborative *Chica-Iranian Project* creates mythical hybrid identities for users to ethnically profile.

In short, Gómez-Peña's works, such as the collaborative *Chica-Iranian Project*, critically prompt and reveal cultural phantasms. That particular project's prompted cultural phantasms invoke provocative identity-oriented image spaces such as "La Llorona" ("the weeping woman," a Mexican legend who drowned her children to be with her lover) and traditional Kurdish women's clothing in light of epistemic domains related to the ethnic identities of the collaborating artist making it. This diversity of epistemic domains representing specific Latino and Iranian worldviews,[11] and an image space blending visuals from both, helps make visible the relationship between culture and technology that has given Gómez-Peña both consternation and inspiration. In this and other works, he aims to reveal problematic cultural phantasms such as the relationship he describes as existing between some Latino subcultures and electronics and computing technologies. He does so through drawing upon complex epistemic domains for both culture and technology as presented through imagery well known in the Latino communities he interacts with and the communities of his collaborators. In this manner, an aim of Gómez-Peña's critical writing and art practice is to help render such cultural phantasms visible.

One epistemic domain contributing to this cultural-phantasm-revealing endeavor is composed of shared values and mental images of Latino people exhibited by the young Gómez-Peña (and presumably like-minded individuals at the same cultural crossroads). These shared values and mental images express the ambivalence that some Latino art practitioners have felt regarding the use of electronics and computing technologies. His work confronts the reasons for this ambivalence head on through incorporating knowledge from other, contrasting, epistemic domains, including those representing power-relationships between the United States and Mexico, personal exposure to technologies, and mutual lack of knowledge regarding the everyday experiences with technology of people on either side of the border. His critique in one of the passages quoted earlier analyzes a second component of this Latino technophobia cultural phantasm. In particular, he addresses shared representations of a romanticized Latino culture, and he expresses this critique using text, imagery, and interactive subjective computing systems. Gómez-Peña's uses of technology are grounded in an epistemic domain quite distinct from those epistemic domains that dominate computer science discourses. His epistemic domain is constituted by a type of shared knowledge that is acquired from life experience in a subaltern category. In addition, the type of relationship that Gómez-Peña has with technology may be invisible for those whose experiences with technology are more privileged and uninterrogated, though they may seem all too commonplace to others. In all of the senses described previously, Gómez-Peña's work is aimed at prompting and revealing the complexities of cultural phantasms related to social identity, diverse experiences, and technology.

Reflections on Cultural Phantasms

Making cultural phantasms in computing explicit, and at times drawing upon them to inform system design, can have powerful benefits. One can only imagine what would result if computer games, or other software applications, were built by developers equally steeped in Gómez-Peña's worldview as they are in topics such as first-order logic. One need not be a member of any of Gómez-Peña's social categories or share his life experiences in order to aid in revealing, or drawing upon, such cultural phantasms. Exposure to systems and ideas grounded in a plurality of worldviews can render cultural phantasms visible for practitioners. Furthermore, technical tools for production simultaneously enable system building while constraining production processes. Programming languages, computer platforms, software applications supporting media development, hardware interfaces, and more all enable and constrain production of cultural computing systems. However, producing cultural computing systems in light of explicit cultural phantasms can help enable unanticipated new designs and reveal unforeseen technical constraints. Cultural computing systems developed with awareness of the cultural phantasms influencing them might stand in stark contrast to "the tradition of rationalism and logical empiricism that can be traced back at least to Plato" that Winograd and Flores argue constitutes a problematic basis for computer science and related fields such as artificial intelligence and cognitive science in the epigraph at the start of this chapter (Winograd and Flores 1986, 14). I now turn to articulating more precisely how cultural phantasms are expressed within technical systems and the goal of developing effective cultural computing systems and, in particular, how overcoming biases against explicitly considering the role of culture while conducting research and development in computing can enable new and innovative practices.

6

INTEGRATIVE CULTURAL SYSTEMS

I tend to think of black culture then as an instrument or an environment that they've invented. . . . It makes things much more complex because instead of talking about black culture, I'll talk for instance a lot about Ghanaian drum choirs, or talk a lot about the African polyrhythmic engine, polyrhythmic percussion engine. And those will be very particular African traits. Sound is a sensory technology, so I talk a lot about black technologies. They're machines.

—Kodwo Eshun, *More Brilliant than the Sun: Adventures in Sonic Fiction*

"It is amazing," he said, "that you found a way to say all that about Yoruba number. It just makes me want to laugh!" and he did! It disconcerted me to find my Yoruba colleagues erupting with laughter as, expecting praise and congratulations, I held up my "discovery." Why does my serious empirical investigation of Yoruba logic make native Yoruba speakers want to laugh?

—Helen Verran, *Science and an African Logic*

Cantonese opera, methods in behavioral psychology, and probabilistic approaches to artificial intelligence are all cultural systems. Each expresses a set of shared features that are used to create material and/or conceptual artifacts that are meaningful to certain social groups. It is an everyday fact that sometimes artifacts and ideas are associated with particular cultures such as Swiss yodeling or Senegalese wrestling. It would be an egregious mistake of time, place, and culture, for example, to confuse a fourteenth-century Aztec pyramid with a classical Mayan pyramid. At the same time, ascribing exclusive cultural ownership to artifacts and ideas can also be troublesome for a variety of reasons to be explored in this chapter. This chapter engages the problems, challenges, and potential benefits of explicitly addressing how cultures are associated with, and are distributed onto, subjective computing systems, later introducing the idea of integrative cultural systems as a central conceptual means toward these ends.

I shall use the term "cultural system" to refer to a type of artifact that can be material and/or conceptual. A cultural system is analogous in some ways to a descriptive cultural model as defined in chapter 5. Like a descriptive cultural model, a cultural system is an abstraction from the complex milieu of everyday life in a given society. Yet a cultural system is productive, rather than descriptive, because it is a conceptual framework useful for *creating material or conceptual artifacts* that express features of a culture.

Defining Integrative Cultural Systems

The term "cultural," as used when describing the concept of the cultural phantasm, does not refer to culture merely as static traditions delineated by national, religious, racial, or other boundaries. Nor does it refer only to traditional practices and social identities. In chapter 3, we saw that meaning production in computational media occurs in an ecology of culture, involving individuals, artifacts, tools, and cognitive phenomena such as thinking metaphorically or inventing new concepts. In light of this observation, while discussing culture we can focus on how such an ecology plays a role in how we make meanings of our world. As such, *cultural systems* may be considered to be production-oriented cultural phantasms that are distributed over many components, some of which may be material such as media. In this manner, cultural systems integrate abstract conceptual and representational (often aesthetic) concepts with material media—they construct cultural phantasms. The core term introduced in this chapter, *integrative cultural systems*, refers to cultural systems that are transmitted through, and enacted within, media.

The concept of the integrative cultural system can be elaborated by an observation. The observation is that some cultural systems are not necessarily tied to particular forms of media. One can obviously sing or play a guitar with a bluesman's sensibilities, but perhaps less obviously, one could also write a novel or direct a play with the same sensibilities. In this manner, the cultural system of the blues is not restricted to a single medium. I shall call such systems *culturally metamedial.*[1] Metamedial cultural systems are not dependent on any particular medium and thus can be expressed and shared via a range of media, including computational media. It is up to the members of a culture and other stakeholders to determine whether the cultural system is still considered to be a representative product of their culture.

Many types of cultural system seem to be specific to both particular cultures and media, such as West African cinema, Egyptian instrumental music, or Japanese computer role-playing games. All three examples represent cultural phantasms, each in its own medium. Works of these types seem to be created based upon their creators' adherence to several factors. One factor is shared cultural style, including issues of representation such as media conventions. Another factor is shared cultural content, including cultural phantasms based upon the content's historical origins. Another factor consists of a shared set of commonly used media and media conventions. Yet the metamediality of integrative cultural systems means that *style and content are more definitive of the cultural system than the medium in which they are produced.* Thus one could create a videogame based on a West African cinematic cultural system, a sculpture based on the sounds of Egyptian instruments, or a poem based on Japanese computer role-playing games, because shared styles, conventions, histories, and content are both prompted by, and generative of, cultural phantasms that media producers subscribe to, invoke, and recombine using media. To give two well-known examples, there are videogames featuring Hollywood-style linear cut-scenes and ample use of the shot-reverse-shot convention; there are also punk magazines ('zines) that feature independently produced, politically oriented, do-it-yourself (DIY) amateur aesthetic sensibilities. Integrative cultural systems like these can now be said to be *cultural systems that are metamedially distributed.* In this chapter, I shall build up to an extended example focused on how cultural systems can be distributed onto computational media.

The next subsection of this chapter discusses three examples illustrating the problems of associating cultures with ideas and artifacts in a simplistic way. The subsection problematizes the concept of cultural "ownership," such as implied by phrases that pair a possessive form of a term for a place or group (such as "Western") with a term for a material or conceptual artifact or form (such as "computing"). Building on this discussion, the following subsection describes historian and philosopher of science Helen Verran's concept of "an African logic" as an illustrative cautionary tale further revealing the complexities of associating material and conceptual systems (in this case, a type of mathematics practice of Yoruba speakers). Bearing these warnings in mind, the next section carefully describes a concept of the *trans-African*,[2] which is carried through the rest of the chapter to help illustrate the idea of the integrative cultural system. The usage of the phrase "trans-African" is also explicated, as it must be made clear that it neither ignores the great ethnolinguistic diversity of African cultures nor refers to an essential characteristic of persons from Africa or with historical connections to the continent. Rather, "trans-African" as used here is a cultural phantasm generative of, and prompted by, material and conceptual artifacts produced by a set of practitioners (who may or may not be self-conscious regarding the relationship between the cultural phantasm and their practice). Author and theorist Ngugi wa Thiong'o's particular model of orature is presented in the next subsection. Ngugi's theory is grounded in his work in Kenyan theater, and his theoretical work on how traits of diverse African cultural forms are retained, transformed, and/or obliterated by issues such as colonialism, postcolonialism, movement into the diaspora, and related phenomena. Ngugi invokes an *integrative view of the arts* (Biakolo 1999; Ngugi 1998) that is crucial for further articulating the chapter's central concept of integrative cultural systems.

The upshot is that Ngugi's model of orature is shown to be relevant to computing practices. In this light, the GRIOT system[3] can be seen as a case study of a computing system featuring a design partially informed by a conception of trans-African orature; thus GRIOT is an integrative cultural system (Harrell 2007a) and a modest example of a cultural computing system. The chapter concludes with reflective broadening discussion on the concept of integrative cultural systems.

Unownable Objects and Ideas: The Complicated Relationships between Cultures and Material and Conceptual Artifacts

Before discussing examples of how specific integrative cultural systems can inform development of computing systems, it is important to be clear about the philosophical orientation here regarding the relationships between cultures on one hand and objects and ideas on the other. It is important to state outright that although the concept of integrative cultural systems touts the value of making the cultural groundings of media systems explicit, it is also necessary to avoid the many intellectual traps laid by the dangers of essentialism, generalization, stereotyping, prejudice, bias, racism, oppressive hegemony, and related disempowering phenomena.

Let us start by picking up on examples related to ideas raised in the previous subsection. Phrases such as "African cinema," "Egyptian musical instruments," or "Japanese role-playing games" are commonplace on the surface, yet strange upon further inspection. Such phrases are commonplace and associate cultural groups on one hand with specific media forms, technologies, and genres on the other. The fact is that such phrases belie a range of types of relationship between cultural groups and media. The simplicity of such phrases can obscure the complex nature and diversity of such relationships. At the same time, the phrase can also seem to imply that cultures can "own" material artifacts like musical instruments and games or conceptual artifacts like styles of cinema. Because of this, during this discussion I shall refer to such terms as "cultural ownership phrasing," while understanding that this "ownership" is a stand in for a variety of types of relationship.

For everyday conversation, it may be expedient to use cultural ownership phrasing, but it is never precise. Such is especially the case when considering different grain sizes between the cultures and media (or other objects and ideas) being related. Nollywood cinema (the popular film of Nigeria) may seem to be a coherent, self-contained category, whereas West African cinema may seem too diverse and expansive to serve as a meaningful category. British figurative art may seem to be a reasonably sized area of analysis to some, whereas Western philosophy, as frequently as the term is used, may be unwieldy as an area of study. Beyond this complication of grain size, there are also biases in academia and society regarding which types of cultural relationship are worthy of scrutiny and which are not. A Caribbean poet such as Derek Walcott might raise a few Afrocentric eyebrows by citing the works of ancient Greece, whereas the Irish author James Joyce would be less often accused of being culturally compromised by classicists[4] when doing the same, even though ancient Greek culture is far removed from the settings of both authors. There may be more at stake in some cases than others, however. Dominant cultures are assumed to have diversity within their media productions, whereas all too often marginalized or underrepresented groups are treated as monolithic. Hence, critically engaged scholars might be *more* likely to question a phrase like "African philosophy" than one like "continental philosophy," despite the overgeneralization in both phrases.[5] All of these reasons suggest that we should always bear in mind the complexities hidden by cultural ownership phrasing.

There are many ways that this complex type of cultural "ownership" can be ascribed. It might be ascribed based on shared style or philosophy. It might be ascribed based on shared historical origins. It might be ascribed based on shared conventions. In any of the cases in our examples, the idea that concepts and artifacts can be owned by specific cultures is overly simplistic. It seems unremarkable to suggest that "African cinema" might imply a category of film based on shared African stylistic or philosophical approaches to filmmaking. It is not shocking to assert that the category of "Egyptian musical instruments" suggests a class of Egyptian music making devices that share historical origins. And it is well known that gamers in the United States unblinkingly use the phrase "Japanese role-playing games"[6] to describe a set of console videogame conventions and play mechanics originating in Japan. These examples illustrate that for many people, the association between culture and media often seems natural and uncontroversial. The complications arise in part because of the many different types of association between cultural groups and cultural systems. Shared stylistic or philosophical approaches, shared historical origins, and shared conventions are each quite distinct criteria for associating a particular cultural with a cultural system. These categories, like many human conceptual categories, do not stand up to strict logical analysis; they remain blurred and complex rather than reducing to what Lakoff would term a "classical category" (Lakoff 1987). Trying to understand a particular work in terms of a shared category based on stylistic or philosophical approaches can often fail. For example, the approach does not help one understand a work such as filmmaker Abderrahmane Sissako's spaghetti western–style[7] film-within-a-film *Death in Timbuktu* (Sissako 2006).

The film segment, embedded in Sissako's feature film *Bamako*, stars the American actor Danny Glover as a cowboy gunslinger in Mali (see figure 6.1). Some of the complications raised by the segment are discussed by film scholar Ryan Spence. For Spence, Sissako's film segment does not seem to count as "indigenous" African cinema, even though African audiences are able to imagine themselves within the film's wild west setting (Spence 2007). However, in contrast to Spence's reading, Sissako himself describes *Death in Timbuktu* as having an aesthetic and content-oriented motivation. As *Bamako* is largely set inside a single courtyard, Sissako states that *Death in Timbuktu*

> serves as a form to make the film [*Bamako*] breathe. An audience can become bored watching the courtyard setting for thirty or forty minutes. The question was to go to something which could make the film breathe, and at the same time have content which would show a metaphor of what I tell in the film. Which is, in general: the domination of a group, of a vision of the world, more than of an identity. And this is why the cowboys are white and black. Through that, I also show, in a perhaps clear way if it had not been understood, that there is a joint

responsibility in Africa. When a white man says that there are two teachers too many, it is the African who shoots. Thus Africa is responsible. [I].e. a policy is imposed only when you accept it. You can refuse it. (Fortin 2007)

Taking Sissako's own words into account, one could ask whether *Death in Timbuktu* could help exemplify a style-based category of African cinema. If not, it suggests that self-conscious quoting of dominant filmic style should be excluded from the category of African cinema. However, such exclusion has the side effect of reserving self-referentiality and ironic satire of style as solely the domain of American, European, or other privileged forms of cinema. *Bamako* is not easily classified as an example of African cinema, or excluded as an example of African cinema, solely on the basis of its style. Style-based criteria for associating an idea of African culture with the cinematic medium are insufficient in light of works such as Sissako's. It is more accurate to see the film segment as an integrative cultural system, distributing a complex cultural phantasm involving a unique African perspective, global racial politics, media domination, and a cowboy metaphor across multiple cinematic styles.

It should be no less controversial to ascribe ownership of ideas and objects to specific cultures solely on the basis of shared historical origins. Scrutinizing categories of musical technologies such as "Egyptian musical instrument" can help explain why. One reason is that technologies blur the boundaries of musical categories. Describing

FIGURE 6.1
Actor Danny Glover played a cowboy in the film *Bamako*.

the sampler as an electronic musical instrument that can replicate, transform, and repeat recorded segments of audio, cultural theorist Kodwo Eshun writes:

> The sampler is the universal instrument, the instrument that makes all other instruments.
>
> The sampler operates . . . like the music heard in Ishmael Reed's Egypt AD '72: "A mixture of Sun Ra and Jimmy Reed played in the nightclub district of ancient Egypt's 'The Domain of Osiris.'"
>
> It's an anchronizer that derealizes time. (Eshun 1998, 57)

In short, audio technologies can produce sounds in ways that defamiliarize listeners with their particular origins as well as recalling specific real or fictitious cultural histories. Eshun's observation recognizes the subjective and imaginative natures of cultural systems. Eshun's statement in the chapter's epigraph also reflects this observation. Eshun argues that "black culture" is an invented instrument, but I would add not only that is it an invented instrument, but also that the instrument of black culture is itself constituted by many more invented instruments and environments. Thus, we see the seemingly monolithic revealed as fragmentary. In addition to the fragmentation of such monolithic ideas, the problem of definition is complicated by sharing among peoples; so, for example, instruments such as the Oud, iconically used in some types of both ancient and contemporary Egyptian music, have been sampled in hip-hop music, and the European violin[8] has been in use in some types of Egyptian music for centuries. It is a matter for debate as to which of these cases is a better example of shared historical origins regarding deployment of an Egyptian musical instrument. It is intellectually richer to consider musical works such as hip-hop tracks sampling the Oud as integrative cultural systems, distributing cultural phantasms evoking ancient historical sounds onto a type of music originating in African American communities in the twentieth-century United States.

It can be equally problematic to ascribe ownership of ideas and artifacts to cultures based on shared conventions and mechanisms for use. Examining differences between types of computer role-playing games can be used to help make this point. Computer role-playing games all tend to exhibit features such as characters that increase in ability with the accretion of experience points, combat, changeable armor and weapons, world exploration, and other related conventions. At the same time, the genre has often been described as being split into "Eastern" ("Japanese") and "Western" ("American") categories. These categories are often seen as quite distinct, with one author on a popular site for game developers even writing that "the gap between Western and Japanese RPGs is so huge that they sometimes don't even seem like they belong in the same genre" (Kalata 2008). Indeed, a popular gaming website has called attention to an advertisement (depicted in figure 6.2) showing purported Japanese gamers holding protest signs with slogans extolling apparently revolutionary virtues of "Western" computer role-playing games (Ashcraft 2010).

Some of the slogans in figure 6.2 read: "The stage has been set. After that, you're free to do whatever!" "The player is weak, the enemy is weak. That's way too convenient," and "Because the story doesn't change, what's the point of playing it again?" thus highlighting the significant conventions that differentiate the fixed-narrative

FIGURE 6.2
This Japanese advertisement for the computer role-playing game *Fallout: New Vegas* reveals stereotypes about Japanese RPGs.

"Japanese"-style games from the open-ended "Western"-style (Ashcraft 2010). This binary division of games by culture is quickly revealed to be inadequate upon further analysis. It has been stated that early popular computer role-playing games created in Japan featured influences from early American computer role-playing games such as *Wizardry: Proving Grounds of the Mad Overlord*. Furthermore, any game, regardless of national origin, could incorporate any particular game feature—and many games do mix and match features. A telling account from a game development magazine states:

> In the past, the Eastern format was arguably more prolific and hence more popular than the Western format, with even some Western games mimicking Eastern ones. Lately, however, the Western format is becoming more popular in the West, rivaling (and occasionally trumping) the Eastern format in popularity, partly due to progresses in technology making arguably more immersive games, and leading Eastern development teams to incorporate more elements from Western RPGs. (T.V. Tropes Wiki 2011)

The idea of these games' mechanics as being associated with culture ignores the impact of cross-cultural exchange, historical trends in game design, and new or subgenres that complicate both the "Western" and "Japanese" categories. For example, games such as the *Etrian Odyssey* series are often described in U.S. gaming periodicals as exhibiting a "retro" style hearkening back to the original *Wizardry*-style games rather than as "Eastern" role-playing games (Bozon 2007; Magrino 2007). These assertions are interesting because they highlight the games' "Western" cultural associations even though the games were developed in Japan and feature random encounters, level-grinding,[9] and illustrations in the manga style originated in Japan. Categorizing the games by culture based on shared play conventions hides many interesting details about the games and their histories. A more ideal approach is to view computer role-playing games, regardless of national origins, as integrative cultural systems distributing cultural phantasms regarding preferences for specific game mechanics over game advertisements, game periodicals, game players, and the games themselves.

The examples of "African cinema," "Egyptian musical instruments," and "Japanese role-playing games" were each chosen for a specific purpose. Each example prefigures topics that I shall explore later in the chapter. The discussion relating the concept of "Africanness" to cinema prefigures a later discussion of the relationship between specific trans-African oral media traditions and computing practices. The discussion of musical instruments prefigures discussion of the GRIOT system, an "instrument" for building interactive computational narratives. Finally, the discussion of computer gaming conventions prefigures discussion of GRIOT's use in creating a form of interactive poetry that inherits some forms of interaction from interactive fiction computer games.

In those later discussions, I shall attempt to have my cake—being against cultural generalization, stereotyping, and bias—and eat it, too, by explicitly discussing some of the trans-African cultural forms that influenced development of the GRIOT system. In particular, the GRIOT system is based in a concept that I shall call *trans-African orature*. We must remember that behind the adjective "African," as with the adjectives "Western" or "Continental" (which in philosophy implies "grounded in one of the diverse epistemologies of the European continent"), lurks a cultural phantasm. Historian Colin Palmer reminds us that

> the appellation "African" was a misnomer until very recent times. Because, generally speaking, the peoples of Africa traditionally embraced an ethnic identification in contradistinction to a trans-ethnic, regional, or continentally based one, it is more historically accurate to speak of Yoruba, Akan, or Malinke diasporas for much of the period up to the late 19th century or even later. The issue becomes even more complicated when one recognizes that individuals also moved from one society in Africa to another for a variety of reasons including being captured in war. Because an African or transethnic consciousness did not exist, the people who left their ethnic homeland were, strictly speaking, residing "abroad." (Palmer 1998, 29)

The adjective "trans-African" is used here because the discussion includes cultural forms related to, but outside of, the continent of Africa. This usage is adopted despite that Ngugi wa Thiong'o's discussion of orature informing the argument here is oriented primarily toward debate in the academies focused more exclusively upon continental Africa and is based on his own cultural traditions such as Kenyan theater. As soon as Ngugi enters a broader African debate than the specific Kenyan context, the discussion is already trans-African. Nonetheless, "trans-African" may be awkward to use here because it seems to impute sameness across a diversity of peoples. Furthermore, it may initially seem to mean only "across the continent of Africa," excluding the African diaspora, whereas I have clarified that the meaning here is inclusive of the diaspora. It may be the case that "transnational" should be preferred. However, "transnational" might imply a focus on the movement of cultural production across *national* borders, rather than focusing on the cultural continuities and affinities, both imagined and historically grounded, between cultural productions of both diverse peoples on the continent and in the diaspora.

In the past I have used the adjective "diasporic" because my focus is inclusive of cultural products produced and transformed by a dispersion of peoples from diverse African locations into diverse nations in other continents. However, the term "diasporic" introduced another potential confusion: as Palmer also reminds us, the meaning of the phrase "African diaspora" is far from clear: "Does it refer simply to Africans abroad, that is to say the peoples of African descent who live outside their ancestral continent? Is Africa a part of the diaspora? Is the term synonymous with what is now being called the Black Atlantic?" (Palmer 1998, 27). Hence, the term "diasporic" may have seemed to exclude the plurality of cultural productions on the continent of Africa itself, which was not my intention.

In light of all of these complications and warnings, there are still strong reasons for using the term "trans-African." The term addresses not only cultural forms produced in specific locations but also cultural forms whose origins cannot be easily located due to the middle passage, emigration from Africa, and movement *within* Africa. In the *Living Liberia Fabric*, our work directly engaged the cultures of ethnic groups, including the "Congo" people in Liberia who were repatriated in Liberia from slavers' ships embarking from Central Africa and from the Caribbean islands. Given the complexity of their history and the interweaving cultural strands that influence them, without going into the particularities of the history of the Congo, the phrase "trans-African" may be nearly as specific as possible for referring to this group. The term "trans-African" is also inclusive of other cultural forms that will be discussed later, such as the martial art/dance called capoeira, examples of which have moved from the diaspora (Brazil, and later North America) back to the continent of Africa in new areas (e.g., practitioners on the Île de Gorée of Senegal).[10] My argument is that the cultural grounding of the GRIOT system is informed by a transethnic perspective oriented toward recognizing continuities between a diversity of African aesthetic forms of cultural production and forms of cultural production in the African diaspora. Like art movements that take up the mantle of Pan-Africanism as a strategic political gesture (rather than, say, the essentializing, though artistically fruitful, Négritude literary movement of the 1930s), GRIOT is rooted in a constructivist notion of orature produced in Africa and the African diaspora based on theory arising from debates about the nature of oral traditions occurring in multiple academic venues in a plurality of African nations, linguistic groups, and ethnicities, and even sensibilities or affiliations.

There is a temptation, abetted by multiple strong reasons, for using phrases that do seem to ascribe cultural ownership. Though perhaps outside the scope of my scholarly argument, I shall describe several of these reasons, along with pedagogically situated anecdotes illustrating them. The first reason why some use cultural ownership is the most simplistic; it is easier to discuss media in terms of sweeping generalizations than to address the full complexities of the relationships between cultures and media in detail. My students, hailing from a range of international locales, initially did not hesitate to discuss the differences between "Western" and "Japanese" videogames. They are generally sensitive regarding issues of making cultural generalizations, so I presume that they use such phrases because they see the matter as a choice between using expedient, well-known generalizations versus cumbersome, mitigating explanations that are unfamiliar[11] to game players and scholars. A careful distinction commonly made in the social sciences between *emic* (terms meaningful to those in the cultural group at hand) and *etic* (neutrally intended terms often used by researchers or other outsiders to the cultural group at hand) descriptions can help in this regard.

A second reason why some use cultural ownership phrasing is that ascribing cultural ownership of ideas and artifacts can be empowering. For people who come from backgrounds that are currently underrepresented in fields such as cinema or computing, it can feel liberating and empowering to encounter concepts that seem to include them. When I co-taught a course on African Cinema and Digital Media with a scholar of West African (and European) art house cinema, a self-identified African American student enthusiastically thanked me ahead of the semester for teaching a technical course in which he felt that his background was celebrated. He was not raised in West Africa, yet he felt empowered by a course that he implicitly felt reflected his own historical and cultural background.

A third reason why some use cultural ownership phrasing is that it can combat covert forms of discrimination. When historical origins of some cultural forms are celebrated while others are erased from memory, it constitutes a form of bias. The case of rock-and-roll music and the contrast between the predominant current image of the "white rocker" and historical discrimination against the form's African American pioneers is well documented. Similarly, disparities in financial compensation between jazz bandleaders racially identified as white and black during the 1930s are also well documented (if not as often discussed). When I taught another course on subjective computing systems, an international doctoral student studying with me was perplexed by the idea that hip-hop music has origins in practices enacted by African Americans. For him, hip-hop was global youth culture, without national or ethnic origins. Yet he balked at the idea that classical music forms with origins in Turkey or France could be equally appropriated and removed from their historical origins—say, by a North American playing a Turkish fasıl (type of suite) or an orchestra in Beijing playing the compositions of Claude Debussy. This selective globalist perspective exhibits a type of bias that cultural ownership-oriented phrasing such as "black music" can guard against, despite the complications that we have seen such phrasing can invoke.

There is a way out, however, and I hope that this chapter can play a small role in contributing to it. This chapter introduces vocabulary and perspectives that allow us to discuss cultural foundations openly, while being cognizant of the traps of cultural essentialization, generalization, and stereotyping. There are many ways to engage the cultures of Africa and the African diaspora while avoiding cultural ownership phrasing and the essentialism it can suggest. Yet it is important to acknowledge the second (empowerment) and third (combating bias) reasons that some use such phrasing. There is often an antiracist impetus for describing African conceptual systems in an essentialist manner. Science and technology studies researcher Ron Eglash notes:

> Opposition to racism has often been composed through two totalizing, essentialist strategies: sameness and difference. For example, Mudimbe (1988) demonstrates how the category of a singular "African philosophy" has been primarily an invention of difference, having its creation in the play between "the beautiful myths of the 'savage mind' and the African ideological strategies of otherness." In contrast, structuralists such as Levi-Strauss have attempted to prove that African conceptual systems are fundamentally the same as those of Europeans (both having their basis in arbitrary symbol systems). (Eglash 1995, 18)

While celebrating antiracist perspectives, we can reject the notion of trans-African orature akin either to the singular African philosophy disputed by Mudimbe or universal African conceptual systems argued for by Levi-Strauss. Instead, our concept of trans-African orature is rooted in *practitioners' subscription to a set of representations, conceptual frameworks* and *shared psychosocial/cultural values of embodied oral performance*. To say that some orature is "trans-African" means that practitioners are informed by diverse sets of experiences and engagements with oral cultural media forms that use specific or carefully conceptualized transethnic African origins as grounding for practices of community-building, self-conceptualizing, and models of cultural production. In other words, *trans-African orature is a cultural phantasm that I have found to be generative of a diversifying computing practice.*

The Case of an African Logic: Remarks on Reifying Cultural Boundaries, Prejudicial Cultural Binaries, Assuming Authority Over Other Cultures, Esssentialization, and Generalization

Beyond associating cultures with specific media forms, some authors have posited associations between more fundamental systems such as in mathematics or computing with particular cultures. Such associations are even more complex to untangle, further revealing the problems in associating technologies with particular cultures. The following discussion looks at the association of culture with mathematics. In particular, this subsection focuses on one researcher's cautionary tale as she encountered problems in attempting to define an "African logic," a specific type of Yoruba mathematics practice. The primary reason for exploring this example here is that presenting the researcher's self-reflections provides a useful, carefully reasoned, cautionary tale. A secondary reason for the example's focus is that mathematics undergirds the computational medium that is a central topic of this book. The example helps show why being explicit about cultural foundations of computing practices cannot be as simple as introducing concepts such as an African (Yoruba) logic or African computing practice. Note that this observation also means that we cannot simply call logic or computing exclusive results of "Western," "Greek," or any other culture either. The analysis of this example concludes by revealing three dangers inherent in associating particular cultures with material and conceptual artifacts, namely *reifying cultural boundaries*, *reenacting prejudicial cultural binaries*, and *assuming authority over another culture.*

Helen Verran, based on her field research, posited a distinct type of African logic (Verran 2001). In her earlier work, Verran argued that there were significant differences between numbers in Yoruba and English that even affected everyday mathematics practiced in societies using the two languages. For example, Verran describes an educator who was disturbed by observing that some Yoruba students had no problem considering the sum of the lengths of a bundle of sticks of uniform size to represent length, whereas for most English-speaking mathematics practitioners "length" necessarily represents a continuous extension, not a collection. At a high level, the differences are rooted in abstract, linguistically based dispositions toward concepts such as "number" and "length" that have impacts on practices. More specifically, Verran distinguishes between Yoruba and English numbers in at least three interconnected senses: numeric base, linguistic use, and embodied basis. I shall discuss each of these differences in turn.

First of all, whereas English (and other Indo-European-based number systems) use ten as a base,[12] Yoruba primarily uses base twenty, secondarily using base ten, and subsidiarily using base five. At the primary level, the system is structured by progressing from one vigesimal (twenty) to the next; tens and fives are used to produce intermediary numerals (Verran 2001, 55). After explaining this vigesimal basis for Yoruba numeral generation, Verran describes the process of generating intermediary numerals as follows:

> The first four numerals of each vigesimal are generated through addition of ones, say 40 plus 1 (41), 40 plus 2 (42), and so on, a process that is fairly familiar to base-ten users.
>
> After 44 we "leap" to 60 take away 10 take away 5 ($60 - 10 - 5$) to generate 45; 46 is ($60 - 10 - 4$), and so on to 49, progressively taking away one less at each step.
>
> Fifty is 60 take away 10 ($60 - 10$), 51 is 60 take away 10 add 1 ($60 - 10 + 1$). This continues up to 54.
>
> Fifty-five is 60 take away 5 ($60 - 5$), 56 is ($60 - 4$), and so on, progressively taking away one less at each step to 59. (Verran 2001, 55–56)

Second, Verran distinguishes between English and Yoruba number systems linguistically, noting that numbers in English are noun-oriented and typically behave adjectivally, whereas they are verb-oriented in Yoruba. Verran describes the Yoruba linguistic usage as follows: "As elisions of introducers and verbs, the names of the counting set of Yoruba numerals have the form of nominalized verb phrases. Saying that the numerals are elided verb phrases identifies that grammatically the numerals function as mode or modal nouns. 'Mode' here is related to the modifying function that adverbs have in sentences. Number names are adverbial in nature, ascribing 'a manner of appearing'" (Verran 2001, 67). To give one of her concrete examples, a Yoruba phrase that would be understood in English as "He gave me four stones" would be literally translated as "He gave me stonematter in the mode of a group in the mode of four" (69). As another example, the Yoruba phrase that would be conventionally translated into English as "One fish is not enough" would be literally translated as "Fishmatter in the mode one does not reach" (69).

Finally, she described the different embodied bases of English and Yoruba number systems and the ways that the body is used in elementary counting, most prominently whether fingers alone are used or if toes are used as well. Verran describes this difference in the following manner:

> We might say that the Yoruba language rules for numeral generation can be taken as modeling the following sequence of specified actions with hands and feet, fingers and toes. Beginning with the finger/toe complement of a person gives the major base ogún (twenty). Shifting from one vigesimal to the next codes for "starting a new set of fingers and toes"—literally "placing out a new set of twenty" in Yoruba. . . .
>
> This is very different from the picture we get with the base-ten numerals used in modern quantifying and mathematics, say in English. There ten implies the one-by-one pointing to the ten fingers. Twenty implies two sets of fingers. Twenty-one begins again: thumb of left hand held up; twenty-two: forefinger of left hand, up; twenty-three: tall man of left hand, up; and so on to twenty-six: thumb of right hand, up; and on up to thirty, which is three sets of fingers. What we see in English is a linear passing along the fingers until the end, keeping tally of how many sets, and then doing it again. (Verran 2001, 64–65)

Verran's account of the differences between Yoruba and English numbering systems is much more nuanced and expansive than the three distinguishing points raised here. These distinctions, however, are enough to give a high-level view of the type of observations upon which Verran based her argument for two distinct, coherent logics.

Ultimately, summarizing her early argument for two consistent logics of numbering, Verran writes:

> I have unpacked natural number as used in the English language and in the Yoruba language and shown them as systems of abstraction created in two disparate systems of categorization. I have argued that the basis of the difference between the two chains of abstraction is the difference between Yoruba and English in the types of actions that bodies engage in that is coded in coming to predicate (use verbs) and so to designate in the language. The sort of contract that natural number is in a particular language has been determined by a set of prior (and ancient) decisions about coding interaction in the material world. (Verran 2001, 186)

In this manner, Verran couches the differences between the two number systems more broadly as a matter of the ways languages are used to engage with the world; the languages entail different epistemic domains for numbers.

Importantly, Verran later strongly criticized and revised her insights regarding an African logic. We shall see how and why she rejected her earlier assumption informing her perspective that Yoruba and English number logics were different, but equal. Verran's revision of her ideas does not mean that different phenomena were not taking place in Yoruba versus English settings. Indeed, her research rigorously demonstrates that there was a notable difference. Yet her revision does mean that the worldview informing the binary division between Yoruba and English (sometimes generalized to a division between "African" and "scientific") was too limited. The second quote in the epigraph at the start of this chapter reveals a part of the impetus for later revising her position. In it, she describes how Yoruba audiences laughed in response to her work. Confused at the time, she also observed "that the most significant response of my Yoruba colleagues was eyes twinkling in amusement, as if a collective laugh was always about to erupt" (Verran 2001, 27). This observation can be traced to her realization that any effort "to teach, say, 'English arithmetic' in one lesson and 'Yoruba arithmetic' in another" would have been ignored as "clearly foolish" (28). The reasons for this are subtle and are based on a Eurocentric worldview underlying her research.

It was not the case that Verran overtly felt that English number logic (which she started by calling "scientific" logic) was superior to Yoruba number logic. Her starting position recognized that the African logic she argued for was consistent and valid. Indeed, her project "began with a desire to refute number's claims to social, cultural, and political neutrality" (Verran 2001, 25). Yet Verran later felt that her earlier account had been ultimately flawed because in it she argued for universal cultural rules about a Yoruba type of mathematics. Her study failed to emphasize that many Yoruba speakers, like many speakers of other languages, simultaneously learn formal textbook mathematics as children and use mathematics informally (for example, involving estimation and approximation) at the market. Many Yoruba speakers, like many speakers of other languages, often come up with creative everyday mathematics problem-solving approaches in addition to learning the professional mathematics practices used in business or engineering. To put it in her own words, Verran failed "to recognize communities of practice as creative and generative" (Verran 2001, 29).

Verran should be celebrated for continuing to critically reflect upon her own earlier observations, especially as the results of that self-reflection are very useful to others. Verran's lessons are useful here; in particular, she found three flaws underlying her approach (which she now pejoratively categorizes as *relativistic*) that will be important to bear in mind in this chapter. For clarity, the following labels and summarizes the errors highlighted by Verran's observations:

1. *Reifying cultural boundaries:*

   "The boundary between 'the Yoruba' and 'the modern' had been hardened and solidified in my analysis as the categories were (re-)defined and delimited. A denial of difference as real or doable *and* a simultaneous hardening of separation are some of the moral outcomes of my relativist way of telling 'a Yoruba logic' . . . my relativist schema merely retells an imperial universalism." (Verran 2001, 30–31)

2. *Reenacting a prejudicial cultural binary:*

   "The abstract 'Yoruba logic' I had revealed could only be taken as an echo, a shadowy form of English logic. The schema reenacts the categories of a universal modernity, originating in European traditions, and a Yoruba echo of a necessarily European modernity. Either way, a distinct 'us' and 'them' are locked forever together, and apart, through the specter of originality/mimicry." (Verran 2001, 31)

3. *Assuming authority over another culture:*

   "I find that, as author, I have assumed the voice of authority. This voice, legislating from a position of certainly, tells the ways contemporary Yoruba should understand themselves and their knowing." (Verran 2001, 31)

The collective amused response that Verran encountered from her Yoruba colleagues hailed from a failure to realize these three errors in her earlier work. Verran's observations also shed light on the entire endeavor of associating material and conceptual artifacts with specific cultures. Verran's discussion highlights the complexities of the relationship between the "system" and the "culture" in the phrase "cultural system." As I discuss cultural systems in the remainder of the chapter, I shall take care to recognize that cultural boundaries are conceptual abstractions, avoid implicit binary observations that privilege one culture over another, express humility, and realize that members of a culture possess a type of authority over that culture.

The discussion and warnings raised thus far regarding associating particular cultures with material and conceptual artifacts are intended to set the stage for careful discussion later in the chapter that relates a constructed cultural phantasm called trans-African orature to computing. Any discussion of broad cultural traditions tends to generalize cultural phenomena, obliterate nuanced concern for the diversity within various traditions, and invite criticism of the very notion of a "tradition" itself. The concept of trans-African orature is problematic first of all because people in all cultures communicate orally. The notion of trans-African orature is, of course, troubled by the difficulties with the term "trans-African," as noted earlier. In addition, there are intersecting communities of practice with features that originated in particular specific African contexts and that persist (often in quite transformed instantiations) in cultural systems throughout the diaspora. I shall be aware of these and related issues and shall proceed sensitively with regard to the broader argument here that emphasizes the explicit grounding of computing practices in culture.

We have seen many examples of the complex ways that cultures are related to ideas and objects. The following remarks provide a set of concluding observations regarding this discussion. Basing technical and creative production upon such foundations can drive technical and artistic innovation. Such innovations will reflect the great variety of particular cultural systems, rooted in their specificities, and drawing upon cultural resources ranging from cultural self-conception to adherence to broad cultural narratives. The concepts presented here may seem to suggest, for some, a binary opposition, like Verran's Yoruba versus English mathematics, pitting the cultures of Africa and African diaspora against the oppressive imperial forces of Western tradition. Although I am fully cognizant of the historical, often brutal, circumstances from which this binary portrait arises, the binary portrait is incorrect. Diverse African traditions, such as the oral aesthetic cultural systems focused on here, are broadly influential in this case impacting traditions including literature of the black Atlantic, African American jazz, syncretist religions in South America and the Caribbean. They also have the potential to influence computing practice, as I shall demonstrate later with some of my own work. The focus on trans-African oral traditions is motivated by the need for a degree of cultural specificity in order to develop effective subjective computing systems (universalism seldom makes good art) and by the fact that research models of orature arising in trans-African settings alike directly and explicitly influenced the development of the GRIOT system (introduced in chapter 3 and described in depth later in this chapter).

Finally, the proposal here is not that computing practices should *mine* diverse forms of cultural production for new models that benefit technologically privileged practitioners and consumers, nor is the aim to view cultures as resources to be exploited by technologists. Instead, I propose that diverse cultural systems can enrich our understandings of our computational practices and that computational practices always are rooted in cultural values. Cultural computing is the inverse of endeavors that propose to export technologies to materially under-resourced "third-world" communities as a humanitarian gesture. Instead, we take the view that diverse cultural values and practices represent legitimate foundations for technically rigorous and artistically effective computing practices. The accounts of trans-African orature and the GRIOT system later in this chapter reflect this focus.

Trans-African Orature: A Cultural Aesthetic System

The remainder of this chapter explores the ways in which culture and media come together as *integrative cultural systems* by focusing on a specific case. This case is that of oral aesthetic cultural systems. Oral aesthetic cultural systems are well known for their importance in trans-African settings. Yet, perhaps because they are not privileged in computing discourse, it has not been common to see them as potential groundings for subjective computing practices such as developing interactive narrative systems. The following discussion describes how trans-African oral aesthetic systems can provide such grounding.

In his essay "Oral Power and Eurupe Glory," author and theorist Ngugi wa Thiong'o describes a cultural system. Ngugi identifies and elaborates a set of principles for analyzing oral systems of communication and a perspective on the deployment of those principles (Ngugi 1998). He foregrounds an oral aesthetic cultural system (based in part on his experience with, and knowledge of, Kenyan theater), including an account of elements essential to an oral performance, namely architectural space, time frame, an oral equivalent to mise-en-scène, and the audience-performer relationship. These elements of performance as described by Ngugi are also central in many forms of subjective computing with their virtual worlds, procedurality, and user-machine interaction. The parallel between an oral aesthetic cultural system and subjective computing fuels the argument that computing technologies hold great potential for contributing to new forms of subjective computing beyond the privileged models typically encountered in engineering practices. Explicitly highlighting diverse cultural foundations is not a radical or revisionist gesture. It holds concrete advantages. There are diverse cultural aesthetic traditions that contain systems of interactivity and generativity that hold the potential to spur innovation in the development of subjective computing systems that engage a plurality of worldviews.

The conception of orature here is informed by a diversity of trans-African cultural traditions. Ngugi wa Thiong'o asserts that the term orature was "coined in the [Nineteen] Sixties by Pio Zirimu, the late Ugandan linguist" (Ngugi 1998, 105). He claims that the impetus for the coinage arose from two debates. The first debate revolved around the elevated status of the English language and English departments in the African academy. The second revolved around the casting of "oral literature" as either folkloric (or worse, primitive) or as the original basis of all textual composition. Those prejudiced perspectives are based in colonial power relationships that associate peasantry with illiteracy and dominance with reproducible text. These African academic debates questioned the secondary role that oral tradition has often come to occupy in relation to literary traditions.

Orature has taken on particular importance in a host of African settings and in the African diaspora. For example, literary theorist Henry Louis Gates Jr. has described "speakerly" texts as a hallmark of African American narrative forms; at the same time he discusses continuities between Yoruba cosmology and African American trickster figures (Gates 1988). One reason for the trans-African prevalence of orature and cultural forms inspired by oral tradition is that crucial bodies of knowledge—for example, narratives of ancestry—a topic of deep cultural and religious significance in many diverse African cultures, have traditionally been transmitted orally. Consider the cultural role of the griot and his female counterpart the griotte, most commonly described as West African praise singers and performers often providing accounts of genealogical ancestry. Yet such descriptions do not tell the whole story; literature scholar Thomas A. Hale writes of the griot's role: "They are also historians, genealogists, advisors, spokespersons, diplomats, interpreters, musicians, composers, poets, teachers, exhorters, town criers, reporters, and masters of or contributors to a variety of ceremonies (naming, initiation, weddings, installations of chiefs, and so on). Although griots are born into their profession, they do not all perform all of these functions, some of which are gender-specific or not as actively practiced today as they were centuries ago" (Hale 1997, 250–251). Furthermore, although the griot's[13] role is often described as if it is uniform across cultures, Hale provides a more complex picture, stating:

> Societies that count griots among their various professions, however, have their own words to describe them: iggio (Moor), guewel or géwél (Wolof), mabo or gawlo (Fulbe), jali (Mandinka), jeli (Maninka, Bamana), geseré or jaaré (Soninké), jeseré (Songhay), and marok'i (Hausa), not to mention a variety of other terms. Within a particular language group or culture there are other non-hereditary performers, such as hunters and Muslim clerics, who operate in some

ways like griots to meet the needs of certain groups. The multiplicity of terms for hereditary griots across the Sahel and Savanna zones of West Africa reveals individual ethnic identities, cultural diffusion from one people to another over an apparently long period of time, and diversity in the variety of these bards within a particular society. (1997, 251)

The griot's role in society is an example of an element of cultural infrastructure for maintaining narratives. Furthermore, in the African diaspora the griot has become a transethnic cultural symbol of storytelling, especially for people whose historical roots may be grounded in an unknown West African locale due to the middle passage.[14] Indeed, academic journals, music groups and recordings, films, media production companies, and more have all invoked the figure of the griot in their titles. To reinforce this idea, consider the following citations and observations by Hale that paint a portrait of the increasingly diverse uses of the word "griot":

> Today, griots perform at a variety of venues in cities such as Paris, London, New York, and Tokyo, as well as at hundreds of universities around the world. They are now having an impact on such diverse musical styles as rock, rap, and even modern symphonic music. The on-line LEXIS/NEXIS Information System available to data users at many sites worldwide lists over 1,500 citations containing the word griot in newspapers and other publications. Many of them refer to African American musicians, storytellers, and elders who increasingly are being compared to griots. For example, the National Association of Black Storytellers gave Mary Carter Smith the title "Mother Griot" at the 1994 National Festival of Black Storytelling (Smith 1996). But griot is not limited to the African diaspora. The author Studs Terkel, whose writings are based largely on oral interviews, now compares his work to that of a griot (Heinen 1995). (Hale 1997, 249)

It is clear that the naming of my GRIOT system continues this trend. At the same time, it is important that we also acknowledge the literal, historical, and contemporary social roles performed by griots, as they are clearly prominent creators of traditions of orature. As such, griots should be acknowledged as the inspiration for a variety of trans-African forms of orature, and even forms of orature with cultural roots outside of West Africa.

Remarks on Orality

Orature is often discussed in relation to literature, paralleling the broader relationship between orality and literacy. As an important example of this broader relationship,

Walter Ong has presented a well-known commentary on those dual modes of communication (Ong 1982). Ong described speech, which is apprehended primarily via our auditory faculty, as being fundamentally related to time, and the written word, apprehended primarily via our visual faculty, as being primarily related to space. He differentiated the irredeemable nature of time from the revisitable nature of space. In the same manner, he differentiated oral utterances (which are lost to time once emitted) from written signs (which are arrested in time). Ong does make a series of sharp observations about common traits of oral exposition such as its frequent use of repetition, contextual situatedness, and reliance on memory. Unfortunately, his larger argument is reductive because he defines cultures solely in terms of their degrees of deploying of orality or literacy. Ong's views also exhibit a type of technological and linguistic determinism, which can be seen in his claims that a culture's use of written or oral media technologies for communication has a singular determining effect upon the nature of the entire culture. Emevwo Biakolo's critique of Ong's work illuminates ways that the binary opposition between oral culture and written culture serves to preserve a system of cultural prejudice informed by a "faulty principle of causality" (Biakolo 1999, 48). Biakolo cites Ruth Finnegan to make this point:

> Much of the plausibility of the "Great Divide" theories has rested on the often unconscious assumption that what the essential shaping of society comes from is its communication technology. But once technological determinism is rejected or queried, then questions immediately arise about these influential classifications of human development into two major types: oral/primitive as against oral/literate. . . . It is worth emphasizing that the conclusions from research, not only about the supposed "primitive mentality" associated with orality, but also about, for example, concepts of individualism and the self, conflict and skepticism, or detached and abstract thought in non-literate cultures now look different . . . [and] once-confident assertions about the supposed differentiating features of oral and literate cultures are now exposed as decidedly shaky (Finnegan 1988, 13). (Biakolo 1999, 49)

Rather than perpetuating the determinism inherent in Ong's work, in this chapter we focus on Ngugi wa Thiong'o's discussion of orature, which does not rest upon the orality/literacy binary opposition.

Ngugi begins with a comparative approach that destabilizes any hierarchy in which literacy is privileged over orality. An oral system is not a "pre-literate" system, it is a different "formal narrative, dramatic, and poetic system" (Ngugi 1998, 117).

The fallacy of such hierarchies created by biases toward media oriented to the ear (orality), eye (literacy), or even language in general, is described by semiotician Daniel Chandler, who argues that "the bias in which writing is privileged over speech has been called *graphocentrism* or *scriptism*. In many literate cultures, text has a higher status than speech: written language is often seen as the standard" (Chandler 1994). Graphocentrism is a charge to which Ong is immune, as we see in Chandler's continued discussion (citing Ong) of this type of bias:

> Graphocentrism often involves an uncritical equation of writing with progress, growth and development. "Pre-literate" societies may be seen as a lower stage of development than our own. Non-literate societies and individuals may be defined negatively by their "lack" of writing. To privilege literacy involves branding half of humankind as "inferior." Walter Ong declares that "Those who think of the text as the paradigm of all discourse need to face the fact that only the tiniest fraction of languages have ever been written or ever will be. Most have disappeared or are fast disappearing, untouched by textuality. Hard-core textualism is snobbery, often hardly disguised" (Ong 1986, p. 26). (Chandler 1994)

After his argument against biases toward the literary (equivalent to what Chandler calls graphocentrism), Ngugi's discussion quickly moves on to articulating a perspective on oral aesthetic cultural systems (Ngugi 1998). Ngugi's work focuses on the factors that come into play in "the actual execution" of oral performance.

Ngugi wa Thiong'o's Model of Orature

Ngugi's view of orature is useful for understanding works in which cultural systems historically associated with Africa are invoked but are deployed in diverse media and new forms in contemporary (often postcolonial) African transethnic settings. In such cases, the material conditions of performance may be radically transformed because the original architectural spaces, musical instruments, costumes, and so on may be unavailable. Furthermore, the cultural situations of participants may be radically transformed; for example, they may speak colonial languages or may even be unaware of the traditions upon which the performance is based. The performance may also exist as an amalgam of multiple media types, including written, cinematic, or computational media. In such cases, orature provides a lens with which to examine cultural continuities within content, worldview, and media usage. Ngugi acknowledges that the characteristics of orature that he discusses—for example mime, dance, masks, and storytelling—are not exclusive to African modes of expression. However, the performative and integrative characteristics of orature do construct a conceptual framework that is based in careful reflection upon continuities of trans-African cultural (Ngugi 1998). However, the performative and integrative characteristics of orature articulated by Ngugi construct a conceptual framework that is based in careful reflection upon continuities of African cultural systems also throughout the diaspora. Such cultural systems can undergird expressive computational practices, as will be described shortly.

Ngugi presents two facets of orature, the *performative* and the *integrative* facets, which I argue may serve as foundations for subjective computing systems. Let us take a look at the performative facet first. Ngugi (1998) describes four elements of oral performance aesthetics in many African contexts:

(1) architectural space,
(2) time frame,
(3) (oral) mise-en-scène, and
(4) the audience-performer relationship.

The architectural space he describes is typically an open space. It is most often a circular space. The choice of a circle is not incidental; rather, it has a symbolic unifying importance within the traditions the Ngugi addresses. He also describes how the time frame establishes the conditions for performance in several ways. The time frame can relate to the functional use of a particular performance—for example, work songs being performed during work time or rite of passage performances coinciding with the necessary time of the ritual. The length of time also establishes conditions for performance. "Oral mise-en-scène" refers to the different ambiences that can be created using costumes, light sources, and so on. Ngugi writes "one can imagine the play of shadows and light on the bodies and costumes of the actors. The sources of light, whether fire, the moon, or the sun, could create different ambiences" (Ngugi 1998, 110). Finally, the most important element is the audience-performer relationship. Ngugi describes how the audience can play varying roles within performances, for example as critics or co-performers, such as in stories "where a choral phrase or song or response" is taken up by listeners who then become a part of the action. In such live performances, production and consumption dynamically intermingle.

Ngugi's second facet of orature, its integrative characteristic, constitutes a more delicate argument. His discussion is based on a transethnic account of African oral practices but is rooted in his experience with Kenyan theater because it arises from a view of orature as a *complete aesthetic system*. Orature uses artistic forms to represent adherence to a set of values (what I would call a cultural system) shared among cultural participants. The conditions of oral performance are connected to the cultural phantasms of its participants. The dominance of the circle (with its symbolic and cosmological connotations) in architectural and performance spaces is an example of such a phantasm. Ngugi comments that "the interconnection between phenomena captured in the image of the circle, the central symbol of the African aesthetic, is consonant with the materialist metaphysics that one finds in so much of the pre-colonial African societies, the remnants of which still condition the African world-view" (116). The emphasis here is that in performances based in such cultural phantasms, the conditions for performance are not accomplished with the stylistic innovation of a singular author or by happenstance. As an example, Ngugi notes that many precolonial Kenyan oral narratives reflect "the interdependence of forms of life in the fluidity of movement of characters through all the four realms of being and their interactions in flexible time and space. Plants, animals, and humans interact freely in many of the narratives" (Ngugi 1998, 117). For cultural practitioners immersed in, or subscribing to, such cultural phantasms, orature is a "complete aesthetic system" in the sense that the content of an oral performance, the material and social conditions of the performance, and the worldview informing the choice of content and conditions are all integrated. This is one sense in which some forms of orature in Africa and the African diaspora is said to be integrative.

Another sense in which Ngugi describes his model of orature as being integrative is its rejection of boundaries of media and conventional artistic form. Orature allows for the integration of diverse art forms. This aspect of the integrative character of orature potentially separates it from its roots in oral communication. Under this view, underlying conceptual cultural aspects of an aesthetic cultural system are deployed through the conditions and form of the performance but do not rely upon them. Indeed, cultural phantasms of participants may be seen as more intrinsic to orature than even the fact of its oral transmission. If a particular form of expression is rooted in a traditional conceptual aesthetic cultural system that is typically expressed as an oral performance, then that form of expression can be said to be grounded in orature. This integrative aspect of orature corresponds to what I termed "metamedial" earlier.

This argument can be exemplified by a case Ngugi raises regarding the black arts movement in Britain. Ngugi references (1998, 114) the author Kwesi Owusu, who writes, "Many black artists work in various media simultaneously, forging creative links, collaborations and alliances. This state of consciousness, a reflection of African and Asian attitudes to creativity, is what is called orature" (Owusu 1988, 2). Acknowledging and putting aside the obvious critique of his generalization about African and Asian attitudes, Owusu's conceptualization demonstrates the idea that particular oral forms of expression can take shape in various eventual media. Understood this way, orature becomes more akin to a communal and improvisational stance toward art than a type of work that is conveyed orally. The term "orature" becomes incredibly expansive, but not vacuous, under such an interpretation.

Some cultural producers implicitly consider oral cultural aesthetic systems to be culturally metamedial—they are integrative cultural systems. Ngugi, in a side remark, even provides a suggestion that orature can be viewed in a culturally metamedial way related to subjective computing systems. He suggests that characteristics of orature may persist in, and serve as foundations for, "cyberspace" media forms.[15] Take the example of "signifyin(g)," the historical African American tradition of verbal competition via a series of escalating, often metaphorical, jibes, that can contribute evocative power even to written forms that employ its oratory tropes and patterns (Gates 1988). A culturally metamedial example of signifying can be seen in the popular *Monkey Island* series of computer games, which feature conversational insult exchange as a combat model called "insult swordfighting." Such gameplay could be considered an oral aesthetic system because of its roots in the tradition of signifyin(g). In cases such as this, actual embodied performances are seen as secondary to preserving some structure of oral communication in the computing system. In this manner, media forms such as computer games can "remediate" older forms, but they do not merely replace old media with new via "absorption" (Bolter and Grusin 1999). That is, computational media do not render oral or textual media into obsolete relics. Forms of orature may be remediated by computational media, but to understand this remediation we must investigate exactly which attributes of orature have influenced the cultural form, and in which ways. Our discussion of one specific model of trans-African orature has provided a description of aspects of orature useful for that purpose.

Remember that the aim in arriving at this expansive definition of orature is to use it as an example of an integrative cultural model that can provide grounding for a subjective computing practice. Arguing that trans-African oral cultural aesthetics can provide a basis for engineering development may seem to be atypical for a computer science practitioner to make. Yet, in the absence of a Eurocentric bias, it is no more exotic than finding roots of AI systems in Descartes's view of the mathematical mind. In fact, the argument here recommends being *more knowledgeable and explicit* in revealing underlying cultural influences than most AI research seems to be. In media theory, the computer is often seen as a metamedium, capable of reproducing other forms (but crucially featuring its own unique characteristics). Here, I use the notion of orature in the African diaspora as a *metacultural* concept, both describing an aesthetic cultural system (e.g., the four conditions for performance described previously) and extending that system beyond its origin in oral performance by applying it to computational media. The GRIOT system, described in the following section, is a cultural computing system constructed within the tradition of computer science, but its areas of application have been greatly influenced by an explicit interest in (and implicit cultural worldview incorporating) the traits of African oral culture in the diaspora (Goguen and Harrell 2005; Harrell 2005).

GRIOT: Design Based on Computational Integrative Cultural Phantasms

Recall that earlier in the chapter I called attention to the metamedial characteristic of integrative cultural systems. The *metamedial* characteristic of integrative cultural systems means that it can be conveyed via a range of media, including computational media. Such systems express and share styles, conventions, histories, and content that are more definitive of the cultural system than the medium it is produced in. By examining the ways it participates in imaginative world and poetic phantasm building, a subjective computing system can be used to illustrate metamedial characteristics of integrative cultural systems. This section exemplifies the concept of an integrative cultural system using the case of the GRIOT system and its relationship to trans-African traditions of orature.

   In any process of cultural production, the author's worldview influences development of the artifact at hand. In the case of the GRIOT system, this process includes its reliance upon particular cognitive science theories and its initial areas of application as a platform for implementing computational poetry and narrative. I stress, however, that its development was a technical practice.[16] GRIOT was developed with software engineering techniques and was influenced by the value systems of the engineering discipline. Yet some of the poetic and narrative models, applications, claims, and goals of GRIOT were based in cultural traditions and values typically absent from computer science discussions, including the tradition articulated by my reframing of Ngugi's model as trans-African orature. The functionality and aims of the GRIOT system were described in chapter 3. The GRIOT system supports authoring of expressive epistemologies that contribute to the production of content, style, and interaction forms based in several related trans-African art forms and aesthetic models. Development of these aspects of the GRIOT system involved critical engagement with several of the issues considered in our discussion of trans-African orature.

GRIOT's relationship to trans-African art forms and aesthetic models, including orature in particular, exemplifies the metamedial characteristics of integrative cultural systems in the following four ways:

1. *Cognitive semantics basis:* GRIOT is a computing system that can model culturally specific forms of discourse as it is based on more general theories of meaning construction. Namely, GRIOT's basis in cognitive semantics allows for an approach that admits concerns such as orature into computational practice.

2. *Culturally specific agency play:* Agency play, which for now can be considered the play of interaction between systems and users (a detailed definition will be given in chapter 7), enables specific cultural modes of interaction between the user and the works made using GRIOT. More precisely, the GRIOT architecture enables authors to implement subjective content generation and improvisational, collaborative relationships with the audience/users.

3. *Computational orality:* Agency play is used to implement interaction models based on oral tradition, even in cases involving only written output. In particular, works built using GRIOT are informed by oral performance and users interact with such works using a call-and-response model as opposed to command execution.

4. *Computational cultural content:* Cultural style and content related to oral tradition is instead represented computationally. Polymorphic poetry implemented in GRIOT addresses issues related to orature in the African diaspora and relies upon expressive epistemologies in which questions explicitly related to the African diaspora are raised.

A discussion of each of these types of relationship between GRIOT and trans-African orature follows.

Cognitive Semantics Basis

GRIOT's knowledge representation structures are rooted in the cognitive science theory of conceptual blending (Fauconnier and Turner 2002; Harrell 2007c). This cognitive science (semantics) foundation helps to support a systematic and general approach to representing culturally specific concepts. I discussed in the introduction how research in cognitive semantics suggests that language activity is only the observable result of backstage cognition processes that exhibit operational uniformity (Fauconnier 1999). This operational uniformity underlying conceptual thought applies to our understanding and creation of cultural products regardless of the culture they are associated with. This perspective contrasts strongly with academic traditions such as cultural anthropology, which often seek to understand cultural productions in their particularities as opposed to their underlying cognitive processes. It is intended that the cognitive semantics foundation of the GRIOT system allows it to be applied to products of oral culture in the African diaspora just as readily as to any other type of cultural production. It is in this sense that the cognitive semantics basis for GRIOT is a metamedial characteristic.

In *Cognitive Dimensions of Social Science*, Mark Turner presents Clifford Geertz's description of the role of the anthropologist to make a similar point (Turner 2001). Geertz describes his brand of analysis as "not an experimental science in search of law but an interpretive one in search of meaning. It is explication I am after, construing social expressions on their surface enigmatical" (Geertz, cited in Turner 2001, 13). The nature of Geertz's enterprise—what Turner calls the "historical retrospection" and "particularity" of the approach—contrasts strongly with the cognitive semantics focus on cognitive operations such as analogical inference, metaphorical mapping, and conceptual blending (Turner 2001).

The cognitive semantics approach is not a case of scientific reductionism though. On the contrary, the focus on operational uniformity provides potential bridges between phenomena in diverse cultures. The approach provides a means for comparative analysis of cultural systems, at the same time providing an experimental analysis based upon "weighing data, making hypotheses, building models, offering explanations, sometimes offering even predictions or tactics for intervention" (Turner 2001, 59). For example, we have seen that George Lakoff and Mark Turner have analyzed poetry by critically examining deployment of culturally entrenched metaphors within particular poems (Lakoff and Turner 1989). The cognitive semantics approach enables researchers to take a perspective on elements of orature in the African diaspora that does not seek to exoticize them but rather to understand their implications when expressed computationally.

Culturally Specific Agency Play

The GRIOT architecture allows computational narrative authors to implement works that generate content at runtime. It also enables implementation of works that exist in an improvisational and collaborative relationship with the audience. Cultural knowledge must be authored as expressive epistemologies. The narrative event structuring component of GRIOT also allows authors to structure the sequence of opportunities for users to provide input. In combination, these features exemplify Ngugi's observation about orature regarding how the audience can play varying roles within performances: "The audience could participate as critics and performers. In stories, for instance, a choral phrase or song or response was often taken up by listeners, who, in so doing, became part of the unfolding action. And the performances were nearly always live, production and consumption affected each other in a very dynamic manner. The oral was connected directly to the aural through performance" (Ngugi 1998, 110). In the case of GRIOT, it is through co-performance that the oral is connected to the textual.

The relationship between user input and system output in GRIOT can be used to express a range of subjective and cultural phenomena. For example, the following GRIOT-based polymorphic poems consider respective effects of user input: in *Loss, Undersea*, user input changes the emotional tone of the output; in *The Girl with Skin of Haints and Seraphs*, user input changes how stereotypical and metaphorical verbal images are recombined; and in *The Griot Sings Haibun*, user input changes the output's thematic focus on particular aspects of a Buddhist view on the qualitative experience of everyday events (Goguen and Harrell 2005; Harrell 2005, 2006, 2007c). These phenomena, expressed through improvisational meaning generation as a collaboration between the system and its users, are motivated by a commitment to trans-African oral media traditions that are complimented by the Japanese literary form of haibun poetry in *The Griot Sings Haibun* and Tibetan Buddhist concepts.

There is another, more abstract, influence of orature upon the research goals that led to the creation of the GRIOT system. GRIOT initially generated only text as output, but it has been expanded to compose video, animation, photographic imagery, and other types of audiovisual media. This expansion can be interpreted as an example of the generalizing from one medium to other media (generalization is a key engineering value), and thus the application of GRIOT to multiple types of media assets also exemplifies the metamedial characteristics of an integrative cultural system.

Computational Orality

Works made using the GRIOT system often replace the common command-and-control interface paradigm with a call-and-response interaction model. Call-and-response is a well-known trans-African cultural form. A hallmark of the form is a type of dialogic participation that structures some form of expression. One previous example was Ngugi describing how audience members spontaneously take up a choral phrase in a song during a performance. Call-and-response structure can be found in musical forms such as field hollers, spirituals, the blues, jazz, and rock and roll, as well as in religious forms such as African American preaching and forms of civic engagement such as political protest. Indeed, dynamic forms of call-and-response can be found in works in the African diaspora as diverse as the songs in the African Brazilian martial art/dance capoeira angola, composer and bassist Charles Mingus's calling out (with drummer Danny Richmond responding) of the segregationist Governor of Arkansas in "The Original Fables of Faubus" (Mingus 1960), the penetratingly satirical fiction of Ishmael Reed, and hip-hop rapping. The call-and-response form that is probably best known consists of a structure of song performance in which a lead singer *calls* out a line and the audience *responds* in unison, often with some improvisation on the part of the lead singer and/or variation on the part of the audience. Works produced in GRIOT inherit some aspects of this call-and-response model. In some works produced with GRIOT, the interaction model is inspired by the call-and-response form in that user input takes the role of a "call," prompting the system to produce variations in its response guided by the user. In other GRIOT-based works, the system's output takes the role of the "call," in that the output has a great degree of improvisational variation and user input is selected from a small number of possible "responses." In either case, user input does not consist of commands intended to control the system to produce specific results. Rather, user input is used to *co-construct output with the system* paralleling the co-construction of content trans-African call-and-response forms. For example, as we have seen in all of the previous examples of works created with GRIOT, user input can guide variations in aspects of output such as theme, emotional tone, or stakeholder perspective, which influences, but does not directly determine, the resulting output.

This model for interaction has been adopted because of its ability to support culturally specific types of content. The polymorphic poem *The Girl with Skin of Haints and Seraphs*, discussed in chapter 3, provides a commentary on cultural specific racial politics, the error of holding simplistic binary views of social identity, and the need for more contingent, dynamic models for self-representation in computational media. We saw that the dynamic nature of social identity is also reflected in the way the program produces different poems, with different metaphors each time it is run, because of the way that the system draws on a set of expressive epistemologies providing structured knowledge about domains such as skin, angels, demons, Europe, and Africa given as sets of axioms. This structure enables interaction with *The Girl with Skin of Haints and Seraphs* to invoke attributes of trans-African orature such as the call-and-response structure just discussed. The output of *The Girl with Skin of Haints and Seraphs* also draws upon African and African American vernacular traditions of signifyin(g) in its deployment of exaggerated stereotypical metaphors and other verbal imagery. Another example of output from *The Girl with Skin of Haints and Seraphs* (Harrell 2005) follows:

The Girl with Skin of Haints and Seraphs (Sample Output 3)

```
> Africa

every night she wakes covered with winged-creature original-
lady sweat

> Africa

she nearly died while choking on lady black candy

skin black ideas and miserable thoughts whipped through her

> Europe

her failure was ignoring her scaled-being sunbather nature

and her pride privilege feet danced

> Europe

she worked raising ashy-skin wintery-skin children of her own

and her mathematics bullet feet danced

> angel

she finally knew that a privilege love woman would never be
loved
```

The output is intended to convey the author's intention to capture the concept of stereotypical cultural binaries in the epistemologies that provide semantic structures in the program—stereotypes and binaries that are to be destabilized as more contrasting poems are generated. Stereotypes of both essential Africanness (the `original lady` with `skin black`) and Europeanness (the `sunbather` with `wintery skin`) are conjugated differently upon each execution. For contrast, another execution with the same user input reads:

The Girl with Skin of Haints and Seraphs (Sample Output 4)

```
> africa
her arrival onto this earth was marked—black ghost knows
longing and fear

> africa
her wax hot drips anansi bitemarks in the flesh and psyche of
hope loss loves

her condition was melaninated impoverished-elder-like

> europe
tears ran relay races between her combination-skin bullet eyes
and her pain entitlement earlobes and back

longing awe ideas and miserable thoughts whipped through her

> europe
when hungry she dined on shame smugness rice and female
imperialist yams

life was an astounding miracle

> angel
her pointed-nose piercing-arrow spirit would live on
```

A parallel structure can be found in many examples of call-and-response orature—for example, in the words of the capoeira angola song "Ê Paraná":

Ê Paraná
Eu não vou na sua casa, Paraná
Ê Paraná
Pra você não ir na minha, Paraná
Ê Paraná
Porque você tem boca grande, Paraná
Ê Paraná
Vai comer minha galinha, Paraná
Ê Paraná
Puxa, puxa, leva, leva, Paraná
Ê Paraná

Paraná está me chamando, Paraná

. . .

The song excerpt translates[17] to English (Harrell 2005) roughly as

Eh, Paraná
I do not go in your house, Paraná
Eh, Paraná
For you go not in mine, Paraná
Eh, Paraná
Because you have a great mouth, Paraná
Eh, Paraná
You will eat my chicken, Paraná
Eh, Paraná
Pull, pull, take, take, Paraná
Eh, Paraná
Paraná is calling me, Paraná

. . .

The repeated invocation of a historic place[18] is a common theme in call-and-response lyrics. As just discussed, when these songs are sung, new lyrics are often spontaneously improvised. The creation of traditionally structured songs with new meanings, especially layered meanings, as in capoeira songs (the songs often have double and triple functions within the art form) also serves to create new identities for postcolonial contexts. The example output from *The Girl with Skin of Haints and Seraphs* was enabled by GRIOT's support of precisely this type of emergent content via participation in its call-and-response structure. GRIOT's implementation of a call-and-response structure in a computational system is an example of a metamedial characteristic of an integrative cultural system.

Computational Cultural Content

In the previous subsection, the example poem illustrated use of GRIOT to implement polymorphic poems in the service of social commentary. In this case, the use was to critique narrow reliance upon power relationships of binary opposition in racial identity politics (e.g., in stereotypical or outmoded oppositions such as male versus female, black versus white, Oriental versus Occidental (Harrell 2008). Similarly, Joseph Goguen used GRIOT to author a polymorphic version of his poem "November

Qualia" (used in the performance of *The Griot Sings Haibun*) to describe moments of qualitative experience from a Buddhist perspective (Goguen 2005a, 2005b). Sample output from this polymorphic poem is (see figure 6.3 for the graphical output):

```
qualia are moments of luminous world,
empty, suffering, compassion
mind body snapshots

neither arising, departing, or dwelling
gone beyond
gone far beyond

6:41 am
mind cloud ocean
unmoved moving trees
connecting blue high, blue emptiness flesh
forever being sky
timeless, perfected tender self

6:53 am
the pipes:
connecting, pipes of compassion
vivid bolted
shining, empty
neither atomic nor not
always connecting
timeless, perfected
beyond being beyond

7:26 pm
save us from fear, wanting
addict & moonlight, wanting & timeless forgotten
bright grasping fear
vultures of mind, forever circling
embracing transient form
ecstatic revulsion, wanting
```

```
1:47 am
translucent flesh, tender, inscrutable
unending mother ocean
biomass being, vital & vivid

all connected, empty, void
burning mind & self
ecstatic tender burning void
```

In both *The Girl with Skin of Haints and Seraphs* and the polymorphic version of "November Qualia" used in *The Griot Sings Haibun*, particular worldviews provide the impetus for the expressive statement being made.

Both polymorphic poems allude to specific cultural philosophies, yet the production of each polymorphic poem was enabled by the medium in which it was created. Emphasizing culturally grounded subject matter, regardless of medium, is an example of deploying an integrative cultural system. The works built using GRIOT deploy particular cultural forms (such as prose poetry or haibun poetry), are informed by cultural worldviews (such as African American or Tibetan Buddhist perspectives), and the authors' statements about these works foreground the ways in which their works are culturally rooted. The simple act of foregrounding such cultural foundations is uncommon within current computing practices. Yet the fact that it has been done with GRIOT provides a useful example because underlying cultural values have had a strong impact upon the research and development of the system.

Furthermore, the polymorphic poems implemented with GRIOT have most often been presented via performance. In *Second Person*, editors Pat Harrigan and Noah Wardrip-Fruin refer to GRIOT-based works as being within the category of performances that "take place in both the digital and real worlds" (Harrigan and Wardrip-Fruin 2007, 108). A notable case of this was an implementation of the polymorphic poem *The Griot Sings Haibun*, which was performed live in collective improvisation with free jazz musicians (Goguen and Harrell 2005; Harrell 2007b). During the performance, the GUI was projected onto a large screen behind the performers for the audience to see and was mirrored on a plasma screen facing the performers so that the musicians and orator could see it. I acted as a polymorphic poem *performer*, improvisationally selecting themes from which to generate text output from the "November Qualia" polymorphic poem and selecting corresponding visual imagery based on what the musicians played. The musicians could also respond improvisationally to the text and images on the plasma screen. In this sense, the performance was a collective improvisation.

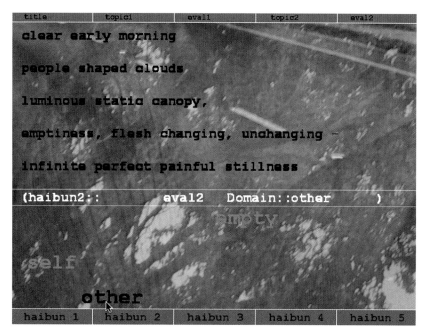

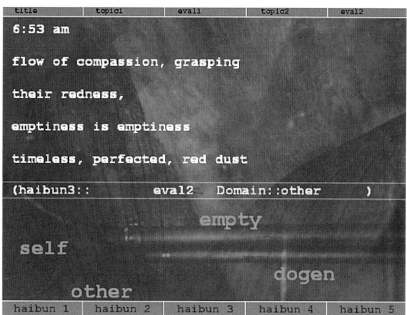

FIGURE 6.3
Two screenshots from *The Griot Sings Haibun* reveal different compositions of text and images displayed during performance.

When using the GUI for *The Griot Sings Haibun* during the performance, the system performer selected the desired clause type using buttons arranged in a row at the top of the screen and then selected a clause by clicking on one of the keywords (e.g., `self`, `empty`, or `other`) on the bottom third of the screen to use one of the particular epistemologies related to Goguen's Buddhist themes of self, other, emptiness, and related concepts. At various times, clauses of only particular types would appear on the screen and would be regenerated on the fly. Thus, because clauses could be chosen and displayed in any order and not just the order determined by the narrative/poetic structure prespecified by the polymorphic poems author, the discourse structure was more dynamic and variable during performance than when using the pure LISP interface.[19] Several examples of haibun poetry were implemented, and buttons along the bottom of the screen allowed the performer to shift from one haibun polymorphic poem to another. These selections also governed the background images.

Such a performance consolidates many of the characteristics of orature presented by Ngugi. The performance took place in a particular architectural environment (on stage), with performers arranged in a circle (including a large screen for feedback to the musicians). The lighting was controlled in order to focus audience attention on different performers at different times. The performance featured real-time generation of output from the polymorphic poem. The timing of particular utterances and musical phrases was orchestrated by the collective improvisation of the group. The rhythm of the polymorphic poem was constructed improvisationally as well, generating lines at a pace determined by feedback from the orator, musicians, and perceived audience response. Finally, the projected backdrop served as a type of performative mise-en-scène in Ngugi's sense. All of these aspects of the performance reflect a concern for the performance conditions of architectural space, time frame, performer-audience relationship, and mise-en-scène. Preserving all of these aspects of oral performance in a computational system is a metamedial characteristic of GRIOT as an integrative cultural system.

Troublesome Phantasms and Further Reflections

In the previous discussion, I stated that new expressive and technical possibilities for computing can be rooted in diverse cultural values and practices. This concept is not new to computing; indeed, computational artifacts are found all over the world. However, computer science research typically leaves its cultural values implicit. When they are made explicit, they typically reflect a privileged value system within

"Western" civilization such as the rationalist tradition so well described by Winograd and Flores (Winograd and Flores 1986). The concept of trans-African orature provides one frame for interpreting the aims and outcomes of the GRIOT system, the cultural value that its architecture exemplifies, and the performative deployment of expressive works created with it.

In constructing this argument, I have tried to anticipate a wide range of potential critical feedback based in a set of heinous and haunting social constructs. I am haunted by ghosts of an essentializing "African primitiveness" exemplified by the "savage mind" critiqued by Mudimbe in the earlier Eglash quotation. I am haunted by the linguistic determinism in the binary view of culture put forth by Ong and others; those views can also be used to stereotype and demean entire cultures as primitive. Furthermore, I have risked criticism for making generalizations about African culture because I have accepted the idea of *explicitly shared* cultural systems (knowledgably invoking cultural phantasms) while rejecting essentialist perspectives that focus on *innate* characteristic of individuals or groups as the sole bases for cultural forms of expression. I recognize that I may be subject to the critique that my own cultural identity is too intertwined with my technical practice, but, as I have argued, all the technical practices that are often viewed as objective are imbued with a cultural basis that is invisible to those who are embedded in it. My cultural values are visible largely because they are not in alignment with the cultural values that are commonly accepted as the foundation of discourse in computing theory and technical practice. Yet the degree to which these criticisms could make it hard for unsympathetic readers to receive the core argument of this chapter is the degree to which the chapter may have succeeded in its aim to provoke and stimulate the fields to which it is addressed. I have attempted to construct a careful argument for the value of making cultural concerns explicit in computing practice. Furthermore, using the case of trans-African orature as an example, I argued that analytical and productive gains have been made.

Reflections on Integrative Cultural Systems

Diverse cultures can inspire innovation in both creative forms and technical insights. When developing computational integrative cultural systems, we want to reemphasize that the design of algorithmic and data structural components always stand in service of some cultural goals and values. Developing effective cultural computing systems depends on addressing the goals and values exhibited by the system at hand. To make this point, I shall contrast the quite distinct aims of two influential researchers in different areas: computer scientist Ben Shneiderman and scholar, composer, programmer, and musician George Lewis. The contrast between the examples will be used to highlight the usefulness of the concept of the integrative cultural system. As a user-interface design expert, Ben Shneiderman writes, "Successful technology developments will come from those who recognize the importance of tools and social systems that support human goals, control, and responsibility. Users want the sense of mastery and accomplishment that comes from using a tool to accomplish their goals" (Shneiderman 2002, 237).

Shneiderman strongly warns against the goals of most artificial intelligence practitioners and the potential sacrifice of human empowerment for the sake of automating traditionally human tasks. Empowering human users is the core value for Shneiderman. In his intentionally lofty, far-reaching concluding chapter, he bravely lauds the nobility of building computers with such goals, stating:

> There are higher human values that we must aspire to serve. We can pursue environmental quality and quality of life. We can strive to resolve conflicts and promote peace.
>
> Responding to these grand concerns may seem to be beyond the scope of users and technology developers, but I believe that you can attain them by focusing on specific and measurable goals such as the following:
>
> >Increase life expectancy
> >Control population growth.
> >Reduce homelessness.
> >Reduce illiteracy worldwide.
> >Reduce automobile accident deaths.
> >Increase air quality in major cities.
> >Reduce the threat of war. (Shneiderman 2002, 239)

In contrast to Shneiderman's anti-AI stance, when describing his interactive computer music system, theorist and musician George Lewis does not mind ceding control to the software: "Voyager functions as an extreme example of a "player" program, where the computer system does not function as an instrument to be controlled by a performer. I conceive a performance of Voyager as multiple parallel streams of music generation, emanating from both the computers and the humans— a nonhierarchical, improvisational, subject-subject model of discourse, rather than a stimulus/response setup" (Lewis 2000, 34). Lewis describes the style and function of his system as rooted in an African American aesthetic of "multidominance," citing painter Robert L. Douglas's trans-African notion indicating "the multiple use of colors in intense degrees, or the multiple use of textures, design patterns, or shapes" (Lewis 2000, 33). Multidominance is at odds with the need for user control, with Lewis attributing further ideological import to his stance:

> Voyager's aesthetic of variation and difference is at variance with the information retrieval and control paradigm that late capitalism has found useful in framing its preferred approach to the encounter with computer technology. As I have observed elsewhere, interactivity has gradually become a metonym for information retrieval rather than dialogue, posing the danger of commodifying and ultimately reifying the encounter with technology:
>
> > Indeed, the rapid development of standardized modes for the relationships between humans and computers is unfortunate for such a young and presumably quickly changing technology. The evolution of the language used to reflect the multimedia revolution is a compelling testament to the power of corporate media. Corporate power assumes an important, even dominating role in conditioning our thinking about computers, art, image, and sound. Much of the descriptive language surrounding multimedia (and related areas, such as "cyberspace") serves to hide the power exercised by corporations. (Lewis 1995)
>
> (Lewis 2000, 36)

Both Shneiderman and Lewis put forth humanistic views of technology use concerned with the empowerment of individuals and communities, though their views may seem at odds regarding issues of automation and control. The key here is culture. Lewis reminds us that technologies based on cultural systems other than those that currently dominate computer science may help avoid some of the dangers of human disempowerment that Shneiderman warns of. Juxtaposing the two researchers' views results in a parable, the story goes that different people have different perspectives about the utility and aesthetics of user control. Some feel so strongly that they even make grand cultural proclamations about what are good or bad users of the computer. Yet, regardless of who is right, either perspective can be better understood when viewed as an expression of a computational integrative cultural system. The final point, which I cannot resist repeating once more, is that a systematic and clarifying approach to making cultural foundations of phantasmal media explicit is necessary and could help further push the aims of this book: diversifying the range of expressive computing practices.

IV

CRITICAL COMPUTING

I have already argued for the power of computers to have an impact on individuals and discussed ways in which that power can be shaped by cultural phantasms. It is clear that computing technologies are often seen as utilitarian tools for doing work (Suchman 1983) and are also sometimes seen as media for entertainment or art (Murray 1997). We have even seen, as in the case of robots and software agents, that computing technologies can be used as human companions (Turkle 2004). However, it is less common to see computing technologies as expressions of human values regardless of how they are used. Part IV of this book helps better understand and design the values built into computing systems. It also helps show how those values affect human societies and how those values can specifically affect society through empowering people. *Critical computing* refers to the analysis and design of computing systems while considering the values they express and their potential to catalyze social awareness and empower people.

Computing technologies have an impact on our societies by the ways in which they operate in conjunction with human bodies, involve multiple people and systems, and affect particular situations. Ranging from collision-detection technologies in aircraft to networking technologies that allow geographically remote musicians to jam together across continents, computing technologies influence our embodied behaviors, distributed communications, and situated activities. It is important to critically examine how the structures of computing systems express values while prompting phantasms that affect societies that use those systems. Such accounts can help design systems to better serve the needs and values of their users. The concept of critical computing can help technologists move beyond the development of utilitarian and productivity-oriented applications without consideration of social values.

The values built into the structures of computer systems can serve to either empower or disempower people. The same technologies that allow one to chat with a loved one across an ocean in a different country, or that customize a user interface based on where one lives, can be used for illegal surveillance and restriction of privacy. The same technologies that can be used for educational training or artful entertainment can be used for online bullying or training soldiers. These technologies can influence people's self-conceptions, sociocultural configurations, and even international relationships. The critical computing concept helps us move beyond acceptance of computing technologies that may disempower people and serve to perpetuate social ills.

In addition to integrating humanities and arts-based approaches to critical engagement with society and the world with computer science and engineering practices, the critical computing approach more broadly calls for heeding useful insights emerging from people in groups that are disproportionately underrepresented in current computer science and related fields. These groups include people from many cultural or ethnic categories, economically under-resourced communities, and women. Such insights can help shed light on the ways in which technologies play roles in perpetuating social inequity as well as the ways in which technologies can combat inequity. Ralph Ellison's novel *Invisible Man*, which provides the epigraph to chapter 1, is one of the most compelling sociological and poetic treatises on the social invisibility of stigmatized groups, capturing both subjective experiences and institutional practices of discrimination (Ellison [1947] 1995). For example, an account of institutionalized discrimination can help developers avoid building such values into the structures of computing systems, an eventuality illustrated by Brawn's Seller Representation and some recommender systems discussed earlier.

Such insights can also offer strategies for how technologies can be used to empower people more generally. For example, we saw in chapter 3 that the artist and philosopher Adrian Piper has developed strategies related to her experience of the phenomenon called *passing* (being seen as a member of a social group, while actually being seen as—by oneself or one's society—a member of another) to expose ignorance and bigotry (Piper 1999). Passing as a member of another group, both intentional and inadvertent, and experiences of ignorance and bigotry are common phenomena in online games and social networks. Unfair stigmatization, marginalization, passing, and ignorance about others are common phenomena explored by artists and thinkers such as Ellison and Piper that also have broad applicability to other social categories as broad as immigrants or even the working class. For the purposes here, insights such as theirs can provide foundations for thinking about such phenomena in computing systems in terms of both subjective human experience and social impact.

Chapter 7 addresses ways to make interaction between users and computing systems meaningful. The chapter argues that in order to better understand and design critical computing systems, we should take into account both users' subjective experiences of the effects of their interactions and users' social and cultural situations. Building on this argument, the chapter presents the concept of *agency play*. Agency play is a model that serves to explain how user agency (enabled by a computer system used in particular situations) works in conjunction with system agency (as interpreted by users in particular contexts). Furthermore, the concept of agency play acknowledges the concept of a user's broader agency within social structures. Chapter 7 argues that *agency play* can guide development of systems that can dynamically change a user's agency to interact with the system for both expressive aims and critically engaged aims related to issues such as understanding both self and society.

Chapter 8 offers specific ways to address these issues by introducing the concept of *critical-computational empowerment*. The chapter begins by showing how the combination of shared mental images and ideology that I have called cultural phantasms play a role in defining social phenomena that can oppress or empower people at the individual, sociocultural, or state (i.e., political, corporate, or military) levels. Chapter 8 helps show how computing systems connect to the real world by articulating the specific technical ways in which computing systems acquire information that refers to society and culture. Chapter 8 then goes on to show how each of the concepts highlighted in the previous chapters can be used for the critical computing aims of social analysis and empowerment.

Critical computing is a socially oriented approach to computing with the ultimate aim of empowering of people. These ideas represent my specific conception of critical computing, which is not the only approach to it. Rather, the ideas of chapters 7 and 8 are offered for researchers and practitioners to take up only to the degree that the concepts support understanding and making ethically sound subjective, cultural computing systems. The ideas can be applied informally or with careful precision to analysis, design, and implementation. The only hope is the ideas in part IV of this book help in the realization of critical computing systems that improve the human condition through a play of agency and empowerment.

7

AGENCY PLAY

In the worldview of utopian navigation, the computer is seen as a value-free conduit, an executor of user agency. Even the use of the word "navigation" is telling—it moves the focus onto the user's movement in some data space and away from the system's active manipulation of that data. The computer is seen as pure communication device, pure medium. Of course in this post-McLuhan age it is considered a given that a medium is not a passive pipe, but rather the active messenger of a worldview.

—Steffi Domike, Michael Mateas, and Paul Vanouse, *The Recombinant History Apparatus Presents: Terminal Time*

You are a young warrior in a sparse landscape. In order to revive your loved one, you must slay towering mythical behemoths, one after another. After scaling a colossus and plunging a sword into its vulnerable point, the giant drops to its knees in melancholy slow motion. You run, jumping this way and that, trying to avoid the veins of energy rising from its body to seek you out. Inevitably, they pierce you and the world turns black . . .

This brief tale of a young warrior's plight describes a segment of play from the videogame *Shadow of the Colossus* (see figure 7.1). Because the scene's ending is predetermined, some may wonder why the game allows the player to perform actions immediately after slaying the monster. Many games would use a noninteractive cutscene instead. Yet allowing the player to move despite being unable to change the

FIGURE 7.1
Veins of energy ravage the player character Wander after defeating giant creatures as shown in this image from the game *Shadow of the Colossus*.

outcome is an effective design choice. It increases the sense of hopeless fate. The segment is an example in which allowing the user only limited interactivity evokes a subjective feeling. Interactivity is skillfully used as an artistic tool—a phantasm conveying the feeling of futility is prompted.

Interactivity is often seen as one of the hallmarks of computational media, but many theorists are cautious about overusing the term because it has become associated with particular limited interaction mechanisms and their results. Examples of such mechanisms and their results include clicking buttons on a controller to select a segment of text to edit or making a selection from a menu on a computer screen in order to open a software application. Such types of interaction may indeed be uniquely computational, though they are not inherently imbued with rich expressive meaning; they may be more akin to choosing a page to turn to in a book than to intellectually engaging with the imaginative world of a book. Yet subjective computing systems such as games are often described as interactive as well. In such systems, the computer allows users to interact *within and upon* imaginative worlds. Rather than focusing on particular mechanisms for interacting with computers, this chapter focuses on expressive uses of agency. That is, I shall explore how the types of interaction within and upon computer-based imaginative worlds and poetic cultural productions produce and reveal meaningful phantasms.

I prefer focusing on the term "agency" rather than "interactivity." There are two reasons for this preference. One type of "agency" can be described as people having the power to perform meaningful interactions within the world (a popular understanding of agency). Another type of "agency" can be described as users having the power to affect the operation of computer systems (a computational media theory understanding of agency). This dual understanding of agency is important, because the approach taken here is to look at computational agency as based in using the second type of agency to achieve the first. This approach allows us to focus on how people interact with computer-based phantasms in ways that are meaningful and impactful in the broader world, in contrast to a dangerous type of phantasm in which agency of the second type stands in for agency of the first type. In such cases, self-determination in the imaginative world of a subjective computing system, such as a computer game, can *suppress* the urge toward self-determination in the world outside of that game. Imagine: in a computer game, a player could learn to engage in conversation with computer-generated characters of other cultures or even lead a civilization to overthrow tyrannical rule in the game world, while in the real world the player leads a sedentary, consumerist life uninterested in cross-cultural communication or social changes occurring at large. Constructing systems that prompt phantasms in which computational agency leads to empowerment, and/or in which computational agency expressively reveals phantasms that lead to oppression, is key to the type of agency ultimately endorsed in this chapter. This chapter describes how authors can implement a range of types of agency based in computational media. Creative and critically engaged deployment of a range of types of agency is what I shall call "agency play," which is the central concept introduced in this chapter.

Agency play emphasizes that agency is best understood through looking at the interaction between user agency and system agency. First, it is important to consider the full range of possible user actions, noting that it may not be possible to name and list all possible actions. Second, it is important to consider effects that user actions have on content and how content is presented. Third, it is important to consider the system's capacity to modify content and presentation of content. Finally, it is important to consider how system agency can support engagement with content in ways that influence users' relationships with cultural phantasms and their societies. Both the user and the system need to be taken into account as part of our discussion of agency. The interplay between these four important points relating the concepts of user agency and system agency to one another provides a starting point for systematically describing new possibilities for creatively deploying agency in subjective computing systems.

In media forms such as the novel, a certain type of user agency has often been considered a novelty. Works such as Vladimir Nabokov's novel *Pale Fire* or Raymond Cortázar's *Rayuela* (*Hopscotch* in English) have been influential in that users are given instructions to read these books that involve jumping between sections, but those works have been seen as singular creations (Nabokov 1962; Cortázar 1966). A type of system agency based on using rule systems to structure the production of literary works also has been largely a niche interest. The experimental writing group Oulipo is perhaps the most notable community of practice engaged in producing literary works built using various mathematical rules (Mathews and Brotchie 1998). However, many features of works in noncomputational media that invoke user and system agency have been incorporated into subjective computing systems such as the point-and-click adventure games of the 1980s or the hypertext fiction of the 1990s. Such works offered users stories in which they could become a character and traverse multiple paths through the story. Full player agency became a type of Holy Grail in the construction of subjective computing works. However, the field has matured beyond that stage, and the deployment of particular types of user and system agency is now a stylistic choice carefully manipulated over the course of a user's experience to facilitate the goals of subjective computing system designers.

The area of interactive narrative[1] research provides an excellent example to highlight potential for new directions in creating systems that use agency. Interactive narrative researchers most often attempt to develop systems that tell effective stories in computer-based imaginative worlds. Researchers Ruth Aylett and Sandy Louchart have introduced the term "narrative paradox" to describe an opposition between the user's free will to move and interact with objects and the system's capacity to provide the user with a well-structured narrative experience (Aylett and Louchart 2003; Louchart and Aylett 2003). Many researchers seek to provide techniques to balance the two sides of this paradox (Cavazza, Charles, and Mead 2001; Young 2007). Indeed, some research takes this perspective to the extreme, viewing the user's free will as existing in an adversarial relationship to the system's operation.[2]

Despite being potentially useful for building certain types of interactive narrative imaginative worlds, this view does not hold for projects with different aims. A problem for those seeking to build other types of computer-based imaginative worlds, narrative or otherwise, is that this "narrative paradox" perspective is rooted in a vision of only one particular type of agency. It is a vision of building imaginative worlds in which users can move through space and interact with characters and objects as a means of taking part in a compelling story. In contrast, user agency can allow for other effects such as varying the *telling* of a story (for example, using a different narrative voice or providing different levels of detail in the exposition) rather than plot. User agency can be judiciously scaled back or augmented. User agency can change over time.

Subjective computing *systems* also exhibit a type of agency. Systems can take over control from users and act autonomously. Systems can prompt phantasms conveying a lack of agency by restricting users' options, which might, in turn, engender critical reflection by users about their agency outside of using the system. As these examples are meant to suggest, the concept of agency play, to be described in detail later in this chapter, expands the notion of agency as it applies to critical computing.

The rest of the chapter provides an expanded discussion of agency and a detailed definition of the concept of agency play. Several subsections recap a range of approaches to agency. The first of these subsections introduces what I have called a situated approach to agency (Harrell and Zhu 2009). By "situated," I mean that user agency must be understood as situated in the particular actions of a subjective computing system's user. For example, an author may deprioritize agency along some dimensions of control such as moving a player character through space in favor of offering agency in determining plot outcomes.

The approaches to agency in the other subsections provide different perspective on the relationships between people and systems. Aside from the agency as free will approach, the approaches summarized are quite different than typical computational media–oriented definitions of agency that focus on interaction with the computer itself. Instead, the other approaches surveyed focus on issues such as power relationships and agency within society, culminating with a discussion of how situated agency can be used for expression. Sections on user agency and system agency follow, emphasizing in particular how the two notions rely upon each other. The following section articulates the agency play construct in detail. Agency play is defined in detail as a set of dimensions along which user and system agency interact with one another. Finally, the chapter relates the concepts of agency play to the broader notion of improvisation in the arts.

A Situated Approach to Agency

Long before being explored in computational media theory, articulating the concept of agency has been a central challenge in diverse areas, including philosophy, anthropology, political activism, and critical cultural theory. The focus here is on providing constructs that allow us to scrutinize user agency in relation to the computational technologies that are used to enable interaction.

There are several precursors that describe a difference between the agency of humans and the agency of systems. The work of Andrew Pickering in the sociology of scientific knowledge is a useful departure point because it makes a distinction between human and material agency. For Pickering, humans have agency and materials also have agency. Pickering describes a "dance" between humans and other materials. He focuses upon a type of human agency consisting of knowledge of how to perform manipulations in a particular conceptual system, such as how to perform elementary algebra manipulations (Pickering 1995). Similarly, Michel Callon and Bruno Latour's actor-network theory is an influence on the concept of agency play because it incorporates both human and nonhuman actors (Callon 1986; Latour 2005). Offering a more fine-grained account of different types of agency, Laura M. Ahearn identifies three major trends in conceptualizing agency over the past few decades: the concepts of "agency as free will," "equating agency with resistance," and "the absence of agency" (Ahearn 2001). At the end of this section, an approach to agency is proposed that is situated in particular cultural contexts and lends itself to a range of expressive applications in subjective computing works.

A Dance of Agency

Andrew Pickering focuses on a duality that he describes as existing between "human agency" and "material agency" (Pickering 1995). Human agency centers upon intentionality and actions taken by humans upon the world. In particular, Pickering is interested in the types of agency exhibited by scientists in the practice of knowledge production. He describes a notion of human disciplinary agency that consists of recognizing and knowing how to use/perform "a series of manipulations within an established conceptual system" (115). Pickering also describes a contrasting notion of "material agency" as the idea that the world is "continually doing things, things that bear upon us not as disembodied intellects but as forces upon material beings" (6). It is a view that sees science as an array of forces that humans typically apprehend through the use of machines. Pickering defines a "dance of agency" as the process whereby humans attempt to apprehend the agency of the material world through the mediation of artifacts and that material world both yields to, and resists, human apprehension. Despite his focus on agency in scientific practice rather than computational media, Pickering's notion that there are symmetrical notions of human and material agency engaged in a dialectical dance parallels the constructs of human agency and system agency as described in this chapter.

Actor-Network Theory

Another useful perspective on the interacting agencies of humans and systems is provided by the sociological approach called actor-network theory, which was initiated by Bruno Latour and Michel Callon (Latour 2005). Actor-network theory is used to examine networks of elements such as people, organizations, and machines involved in the production of technology. Actor-network theory does not distinguish between "human" and "nonhuman" actors for most purposes and uses the term "actant" to reflect this lack of bias. This absence of distinction between humans and machines, though perhaps exaggerated for rhetorical impact, supports our idea that systems are not objective and the further idea that systems have values. The values built into systems can prompt phantasms that affect users in ways that can be empowering, discriminatory, stigmatizing, marginalizing, democratizing, and more. However, as Joseph Goguen observed in reflecting upon the work of Latour, it is the human actants in a network who must perform acts of interpretation, which are, in effect, theories of a system's functioning (Goguen 2003). Understanding a parallel between the user agency enabled by the machine and the system agency interpreted by humans is key to understanding role of agency in critical computing works.

Agency as Free Will

The prevailing approach to user agency in computational media treats the term "agency" as synonymous with users' free will. A straightforward example of such treatment of agency occurs in the rhetoric of free spatial navigation, as in "you can go anywhere you want!" Subjective computing system designers holding this perspective seek to allow users free will in exploring computer-based imaginative worlds such as virtual worlds, interactive narratives, and games. In this example, the operating premise is that users should not be bound to visiting locations in an order predefined by the author. In describing such environments, critics often describe possibilities of spatial exploration and object manipulation as primary constituents of user agency. Literary theorist Marie-Laure Ryan calls this conception of agency "internal-exploratory interactivity" and describes these as systems in which "the user exercises her agency by moving around the fictional world, picking up objects and looking at them, viewing the action from different points of view, investigating a case, and trying to reconstitute events that have taken place a long time ago" (Ryan 2001).

Ahearn reminds us that the agency to take actions and observe their results requires certain concomitant mental states, such as "intention" (Davidson 2001) and "presence of the self" (Segal 1991). As philosopher Jerome Segal puts it, "Hitting a ball is an action, falling down a flight of stairs is not. A theory of action seeks, among other things, to explain the distinctions we make" (Segal 1991, 3).

Taken together, skillful uses of increasingly powerful hardware, more robustly interactive software, and a maturing array of conventions of use have allowed designers to enable users' decisions to produce striking effects within imaginative computer-based worlds. For example, in the computer game *Star Wars: Knights of the Old Republic*, the way a player controls a character through the story determines several different outcomes. Players have agency to affect a character's moral disposition (whether it aligns with the light or dark side of the Force), the set of new skills the character can learn, and which branches of the storyline will be taken.

However, an unchecked focus on free will may lead to unanticipated, and largely undesirable (though perhaps also transgressive), consequences. In massively multiplayer online (MMO) role-playing games, grief players (also called "griefers") perform actions not to advance game goals or for narratively oriented fulfillment but to intentionally aggravate and harass other players. They kill other players' characters, steal weapons and coins, and even form virtual mafias, all in the pursuit of their own enjoyment and free will conception of "agency."

The example of griefers echoes Ahearn's warning to us. "The main weakness in treating agency as a synonym for free will," she argues, "is that such an approach ignores or only gives lip service to the social nature of agency and the pervasive influence of culture on human intentions, beliefs, and actions" (Ahearn 2001, 114). When adopted in the domain of critical computing, this pitfall often transforms into the overamplification of users' freedom to act however they want, while overlooking the importance of meaningful constraints as they relate to the system's content.

Agency as Resistance

The notion of "agency as resistance" characterizes many works in feminist theory and subaltern studies in which traditions of social resistance of the past and present are called into attention. Some feminist theorists assert that in order to demonstrate agency, a person must resist, perform against, and restructure the hegemonic patriarchal status quo (Abu-Lughod 1990; Butler 1990; Haraway 1991). This resistance is an example of a form of oppositional agency that has gradually been adopted by

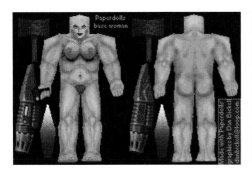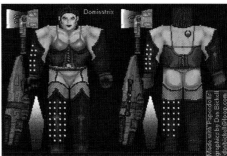

FIGURE 7.2
Images of skins from Sonya Roberts's transgressive "Female Skin Pack Excerpts" are shown here.

some users/artists/hackers of computer-based imaginative worlds. In 1999, for example, Sonya Roberts released "Female Skin Pack Excerpts" (Roberts 1997), a series of female texture maps for the avatars in the game *Quake* because the game designers had neglected to provide any female protagonists (see figure 7.2).

The resultant composition of a female skin on a cartoony muscular male figure, which challenges social norms for body type, prompts a phantasm in the form of the reconfigured player character, while revealing the phantasm in which a gender-biased worldview is implicit in the previously male-only character options. This phantasm prompting and revealing process is a form of resistance to power.

Oppositional agency also finds its way through the voices of protesters in virtual environments, a rich topic for ethnographic exploration (Boellstorff et al. 2012). Users of the virtual world *Second Life* have successfully pressed the system's developer, Linden Labs, to alter the regulations of the Internet-based 3D virtual world in various cases. This resistance was perhaps demonstrated most prominently by two events in 2003: a virtual tax revolt and a protest to allow people to retain IP rights. It is useful to include such notions of agency because they relate user action to broader social, political, and cultural contexts both within and outside of the imaginative worlds of particular subjective computing systems.

Absence of Agency

Another approach to agency is articulated by Michel Foucault's work on power (Foucault 1977, 1978). An extreme reading of Foucault is that omnipresent impersonal discourses so thoroughly pervade society that no room is left for anything that might be regarded as agency, oppositional or otherwise (Ahearn 2001). After playing some games produced by the company Persuasive Games, such as *Disaffected!* and *Airport Insecurity*, it is difficult to not question the existence of agency, both inside the games and out. In these games, a user is pushed to accomplish tasks related to pervasive commercial bureaucracy and protocol, such as standing in line at an airport or fulfilling customer orders in a copy shop, echoing real-life experience. Yet game mechanics are diabolically constructed to thwart the user's aims and the ostensible goals of the game, evoking a sense of the absence of agency both in the game world and in life at large (Bogost 2007). Indeed, game studies scholar Jesper Juul reminds us that failure can be central to game design (Juul 2013). The game renders lack of agency into a palpable phantasm through its consternation-inducing game mechanics.

Situated Agency as an Expressive Tool for Subjective Computing System Design

In light of the discussion thus far, it is important to develop a notion of agency that reconciles the valuable insights provided by these various perspectives on agency. Any unilateral definition of agency is inadequate. As Ahearn proposes, agency refers to the socioculturally mediated capacity to act. In subjective computing environments, a user's agency to perform meaningful actions is mediated through the interaction mechanisms provided by the computational system (Ahearn 2001). At the same time, the user's agency is also mediated by the user's interpretation of his or her actions. A system's capacity to enable actions, impose constraints on actions, and reward or penalize behaviors clearly has great impact on a user's agency. Even though subjective computing systems such as games are often accompanied by strong rhetoric that a player can do anything they like, their game mechanics shape the player's sense of agency. Thus systems such as games implement value systems that determine which actions can be performed, which actions have impact, and why. In turn, these implemented value systems may reinforce or allow for critique of social and cultural structures outside of the game that are evoked by the content of the game. The fact that subjective computing system interaction mechanisms are always related to values outside of the game means that agency is always *situated* in broader society and its cultural phantasms. To say it another way: user agency is situated materially in the mechanisms for user action within computing systems and interpretively in the context of phantasms prompted by use of those mechanisms. The use of agency is one of the means that subjective computing systems authors have to express themselves.

User Agency

Subjective computing systems afford more active roles for users than art forms such as novels or narrative paintings in various ways. Recall that Janet Murray has claimed that increased user agency is a foundational property of computational media (Murray 1997). Just a few examples of user agency are spatial navigation, problem solving, incorporating gameplay actions within narratives, and traversing links in hypertext stories. Murray's theory has influenced many practitioners who set out to explore new expressive possibilities brought by computational media in which agency plays an important part. However, many attempts have been based on the overly simplistic understanding of "agency as free will" mentioned previously (Ahearn 2001).

Computer and console games are subjective computing systems that have entered the popular consciousness; as such, they provide good examples for discussing user agency. In many games, a sense of free will is often conveyed to the user by means of enabling the user to move a character through space and interact with objects in the game world. Understanding agency as this limited type of free will has often led to an obsession with the idea that "the more agency, the better." This phenomenon is exemplified in notions such as "full reactive eyes entertainment" or F.R.E.E., a concept proposed by game designer Yu Suzuki during the development and marketing of the remarkable game *Shenmue* and its sequel *Shenmue II*, which aspired to allow a character to freely interact with many aspects of his environment such as soda machines, videogame arcade systems, and toy dispensers, as shown in figure 7.3.

FIGURE 7.3
In the games *Shenmue* and *Shenmue II*, the player character can interact with objects such as arcade games or toy dispensers.

Yet despite the high degree of free will to interact with objects in such a game, the slow pacing of its plot was consistently viewed by some players as a detraction from the game, with the high degree of freedom perhaps detracting from meaningful narrative development.

Offering the user a sense of free will in an imaginary world is not the only possible goal. Authors could instead build systems that vary user agency over time to evoke a range of experiences. Instead of granting the user control only over a character's physical actions, he or she might be granted control only over the character's mood. Yet another system might grant a user control only over whose perspective a story is told from. Even more radically, a user might be granted control over whether meaning is conveyed through linear storytelling or through more surreal metaphorical poetry. Subjective computing works should grant user agency along whatever dimension helps convey the meaning of the work most effectively.

One interesting expressive strategy, shown in the *Shadow of the Colossus* example that started this chapter, is to limit or even temporarily eliminate user agency to convey a certain theme such as the sense of confinement or helplessness. Such a strategy can be understood better now in light of the earlier discussion. It could be seen as risky by game developers because the lack of agency as free will in game designs has been traditionally associated with computational simplicity. The use of cut-scenes in videogames is a good example. For decades, the game industry has incorporated cut-scenes in which user agency is temporarily suspended. Although scholars have pointed out the narrative utility of noninteractive cut-scenes—such as to advance plot, introduce characters, and even allow the player a bit of a rest (Juul 2001)—recent trends encourage designers to incorporate player interaction within such scenes. One example is the introduction sequence of the game *Fallout 3*, in which, as your player character is born and grows into a toddler, adolescent, and young adult, you must choose a name, gender, and appearance in addition to interacting with people and objects in the environment. The expressive power of critical computing systems lies in communicating meaningful ideas, not in mechanical interaction. As will be argued later, computational techniques can be used to tune user agency according to the expressive needs of the critical computing system.

System Agency

System agency is defined as the capacity of the computer to modify content (data) and to enable users' actions. However, it is important to understand that system agency exists only in conjunction with humans who make sense of the system's actions. Of course computers perform actions, yet that enactment alone does not constitute agency—agency arises from meaningful enactment. Thus system agency is a phantasm prompted when an epistemic space drawn from an epistemic domain attributing meaning to system behavior is integrated with sensory experience of system operation. Computers express their agency, in this phantasmal sense, through procedural rules. The underlying rules of subjective computing systems determine how the systems function. These rules range from simply timing the presentation of text such as in the text animation "The Sea" by Young-Hae Chang Heavy Industries (Young-Hae Chang Heavy Industries 2008) to controlling AI-based characters such as in Michael Mateas's and Andrew Stern's interactive drama *Façade* (Mateas 2002). Screenshots of both works are shown in figure 7.4.

The notion of system agency is related to the discourse accompanying classic AI goals of building autonomous intelligent programs exhibiting humanlike behaviors.

FIGURE 7.4
Rules in the web-based text animation "The Sea" carefully coordinate textual changes with music (above); rules in the interactive drama system *Facade* coordinate multiple AI characters in dialogue with the player character (below).

The term "system agency" as I use it does not imply, however, that a goal driving my framework for subjective computing is the dream of full system autonomy. *System agency is a result of human interpretation in light of a set of situated social circumstances.* System agency is not a property intrinsic to the computer itself. To rephrase the argument that system agency is a phantasm in terms oriented toward system design, we can say that the term "system agency" provides a shorthand way to describe the *human interpretation of properties of the system behavior and capacity, specified by the story author and authoring system designer.* System agency must always be considered in parallel to human agency. The interaction between human and system agency is named "agency play" in order to call attention to the omnipresent interplay between these two concepts. The term "agency play" also is meant to call to mind the possibility for skillful manipulation of the relationship and play between users and systems toward expressive ends.

Social and cultural contexts are indispensable to the understanding of system agency because system agency simultaneously constrains and enables the nature and interpretation of user actions. Computer-based imaginative worlds and poetic culture systems provide a host of meaningful social and cultural contexts, ranging from the hypermedia experiences of many electronic literature works to 3D interactive narrative games. The capacity of the computational system to modify the story world and provide affordances for users actions is referred to as system agency (while understanding, following Callon and Latour, that this agency exists only in conjunction with the roles of human actors).

Though aimed at subjective computing systems in general, this chapter is especially relevant to computational narrative systems that actively generate stories, story worlds, and/or dynamically altered elements of narration, using AI algorithmic and knowledge structuring approaches. Such systems embody a wide range of types of system agency that often fall into two categories, the second a subcategory of the first: (1) system agency as content generation and constraint and (2) system agency as control over actors. The first type refers to the system's capacity to affect what the content is and how the content can be expressed through control of events, objects, and their presentation in the imaginative world. For example, subjective computing systems in the area of computational narrative generation systems have traditionally focused on structuring of events such as in computer scientist James Meehan's early interactive narrative system Tale-Spin (Meehan 1976). In contrast, recent work such as Nick Montfort's interactive fiction platform Curveship (formerly called "nn") has emphasized more complex variation in the expression of content by introducing affordances for narrative variation such as flashbacks, temporal movement of the narrator, and changes in voice (Montfort 2007). The second type refers to the system's capacity to control events through control of actors in the story, often computationally encoding both internal states and external behaviors of actors. This second type of system agency is the type often addressed in the field area of believable agent design, and it is one that gives rise to the illusion of intentional agents acting in a computer-based imaginative world. When both the user and the system compete or collaborate in controlling characters, a new range of opportunities is enabled to study and implement new ways of designing agency toward expressive and aesthetic ends.

Although the notion of system agency seems rooted in the discourse of classic AI (with its goals of building autonomous intelligent agents whose behaviors reveal humanlike intentionality), the term "system agency" does not imply a goal of full system autonomy. System agency is a result of human interpretation in light of a set of situated social circumstances, not as a property intrinsic to a computational system itself. The term "system agency" acts as shorthand to describe human interpretation of properties of the system behavior and capacity specified by the story author and authoring system designer. More important, it suggests that system agency needs to be considered in parallel to human agency, as is accomplished by the notion of agency play.

Defining Agency Play

The concept of agency play redefines agency as a resource that can be varied to result in meaningful aesthetic effects (such as in *Shadow of the Colossus*). In computer-based environments, a user's power to take meaningful actions is mediated through structures provided by the computational system. Aspects of agency that have not commonly been explored, however, include the ways in which dynamically changing the scope, nature, and interrelated degrees of both user and system agencies during execution can serve the expressive goals of subjective computing works. The use of agency is one of the channels for digital authors to express themselves.

Agency play focuses on leveraging the relationship between the user and system in order to create experiences that are meaningful and engaging for users to participate in. Taking the step of expressively using agency play in subjective computing systems is similar to the step that filmmakers took last century when they discovered that varying camera angle, framing, and take length were all effective storytelling mechanisms. This section defines promising dimensions of agency play and provides illustrative examples. The following are multiple layers of agency play, each of which can be used expressively to convey meaning:

• *Agency relationship:*   User actions and system actions operate in relation to one another. This relationship can vary in relative magnitude and degree of dependency between the two types of actions (e.g., an inverse relationship or independent operation).

• *Agency scope:*   Results of either user or system actions may have immediate and local impact (e.g., turning a character left or right) or longer-term and less immediately apparent results (e.g., a series of actions may determine narrative structure itself).

• *Agency dynamics:*   The relationship between possible user and system actions, and their scopes, can vary dynamically during runtime.

• *User input direction:*   The user may establish a pattern of input that directs agency dynamics and/or agency scope.

Figure 7.5 illustrates how the dimensions of agency relate to each other and how each dimension mediates the ones below it.

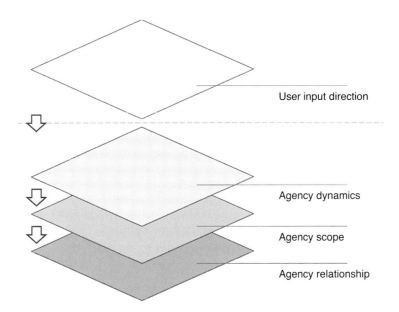

FIGURE 7.5
The dimensions of agency are depicted here as horizontal planes. Arrows indicate the direction of influence between these dimensions.

The dimension of user input direction is separated graphically because it directs the levels below it but is not itself constituted by the layers below it. These layers below are meant to provide vocabulary for more precisely describing such varying types of agency and how they can be manipulated toward expressive effects.

Agency Relationship

Agency relationship is the fundamental dimension of agency play. Agency relationship refers to the relative magnitude of, and dependence relationships existing between, the following:

1. a set of actions allowed by the system to be executed by a user,

2. a set of actions defined by the developer(s) to be executed by the system,

3. a user's desire or need to perform actions,

4. a user's sense of meaningful possible actions, and

5. a range of possible user interpretations of actions.

In analyzing this function, the first two aspects of the function should be considered first, with the understanding that the latter three aspects determine the expressive qualities of the agency relationship. Relative magnitude refers to the relative degree of possible user actions to system-imposed constraints, especially constraints upon actions enacted by the user.

The degree and nature of dependence between user and system control over actions can vary greatly. Primary models include cases in which user and system agency are independent or interdependent. A particular case of interdependent agencies is *inverse* dependence, in which increasing system agency inhibits user agency and/or vice versa. To give an example of independent operation, consider the case in videogames of characters that are controllable by a human player as contrasted to the case of characters that are controlled solely by the system. In this case, independent user agency refers to the ability of the player to make meaningful actions in a computer-based imaginative world. The ability to cause a character to move, acquire artifacts, and interact with other players or NPCs reflects this sense of player agency. User agency can also operate along dimensions outside of the story world, such as in-game camera control. The "meaningfulness" of player actions most often arises from the degree to which a player's actions seem to refer to things in the imaginative world at hand. Thus control over actions that do not have any significant effect on content are commonly described as providing the user with a low degree of agency. Simultaneously, again using videogames as an example, moving a virtual camera in a proper way may reveal to the player a necessary object in the game world. This revealing of the object is an example in which an action outside of the imaginative world's content provides a meaningful result within the imaginative world. As argued earlier, the notion of meaningful agency relies upon situated construal of possible user actions.

An independent model can also describe independent system agency, such as in cases in which a system is capable of autonomously carrying out humanlike action. Consider Rafael Pérez y Pérez's system MEXICA, which is a subjective computing system that generates stories that draw upon Aztec lore (Pérez y Pérez and Sharples 1999). The beginning of a sample story generated by MEXICA reads: "Jaguar knight was an inhabitant of the great Tenochtitlan. Princess was an inhabitant of the great Tenochtitlan. From the first day they met, princess felt a special affection for jaguar knight. Although at the beginning princess did not want to admit it, princess fell in love with jaguar knight" (24). MEXICA itself exhibits independent system agency because it is the system that is doing the "telling." Therefore, the story is not revealed by the user's actions in the story world (such as controlling a character) but rather the system simply autonomously generates stories as output.

The 2005 strategy game *Civilization IV* provides an example of interdependent agencies. When the agency of the player increases in the game as he or she gains more resources (money, weapons, technology, etc.), so does agency of the system because it controls more NPCs with increased capability, and the system must coordinate a more complicated set of game world events at large. Likewise, a system could implement a subset of playable characters that are semi-autonomous, requiring only high-level direction from a player. In this case, the control of character action also displays an interdependent relationship.

As an example of an inverse dependent model, we can look at the IMPROV system by Ken Perlin and Athomas Goldberg, which was developed to allow for the creation of characters that were controlled by users but also expressed their own behaviors (Perlin and Goldberg 1996). For example, one could say that the more an IMPROV-based character can take action in a story world without direction of a player (such as Sid in figure 7.6), the more system agency the less user agency is exhibited (Perlin 1998).

The types of agency independence and dependence described here are meant only to sketch useful points along a range of possibilities, rather than to exhaustively list every possible type of relationship between user and system control of situated action.

FIGURE 7.6
The character Sid was built using the Improv
system. Sid is controlled by a user but also
exhibits his own behaviors.

Agency Scope

The concept of *agency scope* describes the impact and narrative focus of user and system actions, ranging from immediate and local impact, such as spatial navigation ability, to less immediately apparent but more global results, such as shaping the narrative structure itself. Either side of the agency scope spectrum can be used effectively to convey meanings in addition to the actual narrative.

The videogame *Shadow of the Colossus* demonstrates a situation with a high degree of local player agency and a low degree of global player agency. As previously mentioned, at times in the game the player is able to control a character as he tries to dodge bolts of energy coming after him, but no matter the action taken, the player character will still be hit with the bolts and rendered unconscious. The ability to move around (local player agency) but not to change the outcome (global player agency) renders a sense of fate and helplessness.

An opposite relationship between local and global agency can be found in the AI-based interactive narrative documentary *Terminal Time* (Domike, Mateas, and Vanouse 2003). In *Terminal Time*, the last millennium of history is presented according to different ideological biases depending upon audience (a collective group of users in a movie theater) input. In this work, users have only very low local agency through the one-dimensional control mechanism (the volume of the clapping sound of the audience) used to select answers to a few multiple-choice questions. However, there is great variability in the generated output in terms of both media elements composed and displayed and in terms of the rhetorical model that can slant the bias of the output toward a variety of ideologies, such as feminist or antireligious. The contrast, in this case, between low local player agency and high global player agency can be read as a critique of a style of documentary filmmaking featuring a privileged, all-knowing narrator.

Agency Dynamics

The nature of a given agency relationship and the scope of agency impact can vary over time. This change in agency over time is called *agency dynamics*. If these dynamics are orchestrated in order to express a theme such as the increasing emotional maturity of a character, then agency play has become an expressive resource varying according to aesthetic dictates at runtime. Stories that contain fixed levels of agency relationship and agency scope throughout run-time, which could be a conscious and expressive design decision in its own right, have static agency dynamics.

One space to explore the dynamics between player agency and system agency is through semi-autonomous player characters (SPCs). In the domains of interactive narrative and gaming, characters are often categorized as player characters or NPCs. Player characters are often entirely controlled by players, whereas NPCs embrace system autonomy and are not usually subject to player command. Although most characters fall into one or the other category, some games have characters that incorporate traits of both. For instance, some player characters may convey their impatience by foot-tapping, exhibited in an early example by the player character in the 1985 Apple IIe game *Captain Goodnight*; the character also begins playing with a yo-yo or may smile when receiving bonuses to a character's power.

User Input Direction

All of these levels of agency can be directed by user input. For example, in *Pac-Man 2: The New Adventures*, the player does not directly control the Pac-Man character but can direct his attention toward certain objects or tasks—which the character sometimes refuses. The player can also hit Pac-Man with stones from a slingshot to abusively change his mood. Some experiences in the game are inaccessible unless Pac-Man is in the right mood at the right time, but the user can change Pac-Man's mood only through indirect means, as shown in figure 7.7.

FIGURE 7.7
Pac-Man is distraught in the image here from *Pac-Man 2: The New Adventures* because the player has shot him with a slingshot (causing his emotional state to change).

This type of agency dynamics can be used expressively to provide a sense of personality to a player character while simultaneously providing necessary constraints on possible actions. In *Terminal Time*, mentioned earlier, player interaction to determine the ideological bias (e.g., technocentric or white supremacist) is minimal—just clapping. However, the user input is what offers players the strong sense of global agency in the piece because user votes cast by clapping determine the all of the topics of the narrative.

This discussion is a preliminary effort to carefully present a model of agency that includes often overlooked agency phenomena toward the development of theory for design of subjective computing systems. The account of all four dimensions certainly is not comprehensive, and the examples do not cover the entire area of expressive possibilities. Each is an area ripe for further exploration. The modest goal here is to present a new approach to considering the role of agency in expressive works and to provide new vocabulary.

Computer Animation as an Example of Agency Play

Having articulated the notion of agency play, I shall now use it to help explain phenomena of interaction in a common type of subjective computing application. Computer animation used for art or entertainment conveys a special type of subjective experience: it brings life to the screen. At the same time, computer animation is no longer a passive medium. Subjective computing systems like games, interactive narratives, and virtual worlds feature *interactive* animation. Users now are accustomed to both controlling animated characters/avatars and interacting with system-controlled animated AI-based characters (called "agents" in computer science). This shift has naturally led developers to seek to imbue computer-based characters and imaginative worlds with more agency.

In computer science and the computer entertainment industry, there are several strands of research and development resulting in animated CGI exhibiting agency play. One of these research strands includes physics engines or artificial life systems designed to simulate physical phenomena such as gravity. Such systems are deployed in games ranging from automobile racing simulators to the casual game *Angry Birds*, which simulates slingshot attacks (with birds as projectiles) on architectural structures. In this case, there is an interesting agency relationship. Users exhibit some control over characters or moving objects, but because users do not have control over the environment, the rules dictating the results of users' actions might result in quite varied and unpredictable outcomes.

Another example of agency play in CGI is known as *procedural animation*. Procedural animation consists of algorithmic approaches to generate movement. For instance, the work of Ken Perlin uses procedural algorithms to generate lively patterns or rhythms (Perlin and Goldberg 1996). Perhaps the best-known example of procedural animation is Craig Reynolds's influential program *Boids*, a simulator of phenomena such as schooling fish or flocking birds (Reynolds 2001). *Boids* offers users agency to control factors such as the general direction of multiple creatures or, by adjusting the algorithm itself, the density of the flock. At the same time, the movement of individual animals is controlled by the underlying algorithm's specification of factors such as how close a creature should be to the creatures near it. In terms of agency play, users are offered a type of global agency regarding the overall trajectory of multiple creatures, while the system exhibits local agency over individuals at each time step.

Whereas procedural animation focuses on imbuing CGI with rules for movement that do not have to be fully specified by an animator, behavioral animation goes a step further in implementing a type of agency play based on a phantasm in which characters are intended to be believably lifelike in their behaviors. Behavioral animation researchers and developers build AI programs to create animated behaviors. A good example is the work of Joseph Bates's former Oz Project at Carnegie Mellon University, which included endeavors to make AI characters believably and anthropomorphically responsive. In a behavioral animation system, a lazy character could "know" it was lazy (Bates 1992). A user might direct the character to perform an action and it might do so in a begrudging manner (or even refuse to act). These AI behaviors are guided by the system at a high level. Therefore, an animator does not have to fully determine the behaviors or manner of executing actions—the system should have a model of the character's behavior that guides all of its actions. Work in this vein often focuses on creating digital characters with a sense of believable "aliveness," often by modeling internal psychological states of characters (Bates 1992).

All of these approaches simultaneously exhibit agency play to offer more lifelike characters or more dynamic environments, while simultaneously automating functions that animators formerly had to code by hand. Yet these approaches, especially the AI-based approaches, are not without their challenges. Most prominent for the purposes here is the challenge of using agency play to engender social agency through critical reflection on users' own lives. Information scientist Phoebe Sengers has effectively articulated some of the challenges of using AI practices to create such subjective critical experiences. Sengers claims that many agents do not exhibit coherent behavior, even going so far as to say that agent behaviors often seem to users to be clinically schizophrenic when interpreted in human terms. She feels that agents do not properly take into account social and environmental contexts, transitions between behaviors, or reasons for those behaviors. She also asserts that many agent technologies do not account for how behaviors change over time. The following list summarizes Sengers's suggestions for remedies to these issues (Sengers 1998, 2004):

• *Context-sensitivity and negotiability:* Rather than building an agent from conventional context- and communication-independent actions and behaviors, a designer builds agents from context-dependent *signs* and *signifiers*,[3] which are to be communicated to the user.

• *Intentional state entailment:* To explain why the agent's observed behavior is changing, *transitions* are added between signifiers.

• *Diachronicity:* Signifiers can use *meta-level controls* to influence one another, presenting a coherent behavioral picture over time.

Sengers asserts that the key to integrating technology and subjectivity is seeing agent systems as "a form of communication, in terms of the intentions of its designer and how it is experienced by the audience" (Sengers 1998, 211). She goes on to argue: "In this light, the major question to be answered is not "how can we objectively and testably reproduce experience?" but "what are the *goals* of the agent-builder in terms of how his or her agent design should be understood, and how can they be best fulfilled? The major change this philosophical distinction makes at the technical level is that comprehensibility is seen as an essential requirement to be engineered from the start" (211). In terms of agency play, Sengers's argument for comprehensibility could be stated as follows: the agency relationship should be explicitly modeled in system design and agency dynamics must be based on a robust model of behavioral change over time. This agency relationship needs to consider users' real-world situations. Ultimately, her call for comprehensibility of agent behavior is focused on enabling authors to communicate effectively with users. I would go even further and state that comprehensible agent behavior needs to be understood in its relationship to the types of agency and power addressed by thinkers such as Foucault earlier in the chapter. That is, engagement with AI agents should constitute a critical feedback loop that reveals phantasms of human agency through phantasms of system agency—for example, modeling a character who cannot control his violent behaviors as a tool for critical reflection on such violent behaviors and their effects on real people, in the real world. This focus on taking into account the aims of the human author from the start is an important one in critical computing system design. The construct of agency play is a step toward doing so, as agency play focuses on designing the interaction between user and system agency in the way that bests serves an author's goals.

Reflections on Agency Play: Improvisation as Critical Engagement with Society, History, and Emotion

Toward reflecting on the relationship between the agency play model and broader agency within society such as addressed by Foucault, let us begin with two examples of improvisation. To begin with, a description of a scene from the videogame *ICO,* a precursor to *Shadow of the Colossus*, which was discussed earlier in the chapter, reads:

> The cage contains a young girl, Yorda, who sits there quietly. Ico calls out to her and promises to find a way to let her out. He reaches a lever, which lowers the cage close to the ground. Ico makes his way back down and jumps on the cage,

sending it and a dislodged piece of wood crashing to the floor. The impact opens up the cage door, freeing Yorda. . . .

As the pair continue through the castle's many rooms and passages, it quickly becomes apparent that Ico and Yorda need to utilize each of their diverse talents if they want to escape.

In *ICO*, you and your companion are in it together. You must help each other escape; she opens locks and you fight shadows. Except that the "you" just referred to is not *you*. The "you (as Ico)" in the game is a blend between your (player) actions and the videogame character's (a 3D computer graphics boy named Ico) abilities that are implemented in computer code. And "she" is not she. The wraithlike girl named Yorda in the game is a computationally implemented character who operates according to predefined procedures constructing the phantasm of a helpless girl.

Playing the game is an act of improvising within the constraints laid out by that game designer. Furthermore, the rules implemented by computer code are used to evoke a sense of caring for another person. The girl is nearly helpless. You must call her close to you, have her take your hand, and lead her to safety (see figure 7.8). Additionally, a type of imbalanced gender politics is also built into the game; it is a variation of the old "save the princess" trope. Yet a critical impetus toward freedom is also built into the game. All of your improvisational actions are aimed at slipping free from the confines of the phantasmal space of a dismal castle.

FIGURE 7.8
The player character Ico extends an empathetic hand toward the wraithlike girl Yorda in this image from the game *ICO*.

As the start of another example of improvisation, consider the following description of jazz legend Sonny Rollins's music, written by Amiri Baraka:

> In a sense the music depends for its form on the same references as primitive blues forms. It considers the total area of its existence as a means to evolve, i.e., to move, as an intelligently shaped musical concept, from its beginning to its end... shaped by the emotional requirements of the player. . . .
>
> What Rollins (and Coltrane and Coleman and Cecil Taylor, and some others) have done is to reestablish the absolute hegemony of improvisation in jazz and to propose jazz again as the freest of Western music. (Baraka [1968] 1998, 64)

In this quotation, improvisation represents a dream of freedom. It is a deeply cultural and critically engaged view of improvisation. Improvisation serves the subjective needs of the improviser, one of which is his "emotional requirements." At the same time, he also describes the structure of sound as a space to navigate. According to Baraka, using a musical instrument within that metaphorically spatial structure, the improvisor's subjective needs are transmuted into an expressive experience. Poet Kamau Brathwaite evokes a phantasm expressing the same phenomenon of transmuting subjective needs into expression in his poem "Trane":

> Propped against the crowded bar
> he pours into the curved and silver horn
> his old unhappy longing for a home
> (Brathwaite 1995, 14)

In this phantasm, a silver saxophone is used to transmute emotional longing and sociohistorical awareness into the experience of a jazz performance in the "real" space of the poem (a crowded bar). This phantasm integrates an epistemic space drawn from an epistemic domain representing African Americans as diaspora Africans, longing for an historical home, with the image space of John Coltrane playing a silver horn. When Coltrane plays, like Rollins, we know that he uses a musical structure (whether chord changes, riffing off of a melody, or a looser exploration of blues-derived timbre) as a basis for improvisation that allows him to transmute the loss of an ancestral home via the trans-Atlantic slave trade into emotional communication. To forge a strange contrast, reconsider the videogame *ICO*. Clearly *ICO*, at its heart a poignant work of escapist fantasy, is not based upon conveying a profoundly tragic and transcendent history like that of Africans in the Americas like some works of

Brathwaite or Sonny Rollins. The sense of performance and what it means to play "live" is different in each work—in *ICO* the player apparently plays for him- or herself with constraints set up by a game developer long ago, whereas jazz musicians often play for live audiences. At the same time, consider that jazz musicians who are "woodshedding"[4] play for themselves to gain the ability to compose at the speed of thought. Furthermore, jazz musicians often play within commercial structures (e.g., clubs, recording studios, record contracts) that impose strong constraints in the real world. For example, such commercial structures impose both constraints based in racist Jim Crow cultural phantasms that supported segregation and constraints based in cultural phantasms promoting the image of jazz instrumentalists exclusively as male and excluding female performers.

Finally, there is a parallel to be drawn between *ICO* and jazz improvisation. It is the relationship between human improvisational agency to affect the world and the compositional structure imposed by a creative system. Cultural studies and science studies scholar Karen Barad describes this situation via her theory of agential realism, which focuses on agency as a phenomenon, not a property of people or systems. Her perspective can illuminate that for both user and system, agency is performed. As she puts it:

> Agency . . . is an enactment, not something that someone or something has. Agency cannot be designated as an attribute of "subjects" or "objects" (as they do not preexist as such). Agency is not an attribute whatsoever—it is "doing"/"being" in its intra-activity. Agency is the enactment of iterative changes to particular practices through the dynamics of intra-activity. Agency is about the possibilities and accountability entailed in reconfiguring material-discursive apparatuses of bodily production, including the boundary articulations and exclusions that are marked by those practices in the enactment of a causal structure. Particular possibilities for acting exist at every moment, and these changing possibilities entail a responsibility to intervene in the world's becoming, to contest and rework what matters and what is excluded from mattering. (Barad 2003, 826–827)

As the example of *ICO* is meant to illustrate, computers can be used for critically engaged aims—that is to have an impact on what matters for players and their relationships to the world more broadly. Rather than viewing computers as systems to produce objective, mathematical results, computers often transcend their utilitarian origins to critically prompt and reveal phantasms.

Agency play carries with it significant risks. Users' expectations for transparent control over systems can be violated. Dynamic agency may cause the computer to seem unpredictable in response to users' input. Under such circumstances, users input may seem less meaningful if it is often seemingly ignored by the system. Users may need indication of exactly when their agency has given way to system agency, and why. Yet agency play is a promising expressive tool because subjective computing works have matured to the stage that users are accustomed to many conventions of interaction and user agency. Remember, this type of improvisation is not simply free will (just as in jazz playing, "free" does not just mean mindlessly creating sounds at will). Self-reflexive, challenging, and provocative play with conventions at the intersection of users and systems can yield new expressive directions. Agency play, again, is one of the hallmarks of exemplary critical computing systems.

Finally, agency play exemplifies the ways in which critical computing systems can be improvisational. Such systems create new experiences each time they are encountered. Usually, the meanings generated by each experience build upon each other in order to reveal emergent visions. Improvisational uses of the computer require interplay between human meaning and machine data. The computer can structure, change, and respond to data. Human input can drive the computer's data processing to result in new experiences for users. The phenomenon of user input and system operation working hand in hand represents an intersection of human subjectivity and computational structure. This intersection is the meeting point between two sides of a longstanding divide in the arts: improvisation and composition. Examining the interplay between improvisation and composition can be very fruitful. Rather than seeing improvisation and composition as opposites, I argue that the interaction between *types of freedom* and *types of structure* is a space where a great deal of creative expression emerges. This chapter argues that this space is a creative zone for building critical computing systems, just as in other media.

Just as agency play is not built on a model of agency as free will, the type of improvisation it enables in critical computing systems is not merely a naïve sense of freedom. It is improvisation as a sense of freedom that is understood only as it operates in relation to structure. It is a play of different types of freedom and different types of structure. It is improvisation as a system of exchange. Embracing the aesthetic sensibility of improvisation and its ability to engage with cultural phantasms will play a part in enabling the computer to reach its potential to reflect the tragedies and triumphs of the human condition.

8

CRITICAL-COMPUTATIONAL EMPOWERMENT

For seasons and seasons and seasons all of our movement has been going against our self, a journey into our killer's desire.

—Ayi Kwei Armah, *Two Thousand Seasons*

Many of the constructs that humans cling to as reality are, in fact, products of the human imagination. Power relationships and social stratification, along with the political processes, policing institutions, economic systems, and the human interactions they intertwine with, are all real-world phenomena. Yet these phenomena are rooted in the imagination; they are rooted in the human ability to construct cultural phantasms. Manifest destiny, Rudyard Kipling's "white man's burden," flower power, and the slogan *Ash-sha 'b yurīd isqāṭ an-niẓām*[1] (a rallying slogan of the Arab Spring that means "the people want the fall of the regime") are all socially, politically, and emotionally charged phrases. For many people, they respectively conjure a set of images: nineteenth-century covered wagons pioneering their way to Oregon; the gritty necessities of European imperialism over devilish, childish natives; anti-establishment youth in psychedelic colors with flowers in their hair; and groups of protestors from Tunisia, Egypt, Yemen, Libya, and beyond with handwritten signs and fingers on mobile phones. These socially, politically, and emotionally charged examples—*embodied* by people in wagons, on ships, in parks, and on the street, *distributed* across media, and *situated* in specific cultures—are all products of imaginative cognition. They are phantasms.

The phrases are also charged with ideology that means different things for different people. Some would assert that manifest destiny and the "white man's burden" are, respectively, a theologically inspired argument for genocide of Native American peoples and a racist justification for colonial conquest. Those who unquestioningly sing "from sea to shining sea" or who excuse Kipling's poem as mere satire might disagree. Some might say that "flower power" and "the people want the fall of the regime" are, respectively, a justification for an irresponsible lifestyle rife with illicit behaviors and a rallying cry for change that might end even cursory protections for religious minorities. Those who saw the countercultural movements of the 1960s United States as contributing to the end of the Vietnam War or the Arab Spring as leading to the collapse of oppressive regimes might likewise disagree.[2] These examples have serious real-world implications for lives and livelihoods, for bodies and histories. Through all this, we must remember that ideologies are conceptual artifacts produced by humans. The power that we have to define our own destinies in light of the social structures we inhabit, and the power that is exerted over us to restrict our social destinies, are both rooted in embodied, distributed, and situated cultural phantasms.

This chapter looks at the intersection of critical engagement with society and computing. More specifically, I shall address issues of empowerment. These topics include the ways power is maintained, abuses of power, and means to positively take part in the empowerment of the disenfranchised. I shall first focus on the relationships between the computing systems and the cultural phantasms that maintain or change real-world power relationships. Then I shall focus on developing computing systems that explore the strong correlation between imaginative conceptual change and social change—again with a view toward empowerment. It is useful to take a moment to first distinguish the orientation of this chapter from several parallel or related aims involving computers and empowerment. The orientation here is not specifically toward using computers for civic engagement, activism, or international "development," although there are clear parallels with these aims. Those using computing to pursue civic, activist, and international development aims often see themselves as using computers to support citizen participation in social change, to implement cause-oriented applications or interventions, or to provide technological support for economically and infrastructurally under-resourced environments. In contrast, this chapter aims to explore, through both example and speculation, how *phantasms involving computing technologies can play roles in social empowerment and how we can reveal the ways that they sometimes disempower.*

The next section presents a brief discussion of power and empowerment. After discussing the complexities involved in developing an account of power, a distinction between three interrelated levels of power is introduced, namely individual, sociocultural, and state levels of power. The three levels are an introductory rubric that provides us useful orientation for ensuing exploration. A brief survey of approaches to power and empowerment follows, elaborating upon each of the three levels and their relationships to one another. A short discussion of contrasting broad strategies for empowerment ranging from the conservative to the radical follows. This discussion leads to open-ended and speculative reflections on the critical computing approach to empowerment argued for in this book. This high-level discussion gives way in the following section to an introduction of the concept of *social-computational flow*, which describes the type of exchange that enables computing systems to acquire information regarding phenomena in the external world, including power relationships. Social-computational flow is a useful conceptual tool for revealing the connections between social critique and change, on one hand, and technical aspects of computing systems, on the other. The subsequent section envisions future possibilities for understanding and designing critical computing systems. An in-depth example is then presented and analyzed to reveal its potential to empower and to challenge disempowering phantasms. The analysis of these examples is driven by the previously introduced concepts of *expressive epistemologies*, *polymorphic poetics*, *cultural phantasms*, *integrative cultural systems*, *agency play*, and *social-computational flow*. A speculative discussion follows that explores the potential of using critical computing systems to achieve empowerment.

Power and Empowerment

Understanding the concept of empowerment means understanding the nature of power. Social scientists and activists alike have developed many nuanced and comprehensive approaches to understanding empowerment. Indeed, some social science and activist approaches argue that empowerment cannot be apprehended as a holistic concept. Despite the broad scope of the terms, I nonetheless use the terms "power" and "empowerment" because of their clarity. I argue for empowerment because the word captures the essence of my humanistic conception of critical engagement. It is in this spirit that I begin the following discussion of power and empowerment, with the hopes that readers might find resonance with, or at least greater understanding, of my aims regarding critical computing practice as a desirable phantasmal media endeavor.

There is no consensus definition of power. To highlight this fact, let us consider social worker and researcher Elisheva Sadan's survey of influential theories of power. Sadan's survey cites influential theories of power from researchers such as Robert Dahl, Peter Bachrach and Morton Baratz, Steven Lukes, Michel Foucault, John Gaventa, Michael Mann, Stewart Clegg, and Anthony Giddens (Sadan 2004). Her analysis reveals the inherent contradictions in many of the scholarly definitions of power, as can be seen in the following summary (Sadan 2004):

• Power has to be acquired. Power may only be exercised. Power is a matter of authority.

• Power belongs to an individual. Power belongs only to the collective. Power cannot be attributed to anyone; it is a quality of social systems.

• Power involves conflict. Power does not involve conflict in every case. Power generally involves conflict, but not necessarily.

• Power presupposes resistance. Power, first and foremost, has to do with obedience. Power is both resistance and obedience.

• Power is connected with oppression and rule. Power is productive and makes development possible. Power is an evil, a good, diabolical, and routine.

The contradictions and complications raised in her summary illustrate that power has so many meanings that it is difficult to pin down in scholarly terms.

Like the challenge in defining empowerment, it may be an impossible task to develop an effective overarching definition of power. For this reason, it is necessary to orient our discussion toward the types of power that are relevant here. Although it is restrictive in many ways, a three-level distinction between individual, sociocultural, and state power can begin to serve this purpose. To some thinkers, power is an individual condition. Under such a perspective, empowerment could mean enabling an individual to be and to feel capable of acting autonomously within the world. For others, power is a sociocultural phenomenon. For this second type of thinker, power refers to the ability to construct shared ideology and to influence the norms, values, and group relationships within a society. Empowerment in this sense would refer to prompting people to critically analyze and change a society's norms, values, and social configurations rather than unquestioningly accepting dominant ideology and group relationships. It would also mean the ability to construct ideology that others adopt. It would also mean enabling subordinated groups to maintain their own ideologies without being dominated or oppressed. For a third type of thinker, true power is a function of the state—those organizations that can manufacture consent and acquiescence through military, economic, or political might. For those oppressed by such organizations, empowerment could mean either resistance to, revolution against, or gaining influence over those state organizations. I shall call these three types of power the *individual, sociocultural,* and *state* levels of power.

Obviously, a much more nuanced account is possible than this three-level distinction provides. A more nuanced account might begin with descriptions of how these three (and other) types of power interrelate. A careful account of power must also include discussion of issues such as how power changes the nature of those with power, how power relationships can reverse in some situations, and how individuals and groups may have some types and degrees of power in some situations but different types and degrees of power in other situations. There are many topics that must be addressed in a complex formulation of the concept of power. Yet it is still useful to distinguish between individual, sociocultural, and state levels of power, as these three levels of power represent the most common ways that power is discussed (recognizing that researchers sometimes address power at one level at the expense of the others, as suits their varied perspectives). The three-level distinction can at least provide some initial orientation that can help us avoid this problem. So I shall use the three levels of power as a crude conceptual tool in order to help us begin discussion, while acknowledging that it is an oversimplifying framework. In this manner, I shall touch upon several notions of power to provide a sketch, rather than a definition, of the types of power and empowerment addressed by critical computing practices described later in the chapter.

To continue this discussion in more depth, let us consider the results of another survey of approaches to defining power before elaborating upon each of the three levels and the relationships between them. Psychologists Dacher Keltner, Deborah Gruenfeld, and Cameron Anderson also have surveyed many approaches to understanding power (Keltner, Gruenfeld, and Anderson 2003). Their survey helps reveal the relationships that power has to *cognitive processes* such as stereotyping and interpretation of nonverbal behavior, along with *social behaviors* such as emotional display, sexual aggression, and teasing. These types of cognitive processes and social behavior describe ways that power relationships influence daily interactions, typically in ways that benefit those with power, to the detriment of those without.[3] For Keltner, Gruenfeld, and Anderson, the concept of power is distinct from the concepts of status, authority, and dominance, though all three can play a role in determining power.

Keltner, Gruenfeld, and Anderson also provide their own definition of power, synthesized from many previous theories. Synthesizing a number of definitions from sociology and psychology, Keltner, Gruenfeld, and Anderson define power as "an individual's relative capacity to modify others' states by providing or withholding resources or administering punishments. Resources can be both material (food, money, economic opportunity) or social (knowledge, affection, friendship, decision-making opportunities), and punishments can be material (job termination, physical harm) or social (verbal abuse, ostracism)" (265–266). Without dismissing the value of other definitions, I shall use their definition as a catalyst for discussion that expands the notions of individual, sociocultural, and state power and relates the three levels to one another.

Interrelated Levels of Power

The Keltner, Gruenfeld, and Anderson definition raises a question regarding empowerment related to the individual level of power: does power necessarily involve modifying others' states, or can it refer to the capacity for self-determination regarding resources and punishments? That is, can power be a characteristic of an individual? The answer to this question has strong bearing on the potential for self-empowerment. Furthermore, we must consider whether power can be a feature of individual cognition in the form of dispositions toward, and perceptions of, resources and punishments. To give an extreme example, one might argue that even under extreme duress, such as torture, people could possess power by refusing to acquiesce or change their beliefs and attitudes. For some thinkers, the ability to determine one's own one way thinking (to the extent that it is possible to do so) is a key to self-empowerment. Under this view, individual cognition is where the locus of power lies.

Yet cognitive processes should not be analyzed by focusing only on what is "inside an individual's head" because they are also distributed onto other people and artifacts. Cultural phantasms, such as manifest destiny or flower power, are results of imaginative cognition processes that have become socially entrenched. Cultural phantasms have the capacity to maintain and change power relationships. The degree to which individuals can participate in the creation of effective cultural phantasms constitutes a type of power. In this sense, influential cultural phantasms can enable some people to exert power over others, at the same time as they are rooted in individual cognition. Likewise, individuals can construct and reveal cultural phantasms in ways that are designed to disrupt the entrenchment of cultural phantasms as a means of addressing sociocultural power.

Cultural phantasms can support a pervasive form of power when they serve to modify others' (material or social) resources or punishments. Part of the dangerous nature of cultural phantasms is that they can exert this type of sociocultural power invisibly. For example, the invisible premises and values in the phantasm of manifest destiny enabled many nineteenth-century U.S. citizens to support and participate in genocide and relocation of indigenous groups without questioning the values of manifest destiny underlying the slaughter and oppression. This last statement reveals also that cultural phantasms can have bearing upon state power. The sociocultural and state levels of power are also interrelated. The matrix of intertwining sociocultural and state levels of power impacts groups conceptually (such as establishing norms) and materially (such as killing in state sponsored wars). The concept of the cultural phantasm exemplifies the relationship between individual (cognitive) power and sociocultural power. I shall now explore some of the relationships between sociocultural and state power.

One way that cultural phantasms maintain invisibility is through the fact that they are partially constituted by shared norms. The ability to maintain the invisibility of cultural phantasms contributes to their use as a means of maintaining power. This type of invisible exertion and maintenance of power contrasts with means of exerting and maintaining power based on the use of physical power that also characterizes state power. Antonio Gramsci was a Marxist thinker who addressed the issue of how shared norms contribute to maintenance of power. Toward this end, Gramsci identified two social levels that he called the "civil society" and "the State," (corresponding to sociocultural power and state power in our terms) and used the concept of hegemony to describe a type of power relationship between the two. In Gramsci's words: "What we can do, for the moment, is to fix two major superstructural 'levels': the one that can be called 'civil society,' that is the ensemble of organisms commonly called 'private,' and that of 'political society' or 'the State.' These two levels correspond on the one hand to the function of 'hegemony' which the dominant group exercises throughout society and on the other hand to that of 'direct domination' or command exercised through the State and 'judicial' government" (Gramsci 1971, 12). In the broadest sense, the concept of hegemony is well known as referring to the dominance of one group over others in a manner sustained by the consent of both the dominant and dominated. Shared worldviews between dominant and dominated, to the benefit of the dominant, are some of the sharpest and most durable weapons of hegemony. Although this domination can be economic, political, linguistic, and so on, many theorists find the most pervasive form of hegemony to be cultural. To give an example of the type favored by critical theorists such as Jean Baudrillard (1983), if products such as name-brand T-shirts, blue jeans, and designer handbags become globally desirable in part due to spectacular cultural phantasms, it leads individuals globally to unthinkingly support the economic and political systems that make such products available. Such products convey fashion-oriented mental imagery that becomes invisibly intertwined with ideology. Clearly, cultural phantasms play a role in the maintenance of hegemony. We should note here, however, that hegemony is not maintained only by cultural phantasms, though they are one such means. Cultural phantasms depend on mental/sensory images, but the consent that sustains hegemony has very real and immediate implications (even if that consent most often does at least partly depend on phantasms). Additionally, cultural phantasms can be used either to reinforce or destabilize hegemony through the imagination, particularly because the concept of the cultural phantasm emphasizes its roots of phantasms in individual cognition, whereas hegemony foregrounds the relationship between culture and state power.

We can take a moment now to discuss the nature of state power. In the 1950s, sociologist Charles Wright Mills introduced seminal research on state power. Mills highlighted that the power to make history, akin to providing or withholding resources in the Keltner, Gruenfeld, and Anderson definition of power given earlier, is restricted to "national spokesmen, power elites, and policy makers" (Mills 1958, 53). Though perhaps his statement contains what might be considered a gender-biased anachronism, which can be evaluated for its accuracy, his statement was intentionally gendered. His argument describes the locus of power existing in a small number of *men* called "power elites": "The power elite is composed of men whose positions enable them to transcend the ordinary environments of ordinary men and women; they are in positions to make decisions having major consequences. Whether they do or do not make such decisions is less important that the fact that they do occupy such pivotal positions: their failure to act, their failure to make decisions, is itself an act that is often of greater consequences than the decisions they do make" (Mills [1956] 2000, 3–4). It is useful to consider whether his concept reflects his patriarchal view of society, his view of societies that are patriarchal, or both. Regardless, beyond noting how analyzing Mills's phantasm called the power elite reveals the ways in which accounts of individual identity cannot be separated from issues of power, Mills's phantasm is useful here because it completes a circle of the three levels of power we have been discussing. Power elites are *individuals* who exercise what we have been calling state power. It is important to be clear about what is meant by "state power." Mills's concept of the power elite can also help with this. Mills's power elite do not just represent nations; they run corporations and military forces (which in some nations operate with relative autonomy and in others constitute the government). What links the elites in these arenas is that "they occupy the strategic command posts of the social structure, in which are now centered the effective means of the power and the wealth and the celebrity which they enjoy" (Mills [1956] 2000, 4). At the same time, Mills also reminds us that state power should not be viewed in a monolithic way. He begins by revealing that the power elite are abetted by lackeys: "The power elite are not solitary rulers. Advisers and consultants, spokesmen and opinion-makers are often the captains of their higher thought and decision. Immediately below the elite are the professional politicians of the middle levels of power, in the Congress and in the pressure groups, as well as among the new and old upper classes of town and city and region" (Mills [1956] 2000, 4). However, even more telling is Mills's contention that

> no nation-state is a homogeneous entity, that none is in itself a history-making agent. "It" does not possess decision or will or interest or honour or fight. "Nation" refers to a people occupying a more or less defined territory and organized under the authority of a state or, with some chance of success, claiming such an autonomous organization. The "state", a dominating apparatus, refers to an organization that effectively monopolizes the legitimate means of violence and administration over a defined territory. "Legitimate" means: more or less generally acquiesced in by publics and masses, for reasons in which they believe. In the case of the nation-state these reasons are the symbols and ideologies of nationalism. (Mills 1958, 53)

More recent thinkers have discussed further complications in the monolithic and homogeneous nature of state power. In particular, exploring the relationship between computing technologies and state power reveals profound transformations just hinted at in the 1950s analyses of Mills. The influential radicalized group of artists called the Critical Art Ensemble asserts that the state has adopted many of the distributed, mobile, deterritorialized characteristics that were formerly the realm of the dominated and those resisting power. Citing Mills's difficulty in getting empirical information about the power elite, the Critical Art Ensemble states that "even in 1956, when C. Wright Mills wrote *The Power Elite*, it was clear that the sedentary elite already understood the importance of invisibility" (Critical Art Ensemble 1993, 17). Whereas formerly state power could be characterized by the large formations adopted by nation-states with standing armies, guerrilla warfare was characterized by a kind of nomadic mobility. But today, the power elite could be described as the "nomadic elite" (17), "networks fighting networks" as media theorists Alexander Galloway and Eugene Thacker put it (Galloway and Thacker 2007, 18). The Critical Art Ensemble writes:

> The nomadic elite itself is frustratingly difficult to grasp. . . . As the contemporary elite moves from centralized urban areas to decentralized and deterritorialized cyberspace, Mills' [sic] dilemma becomes increasingly aggravated. How can a subject be critically assessed that cannot be located, examined, or even seen? Class analysis reaches a point of exhaustion. Subjectively there is a feeling of oppression, and yet it is difficult to locate, let alone assume, an oppressor. In all likelihood, this group is not a class at all—that is, an aggregate of people with common political and economic interests—but a downloaded elite military consciousness. The cyberelite is now a transcendent entity that can only be imagined. Whether they have integrated programmed motives is unknown. (17–18)

The Critical Art Ensemble offers a strong warning regarding the limitations of using computational media for empowerment. They argue that computational media (and the older "electronic" technologies upon which they are based) enable the nomadic elite to regulate the lives of the ordinary people who constitute the underclass. Nations, corporations, and military forces alike, they argue, mediate control of resources (and presumable punishment) using information technologies. The Critical Art Ensemble continues their argument:

> As the electronic information-cores overflow with files of electronic people (those transformed into credit histories, consumer types, patterns and tendencies, etc.), electronic research, electronic money, and other forms of information power, the nomad is free to wander the electronic net, able to cross national boundaries with minimal resistance from national bureaucracies. The privileged realm of electronic space controls the physical logistics of manufacture, since the release of raw materials and manufactured goods requires electronic consent and direction. Such power must be relinquished to the cyber realm, or the efficiency (and thereby the profitability) of complex manufacture, distribution, and consumption would collapse into a communication gap. Much the same is true of the military; there is cyberelite control of information resources and dispersal. Without command and control, the military becomes immobile, or at best limited to chaotic dispersal in localized space. In this manner all sedentary structures become servants of the nomads. (Critical Art Ensemble 1993, 16–17)

In light of these observations, let us recall the aim of this section: we seek to address the role of computing systems in issues of power and empowerment. We can now ask how computing systems can play roles in positively empowering people against domination and oppression, especially when power against them is exercised by dominant groups using computing systems as well. Domination of individuals is perpetuated using computing systems by prompting individual phantasms. For example, many teenagers construct self-images based strongly upon musical taste. One might assume that if they have access to a large number of musical choices available over computer-based retailers, they have wide latitude with which to self-represent through music. However, this is not the case. In this example, teenagers' self-images might be affected by music through pervasive computing technologies such as recommender systems because of their homogenizing effect on listening and purchasing preferences. Furthermore, such teenagers' self-images might be impacted by mass marketing involved in corporate production of musical products and fashions, which gives much greater prominence to hegemonically determined tastes than to more marginalized, subaltern, or oppositional options. Such teenagers are also influenced by the dominant and highly regulated computational distribution outlets for those musical products and fashions. In these examples, sociocultural domination is perpetuated using computing systems that can manufacture hegemonic consent in taste, as we saw is possible with collaborative filtering technologies in chapter 5. State domination is perpetuated through the control of information resources and increasingly autonomous computing technologies to execute war operations. Any notion of empowerment using computing technologies, as I argue for in the concept of critical computing, cannot be a technological determinist concept. The use of the computer alone, say by making media more "interactive" and therefore "transformative," is not enough to unilaterally empower people. We can instead try to identify strategies and approaches to developing and using computing technologies that are efficacious in empowering people at multiple levels of power.

Empowerment Strategies

Just like in all other dimensions of life, there are many approaches to empowerment using computing technologies, ranging from conservative and reactionary to radical and destructive. I shall characterize several examples of these approaches in turn, ending with a strategy that I believe is especially effective as an empowering critical computing practice.

A very conservative route might suggest that the disempowered participate in society and use computing technologies in accordance with maintaining existing order, while achieving some modicum of comfort in the meantime—perhaps even with a sense of self-actualized achievement. This is often what social philosopher Cornel West has called an "assimilationist" strategy (West 1990). While discussing the disempowerment of African American ("black") people in particular, he describes one realization of an assimilationist strategy as the "manner that set out to show that Black people were really like white people—thereby eliding differences (in history and culture) between whites and Blacks," which he argues "subordinates Black particularity to a false universalism" (West 1990, 27). For example, this might mean that a person identifying as "black" would aspire to have a lucrative career in a mainstream corporate computing technology company as the most effective route toward social acceptability. This aspiration would entail adopting "universal" epistemic domains, including styles, behaviors, material possessions, perhaps even beliefs, and more in order to accommodate the norms and values of corporate culture. This type of assimilation, entailing adopting norms and values that are believed to be universal though they are in fact the norms of the privileged, would be deemed as an appropriate aspiration of such a person. This is the case even if the assimilation occurs at the expense of particular forms of cultural engagement that the person previously identified with as an element of some type of black (or any other) culture. Such strategies assume that membership in marginalized groups is a disadvantage. This strategy can be deployed in computing technologies as well. Computational subordination of cultural particularity can be exemplified by naïve arguments often made about computer-based virtual worlds.

For instance, I have often argued that providing users with a greater range of self-expression in customizing avatars (not only graphics, but also behaviors and affordances) and social networking profiles (not only content of predefined fields such as "gender" but also new fields) is a useful tool for empowerment because it enables less privileged social categories that system designers might not have considered at implementation time to be represented. Furthermore, many existing computational avatars or profiles representing less privileged social categories can stigmatize users (Harrell 2009a, 2010c, 2010a, 2010b, 2010c; Harrell, Vargas, and Perry 2011).[4] At times I encounter a counterargument that goes: because users can choose the avatars they want to represent themselves, they need not be marginalized on the Internet because they can hide any traits that could lead to their marginalization. This counterargument is flawed because it effaces differences of power, as argued in depth by media theorist Lisa Nakamura

(2002, 35).[5] It is a form of the more general counterargument that goes: computational environments such as virtual worlds and social networking sites create spaces where real-world opression applied in virtual worlds perpetuates anachronistic social divisions. Under this view, for example, if a feminist thinker experiences marginalization as a woman, then she need no longer worry because in a virtual environment she can represent herself with an avatar of a man, an ungendered robot, or even an unadorned cube if she wants. Such counterarguments are flawed because they ignore the default assumptions users have about other users. Implicit in this objection is the idea that most users make no assumptions regarding the diversity of groups other users are from, when in fact the default assumption of most users may be that others are from the dominant group, whose members should all be treated equally. However, if this woman is required to hide her own identity to be treated as an equal, do we really want to consider that to be empowerment? As revealed by the discussion of Adrian Piper's work in chapter 3 and the introduction to part IV, passing as a member of a hegemonically privileged group does not preclude the experience of encountering bigotry, but it does create the dilemma of deciding whether to address bigotry when it occurs. Furthermore, the ability to look like someone different in a virtual world does nothing to alter real-world inequities in allocations of resources and punishment.

Instead of such conservative approaches, West proposes a route toward empowerment based in multiculturalist ideology. His proposal is geared toward building coalitions between those in both oppressed and privileged groups. His proposal offers specific strategies that are especially cognizant of the positions of those people from oppressed groups who find themselves working within (and receiving benefits from) mainstream institutions, yet who are also aware of the compromises to their own power in order to do so. He proposes what he calls "a new cultural politics of difference" and recommends that people pursue a strategy of empowerment based on "demystification." Demystification can be summarized as follows (West 1990):

• Producing social structural analyses of empire, class, race, gender, nature, age, sexual orientation, nation, and region (as a springboard—not ending point)

• Keeping track of the complex dynamics of institutional power structures in order to disclose options and alternatives for change

• Highlighting the role of human agency (e.g., as engineer, artist, critic, or audience).

At the same time, West warns thinkers to avoid single-factor-based analyses, such as those focusing solely upon factors such as race, class, gender, and the like, which inevitably result in a type of reductionism. His approach is simultaneously radical and middle-of-the-road. West argues that the disempowered person should take on a role that he calls the "critical organic catalyst," that is, the role of one who "stays attuned to the best of what the mainstream has to offer—its paradigms, viewpoints, and methods—yet maintains a grounding in affirming and enabling subcultures of criticism" (West 1990, 33). Institutionally supported endeavors that aim to support changes of individual perspectives using computing technologies are good examples of this approach. The game *A Closed World*, produced by the Gambit Game Lab at MIT (GAMBIT Singapore—MIT Game Lab 2011) to reveal dilemmas of revealing diverse sexual orientations to others (colloquially called "coming out"), constitutes a social structural analysis in the form of a computer game (see figure 8.1). Games like *A Closed World* are examples of what Mary Flanagan calls "critical play," in their use of play environments for "careful examination of social, cultural, political, or even personal themes" (Flanagan 2009, 6).

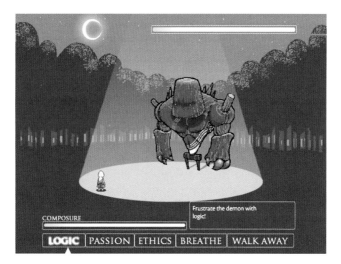

FIGURE 8.1
This screenshot from the game *A Closed World* depicts the player character interacting with an NPC.

Other Gambit projects include games that support individual empowerment through engendering better understanding of issues such as addiction and mental illness. Taken together, such projects not only aim to support the agency of players but also highlight the agency of engineers and artists who make the games, as well as the audiences and critics that judge the games in independent games competitions. More broadly, trends with names such as "serious games" or "games for change," often pursued with strong relationships to universities and nongovernmental organizations (NGOs) further exemplify West's demystification-based, critical organic catalyst approach to empowerment in the context of critical computing systems. The key term "demystification" in West's approach is important because rather than celebrating some abstract empowering ideals, it reduces the mystique and power of the mainstream as well as the potential of hegemony to exoticize and isolate the marginalized. Instead, demystification supports ensuring that a range of cultural options are seen as valuable, made apparent, and kept open for diverse types of people to partake in.

Some practitioners also take up more radical approaches. Computer-based activists (often called "hacktivists") who use techniques such as denial-of-service attacks,[6] online pranks, and computer viruses view their efforts as anti-establishment agitation against state power. For example, in early 2012 the *New York Times* reported that "hackers affiliated with the loose collective called Anonymous had at various times taken down the Web sites of the Justice Department, the Federal Bureau of Investigation, the White House, the Motion Picture Association of America, the Recording Industry Association of America, the United States Copyright Office, CBS.com, Warner Music and Universal Music" (Perlroth 2012). These actions were undertaken by Anonymous to protest the broadly maligned (as severely impacting freedom of expression and privacy) U.S. bills called the Stop Online Piracy Act in the House, the Protect Intellectual Property Act in the Senate, and the Anti-Counterfeiting Trade Agreement (Perlroth 2012). Let us consider another radicalized example that is in dialogue with critical theory and histories of performance, conceptual, and theatrical art practices. The Critical Art Ensemble cited previously has theorized, and at times called for, strategies of resistance that they sometimes call "electronic disturbance." An account of electronic disturbance follows:

> Nomadic power must be resisted in cyberspace rather than in physical space. The postmodern gambler is an electronic player. A small but coordinated group of hackers could introduce electronic viruses, worms, and bombs into the data banks, programs, and networks of authority, possibly bringing the destructive

force of inertia into the nomadic realm. Prolonged inertia equals the collapse of nomadic authority on a global level. Such a strategy does not require a unified class action, nor does it require simultaneous action in numerous geographic areas. The less nihilistic could resurrect the strategy of occupation by holding data as hostage instead of property. By whatever means electronic authority is disturbed, the key is to totally disrupt command and control. Under such conditions, all dead capital in the military/corporate entwinement becomes an economic drain—material, equipment, and labor power all would be left without a means of deployment. Late capital would collapse under its own excessive weight. (Critical Art Ensemble 1993, 25)

However, in practice the Critical Art Ensemble has preferred staging interventions using art and the specter of electronic disturbance to call attention to social power relationships rather than deploying actually socially destructive technologies. In other words the rhetoric of disturbance is, in fact, used as a constructive practice related to West's notion of demystification.

There are other radical approaches to critical empowerment beyond those we have seen so far. A good example of this is the nonprofit organization called the Free Software Foundation. The Free Software Foundation argues for free software "in the sense of free speech," which means "users' freedom to run, copy, distribute, study, change and improve the software" (Free Software Foundation 2012). Their effort can be considered to be a type of resistance against (corporate) "state" power. To provide a slightly summarized account, the Free Software Foundation's (2012) core activities are as follows:

• Maintaining articles covering free software philosophy and a definition of free software

• Sponsoring the GNU project to provide a complete free software operating system licensed in addition to supporting other free software development

• Holding copyrights to defend against efforts to turn free software proprietary, collecting copyright assignments that are registered with the U.S. copyright office, and enforcing the license under which they distribute free software

• Publishing a free software license

• Campaigning for free software adoption and against proprietary software

• Providing resources to the community regarding how to obtain free software.

Their efforts to provide resources for users to find free software aims to empower individuals and challenge the state power vested in dominant software-producing corporations. They also aim for sociocultural empowerment through campaigning activities against the cultural hegemony of proprietary software and freedom reducing software practices. Although some of the campaigning activities of the Free Software foundation include nondestructive forms of electronic disturbance (avidly distributing slogans and disparaging corporations that they see as reducing user freedom) and stridently inserting their unsolicited beliefs into any online or offline conversation they deem relevant, they also pursue their aims through well-known channels of political advocacy and working within governmental systems to legitimize their views. Their creation and enforcement of a free software license through the U.S. copyright office is an example of such efforts. Furthermore, their efforts to create and articulate a clear ideology of free software represent another form of sociocultural empowerment. Yet, of all of their endeavors, what is most striking is the Free Software Foundation's strategy of sponsoring and developing free software. The mobilization of communities to create alternative material resources to those of corporate/state-power-produced resources is a profound type of empowerment.

There are many strategies for using computing for empowerment beyond the four we have just examined (assimilationism, demystification, electronic disturbance, and development of alternative technologies). However, the four strategies provide snapshots that illustrate an intentionally extremely diverse political spectrum of approaches to empowerment at the individual, sociocultural, and state levels using computing systems. Bearing this broad spectrum of political perspectives in mind, we can ask which levels of power the critical computing perspective on empowerment here refers to. After all, we have seen that some approaches highlight empowerment as only change to individual minds; others highlight empowerment as resistance to hegemony; still others highlight empowerment as having the type of impact upon others exercised by the power elite (even in its newer nomadic formation) or to exercise radical disturbance against abuses of state power.

The critical computing approach, as you might guess, suggests that empowerment must occur at individual, sociocultural, *and* state levels. Furthermore, critical computing must attend to the interrelationships between these levels. Toward stating how critical computing might be used for empowerment, we can say that the focus on *phantasmal media* highlights the potential of computing to aid in prompting constructive imagination to empower people and disrupt invisibly operating phantasms that constrain imagination thereby oppressing people. In particular, the book has highlighted the creation of imaginative worlds that participate in prompting cultural phantasms explicitly grounded in diverse worldviews. Truly empowering cultural phantasms do not replicate the conditions of oppression; rather, they create capacities for individual thought, collective action, and resistance against domination and exploitation. Empowering cultural phantasms support the oppressed in opposing unequal and unfair distribution of resources and punishment in comparison to the privileged. Critical computing empowerment is not reactionary. *Empowerment is the process of becoming a culture maker.* The challenge for culture makers, using the computer and otherwise, is whether empowerment is possible in the face of dominating abuses of sociocultural and state power. I believe that empowerment is possible because individual, sociocultural, and state power are all rooted in imagination, and because we all have capacities to imagine. I attribute a great locus of power to the individual.

The phantasmal media approach begins with the role of individual cognition. We consider the ways that the cognitive processes that prompt phantasms relate to the hegemony (cultural phantasms) and to the power elite (including their power as sustained through decentralized and distributed computing systems used for control). I argue for a multipronged approach to empowerment. First, subjective computing system developers must construct demystifying computational phantasms: we need computing systems capable of expressing imaginative visions. Second, cultural computing practitioners must lay bare the worldviews (epistemic domains) underlying both expressive and utilitarian computing systems: we must account for how computing systems entrench phantasms. Furthermore, cultural computing practitioners must build computing systems that learn from the strategies diverse groups have employed for survival in the face of oppression. Third, critical computing practitioners must develop technologies that reveal disempowering social structures to resist domination by the nomadic elite: we must scrutinize the technologies that we use and develop their potential to disempower and implement computing models that exhibit values that support the oppressed, the disenfranchised, and the marginalized. We must recognize the potential value in the creations, worldviews, and imaginative potentials of the members of those groups.

At the same time, developers and analysts of phantasmal media must realize that there is a locus of power in the human, independent of technology. As such, we must realize that our endeavors are just a piece of the puzzle when it comes to empowerment. We must support endeavors on multiple fronts that support social justice, economic equity, intellectual liberation, political self-determination, and related aims that support empowerment simultaneously at individual, sociocultural, and state levels.

Social-Computational Flow

The discussion thus far has described far-reaching aims of using computers for empowerment. To make that vision into a reality, we need to shift gears now to discuss more specific aspects of computing systems. A crucial aspect of understanding how computing systems can have an impact on society is accounting for how subjective, cultural, and critical computing systems refer to, and acquire information from, situations and objects in the external world. The concept of *social-computational flow* introduced in this section is intended to help develop this type of account. After the previous section's broad discussion of empowerment and social action at multiple scales, this discussion is more specifically oriented toward understanding technologies themselves rather than the use of technologies in social critique or activism. However, the idea of social-computational flow is a useful conceptual tool for revealing specific aspects of computing systems that can be used for empowerment through both conceptual and social change. This concept will be made clear as we explore examples of a system illustrating how each of the chapter topics of the book can specifically empower people.

In the computer science subfield of computer networking, *flow* refers to the transfer of information between a source and destination. This information is subdivided into units called "packets," and the source and destination require a shared specification for how the transfer should take place—a type of shared set of formats and rules called a "protocol." The idea of social-computational flow in this subsection metaphorically builds on the concept of flow in computer science in order to discuss the transfer of information between external world experiences and formats and rules on a computer. The focus of social-computational flow is articulating the nature of the source and destination. As such, social-computational flow is a concept useful for addressing the relationships between computing systems and content (such as imaginative worlds and poetic phantasms), sign systems, culture, and social phenomena such as power relationships. Social-computational flow can be used for bidirectional analysis, from the world to the computer or vice versa, and can involve multiple external world experience and multiple systems.

Although the term could be more broadly applied, in this chapter I shall use "social-computational flow" in a more restricted way to refer to a relationship between the social world of human understandings and computational algorithms and data structures. To help make this clear, let us take three brief examples of subjective computing systems related to war (see figure 8.2): *America's Army*, "the official

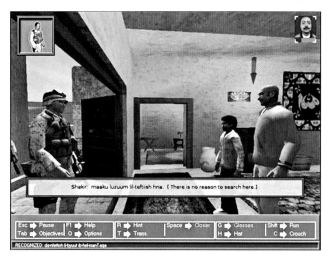

FIGURE 8.2

America's Army 3, Call of Duty: Black Ops II, and the *Tactical Language and Culture Training System: Mission to Iraq* each address war.

U.S. Army game," the *Call of Duty* modern warfare third- and first-person shooter videogame series, and the *Tactical Language and Culture Training System: Mission to Iraq* software for "language and culture training for defense, national security and intelligence applications" (Alelo Inc. 2008a, 2008b).

Social-computational flow can help describe how computing systems such as these intersect with external world social issues of power. These issues include individual power involving combat or communication, sociocultural power involving hegemonic patterns of behavior and national identity affiliation, and state power involving international conflict. Players' experiences with these technologies have social impact in the world at large. Players might join the U.S. Army or develop weapons skills through simulations. Players might become more aware of the customs and manners of another culture—or players might more efficiently engage in military operations against members of that culture. Players might begin to believe stereotypes about members of other cultures. Players might share in cultural phantasms comprising a heroic vision of combat and a demonizing vision of another culture. All of these potential outcomes can have lasting effects in terms of player empowerment. Furthermore, when these players do not engage systems for entertainment, but use the technologies as means of training for actual engagement in war, even more is at stake. Indeed, historians of science Tim Lenoir and Henry Lowood have contended that the "military is using newly-minted best practices of game design and business models to compete in the arena for young highly-trained cyberwarriors" (Lenoir and Lowood 2005, 454). What social-computational flow can help reveal is how these social issues of power are connected to technical aspects of the games such as gameplay mechanics, graphics, and voice and text communication systems.

Toward identifying several notable types of social-computational flow, let us continue with the war-related theme of the previous examples. Imagine a war-oriented videogame in which players encounter both allies and enemies from multiple countries. Aspects of the game's content such as allegiance and enmity between countries could be determined in many ways. The choices of who can be an ally versus who can be an enemy could be the individual decisions of a game player or developer. There are other possibilities, too. Changes to allegiances and enmities could alternatively have been based on collective updating performed by networked game players, algorithmic modeling based on players' actions in the game world, algorithmic modeling based on players actions multiple different games featuring similar themes and settings, or even algorithmic gathering of information from outside sources such as real-world online news sites. If an individual game developer predetermines allegiance and enmity in a game, the game promotes the values of that developer, which may or may not be instilled by hegemony. If a corporate or military institution predetermines allegiance and enmity based upon its own values, the game serves to perpetuate the values of state power. If allegiance and enmity determined dynamically from an algorithm operating on one or more news sites, the game's values may change over time and could end up serving to maintain or destabilize power relationships depending on the ideologies inherent in the news sites used. What all of these examples reveal is that the ways in which these games represent and affect power relationships are influenced by where they acquire their information and associated values.

Understanding where the game acquires such information has important implications for assessing the potential social impact of the ideology underlying the game. The game supports a particular social order based on its content. Aspects of a system's structure can also be configured and reconfigured based on the ways that they encode real-world information. The interface of the war-oriented game itself could change based on shifting allegiances in the real world, perhaps showing different opportunities for action depending on the current state of world political relations. As discussed in chapter 4, the structure of a computing system reflects a set of priorities that encodes the values of the system's designers and users.

What these examples help reveal is that both computational content and structures can connect to real-world ideology in a number of ways. Social-computational flow reveals different categories of transfer between such computational content and structures and real world events and patterns. "Computational content and structure" used in this sense includes a computing system's media elements (stored and generated), data structures, and algorithms. We can now define several of the most notable types of social-computational flow as follows:

• *Individual* social-computational flow (humanly defined transfer from a single human author to computational content and structure)

• *Cooperative* social-computational flow (humanly defined transfer from multiple human authors to computational content and structure)

• *Collective* social-computational flow (human-designed or algorithmically facilitated transfer from multiple human authors treated in aggregate to computational content and structure)

• *Intertextual* social-computational flow (algorithmically defined transfer from thematically related and/or similarly structured external systems to computational content and structure)

• *Semiotically socketed* social-computational flow (algorithmically defined transfer from external systems used as information resources to computational content and structure)

• *Perceptual* social-computational flow (algorithmically defined transfer of motor-sensory technologies that act upon the external world to computational content and structure)

Each of these types of social-computational flow involves a different form of connection between the content/structure of the world outside of a system and the content/structure implemented within a system. It is important to reiterate that although social-computational flow abstractly describes relationships between a computing system and the external social world, they do not imply either a technological determinist or a social determinist bent. Social computational-flow is just one aspect of how computing systems acquire meaning within broader socio-data ecologies (as described at the start of chapter 3). Although these six categories are not exhaustive of all the ways that the content and structure of computing systems connect to the external world, they represent some of the most pervasive forms of such connections between meaning within subjective computing systems and meaning in society.

   We have already seen examples of some of these. In chapter 4, we saw that the imaginative world of *Passage* is an example of an individual social-computational flow, mapping Rohrer's ruminations on mortality into a game. In this case, the source is Jason Rohrer and the destination is the game *Passage*. The epistemologies used in the *Living Liberia Fabric* (in chapter 3) provide examples of cooperative social-computational flow because they acquired their meanings through joint authorship by a team of researchers and from other individuals who contributed multimedia content. In this case the source is my research group, the Imagination, Computation, and Expression Laboratory, and the destination is the interactive narrative memorial the *Living Liberia Fabric*. Collaborative filtering algorithms in online commerce systems such as explored in chapter 5 are examples of collective social-computational flow because they use algorithmically collected information about an aggregate of independent users. In this case, the source is shopping preferences and actions of many users and the destination is the recommender system and the application it is situated in. Intertextual social-computational flow is somewhat less common; however, an example can be found in the computer role-playing game *The Bard's Tale III*, which allowed players to import characters from other games such as *Wizardry I–III, Ultima III* and *IV*, along with those from earlier *Bard's Tale* games as is shown in figure 8.3 (Interplay 1988, 97; Addams 1989).

Т he first thing you need to do is read the Command Summary Card, which tells you how to get Thief of Fate running on your computer. It also tells you how to use the disk utilities and how to transfer characters from The Bard's Tale I, II, Ultima III, IV and Wizardry I, II, III (The option to transfer characters may not be available on all computers). In addition, it lists the keystroke commands you'll be using.

FIGURE 8.3
The manual from the game *The Bard's Tale III* indicates the option to transfer characters from other games.

In this case, the source is one computer game such as *Ultima IV* and the destination is the game *The Bard's Tale III*. Fantasy sports games, in which statistics about real-world professional sports players are converted into game statistics for fictitious teams, represent examples of semiotically socketed social-computational flow. In this case, the source is a statistical database about sports performances in the real world and the destination is a sports computer game. Haptic feedback systems for laparoscopic surgery or gaming systems that use cameras and motion-sensitive devices to affect their imaginative worlds are examples of perceptual social-computational flow. In this case, the source is real-time or recorded technologically acquired sensory information about the real world, such as users' gestures, and the destination is a system, such as a gesture-driven game that drives a player character or camera's behavior based upon those gestures.

Although systems that are individually, cooperatively, and collectively connected to the external world are quite common and can be found in noncomputational media as well, intertextual, semiotically socketed, and perceptual systems, as defined previously, are always computational and perhaps less common. For this reason, I shall examine the meanings of these latter three terms in more depth. The phrase "intertextual system" here *is* intended to refer to *systems featuring actual structural connections that enable their content and/or structure to be affected by a thematically related system.*[7] The idea of a semiotically socketed system metaphorically draws upon the computer science notion of a socket, which is the endpoint of a networked communication link. The phrase "semiotically socketed" builds upon this concept in a more general way to refer to *systems featuring actual structural connections that enable their content and/or structure to be affected by external systems that are treated as data resources.* Semiotically socketed systems are in some ways similar to intertextual systems. However, semiotically socketed systems have a relationship in which one system is treated merely as a resource for the other, such as a computer artwork that queries a database or conducts a search of the Internet. Intertextual systems feature relationships between more or less similar types of technologies in terms of form and possibly even genre. For example, we saw that the fantasy computer game *The Bard's Tale III* could be influenced by the information and actions within the fantasy world of another computer game such as *Ultima IV*. Finally, perceptual systems take input from the external world via technologies such as cameras and other surveillance technologies, accelerometer- and gyroscope-based motion sensors, haptic feedback devices, and biofeedback technologies. In practice, many systems inhabit multiple categories. Furthermore, these connections between computing systems and the external world can be further distinguished through factors such as their degrees of liveness (real-time input and output) and their degrees of autonomous system agency.

Knowing the ways that the content and structures of subjective, cultural, and critical computing systems are acquired from the real world reveals only a small part of the picture regarding how these systems critically influence societies. After we know how computing systems acquire content and structure, along with who (or what) provides that content and structure, we want to know how the systems have an impact on our lives. Computing systems can, and are, used to play roles in revealing and changing social order. Certainly, there are also other ways that computers influence our lives, such as affecting the natural world through pollution made by their production or by providing respite from real-world social ills through escapist entertainment. However, even human dispositions toward aims as diverse as environmental activism or escapist entertainment are structured by the imagination. The computer can play a role in people's development of activist identities or slacker identities, even if our potential to achieve impact in such areas is partially determined by our roles within existing social order. As such, this chapter addresses how computing can be used to reveal phantasms that disempower people and to generate phantasms that can produce empowering conceptual and social change. As already noted, values are embedded within the structures of computing systems. Understanding how computing systems acquire structure and content is a first step toward revealing phantasms of social order. The next step is to envision how such systems play a role in moving people's minds and bodies to work for social change.

Designing Critical-Computational Phantasms

Two Philosophies for Design

There are multiple philosophies informing individual and collaborative social-computational flow in the design of subjective, cultural, and critical computing systems. I shall discuss two prevalent philosophies here. One philosophy can be called *structuralist* and the other can be called *simulationist*. They can be summarized as top-down (starting from an overarching plan to guide and structure experiences) versus bottom-up (starting from individual elements and letting experiences emerge from how the elements interact) approaches. Various authors have used different terms for these philosophies, but the underlying issues are the same. For example, media studies scholar Henry Jenkins's philosophy makes a distinction between embedded (top-down) versus emergent (bottom-up) narratives in games (Jenkins 2004). Popular media journalism and academic research alike refer to similar distinctions between highly narrative "on rails" games and "sandbox games."

In top-down critical computing system design philosophies, the emphasis is on rules systems that structure the presentation and traversal of assets. The term "structuralist" used in this sense comes from literary theory and denotes approaches to understanding stories based on structural, or formal,[8] arrangements of assets. This type of work attempts to develop grammars that describe the regularities in how assets are composed. The most famous of these, quite often taken up and implemented by burgeoning interactive narrative designers, is that of folklorist Vladimir Propp (Propp 1928). Propp noted thirty-one different components (which he called "functions") that form a partial ordering of story elements that are found in all the Russian fairy tales that he analyzed. These functions contained constants (actors) and variables such as particular imagery or motivations of characters. Propp also describes *transformations*, which structurally capture how multiple story versions appear over time. Others have developed more nuanced structuralist approaches for narrative; for example, semiotician Algirdas Greimas proposed his own structuralist terminology, developing a more complicated system that also separated form from rules (Greimas 1971). Similar approaches can be adapted for other forms of discourse beyond storytelling.

Computational media can directly implement such systems using media assets to produce critical expressive works algorithmically. An example of such an approach is Interplay's classic computer role-playing game *Wasteland* (see figure 8.4), which, in part, provides critical commentary on nuclear war via its postapocalyptic setting. During gameplay, at certain points within the game, the player is prompted to read paragraphs from a booklet.

While you're playing Wasteland, you'll be referring to paragraphs in this book. We know that as a Desert Ranger who enjoys the best of challenges, wouldn't randomly read these paragraphs in search of clues. But intense radiation, coupled with the blazing sun, can impair your good judgement, rendering you totally unable to resist. Fight your best fight here – try not to read a paragraph you're instructed to. You'll get a lot more out of Wasteland this way. Once you successfully complete Wasteland, you can then kick back in your best lounge chair under a shady cactus and read the rest of the fictional vignettes.

1 You creep up to the window and, in the soft, muted tights, you see a tall woman with long, blond hair. She sits before a mirror and brushes her hair, then stands and walks over to the sunken tub off to her left. She kneels and her blue, silken robe drops to the floor. She turns the water on and steam slowly fills the air. You watch in fascination as she reaches down into the tub, whirls, and points an Uzi in your direction. "Stop reading paragraphs you're not supposed to read, creeps." She sighs deeply. "Next time I'm going to demand they put me in a Bard's Tale game, this Wasteland duty is dangerous."

FIGURE 8.4

The game *Wasteland* exhibits a structuralist design philosophy in that the player is told to read selected texts assets (above) in the form of numbered paragraphs (below).

FIGURE 8.5
World creation in the game *Legend of Mana* consists of placing artifacts as is shown here (left). A detail from the screenshot depicts the distribution of magical energy types (right) and helps reveal a simulationist design philosophy. Images © 1999, 2000 SQUARE ENIX CO., LTD. All rights reserved.

In bottom-up design philosophies, the focus is on rules systems that determine interactions between assets in order to result in generation of new assets or assets configurations that are not predetermined. The world construction game mechanic in the console role-playing game *Legend of Mana* (see figure 8.5) is an example of the simulationist philosophy: players place artifacts on a map determining their location in the game and the distribution of eight types of magical energy in the game world (Square 2000).

Only within these map locations, which can be accessed in a user-determined sequence, does the game implement more structured subjective computing experiences. For example, one level of the game called "The Infernal Doll" consists of a junkyard filled with discarded toys as a metaphor for dead soldiers lost during a war. The poignant metaphor effectively conveys pathos but does not contribute strongly to a central narrative and does not have a strong relationship to narratives in most of the other locations.

I call the design approaches sketched thus far *philosophies* because in practice they are guiding principles, not pure aesthetic dictates. Subjective computing systems are rarely solely one or the other. *Legend of Mana* is also structuralist in that the player travels to locations in the game and experiences small narrative events that are cataloged numerically in an in-game journal. In *Wasteland*, and indeed most computer role-playing games, combat is largely simulationist in nature because player characters and NPCs interact via rule systems to compare their statistics to one another's (usually with some degree of randomness used to modify results so that outcomes are not completely deterministic). Furthermore, simulationist system designers often begin with an idea of the type of coherent experiences that they mean to evoke, and designers of such systems often do not seek to achieve extremely high degrees of surprising and unanticipated outcomes. For example, battle systems in role-playing games are not deterministic, but they are often probabilistic and are highly predictable in many ways.

Each design philosophy has benefits and pitfalls. A major concern to address in structuralist designs is the issue of grain size of assets. A system using large-grained assets composes content out of clearly recognizable clips, text fragments, sprites, or other types of media. A subjective computing system producing output composed of smaller-grained fragments uses very short clips or stills, words instead of paragraphs, sprite elements, and so on. Large-grained assets like the paragraphs in *Wasteland* can effectively convey well-designed content, yet they often make the rule systems for composing assets very obvious. When assets recur, they are quite noticeable; these systems are often less replayable for this reason. On the other hand, though small-grained assets can produce high variability, they typically require more complex algorithmic approaches in order to achieve coherence (or they may simply produce less seamlessly coherent experiences).

Simulationist systems can offer high degrees of variability between user experiences and in some sense can be seen as structuralist systems with complex rule systems and extremely fine-grained assets. Simulationist systems are often based on modeling experiences using systems of underlying variables, such as a fight in a role-playing game with outcomes determined by values for offensive attributes, defensive attributes, and vitality (a number of points at which life is indicated by a positive value). A design problem is that although such variables are often given descriptive names such as "strength," "armor class," and "hit points," simply representing their values on the screen does not result in compelling critical commentary or immersive worlds. Consider that instead of those combat-oriented variable names we could have instead chosen "seduction points," "rejection points," and "love value" in a critical computing system aimed at providing insight into power relationships between lovers. In such a game, a player character might try to woo potential lovers, succeeding when "love values" reach a certain threshold. A straightforward implementation could result in players doing no more than watching bar graphs change as values change, just as when the theme is battle instead of love. An effective simulationist design would need to generate critical expressive phenomena, events that translate changes in underlying variables into meaningful action units. A game in which combat results in a character limping, breathing heavily, weeping, cowering, and/or a future reluctance to fight is potentially more interesting in terms of critical engagement (as it is more likely to compel a player to consider the costs of aggression) than one in which combat merely results in the shrinking of a green bar representing hit points. This is not to say that the hit point mechanic is not effective in terms of strategic gameplay; it is offered merely as an illustration of a difference between simulating critically meaningful events and offering a visualization of underlying statistical information.

Underlying both structuralist and simulationist approaches to critical computing is a need to computationally represent the meaningful information about the imaginative world being evoked in order to ensure that it affects users' imaginations, and through user actions, potentially has an impact upon the real world. We have explored a number of topics in this book, including *expressive epistemologies, agency play, cultural phantasms, integrative cultural systems, polymorphic poetics,* and *social-computational flow.* Let us take time now to consider how these concepts can help us understand and design computing systems for empowerment. In particular, I shall consider the capacities of computing systems to play roles in revealing cultural phantasms and prompting *critical phantasms.* Critical phantasms are those phantasms that challenge oppressive norms and play roles in empowering people. I now shall consider one system with such aims.

Blue Velvet: Phantasmal Media Analysis

After discussing the game *Passage* in chapter 4, I mentioned that computing systems can help us understand aspects of the human condition such as the relationships between socioeconomic policies, race, history, and more. An example of such a critical computing system is the collaborative multimedia academic research project *Blue Velvet* by researchers David Theo Goldberg and Stefka Hristova and designer Erik Loyer (Goldberg, Loyer, and Hristova 2008), published in the groundbreaking online multimedia journal *Vectors* (with media scholars Tara McPherson and Steve Anderson as editors). *Blue Velvet* scrutinizes the factors that contributed to the disaster known as Hurricane Katrina that devastated the city of New Orleans in 2005. *Blue Velvet* examines the effect of the hurricane on the city and "underscores . . . that the tragic events that unfolded in New Orleans and along the Gulf Coast were possible precisely because of years of [economically] neoliberal policies that underwrote the necessary conditions for such devastation in the first place" (Goldberg, Loyer, and Hristova 2008). I shall analyze *Blue Velvet* to better understand its capacity to prompt and reveal critical phantasms and as an example of phantasmal media design.

The most striking aspect of *Blue Velvet* is the initial interface metaphor that users encounter upon interacting with the system (shown in figures 8.6 and 8.7) and the way that it constructs a cultural phantasm of a flood at the same time as revealing cultural phantasms regarding the reasons that the flood caused so much destruction. Let us look in depth at the system's design and the design process leading to its effectiveness.[9] Toward this end, I shall first provide a close reading of my experience with this aspect of the system. When *Blue Velvet* begins, after a brief load screen, a rightward wipe reveals a title screen in which the bottom third is a New Orleans cityscape consisting of three skyline silhouettes in shades of pale green-beige. The imagery in some ways reminds me of backgrounds of Aaron Douglas's paintings from the Harlem renaissance, though with the uniform slickness often imposed by vector graphics. This cityscape fades into the middle third, which is a blue sky. The blue sky fades to gray in the top third, signifying impending rain. Though the silhouettes are evenly colored, the image of the sky above has the texture of high-quality rag paper. The audio track plays the sweeping sound of a hurricane—spiraling wind and rain. The desaturated colors, lack of humans in the cityscape, color gradient implying rainclouds, and sound of rain together contribute to a desolate, apprehensive feeling. Near the credits there is a red "begin" button. After I click this button, a bar consisting of the repeating charcoal gray and black text "1:NEWORLEANS 2:PREFERENCES" begins to scroll leftward across the screen.[10] A small set of instructions appears, indicating that I should use headphones for an optimal experience (which I do) and that highlighted words can be clicked upon; the instructions soon fade away. After a few moments, several small very pale gray (nearly white) text fragments begin to fall from the word "PREFERENCES" such as "perennial anxiety," "America's outlet," "subtropical swampland," "gumbo ingredients," and "structure." These words appear to be associated with perspectives of the city of New Orleans and their downward motion resembles rainfall. Pale pink words (later they fade to near-red) such as "sociality" and "neo-conservatism" begin to scroll both leftward and rightward across the top of the blue middle third of the screen. These words suggest that the system is constructed to represent a perspective on the politics and economics of New Orleans in light of the social context of the city at the time just before Hurricane Katrina hit. These elements can be seen in figure 8.6.

When the mouse cursor is near words at the top of the screen, moving the mouse horizontally influences the direction and speed of their scrolling based upon how

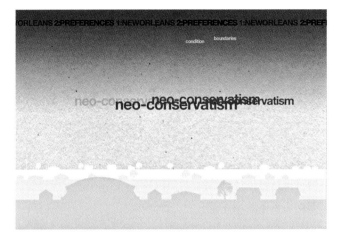

FIGURE 8.6
This type of screen appears in *Blue Velvet* after the initial title screen.

close the mouse cursor is to the edge of the screen (the words move toward the opposite edge of the mouse cursor). Moving the mouse cursor over these words highlights them by turning them white. Clicking on the words causes many more of the rain-drop-like words to fall. They fall at different rates and begin to overlap, resulting in a sense of blurring as they obscure one another. The pale gray words fade away just before hitting the red words. There is no change in the audio when the pale gray words fall—this gives their descent a gentle feel. The pale gray words cause the semitransparent red words to become more opaque. Mousing over the red words highlights them. There are many nearly red words in the center of the screen now; they subtly bounce back and forth horizontally, confined by the bounds of the screen, unlike those at the top of the screen. Though the sound of the storm roils in the background, there seems to be a long time limit for exploring this section, if there is one at all. The sense of an impending storm extends. I click "neo-conservatism."

The effects are jarring. There is an abrupt shift as the clicked word suddenly and rapidly falls downward. Simultaneously, a dramatic musical drumbeat and other percussive sounds begin to play. The word hits the silhouette of the city and the rest of the screen turns black; the city shifts to tan and gray and is overlaid with a semitransparent photographic cityscape. The silhouette contorts, rippling like an exaggerated liquid surface. "Neo-conservatism" fractures into several words like "conservative," "con," "serve," and "vat"; the latter two words are so close to one another, and they fall so quickly, that at first glance it looks like "servant." This illusion is important to mention because the transition is so sudden and unexpected that it can be read only at first glance. There is no way to control this rapid descent—I want to stop it; I feel as if I have set a destructive event in motion and I attempt to rapidly to assess every minor event as it happens. When the scene settles, below the cityscape that is now out of view, other text appears. Photographic assets appear too, which scroll horizontally near the bottom of the screen. At the very bottom of the screen is the bar of text that was formerly at the top. The music remains rhythmic and dramatic. Figure 8.7 depicts this transition and the resultant screen.

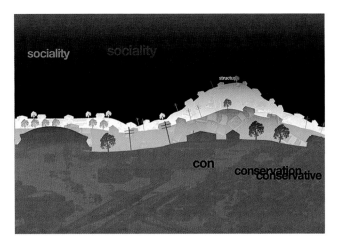

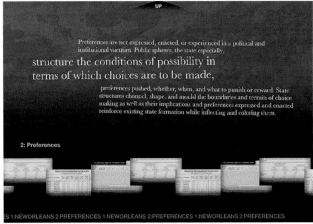

FIGURE 8.7
The top image depicts how, after a click, *Blue Velvet* plays an animation showing the scene submerging beneath floodwaters. The bottom image depicts how multimedia files are then presented for user navigation.

I find the metaphors of a storm, rapid submergence, and depth to be quite affecting. The sense of loss of control and the desire to go back and reread the associative text, as the word "neo-conservatism" broke apart, parallels my desire to go back to the way things were before the disaster. And yet before the disaster, the storm loomed—all was not well. This situation is paralleled by the social, economic, and political descriptors that scrolled and hovered before the submergence: the many intersecting factors that exacerbated the hurricane's effects. These factors, looming above and within the blue-sky layer in the interface, transformed the hurricane's effects from perennial natural damage to a devastating disaster. The cityscape's lack of texture contrasts with the sky's more organic rag paper texture, perhaps intending to signal the artifice of the human-constructed environment. Yet this is the only factor that slightly mitigates the emotional impact of the experience. The slickness of the vector graphics silhouette feels incongruous because it belies the urban grit of the city. However, the vector graphic cityscape enables the most aesthetically arresting moment—the onset of the ripple effect—and it is soon overlaid with a photographic image. In this regard, even this aspect of the system has metaphorical import, as the cityscape (tragically in real life) loses its luster after it is flooded.

Let us now consider how this impactful metaphor was realized in terms of phantasmal media. In other words, we can analyze it as a case of cooperative social-computational flow from the disaster, to the system's authors' conceptualization of it, to its realization in a critical computing system. As discussed in chapter 4 in the case of *Passage*, this analysis can be done effectively using morphic semiotics. This section will present a careful analysis of *Blue Velvet* using this approach.

As previously mentioned, one of the benefits of morphic semiotics is that it can be applied at different degrees of formality and abstraction. Because the aims of this system differ from those of *Passage*, the analysis of *Blue Velvet* will proceed at a different level of abstraction than the earlier analysis of *Passage*. More specifically, I shall focus somewhat less on preservation properties of the semiotic morphisms involved and more on how the semiotic morphisms allow us to trace how the core ideological and metaphorical concepts of the system are realized in its interface, implementation, and capacity to prompt and reveal phantasms.

First, let us rationally reconstruct the system's initial design concept. I shall begin with the concept of the flood, which I can describe structurally, and proceed to look at how it provided a metaphor for the design concept. The structure of the flood is described very simply by a semiotic space (figure 8.8). The elements in the relations and functions are sorts; water level is a data sort because it just provides information about water.

Simple New Orleans Flood Model
produces (hurricane, strong winds)
produces (hurricane, heavy rain)
causes (heavy rain, function: water level increase)
causes (flood, submergence)
broken (levee) = {true; false}
water level = {low; high; catastrophic}
flood conditional function: if broken (levee) = true AND water level = catastrophic then flood

FIGURE 8.8
This semiotic space describes the flood's structure.

As a step preceding the design of the interface metaphor, it seems that this semiotic space was blended with the conventional conceptual metaphor DOWN IS BAD. Figure 8.9 depicts this design as a blend between the DOWN IS BAD image schema and a simple model for a flood described as a semiotic space consisting of relations and functions. The result represents a concept in which submergence, which is bad, is caused by the flood and conditions leading to it. The blended semiotic space in figure 8.9 uses a different illustrative notation than we have seen so far, particularly with respect to one of the input spaces and the blend space. The DOWN IS BAD metaphor is represented by an input space depicted as a downward facing arrow indicating the pattern of motor-sensory experience it entails. This motor-sensory pattern is the "motion along a path" image schema that the metaphor maps onto the concept of being "bad." In the blend space, the sort hurricane is grouped with heavy rain and strong winds, which are subsorts of hurricane ordered by priority. The other elements in the semiotic space (which is shaped like an arrow to represent a top sort, which is a downward vector mapped from the DOWN IS BAD image schema) are organized by priority, representing a causal chain of events.

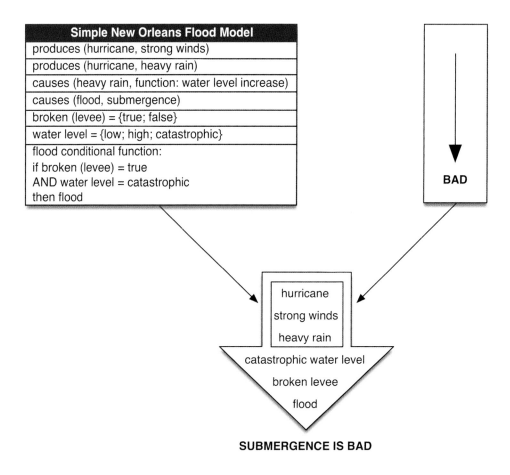

FIGURE 8.9

This blend depicts a metaphor in which submergence, caused by the flood and conditions at the time, is represented as a down trajectory and is also considered to be bad.

In the interface design, this blend provides a basis for a simultaneously literal account of what happened to New Orleans and a metaphorical account represented by sinking words related to underlying deeper causes.

Let us now look at a semiotic morphism from this idea, which is based in a model of real-world experience, to the system's GUI. Some elements were mapped onto an image space representing visual components of the screen. Figure 8.10 illustrates this semiotic morphism. The screenshot images are taken from design documents produced as the developers planned *Blue Velvet*. I have added the text in the rectangles outside of the diagram to describe elements in the final GUI that were not described in those particular design documents. The downward trajectory in the source space (represented by the large arrow and parenthesized word "down") is mapped onto the scrolling motion in the GUI target space that gives the users a sense of moving downward. The hurricane and its subsorts, strong winds and heavy rain, are mapped onto the upper third of the screen (which looks like rainclouds), the wind audio track, and the rainlike falling text. Catastrophic water level is mapped onto the opaque red text; the rising water level in the city maps onto increased opacity of the image. The onset of the flood is mapped onto the transition from the initial scene to the dark scene after the downward motion begins. The breaking of the levees is mapped onto the simultaneous ripple effect that is applied to the New Orleans cityscape silhouette. The notion of SUBMERGENCE IS BAD is mapped onto the darker black, gray, and tan color palette and the ominous soundtrack that also simultaneously appears with the onset of the flood and breaking of the levees. To summarize, all of the elements of the source space metaphor of "bad submergence caused by the flood and conditions leading to it" are mapped onto a sensory (visual or auditory) representation in the GUI.

The GUI design of *Blue Velvet* eventually had to be implemented in a way that preserves the conceptual structure that the authors wanted to convey. The implementation was required to respond interactively to user input and to draw upon several databases in order to select assets and text for display. To account for these aspects of the system, we can describe how the system developers' design concepts were realized in particular computational components. To give a small example, the planning documentation reveals that several key GUI interactions described are handled by what the designers call the "aquarium" (so called, probably, because it provides a model for the transition between being above and below the water). The aquarium model keeps track of current state information about the above- and below-water views and the submerging and surfacing transitions. This information can be seen in

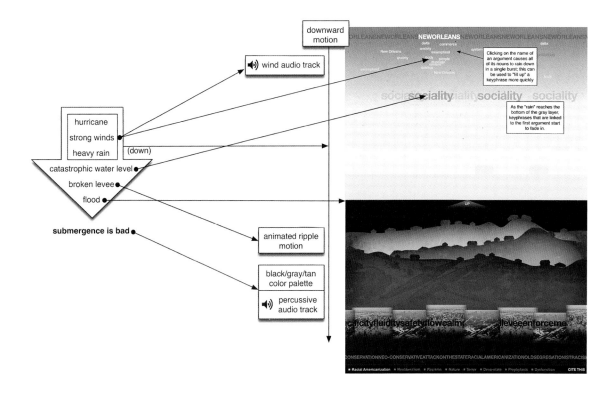

FIGURE 8.10
This image illustrates a semiotic morphism from "bad submergence caused by the flood and conditions leading to it" to the GUI image space.

AquariumModel
COMMENCING:String
ABOVE_WATER:String
UNDERWATER:String
SUBMERGING:String
SURFACING:String
isHibernating:Boolean
isDaytime:Boolean
currentState:String
tableau:Tableau
setState()
setHibernation()
setDaytime()
setTableau()

FIGURE 8.11
This element from the aquarium class diagram
reveals state information variables and functions
implementing elements of the GUI design.

several of the variable names in the aquarium class[11] shown in figure 8.11. For example, the state of transitioning into submergence is identified by the SUBMERGING variable, the current color palette is identified by the Daytime variable (the initial palette is indicated by "True"; the black/gray/tan palette is identified by "False"), and downward motion is identified by the SUBMERGING String variable.

Furthermore, the particular words and assets appearing in the GUI are structured according to a set of "arguments" as to the underlying causes of the devastation caused by the natural disaster—the ways in which human society caused the hurricane to have more catastrophic effects than it would have otherwise. In particular, an epistemic domain for the social conditions contributing to the disaster has been represented as an expressive epistemology for arguments. In particular, *Blue Velvet* presents its interactive content in the form of twenty-four arguments. "Keyphrases" are associated with each argument. The argument names are the terms that scroll horizontally across top of the screen in what the designers call the "tableau" (the repeating text "1:NEWORLEANS 2:PREFERENCES," mentioned in the close reading). The keyphrases correspond to the red text that scrolls horizontally near the center of the screen. Through selecting these keyphrases, the user can access a variety of media assets including maps, images, graphs, videos, audio files, and text that becomes available to explore when the scene submerges.[12] Figure 8.12 shows the arguments and keyphrases constituting this expressive epistemology (Goldberg, Loyer, and Hristova 2008).

Argument	Keyphrase
New Orleans	Sociality
Preferences	Neo-conservatism
Liberty	Homogeneity
Activist segregation	Segregation
Redlining	Redistrict
Conservationist segregation	Race neutrality
Racial privacy/Privatizing race	Born-again racism
Catastrophe	Disaster relief
Apparitions	Signs
Politics of fear	Fear
Crisis management	Vulnerability
Emergency	Immobility
Carcerality	Structural racism
Exposure	Civility
Violence	Special treatment
Skin	Condomization
Misrecognition	Immigration
Surviving	Live free or die
Militarization	Redistribute
Insecurity	Security
Invisibility	Pollution
Disenchantment	Privatization
Singing the blues	Surgical
Redress	Homogenized apartness

FIGURE 8.12
Arguments and keyphrases from *Blue Velvet* constitute an expressive epistemology.

These keyphrases are not mere keys providing access to an objective encyclopedic ontology about the hurricane, the preconditions for its devastating effects, and its aftermath. Rather, they are subjectively chosen entry points to Goldberg's arguments.

There are also epistemologies used to express the epistemic domain of wordplay.[13] To enable keyphrases to break into multiple words upon submergence, as with "neo-conservatism" in the close reading, data structures called etymologies have been implemented. These etymologies reveal several words related to the keyphrase and how those words can break down further into other related words. Figure 8.13 depicts the etymology for "neo-conservatism" from *Blue Velvet*'s design documentation.

Let us now assess what insights we can glean from our analysis of *Blue Velvet* so far. The creators of *Blue Velvet* recognized that different users of their system would have different needs and values. Several of the cultural values found within some sectors of academia are embedded in the structure of *Blue Velvet*'s epistemologies:

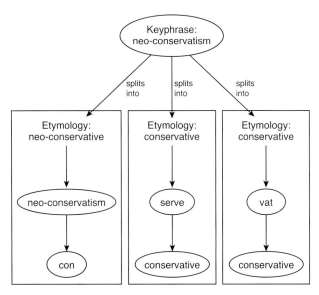

FIGURE 8.13
The etymology for "neo-conservatism" depicts how the keyphrase
can be broken up into three related etymologies, each of which
describes how the name of the keyphrase can be further subdivided.

systematic argumentation, a political orientation, and wordplay. Specific arguments
and specific etymologies represent epistemic spaces drawn from epistemic domains
represented by these epistemologies. In the ways that *Blue Velvet* has embedded these
needs and values into its structure, it is an integrative cultural system that preserves
academic and political values in its architecture. The discussion has also illustrated
how a poignant metaphor of submergence was designed to work in conjunction with
the system's arguments and etymologies—the content would not be nearly as emotionally impactful were it not tightly coupled with the image space, dynamically illustrating the flood, the cityscape's submergence, and the downward motion suggesting
how bad (devastating) it was. Furthermore, the system would be neither convincing
in its argumentation nor effective in its presentation if the structures of the epistemologies and image space did not correspond extremely tightly with one another.

Agency play also plays a role in the construction meaning that occurs when using the system. Initially, there was a great deal of user agency to cause many more words to rain by clicking a keyphrase and to affect the scrolling of words. Yet, when a keyphrase falls, agency is shifted to the system, as the submergence implemented in the aquarium class is rapid and cannot be halted. This event represents a sudden shift of agency relationship—prompting a phantasm of a disaster that is human caused, but inexorable in its progress after it starts.

Agency play also plays a role in prompting critical phantasms in *Blue Velvet*. Accessing arguments in a user-determined order could give some users a *sense* of empowerment because their clicks drive the order in which content is presented. On its own, this type of navigation is merely a type of instrumental means of information access. In *Blue Velvet*, this means of interaction enables a type of local user agency such as the ability to flip to any chapter of a book at will rather than reading the book page by page from start to finish. However, if local user agency in the form of constructing self-ordered readings supports users in the processes of thinking through an argument, drawing their own conclusions, and building up knowledge in their own ways, then the interaction mechanism becomes a useful tool for individual empowerment. This strategy for supporting user empowerment does not suggest that critical computing system developers should always present all points of view as equal, thus intentionally supporting the possibility that user interaction might help users come to conclusions that support oppressive worldviews. Rather, critical computing systems are more likely to engender lasting conceptual change in users through what psychologists call the central route of persuasion (Petty and Cacioppo 1986), which entails allowing and encouraging users to more richly engage, explore, and even challenge an author's argument. If an argument can withstand robust local user agency, and remain convincing, it may be even more compelling. On the other hand, such local agency may diminish the rhetorical force of the system's arguments if they rely upon a chain of reasoning to be convincing. In *Blue Velvet*'s case, by involving users in a process of critically engaging the social issue at hand, the types of agency relationship shift and local user agency goes beyond mere instrumental navigation. The metaphorical interface structure imposes meaningful order on the user's experiences even when the arguments are not presented in sequential order from one to twenty-four.

In order to examine the ways in which *Blue Velvet* serves critical computational empowerment, it bears emphasizing that *Blue Velvet* argues that economic, political, social, and infrastructural policies and structures laid the groundwork for Hurricane

Katrina's devastation to occur. Furthermore, the system's argument is based on the premise that the devastation *revealed* the impacts of forces like neoliberal economic policies, neoconservative political positions, structural racism, and segregation. The authors argue that these forces devalued and immobilized economically impoverished African Americans and otherwise marginalized people in New Orleans in the face of an emergency. The system presents its argument through attempting to prompt a critical phantasm consisting of shared values (e.g., a stance against conservative politics and neoliberal economics), shared knowledge (e.g., empirical evidence about the existence of discriminatory zoning and housing policies, disaster relief policies, and structural and historical racism), and shared representations (a combination of animated imagery photographic imagery, video, music, and more that cumulatively result in a coherent aestheticized vision of the conditions and events of the hurricane). Because this critical phantasm contrasts with the cultural phantasm of a hurricane as a purely *natural* disaster, we can say that the contrast between the view of the devastation as rooted in rooted in human societal conditions and actions, as opposed to only meteorological conditions, reveals the usually implicit (and therefore invisible) natural disaster phantasm.

The design and implementation of the system was motivated by the fact that some people might initially have a different point of view than the authors' own. They realized that many users might begin using the system believing that the hurricane was purely a natural disaster. Some users might be predisposed to think that any other point of view unfairly places the blame for a natural disaster on issues of politics, race, or economics. In short, though they probably would not use the terminology I am using, *Blue Velvet*'s authors were aware that other cultural phantasms exist that allow the disaster to be perceived in different ways. They wanted to reveal those cultural phantasms to those for whom they were invisible and replace them with other critical phantasms that the authors felt respected the needs of the disempowered and oppressed.

Finally, the system's design is based on a balance of both structuralist and simulationsist philosophies. This balance between the two design philosophies allows the system to further serve diverse user needs. For example, some users would be more accustomed to reading content such as *Blue Velvet*'s in traditional academic articles in print journals. Other users may be accustomed to engaging with dynamic computational media works. To serve these multiple needs and values regarding interaction with the system, as in our discussion of agency play in *Blue Velvet*, the assets and their order of reading have been decoupled (what Espen Aarseth [1997] calls the "textons"

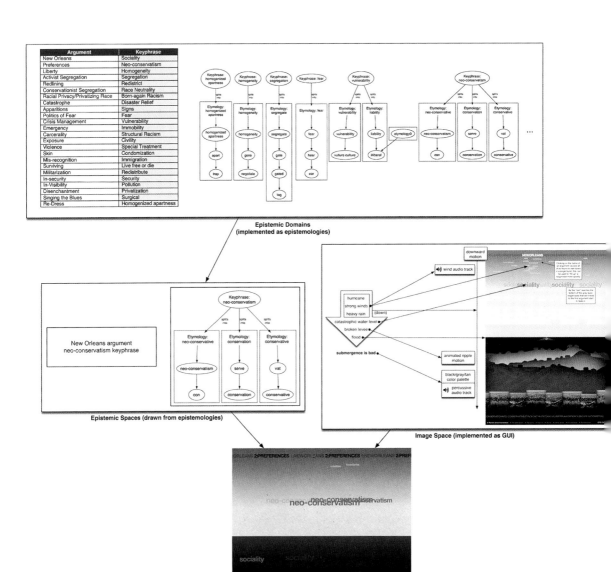

**Epistemic Domains
(implemented as epistemologies)**

Epistemic Spaces (drawn from epistemologies)

Image Space (implemented as GUI)

Phantasms (prompted and revealed by use of the *Blue Velvet* system)

FIGURE 8.14
The *Blue Velvet* system has the
capacity to prompt complex
phantasms.

and "scriptons," respectively). Serving traditional readers, the default order of engaging with the arguments in consecutive order from one to twenty-four programmed into the system is a structuralist design element. Yet, after the third argument appears, instructions are given on how to bring up all arguments at once (or start over from the first argument only); thus hidden affordances to produce out-of-sequence access to the arguments are revealed. In this manner, *Blue Velvet* exhibits a simulationist design philosophy in the way that its assets can be reconfigured and revealed through exploring a series of interconnected epistemologies in a user-determined sequence.

This analysis of *Blue Velvet*, performed using the conceptual framework presented in this book, illustrates a computational media experience reliant upon prompting and revealing phantasms. To summarize, in *Blue Velvet* the sensory experience of the submergence metaphor is understood simultaneously as an intellectual argument regarding the social, political, and economic factors causing the Hurricane Katrina disaster (see figure 8.14)—a subjective, cultural, and critical play of prompting and revealing phantasms.

Loyer has described his system design goal with *Blue Velvet* as searching for an interaction metaphor that is just one level of complexity greater than the average user might expect from such a system, so that people can use it without trouble but not everything is simplistically revealed. I believe that Loyer's design goal is driven by a desire to implement interfaces that are uncannily evocative in terms of imagery and interaction but that always offer clear exploration of both scholarly and poetic ideas. We could rephrase Loyer's design goal as a search for a semiotic morphism that preserves just enough of the rich and abstract source space structure in the target so as to attain a poignant metaphorical connection to the real-world phenomenon being addressed. Furthermore, real-world content described by the source space is mapped via both individual and collaborative social-computational flow. Goldberg collected, orchestrated, and wrote the initial content in the form of an academic article. The three collaborators then combined to provide and organize the specific content as it was segmented and embedded in an interactive animated interface in *Blue Velvet*.

Blue Velvet: Speculative Design and Implications

Blue Velvet's authors would agree that there are some aspects of their critical computing system that could be improved, like any other human cultural artifact. They also would likely agree that there are exemplary aspects of the system that effectively engage the imaginations of users and will stand the test of time. Rather than critiquing the system, the aim here is to illustrate how *Blue Velvet* and other critical computing systems can be used to effectively prompt critical phantasms. In this spirit, it is worthwhile to speculate about what we can learn from *Blue Velvet* about critical computing system design in terms of social-computational flow as an exercise to think about the roles of critical phantasms in empowering people and to illustrate the role of social-computational flow in doing so.

Blue Velvet is a system about a real-world event, along with the event's preconditions and aftermath. In the previous discussion, we extrapolated that an aim of the authors was to use the system to help reveal cultural phantasms that the users might unknowingly possess. For example, the term "Hurricane Katrina" might initially prompt some users to imagine sad brown people being rescued from the rooftops of bungalows, along with a perspective that politics, race, and economics might have played little or no role in the events that unfolded around the hurricane. Recall from chapter 5 that approaches to collective intelligence, such as collaborative filtering algorithms, prompt shared values and preferences, which are building blocks for cultural phantasms. Such approaches could also be used to *reveal* cultural phantasms. Applying a collaborative filtering approach to characterizing user beliefs for the sake of transparently exposing them, rather than opaquely using them to support consumption, would be a transgressive and powerful use of the technology in a critical computing system.

In such a manner, a critical computing system such as *Blue Velvet* could also use collective social-computational flow to better serve the needs and cultural phantasms of its users. For example, the navigation of such a system could be structured in such a way that users must initially articulate what they believe the causes of an event to be. The user would then need to trace a path through content, engaging with media assets presenting perspectives of the event that the user finds to be most compelling. Eventually, patterns of use might emerge from users of the system in aggregate, revealing dominant and underlying user preconceptions in the forms of needs, values, and cultural phantasms. It would also be informative to collect this information from certain target groups. For example, in the case of *Blue Velvet*, such a group could be selected to represent the demographic distribution of pre-Katrina New Orleans as contrasted with post-Katrina New Orleans. The system could then be more targeted in choosing which cultural phantasms to help reveal and which critical phantasms to help prompt. A rich dialogue could occur between the critical phantasms of the system's authors, aimed at engendering conceptual change in users and the cultural phantasms of its users that have invisibly shaped how they understand the hurricane and the reasons for its impact. The system would not only try to indoctrinate users with the authors' perspectives; rather, as mentioned earlier, users could engage, explore, and even challenge the authors' argument with greater subjective nuance.

Systems like *Blue Velvet* can also connect to the real world through other systems. For example, consider again Domike, Mateas, and Vanouse's interactive narrative system *Terminal Time* mentioned in chapters 3 and 7 (Domike, Mateas, and Vanouse 2003). Both *Terminal Time* and *Blue Velvet* deal with issues of social ideology primarily through using their expressive epistemologies to reconfigure how users access media elements. An additional epistemology-related parallel is that *Terminal Time* algorithmically determines the persuasive rhetorical style of its output, while *Blue Velvet* algorithmically determines wordplay in its output. However, a difference between the two is that *Blue Velvet* is focused on the ideologies around a single event and *Terminal Time* is focused on providing ideologically tinted perspective on history over the relatively long time scale of a millennium. If both systems were adapted to use the same epistemic formats, however, rich new possibilities could emerge for both systems through the resultantly enabled intertextual social-computational flow. The impact of revealing cultural phantasms with *Blue Velvet* could be extended by situating the cultural phantasms within broader ideological perspectives on history in general provided by *Terminal Time*'s expressive epistemology, further revealing the pervasiveness of the cultural phantasms. For example, worldviews supportive of neoliberal economic policies or racism could be shown to have had broader implications over time than just for the devastating effects of Hurricane Katrina. A modest way in which enhanced intertextual social-computational flow could extend *Terminal Time* is to incorporate the events surrounding the hurricane within the histories it narrates. A more profound extension using *Blue Velvet*'s content to complement *Terminal Time*'s output would be to reveal the immediate, real-world impacts of the historical ideologies that *Terminal Time* addresses through particular, relatively contemporary events such as Hurricane Katrina. Highlighting the emergent contrast between phantasms in *Terminal Time*'s macrohistorical time scale and phantasms in *Blue Velvet*'s focus on recent sociopolitical realities is a powerful way to reveal cultural phantasms and prompt critical phantasms.

We have seen that there are cultural phantasms that the authors of *Blue Velvet* see as problematic and seek to reveal along with critical phantasms that they seek to prompt. Data to support either aim could readily be found online to extend the system using semiotically socketed social-computational flow. Simple Internet searches can reveal encyclopedia definitions of terms such as "neoliberal" and "redlining," inflammatory and biased comments left by readers about news articles regarding Hurricane

Katrina, demographic information about the city of New Orleans, images of hurricanes, blog posts about police brutality and failures of the emergency response after the storm hit, and much more relevant content. All of this information, in theory, could be integrated algorithmically into a system such as *Blue Velvet* in the form of assets that the system could present to users. In practice, however, such an approach runs into a pitfall of simulationist design, as algorithmically selecting and composing such content at run-time tends to degrade the aesthetic coherence of critical computing systems (because the authors do not know what the algorithms will find ahead of time). Still, it is possible for a well-designed simulationist critical computing system to process and use such assets to more strongly connect the system to dynamic real-world events. For instance, a system could contrast online discussions of the causes of the hurricane's devastation posted in its immediate aftermath to posts about the city of New Orleans at the time it is being used, even if years have passed. Designing for such specific contrasts could make the system more timely for users regardless of when they engage with the system. This discussion just begins to suggest the potential of semiotically socketed social-computational flow to help enable critical computing systems stay in effective dialogue with real-world issues.

Even more speculatively, the system could be extended using perceptual social-computational flow. The same types of surveillance technologies used to monitor hotel lobbies, elevators, street corners, and retail stores in cities such as New Orleans could perhaps be used by citizens to aid in monitoring issues like racial profiling and bias. Just as composite profiles of criminals are generated through such technologies, composite profiles of individuals victimized by institutions engaging in illegal discriminatory practices could be fed into the knowledge base of a critical computing system. Aggregate superimposed face portraits of victims of such discrimination could be created by concerned citizens within communities of the city as subdivided by district. Such images could help show the haunting, collective "face" of those discriminated against within particular communities, which could then be compared and contrasted with the amount of social opportunities present in those communities. A portrait of institutionalized discrimination could emerge. These ideas are all just speculations on how perceptual social-computational flow could be used to enable new types of critical phantasms. I leave it to readers (for now) to envision more new ways that different types of social-computational flow could enable *effective* prompting of critical phantasms and revealing of oppressive cultural phantasms using systems like *Blue Velvet*, and more important, other new types of systems unanticipated by any critical computing system yet invented.

Reflections on Critical Computing for Transformative Empowering Impact

There are many ways that expressive epistemologies, polymorphic poetics, cultural phantasms, integrative cultural systems, agency play, and social-computational flow can help in the understanding and design of critical computing systems for empowerment. Expressive epistemologies can be used for sociocultural empowerment by helping to reveal cultural phantasms. They can play a role in revealing cultural phantasms by allowing content to be explored from multiple perspectives with meaningful differences between them. Polymorphic poetics offers a potential means of expressing a different type of social commentary than research in engineering or the social sciences typically do. Polymorphic poetics accounts for how authors can convey precise critical phantasms designed to prompt both subjective experiences and conceptual change.

The novel *Invisible Man* has been used throughout this book as an example of a media work that prompts readers to carefully construct imaginative worlds and poetic phantasms as a form of social critique. The broad impact of the book has enabled those phantasms to become cultural phantasms. The *Living Liberia Fabric* and *Blue Velvet* might begin to suggest that expressive epistemologies could be used to support design of critical computing systems also capable of prompting nuanced and subjective critical phantasms. In particular, the *Living Liberia Fabric* is designed to prompt critical phantasms as an integrative cultural system that is grounded in the worldviews of its stakeholders, whose needs it is designed to serve. A truly effective critical work of phantasmal media could achieve the type of long-lasting cultural impact of a work like Ellison's novel.

Agency play can also be a powerful tool for understanding the nature of power and empowerment. In the famous "Battle Royal" scene from *Invisible Man*, the unnamed protagonist is prepared to give an assimilationist speech about humility and social responsibility. Instead, however, he is compelled to participate with nine other African American boys in a blindfolded group fight. The battle royal was an evening's entertainment for "all of the town's big shots" who "were there in their tuxedoes, wolfing down the buffet foods, drinking beer and whiskey and smoking black cigars" (Ellison [1947] 1995, 17). The combatants' payment was eventually given in the form of gold coins strewn on an electrified carpet—they received painful shocks with each reward. The protagonist had a limited form of local agency in the competition: He could fight in any way that he wanted to. Yet, not knowing the conventions of the battle, he was left as one of the final two combatants after the others had left. He had no global agency to reject the battle once in that situation. The protagonist thought: "Blindfolded, I could no longer control my motions. I had no dignity" (22). He also had no global agency to assert himself as a valuable and dignified human being. This lack of agency is reinforced by the fact that the battle royal was keeping him from giving the impotent (though inspired in his own mind) speech he had planned to give later (to an audience that would ultimately be revealed as unsympathetic, ignorant, and oppressive). The poignancy and sharp social commentary of the battle royal scene suggests that agency play is a powerful technique for critically interrogating power relationships.

Placing the user or player in the role of a protagonist in a critical computing experience addressing issues as in *Invisible Man* can be a mode of social critique. In such a system, agency play could be used to support individual empowerment through the creation of virtual selves embedded in virtual experiences of real-world social phenomena like racism. For example, social networking profiles, videogame characters, virtual world avatars, and even online accounts have potential to play roles in enabling critical imagining of oneself, as well as the social identities and life stories of others. However, merely customizing graphical representations and text fields based upon the intuitions and assumptions of system developers is insufficient to convey such a sense of self and social identity. Rather, such systems need robust models of what I would prefer to call self-imagination.

Self-imagination is not limited to normative identity categories. Instead, it recognizes the phantasmal nature of social identity and the fluidity with which social identities are constructed, revealed, and transformed. Self-imagination is an example of a conceptual tool, grounded in the cognitive and social sciences, as well as aesthetically sophisticated approaches for realizing them in phantasmal media, that can empower people by enabling them escape from the cultural phantasms that constrain them. Meaningfully prompting and revealing phantasms in which human agency exists in a dynamic expressive relationship with system agency—informed by humanities, arts, and social science accounts of imaginative phenomena—is one tool for self-imagination.

Critical computing systems operate in interconnected webs of information and power. Such critical computing systems can dynamically respond to the changing information produced by state powers and individual bodies of computer users alike, both of which leave traces of their activities in publically available forms online. We now have access to profound collective bodies of information, and technologies of control that shape our desires into forces that kill, or liberate, ourselves. It is our challenge to imagine new ways to understand how these systems function, reveal their oppressive cultural phantasms, and, as critically aware culture makers, to develop alternative critical phantasms that serve our needs and values without trampling upon those of others.

V

CONCLUSION

9

PHANTASMAL MEDIA AND THE HUMAN CONDITION

The novel begins in a railway station, a locomotive huffs, steam from a piston covers the opening of the chapter, a cloud of smoke hides part of the first paragraph.

—Italo Calvino, *If on a Winter's Night a Traveler*

Smoke from the pyramidal sawdust pile
Curls up, blue ghosts of trees, tarrying low
Where only chips and stumps are left to show
The solid proof of former domicile.

Meanwhile, the men, with vestiges of pomp,
Race memories of king and caravan,
High-priests, an ostrich, and a juju-man,
Go singing through the footpaths of the swamp.

—Jean Toomer, *Cane*

Illusion and transformation are twins of meaning making. Media forms that involve illusion and transformation can give aesthetic power to expressive statements about the human condition. We imagine worlds using media in order to make sense of the human condition, whether through everyday thought, creative conversations, densely meta-phorical poetry, or highly fantastic literature. These imaginative worlds are contingent and dynamic, changing with our shifting emotions, contexts, interactions, and experiences. Subjective, cultural, and critical computing systems are media forms that can conjure illusions that prompt or reveal phantasms. Subjective, cultural, and critical computing systems can enable transformation through polymorphic poetics, creatively structuring and processing symbolic information. Subjective, cultural, and critical computing systems have the potential to contribute to changing our conceptions of our world and energizing our capacities to change it, just as all other expressive media can.

Written to nurture these twins of illusion and transformation, this has been a book about how to understand and create evocative story worlds, poetic metaphors, critical conceptual blends, haunting visions, and empowering cultural experiences using the computer. Computing systems hold the power to improvisationally and dynamically combine formal information elements in meaningful new ways while responding to users' interactions. When this power is deployed, the unlimited human imagination is prompted by the limited symbolic ways that machines encode meaning. This balance between the structures that computers can manipulate and the ghostly, subjective forms of imagination that humans produce is at the heart of the expressive potential of computing.

Limited, humble computing systems can intervene beautifully in the processes of human imagination. When the capacities of computing systems to structure, change, and respond to information and user input are orchestrated with sensitive consideration of the slippery processes of human interpretation and experience, phantasms emerge. Carefully designing the interplay of formal computational structures and human subjectivity is the key. So far, I have emphasized several ways in which this type of design can be pursued with groundings in research from fields such as computer science and cognitive linguistics. However, my deepest inspiration comes from a range of artists and their works in other media. After all, there are many media forms in which humans have much more experience in catalyzing salient experiences than computational media.

The concept of *phantasmal media* is inspired by the balance between orchestrated form, improvised chaos, and political forthrightness in Charles Mingus's compositions, such as the "Original Fables of Faubus" (Mingus 1960). This book was inspired by the balance between rich lyrical poetic content and rigid experimental structure in Vladimir Nabokov's novel *Pale Fire* (Nabokov 1962). Similarly, Samuel R. Delany's "The Tale of Plagues and Carnivals" (Delany 1994a) also provides inspiration for the ideas here. Delany's short story features an experimental formal structure based on his aim of expressing 1980s anxieties about HIV (then only called AIDS); Delany blended a tale of plague in a swords-and-sorcery world with contemporary social concerns in order to create an imaginative world that portrayed the conditions at the time with evocative precision. My most transformative experience with classical European music occurred when I encountered how romantic melodies could be combined with highly theorized twelve-tone compositional techniques in the works of Alban Berg (Berg 1995). Similarly, I learned that lush prose can coexist with algorithmically structured form from works such as Italo Calvino's novel *If on a Winter's Night a Traveler* (Calvino 1982a). Jean Toomer's book *Cane* (Toomer [1923] 1969) is another effective phantasmal media work in the print medium. Recall that *Cane* structurally jumps from poetry to prose with abandon, narrating a story that is able to reveal phantasms from the history of the south in the United States, in part because Toomer wrote from multiple ethnic perspectives simultaneously.

The Italo Calvino and Jean Toomer epigraphs that start this chapter are excerpts from works that can exemplify the phantasmal in print literature, though I have focused on computational phantasmal media, including computational systems such as interactive narratives, games, electronic literature, computer-based artworks, social computing systems, and even utilitarian systems used for commerce. Such computing systems put people into dialogue with one another's mental/sensory images, ideologies, and epistemologies (Harrell 2009b). Computational phantasmal media hold the potential to support new modes of addressing, analyzing, interrogating, criticizing, and transforming the human condition, just as is accomplished by the best of the literary and other arts and the worst of other communication technologies used to facilitate conflict and oppression. Let us move toward concluding this book by reflecting upon the nature of the phantasms prompted by the works of Calvino and Toomer, which can help engender better understandings of the natures of, and future possibilities for, phantasmal media to support empowering people through the imagination.

Smoke drifts over these pages, smoke from outside of sawmills in Jean Toomer's classic Harlem Renaissance–era manticore of prose and poetry. Those tendrils of smoke drift through his descriptions of the rural Georgia he explored during a fitful (if temporary) self-examination of his many ethnic roots. Webs of smoke now drift onward to the railway station, wafting over from Italo Calvino's second-person, self-reflexive narration of *you*, the reader, seeing the smoke. In both texts, smoke is evoked as a phantasm—in two parallel senses of the term. Phantasms are imaginary constructions that structure human behavior and ideas. At the same time, phantasms are also cognitive sensory-images. Phantasms are composed of both of these aspects, and thus the unstable nature of smoke is an apt metaphor for these expressive mental images conjured by artworks, clearly apparent, yet without the material presence of a solid object or even the stability of a memory (because memories point to objects and events that have occurred in the real world).

The metaphor goes further, however. It can address power relationships that have affected real lives. As I read Toomer's *Cane*, the phantasm of smoke also stands in for a history of cultural theft, a sense of mournful loss encountered by people of African descent and others who are touched by some of the more depraved historical legacies of the United States. Smoke initiates a political image recalling ages of slavery and nobility in turn. For Calvino, the smoke phantasm blends two parallel stories. The first story in the blend is a narrative description of a man reading a book in a railway station scene. The second story in the blend is the experience of *you*, the person in the real world reading the story (regardless of your gender and your own narratives of personal experience). The books by Calvino and Toomer from which the quotations are excerpted reveal how phantasms can support conceptual and social change in several ways. The books prompt readers to construct rich, detailed, and sustained imaginative worlds in dialogue with the texts. The books interrogate socio-cultural norms and values. The books also skillfully deploy experimental new structural literary and linguistic conventions while maintaining the evocative force of the phantasms they prompt. This notion of the phantasmal based on an interplay of formal structure and imaginative cognition is at the heart of many powerful literary works. This characteristic crucially distinguishes imaginative world and poetic phantasm construction with computational media from many other forms of media expression. It is the heart of phantasmal media expression. Yet, because of this focus on *computing* systems, the theory of phantasmal media must seek to account for how *data-structurally and algorithmically based constructions* can prompt mental imagery in the context of diverse epistemologies of users and developers.

In light of this goal, the theory of phantasmal media must serve two purposes for subjective, cultural, and critical computing research and practice. First, the theory of phantasmal media provides an interdisciplinary framework incorporating cognitive science, computer science, and the arts to articulate how computing systems can function as mental images and ideology-based semantic systems. Second, the theory of phantasmal media illuminates an underdeveloped potential of computing systems: their ability to address the human condition, including social ills, cultural imaginaries, and empowering values.

Because I ultimately argue for the power of *individual* imagination, let us recall the role of the imagination in understanding the self. Self-imagination, the combination of social identity, life story, and self-conception, is a central feat of human cognition. The fallout from this observation is striking. First, if our identities are largely imaginative, the implications are grand—we can reinvent social categories in creative empowering ways. Second, a theoretical account of phantasms can aid in elucidating the types of ideologies, social behaviors, political configurations, and global power relationships that shape our everyday lived experiences in our individually perceived realities.

Phantasms have a unique ability to articulate and reveal nuanced subjective experiences of phenomena such as self-imagination. Subjective, cultural, and critical computing systems are uniquely poised to enable people to participate in dynamic and transformative experiences enabled by *expressive epistemologies*, *polymorphic poetics*, *cultural phantasms*, *integrative cultural systems*, *agency play*, and *critical-computational empowerment*.

Recall that a theory of phantasmal media must also address a gap, the striking chasm between current forms of computational media expression and more mature media forms that have much more established conventions and strong communities engaged in meaning making, interpretation, criticism, and theorizing. Computational media systems all too often remain focused on self-reflexive exploration of the media themselves, as opposed to producing transformative content. Observing this chasm between computational media and more mature media does not require devaluation of the many ingeniously creative computing systems that already exist and that expand the range of what the medium can do. This observation also does not seek to undermine the accomplishments of popular or influential subjective computing systems such as games or computer-based artworks that stir rich emotional and dramatic experiences of sensory imagination for players and audiences. Currently existing exemplary subjective computing systems are valuable not just because of the stunning content they can produce but also because they provide insight into the challenges of using data structures and algorithms as bases upon which we can build dynamic new expressive computing forms. Rather, acknowledging the chasm between computational media and more mature media forms is just an invitation for us to build systems that serve human needs even better. Acknowledging that there is still work to do in inventing new expressive computing systems is an exhortation for us to strive to do better at protecting the tender experiences of life that we treasure using a cloak made from the best of what the human imagination can conceive. We can ground our subjective computing systems in diverse cultural models that take full advantage of the characteristics and affordances of computational media.

Cognitive scientists have begun to show that cognition depends on fundamental imaginative processes—including event stories, action stories, metaphor, metonymy, conceptual blending, parable, and more. Understanding how the processes underlying imaginative cognition create the building blocks for phantasms can serve as a bridge to understanding how to build increasingly effective computational phantasmal media systems. Modeling the aspects of these cognitive processes that are regular and structured enough to be amenable to data-structural and algorithmic implementation, and leaving the rest up to the facilities and experiences of human artists, is an approach that can undergird a range of new types of computational phantasmal media that can express and have impact upon the human condition. After all, many tragedies and triumphs of the human condition, ranging from intense personal melancholy to grand battles against oppressive worldviews that see humans as mere resources to exploit, are all phantasmal feats of imaginative cognition.

Realizing that substantial aspects of our life experiences are phantasms has profound implications. The supposed real world curls up and drifts away, spectrally, like a pale line of smoke. Data structures no longer are attempts to capture objective truths but are instead subjective forms to be manipulated. Algorithms become expressive tools, limited by the constraints of the Turing machine but robust in their abilities to transform content within those confines. The key for harnessing computing systems to produce meaningful, potentially transgressive and transformative phantasms is this: we must better understand the patterns underlying imaginative cognition and we must better understand where there are no such patterns. At the same time, we must never lose sight of the facts that all computation is composed of mere smoky, subjective phantasms and all meaning, including computationally prompted meaning, is ultimately human imagination.

SUMMARY

1 DEFINING PHANTASMS

The concept of phantasmal media is the central topic of this book. Phantasms are combinations of mental imagery and ideology constructed by embodied, distributed, and situated cognitive processes. The concept of the phantasm captures the insight that many of the constructs people see as socially real are in fact rooted in processes of imaginative cognition. Phantasmal media is a term to describe media systems that prompt phantasms—with a focus on computing systems (computational media).

Key design concept: The idea of the phantasm provides an orienting perspective for developers focused on issues of content and imagination in the design of computing systems.

2 IMAGINING AND COMPUTING PHANTASMS

This book focuses on understanding and designing computer systems that prompt phantasms. I explore how computers prompt phantasms through an articulation of how computers can be used for the subjective, cultural, and critical aims of understanding, and improving, the human condition.

Key design concept: The ideas of subjective, cultural, and critical computing can guide development of new types of computing systems.

II SUBJECTIVE COMPUTING

The computer is usually seen as an objective machine, yet it can be used for subjective aims such as expression. A key aspect of using the computer for subjective aims (subjective computing) is understanding its ability to represent imaginative worlds, ideas, and worldviews through data structures (expressive epistemologies). Furthermore, computing systems can express values (such as preferences of designers, norms of societies, or traditions of civilizations). Another key aspect of subjective computing is precisely describing some of the ways that values can be embedded in the structures of computing systems. We can also account for how computing systems express different meanings and values through different structures (polymorphic poetics).

3 EXPRESSIVE EPISTEMOLOGIES

The computer can be used to construct imaginative worlds and prompt forms of imagination called poetic phantasms (meaningful mental imagery and ideas involving metaphor, narrative, categorization, etc.). Imaginative worlds and poetic phantasms are results of subjective forms of computational expression (subjective computing systems). "Expressive epistemologies" is the name I give to data structures based on subjective human worldviews that are useful for implementing computer-based imaginative worlds and prompting poetic phantasms.

Key design concept: The idea of expressive ontologies can guide development of knowledge representations used for subjective purposes.

4 POLYMORPHIC POETICS

The mathematician and computer scientist Joseph Goguen developed a theory called algebraic semiotics that is useful for precisely describing the structures of systems that convey meaning such as languages, graphic designs, and user interfaces. A key aspect of this theory is the concept of a mapping from one sign structure to another. In computing system design such mappings are often from an abstract idea of a system to a specification for a system's implementation. At the same time as reflecting a philosophical commitment to acknowledging the limitations of highly structured mathematical approaches, algebraic semiotics utilizes highly mathematical formalisms (from the areas of universal algebra and category theory). *Morphic semiotics* is a formulation of algebraic semiotics that is intended to be more generally accessible to non-mathematicians. *Polymorphic poetics* is an approach developed to use morphic semiotics concepts to aid in understanding and designing expressive computing systems by considering how different structures might encode different meanings and values.

Key design concept: The idea of polymorphic poetics involves using a precise language to design systems to reflect users' values. Morphic semiotics is the precise descriptive language used.

III CULTURAL COMPUTING

After having observed that computers can be used for subjective purposes such as prompting phantasms, it is important to consider that the very foundations of computing depend on cultural phantasms shared among people. All technical systems are cultural systems. However, computing systems are based on cultural assumptions that are usually left implicit. For example, hardware and software development are influenced by historically and culturally specific ways of talking and writing about systems. Technologies are produced in historical-cultural contexts and are informed by underlying philosophical perspectives. Computers play a role in shaping culture through facilitating the construction of shared knowledge, shared beliefs, and shared representations (cultural phantasms). More explicit accounts of how computing systems are grounded in culture can help us better understand the limitations of systems and design a greater diversity of systems. Furthermore, computing systems can be designed based on particular cultural models (comprising *integrative cultural systems*). This diversity in design approaches may yield new innovations based in cultures that are not currently privileged in computer science.

5 CULTURAL PHANTASMS

Computing systems, whether used for expression or more utilitarian aims such as commerce, play a role in shaping culture. However, culture is a challenging concept to pin down. There are many definitions from fields such as anthropology, sociology, literature, and more. After integrating aspects of definitions of culture from different fields, the idea of a *cultural phantasm* is introduced to describe one particular way that computers can affect and shape culture at large. Cultural phantasms are socially entrenched phantasms that not all members of a society are equally aware of. In this last regard, we can say that cultural phantasms are only semi-visible. Computing systems can be designed to entrench cultural phantasms within a society—for example, by influencing unaware users to come to consensus. Computing systems can also be designed to reveal cultural phantasms by enabling users to take perspectives outside of their own experiences.

Key design concept: The idea of the cultural phantasm can help guide development of systems that play roles in shaping shared user knowledge, beliefs, and representations.

6   INTEGRATIVE CULTURAL SYSTEMS

A *cultural system* is a model providing an abstraction from the complex milieu of everyday life in a given society. Cultural systems are useful for informing the creation of material or conceptual artifacts that express features of a culture. *Integrative cultural systems* are cultural systems that are transmitted through, and enacted within, media. However, the relationship between cultures and systems is complex. It is not the case that different cultures, or people of specific cultures, have certain essential characteristics that can then be found in media systems produced in those cultures. Rather, material and conceptual artifacts associated with cultures can consciously or unconsciously have an impact upon the structure and operation of computing systems. Developing computing systems explicitly based on cultural models can result in new and innovative designs. My GRIOT system for constructing interactive and generative multimedia narratives is presented as a modest example of a computing system with novel features explicitly grounded in a cultural model, in this case a carefully defined model called *trans-African oral literature (orature)*.

Key design concept: The idea of integrative cultural systems can help guide development of computing systems that are explicitly based on particular cultural models. The idea of metamedial cultural systems in which style and content are more definitive of the cultural system than the medium serves this purpose.

IV   CRITICAL COMPUTING

Building on the ideas that computers can powerfully affect individuals in subjective ways, and the argument describing how that power can be shaped by cultural phantasms, I look at how computers can have an impact upon society. By examining the relationship between computing systems and agency within culture and society, it is possible to better understand, use, and design cultural computing systems to serve human needs and values. The ways that users interact with computing systems are situated in society and can be used for expressive personal and social impact (agency play). Furthermore, computing systems can be used to enable critical reflection and engender conceptual and social change (critical computing systems). Finally, computers can play a role in empowering people (*critical-computational empowerment*).

7 AGENCY PLAY

It is well known that humans can interact with computers in a variety of ways. However, it is also clear that interaction is not intrinsically meaningful. It is more telling to investigate how interaction can be used for expressive aims, critically taking into account users' experiences of how interaction produces meaningful effects. *Agency play* is a concept for understanding how different forms of interaction can be used for expressive and critical aims. Agency play is a model of how user agency (enabled by a computer system) works in conjunction with system agency (interpreted by users).

Key design concept: The idea of agency play can guide development of systems that feature changing a user's agency to interact with the system over time for expressive aims. In particular, the concepts of agency relationship, scope, dynamics, and user direction serve this purpose.

8 CRITICAL-COMPUTATIONAL EMPOWERMENT

Now pervasive in society, computers have values and meanings built into their structures. Hence, computing systems play powerful roles in establishing, maintaining, and transforming social structures. We must critically consider the ways that computing systems can affect social power relationships—whether for oppression or empowerment. Toward this end, a theoretical account of power and empowerment is developed, drawing on a range of social theories. Informed by this account, we can explicitly design computing systems to aid in empowering people. A starting point is understanding the ways that real world information is mapped onto, and instantiated by, computational data structures (social-computational flow). Using this framework as a lens, we can then speculate on each of the concepts explored in the chapters of this book—*expressive epistemologies, polymorphic poetics, cultural phantasms, integrative cultural systems, agency play,* and *critical-computational empowerment*—in light of specific systems that address issues of social power.

Key design concept: The idea of social-computational flow can guide developer strategies for importing real-world content into computing systems. The idea of critical-computational empowerment, in turn, can help guide developers in considering how their systems can prompt social change and user empowerment.

V   CONCLUSION

9   PHANTASMAL MEDIA AND THE HUMAN CONDITION

I hope that the concepts of phantasmal media, and subjective, cultural, and critical approaches to computing, can lead to new possibilities of using the computer to better understand, and improve, the human condition through each of our human capacities to imagine.

Key design concept: The idea of phantasmal media can help guide system development driven by a desire to explore, and transform, the relationship between the computer and the human condition.

GLOSSARY

Agency play A set of dimensions along which user and system agency interact with one another. These dimensions are defined as follows:

• *Agency relationship:* User actions and system actions operate in relation to one another. This relationship can vary in relative magnitude and degree of dependency between the two types of actions (e.g., an inverse relationship or independent operation).

• *Agency scope:* Results of either user or system actions may have immediate and local impact (e.g., turning a character left or right) or longer-term and less immediately apparent results (e.g., a series of actions may determine narrative structure itself).

• *Agency dynamics:* The relationship between possible user and system actions, and their scopes, can vary dynamically during runtime.

• *User input direction:* The user may establish a pattern of input that directs agency dynamics and/or agency scope.

Critical-computational empowerment Using phantasms involving computing technologies for social empowerment and revealing the ways in which they sometimes disempower.

Critical computing Research and practice focusing on the design and use of cultural computing systems in light of social phenomena and to effect conceptual and/or social change.

Critical phantasm Phantasms that engender critical awareness, often challenging oppressive norms and playing roles in empowering people.

Cultural computing Research and practice engaging commonly excluded cultural values and practices to spur computational innovation and invigorate expressive computing research and practice. Cultural computing research and practice focuses on rigorously understanding and articulating the groundings of computing systems in culture.

Cultural phantasm A phantasm that is shared within a group that can be described according to a cultural model. In this regard, cultural phantasms are culturally entrenched phantasms.

Elastic anchor A dynamic material anchor that holds information in place, but not in shape (Chow and Harrell 2009b). Elastic anchors are characterized by the following properties:

• *Material-based imagining:* consisting of material images;

• *Imagination triggering:* holding dynamic information or sensation in place for perceivers, yielding imaginative images;

• *Action inviting:* inviting perceivers to take motor action, such as interaction using a graphical user interface;

• *Motor-sensory connecting:* constituting iterative motor-sensory feedback loops, such as those in sketching of architectural designs, pencil testing of hand-drawn animation, engaging in shadow play, or previewing real-time computer animation; and

• *Spatiotemporal patterning:* providing, when the motor-sensory feedback loop runs spontaneously and continuously (as in computer animation), not only spatial and structural patterns, but also temporal patterns.

Epistemic design process Design approach used for producing computing systems based on research understandings of how users interpret output with the aim of designing for a range of interpretations.

Epistemic domain An abstracted, structured description of salient aspects of a worldview for a purpose at hand.

Epistemic format A structured format for an epistemology designed to suit the computational expertise of artists who use a system.

Epistemic semantics algorithm A computational procedure for mapping, generating, or making inferences between epistemologies using a knowledge base; such procedures can be tuned for expressive goals (e.g., meaningful difference between instances of output, providing multiple perspectives scenarios, or producing surprising results within specific social situations).

Epistemic space A smaller, more concise packet of information (called a mental or conceptual space in cognitive science) for making meaning of a situation at hand that is drawn from an epistemic domain.

Epistemology In a new parallel with the computer science term *ontology*: a structured specification describing an epistemic domain that represents what is known and believed in a conceptualization under a specific worldview.

Expressive epistemology An epistemology used in an expressive form of cultural production such as a work of art.

Image space A representation of a sensory or mental image.

Imaginative world construction Modeling reality by drawing upon subjective worldviews; constructing phantasms that convey enough consistent imagery and information to evoke a coherent sense of a (mostly) coherent world.

Integrative cultural system A cultural system that is transmitted through, and enacted within, media. The term "integrative cultural system" can be used to describe how cultural knowledge, beliefs, and representations are distributed onto material and conceptual artifacts, with a focus on computational artifacts.

Morphic semiotics A language for describing sign systems in terms of the relationships formed by semiotic morphisms between semiotic spaces (Goguen 1998).

Phantasm A combination of imagery (mental or immediate sensory) and ideas. More specifically, a phantasm is blend of epistemic spaces and images spaces through backstage cognition processes; these processes operate at the levels of both sensory imagining and conceptual thought and occur in understanding aspects of the world ranging from basic events to complicated forms, such as work in the arts.

Phantasm space See *phantasm*.

Phantasmal anchor A mental image that strongly preserves the structure of a sensory image such that constraints from the environment (static or dynamic) have been internalized, enabling cognitive processing in a manner similar to that of material and elastic anchors.

Poetic phantasm construction The shaping of poetic phantasms in ways that hold aesthetic considerations as centrally important to meaning construction.

Polymorphic poetics Approaches to understanding how the dynamic nature of computational media representations can be used for expressive communication. A specific form of polymorphic poetics consists of accounting for how the choice of a semiotic morphism, or multiple semiotic morphisms, has an impact on the expressive effectiveness of a computational media work.

Semiotic morphism A mapping from one semiotic space, called the source space, to another semiotic space, called a target space. More specifically, a semiotic morphism is a mapping between sign systems, mapping sorts, constructors, predicates, and functions of one sign system to sorts, constructors, predicates, and functions of another sign system, respectively.

Semiotic space Composed of type declarations (called sorts) and operation declarations, usually including axioms and some constants, plus a *level ordering* on sorts (having a maximum element called the *top sort*) and a *priority ordering* on the constituents at each level. Loose sorts classify the parts of signs; data sorts classify the values of attributes of signs (e.g., color and size). *Signs* of a certain sort are represented by terms of that sort, including—but not limited to—constants. Among the operations in the signature, some are *constructors*, which build new signs from given sign parts as inputs. Levels express the whole-part hierarchy of complex signs, whereas priorities express the relative importance of constructors and their arguments; social issues play an important role in determining these orderings. Conceptual spaces are the special case in which there are no operations except those representing constants and relations, and there is only one sort (Goguen 1998).

Social-computational flow   The transfer of information between real-world experiences and formats and rules on a computer. Social-computational flow articulates the nature of the source and destination between computing systems and content. Social-computational flow can be used for bidirectional analysis from the external world to a computing system or vice versa and can involve multiple real-world experience and multiple systems. Types of social-computational flow include the following:

• *Individual social-computational flow:*   humanly defined transfer from a single human author to computational content and structure;

• *Cooperative social-computational flow:*   humanly defined transfer from multiple human authors to computational content and structure;

• *Collective social-computational flow:*   human-designed or algorithmically facilitated transfer from multiple human authors treated in aggregate to computational content and structure;

• *Intertextual social-computational flow:*   algorithmically defined transfer from thematically related and/or similarly structured external systems to computational content and structure;

• *Semiotically socketed social-computational flow:*   algorithmically defined transfer from external systems used as information resources to computational content and structure; and

• *Perceptual social-computational flow:*   algorithmically defined transfer motor-sensory technologies that act upon the real world to computational content and structure.

Subjective artificial intelligence   Artificial intelligence research and practice oriented toward subjective computing systems.

Subjective computing   Research and practice focused on users' experiences prompted by computing systems. Subjective computing provides ways to develop and analyze computational systems that prompt phantasms. Subjective computing is based on better understanding and designing the interplay of data representations of imaginative meaning and artful uses of algorithms to process such representations with computational media. Subjective computing systems evoke poetic and figurative thought processes.

System agency The capacity of a computing system to modify content (data) and to enable users' actions; system agency requires human interpretation that enables the system to be seen as exhibiting agency.

User agency The ability of humans to perform meaningful actions using the affordances of a computing system; "meaning" in this sense must be understood as situated in the particular actions and understandings of the computing system's user.

NOTES

PREFACE

1. It is reactionary because drowning (or rising) in a lake of whiteness is a generalizing metaphor that fails to capture the ethnically, linguistically, culturally, and ideologically diverse nature of Europe. It also incorrectly conflates the phantasmal concept of racial whiteness blended with literal whiteness and the concept of Eurocentric bias. However, the often Eurocentric historical framing and uninterrogated metaphor "RACE IS COLOR" were somewhat overbearing in my studies at the time—hence the daydream of a game that could help reveal and counter both through the use of metaphor.

1 DEFINING PHANTASMS

1. The concept of double and hidden meanings is not new; indeed, thinkers such as Ferdinand de Saussure and Roland Barthes are well known for presenting concepts such as connotation and "myth" to describe these phenomena (Barthes 1967, [1957] 1972; Saussure 1959). However, the concept of the phantasm differs in several important ways. In particular, "phantasm" differs from earlier related concepts (from the field of semiotics in the case of Saussure and Barthes) in its philosophical emphases and intellectual heritage.

2. Again, these types of imaginative thought include analogy, metaphor, narrative, parable, conceptual blending, and related phenomena usually associated with artistic creativity and expression. I shall explore the concepts of figurative and poetic thought in more depth in chapter 3.

3. Multiple disciplines explore the idea of compound meaning construction. I shall examine the relationship the phantasm has with ideas from other fields such as conceptual metaphors and blends from cognitive science or signs from semiotics in subsequent chapters.

4. Chapter 3 provides a structured approach to representing meanings as sign systems.

5. Constructing an even more specific analogy regarding the radical growth of diverse musical forms, Tzadik Records initiated a "Great Jewish Music" series, which Zorn purposely titled to parallel "Great

Black Music: Ancient to the Future," the earlier motto of the Art Ensemble of Chicago, a group of African American musicians performing music that exceeds the bounds of the label "jazz."

6. A Turing machine is seminal computer scientist Alan Turing's hypothetical machine, which consists of an infinite tape, read/write head, and instruction set. It has been shown that given enough time, anything that can be computed on a modern computer can be accomplished on a Turing machine (Barker-Plummer 2011).

2   IMAGINING AND COMPUTING PHANTASMS

1. Although this book does not primarily address embodied meaning of the type evoked by abstract, nonfigurative works like "Arabesque," many of the ideas here can also help us better understand such art forms. There are many accounts of the nature of abstraction in fields such as art theory, aesthetics, design, and visual studies. Drawing upon cognitive science notions such as the image space can help describe how certain types of abstract media works, including computing systems, convey meaning. Making sense of some such works may require understanding, for example, how they effectively invoke phenomena such as rhythmic repetition, pattern, sensation, and affect. Highly generative screen savers, ambient computer art, computer-based video jockeying performances, and some rhythm videogames are all types of subjective computing systems that often convey embodied meaning through abstract patterns of sounds and images.

2. The definition of "phantasm" used here is couched in contemporary cognitive science (in particular, the subfield of cognitive linguistics). But there are also other uses of the term that differ in some ways from what is meant here. Though not the reference point here, psychoanalysts introduced a use of the term "phantasm" in a similar spirit as is taken here. Jean Laplanche and J.-B. Pontalis used "phantasm (for the 'deep' structure) and fantasy (for the more superficial fantasy or daydream)" when discussing the imagination. They claimed: "From its very beginnings, psychoanalysis has been concerned with the material of fantasies/phantasms (fantasmes). "Fantasy," in German "Phantasie," is the term used to denote the imagination, not so much the faculty of imagining (the philosophers' Einbildungskraft) as the imaginary world and its contents, the imaginings or fantasies/phantasms into which the poet or the neurotic so willingly withdraws" (Laplanche and Pontalis 1964). Now seen as influential concepts in literary theory (rather than scientifically grounded knowledge), this concept of the phantasm is nonetheless useful for describing a powerfully expressive type of thought.

3. The concept of *prototype* here is based on the work by Eleanor Rosch and elaborated upon by George Lakoff, who describe categories based on an idea of central members, family resemblances to those members, gradient membership in those categories, and related phenomena of category formation that are not based on establishing top-down, complete sets of descriptive attributes (Lakoff 1987). I find this model to be useful for media analysis, because establishing definitions for media forms such as games, interactive narratives, computer art, and so on is always contentious due to the fact that these are not objective forms—rather, they are socially agreed upon forms in a dynamically shifting society: one man's play is another woman's game; one person's activist art is another person's subversive computer application.

4. For some, this is the distinction between "computer science" and "computing," which is the reason that this book often uses the term "computing." Furthermore, sometimes this book uses the term "the computer" as a general term, but more often it uses "computing system." Though the terms are largely synonymous, computing system is often preferred because it emphasizes that "the computer" is not just a single machine or type of machine but consists of many types of computer embedded in many

technologies. The term "computing system" also emphasizes that computers are often networked and that they function within broader systems of society and culture. The term "computational media" is used when focusing on the role of computing systems as media for communication and/or expression.

5. In this book, terms such as "developer," "author," "artist," designer," "implementer," and "researcher" will each be used as befits the context of the particular sentence. In practice, many of these roles overlap or are even synonymous. "Developer" is often a useful term because it encompasses both design and implementation. Similarly, terms such as "user," "player," and "audience" will be used as befits the context of the statement being made.

6. The term "computer-based art" is synonymous with what many people would call "digital media art," "computer art," or, sometimes, "new media art."

7. "Computational narrative" is the preferred term here because it includes interactive and generative narrative, as well as systems for aims such as story analysis, understanding, and reconfiguration of the process of "narration" (as opposed to configuring the "story" being narrated). Sometimes the term "interactive narrative" will be used, however, as it is the more popular term and is often the term developers themselves use to describe their systems.

8. My colleague Gerald Sussman suggested this analogy to me during a personal conversation. His work in computer science pedagogy with Hal Abelson fundamentally influenced my approach to computer science (and thousands of other students).

9. Incidentally, this aim would not preclude AI researchers seeking to develop a "truly" intelligent system, given some objective definition of "truly." Indeed, researchers as venerable as Alan Turing have recognized that human interpretation of a system as intelligent is a useful test for determining the success of the system. Achieving truly intelligent systems (so-called strong AI), however, is *not* my goal.

10. Intuition is usually interpreted to mean some type of irrational meaning making. However, Guy Claxton has described intuition as an embodied sense of "rightness" resulting from an accumulation of experience (Claxton 1999). This type of "gut feeling" can perhaps be explained in cognitive science as the result of an embodied emotional experience and unconscious framing, conceptualization, and remembered patterns of motor-sensory experience.

11. Furthermore, as engineering artist and theorist Simon Penny reminds us, some insights can be gained by considering the relationship of technologies to their intended uses at the times of their cultural origins (e.g., between some computing technologies and the military-industrial complex), and distinctions between disciplinary values in expressive forms of cultural production versus more utilitarian engineering endeavors (Penny 1997).

12. Of course, the social identity representations in these cases *are* limited by the capabilities of the systems as implemented by system developers. Some online commerce sites, forums, and similar technologies do, in fact, allow users' self-representations to be affected by other users. This feature is provided via techniques such as allowing users to evaluate the performance and actions of others and making the cumulative results of these evaluations apparent for other users.

13. When comparing profiles, *DefineMe* is designed to match lexical items and logical relations directly, or it can compare the structures of profiles following insights from the analogical structure-mapping engine (SME) developed by Ken Forbus and collaborators (Forbus 2001; Gentner 1983). Following the work of Eleanor Rosch as cited by George Lakoff, the labeling system can also be used to define aspects of categories themselves. For instance, a "robin" tag can be added to the category "birds" to define the prototype of that category (Lakoff 1987).

3 EXPRESSIVE EPISTEMOLOGIES

1. Figure 3.3 was designed by Jichen Zhu.

2. Phantasmal media, as discussed in later chapters, should also demonstrate sensitivity to their cultural milieus and critical awareness.

3. Criticism leveled at such approaches can be found in works such as Agre 1997; Dreyfus 1992; Sengers 1998; and Winograd and Flores 1986.

4. The ConceptNet system was developed at MIT for representing common sense knowledge computationally. ConceptNet's database of information was collected from volunteers over the Web via a project called the Open Mind Common Sense Project. Information in ConceptNet includes relations such as "people desire not to be depressed" or "meat is defined as the flesh of an animal." These relations could be written more formally as: (DesireOf 'person' 'not be depressed') and (DefinedAs 'meat' 'flesh of animal').

5. It is entirely possible that the types of representations used in ConceptNet and similar projects may also be useful for structuring expressive epistemologies. The focus of this discussion has been on contrasting the research goals, not the effectiveness, of particular algorithms or data structures. If the knowledge bases are extensible and rich enough, developing methods for deciding which subsets of large knowledge bases are appropriate for specific contexts would allow such systems to be used effectively as expressive epistemologies.

6. WordNet is focused on relationships between words; Cyc is focused on relations between concepts.

7. Zhu and I examined AI and AI-like systems according to their computational complexity, process opacity, behavioral coherence, and narrated intention during her Ph.D. dissertation work as my advisee (Zhu 2009).

8. Chow and I considered the motor-sensory loop feedback between users and systems and the deployment imaginative motion metaphors through the interaction between embodied gestures and multimedia feedback (Chow and Harrell 2009b) during his Ph.D. dissertation work as my advisee (Chow 2010).

9. The name of the system, because it can be used to generate stories, is taken from the name of West African storytellers called *griots*. More background information about griots is provided in chapter 6.

10. A wildcard consists of two or more parts, including the asterisk marker, which indicates that it is a wildcard, and a variable that determines whether it is to be replaced by another phrase (denoted by the prefix `p-` attached to a clause type name) or by content generated using the Alloy algorithm (denoted by the prefix `g-` attached to a grammatical form name such as `singular-noun`). Optional variables can be used additionally to constrain domains or axioms selected as input to the Alloy blending algorithm (denoted by `d-` and `a-` prefixes, respectively, though in practice axiom-determining variables have not been used). Optional variables can also be used for structural effects such as forcing repeats of wildcard replacement text from earlier in the poem.

11. The Event Structure Machine has the following format:
    <Event Structure Machine>::= "(structure" <clauses> ")"
    <clauses>::= <clause> {<clauses>}
    <clause>::= "(" <name> <number-pair> <subclause> <exit-to-clause> <read-flag> ")"
    <name>::= *an atomic clause name*
    <number-pair>::= "(" <minimum-number> <maximum-number> ")"
    <subclause>::= "(" *an atomic clause name* ")" | "()"

<exit-to-clause>::= "(" *an atomic clause name* ")" | "()"

<minimum-number>::= *a positive integer*

<maximum-number>::= *a positive integer*

<read-flag>::= *read* | *n*

12. Indeed, categories including such diverse members are psychologically real phenomena. For example, Eleanor Rosch (1975) has discussed how many people understand bats as birds, based on their overlapping characteristics with prototypical birds such as their ability to fly, despite that biologically bats are not types of birds.

13. Without going into detail here, Alloy creates such blends based only on the structures of the epistemic spaces given with input that consists of generic information describing shared structure between the epistemologies (e.g., including general relations about People, Objects, and Emotions not limited to the specific domains of angels and skin) and optimality constraints. These optimality constraints prioritize output in which (1) no constants change type from one to another (e.g., seeing the "girl" as an Object rather than a Person), (2) constants and relations are blended if they are similar at the more generic level, (3) content in both of the input epistemic spaces is maximally maintained in the blended space. Details are available in Goguen and Harrell 2009 and Harrell 2007c.

14. The following references were key references in understanding this context and aim: (1) *Truth and Reconciliation Commission Final Report (unedited)* (TRC 2009); (2) *Oral Narratives: The Mobile Story Exchange System* (MOSES), a Georgia Tech project developed to collect oral narratives in rural areas of Liberia, led by Michael Best (who suggested the idea of a Liberia memorial in early meetings and provided valuable experience and connections) and Monrovia-based project manager John Etherton (Best et al. 2008); (3) *An Informal Field Study: Atlanta Friends of the Liberian TRC*, in which we conducted semistructured interviews with a focus group to learn about the experiences and opinions of diaspora Liberians; (4) Guest Speakers Commissioner Massa Washington, journalist and member of the Liberian TRC; Tom Flores, Director of External Relations for the Initiative in Religion, Conflict, and Peace-Building at Emory University; and Peter Nehsahn, author of a memoir collection by victims, survivors, and ex-combatants. We also licensed interview footage from an award-winning documentary film directed by Gini Reticker (2008) to provide additional powerful content in the implementation.

4   POLYMORPHIC POETICS

1. Goguen also described the term "morphic semiotics" as synonymous with "algebraic semiotics," but in practice preferred the latter term.

2. The term "sign" is used here to refer to the kinds of meanings produced when one thing (what the seminal semiotician Ferdinand de Saussure called the signifier) represents another (what Saussure called the signified). Recall that I have described a sign as "the associative total of a concept and an image." The terms are used in a similar sense as those of semioticians such as in the upcoming discussion of the work of the Roland Barthes (chapter 5).

3. I shall make it clear later that the added precision of this approach is not inherently *better* than more informal approaches to semiotics. Although formalisms are advantageous for computational implementation, they are also often more unwieldy for some everyday purposes.

4. Though we might presume the seller to be a real person, sometimes profiles represent stores rather than individuals. On one hand, the seller's appearance on eBay includes information that is not available in the real world. It includes a numeric rating based upon feedback provided by a comprehensive set of

buyers over a set period of time. In fact, the green star indicates a positive rating from between 1,000 and 4,999 buyers. On the other hand, a semiotic space is a syntactic structure. It models the structure of things in the real world; the actual labels used like "name" and "feedback" score are just tokens that are meaningless without human interpretation.

5. In mathematics, a space is a set plus some additional structure.

6. "Morphism" is a term used in the branch of mathematics called category theory to describe a structure-preserving mapping.

7. The cognitive science research on concepts, mental spaces, metaphor, and blending (referenced in chapter 1) addresses issues of meaning that overlap with those in semiotics. However, many of the cognitive linguistics results differ from the earlier semiotics approaches in historical development, desire to reconcile constructs with empirical neuroscience results, philosophical commitments, and recent emphasis on issues of embodied, distributed, and situated cognition.

8. Note that this swastika is tilted at an angle. This is a cue that the signifier actually refers to the swastika tilted at a 45-degree angle used by the Nazi Party.

9. The discussion of the philosophical orientation here is taken from joint work between Joseph Goguen and me, but the primary elements are derived from Goguen's earlier work in algebraic semiotics.

10. The notion of a singular, unified Western culture is itself a generalization and phantasm.

11. Note that in the humanities, approaches such as semiotics have been called *structuralist* theories because they attempt to add a type of rigorous regularity to analysis of systems that produce meaning in fields such as literary studies and linguistics (indeed, an early book by Roland Barthes was called *Elements of Semiology*, implying a science of signs). In contrast to those earlier approaches, humanities scholars might call the approach taken in morphic semiotics *strategic structuralism* because we take advantage of the utility of structuralist approaches without subscribing to the modernist holism and desire to create totalizing systems that ultimately lead to the failure of fields such as semiotics to produce a science of meaning.

12. It is worth noting that, like the earlier example of the Simple Seller Representation, days based on the same underlying system can be represented in multiple ways. For example, the twenty-first day of March in the year 2011 could be represented just as well as 3/21/2011 (as is conventional in the United States) or 21/3/2011 (as is conventional in the United Kingdom).

13. In computer science, parameters are variables that provide input to functions.

14. Algebraic semiotics uses logical sentences to define axioms mathematically.

15. Mathematicians will recognize this hierarchy as a partial ordering.

16. A first-person shooter (FPS) is a game that positions a virtual camera such that it simulates a first-person perspective. FPS gameplay typically focuses on skillful killing of enemies with a gun.

17. The Atari 2600 console, as it is popularly known, was originally called the Atari Video Computer System (VCS) and was renamed later for its part number CX2600 after Atari released another console.

18. In his book *Cybertext*, Aarseth (1997) is critical of several efforts to apply traditional semiotics to computational systems or to develop new types of computational semiotics.

19. It is also worth considering how the semiotic space presented in abbreviated form in figure 4.16 came to be. The semiotic space is a description that I developed based on the game itself. Finding a useful description of the structure of a real-world sign system is the inverse of the design problem. It is the *analysis* problem. A scholar describing the rhythmic structure in music or poetry is pursuing this type of analysis problem. Morphic semiotics is useful for both design and analysis problems, though the focus here has been on design.

20. The quotation describes the design problem. In the article it is taken from, Goguen continues to describe the analysis problem as follows: "Conversely we may be given some situation and want to and the best way to describe [the user interface for a computer system] in natural language or in some other medium or combination of media such as text with photos, or cartoon sequences, or video or online hypertext, or hypermedia" (Goguen 1998, 5).

21. The number values such as 40 + 8 represent hue and luminosity in order to designate a color for the National Television System Committee (NTSC) standard.

22. The process of tackling this type of design problem can be undertaken informally, as a way to think about the design process. It could also be done very formally, using mathematical notation if the designer is developing a high-stakes application such as the interface for an aircraft.

23. Furthermore, all of the constants like `ashy-skin` or `yam` can participate only in the types of relations (axioms) that are preserved in the target space.

24. "Structural blending" refers to the blending of semiotic spaces as is described here, whereas Fauconnier and Turner's "conceptual blending" refers to blending of actual human concepts. The concepts are analogous in some ways because semiotic spaces can be used to model conceptual spaces, enabling the algorithmic approach to modeling conceptual blending that Goguen and I have pursued.

25. The excerpt from the poem "The Road Not Taken" that Lakoff and Turner reference reads:

> Two roads diverged in a wood, and I—
> I took the one less traveled by,
> And that has made all the difference.
> (Frost 1920)

26. *Passage* was developed for a contest with the constraint that all games be displayed in 256 × 256 pixels or less. The labels of elements in this diagram will be used as names of constructors for a semiotic space later in the chapter.

27. The table does not explicitly represent states and state transitions; rather, it informally describes changes in state in the axiom section. In algebraic semiotics, an additional mathematical tool, called "hidden algebra," is necessary to represent state. In morphic semiotics, brief descriptions of functions as axioms for the semiotic space will suffice, though it is not mathematically precise to do so. This trade-off allows for representation of dynamic systems without adding complexity to the definition of semiotic spaces.

5   CULTURAL PHANTASMS

1. In computer science and artificial intelligence, the meaning of "objectivism" can be stated as the assumption "that reason and cognition consist of symbol manipulation, where symbols get meaning through a correspondence to the real world (or possible worlds) objectively defined and independent of any interaction with human beings" (Di Donato 2010, 530).

2. For example, the neighborhood-based collaborative filtering algorithm creates predictions as follows: "calculate the similarity or weight, $w_{i,j}$, which reflects distance, correlation, or weight, between two users or two items, i and j; produce a prediction for the active user by taking the weighted average of all the ratings of the user or item on a certain item or user, or using a simple weighted average" (Su and Khoshgoftaar 2009, 5).

3. Of course, "culture-building" has not yet been precisely defined.

4. Remember that our definition of "conceptual" includes embodied and distributed aspects. Hence perception, emotions, representations, interpersonal interactions, and artifacts all play roles in these conceptual frameworks.

5. Many other types of cultural model are possible to imagine. For example, a *prescriptive cultural model* would propose a conceptual framework that societies should strive for. *Fictional cultural models* are constructed in many works of art. However, the account mentioned previously is not meant to be comprehensive; rather, it is intended just to call attention to several notable uses of the term.

6. I have not independently verified the assertion that this is the singular source of these three categories.

7. Barthes prefers to say that such images make ideas "innocent" and natural.

8. I leave it as an exercise to analyze the use of the metaphor of sheep for users of such systems, as provocative as the ovine metaphor may be, as our focus is on values built into the structures of systems.

9. There is some controversy over the origin of the stored-program architecture.

10. For the sake of comparison, the work of George Lewis, referenced in the introduction, serves a cultural role that parallels Gómez-Peña's efforts to share cultural information through subjective computing systems. A distinction is that Lewis programs his systems as a means of representing cultural models of improvisation.

11. It is important to also be aware that the blending of Iranian and Kurdish identities is itself a phantasm.

6 INTEGRATIVE CULTURAL SYSTEMS

1. Media theorist Henry Jenkins has used the term "transmedial storytelling" to describe a process in which a narrative is distributed across media (Jenkins 2006). One difference between Jenkins's use of the term "transmedial" and the term "metamedial" here is that the latter refers to the *potential* to be expressed across media, not the process of *deployment* across media.

2. As I shall discuss later, "orature" is a relatively recent coinage that refers to what used to be called (oxymoronically) "oral literature." Important reasons for the use of this term are bound up in a response to some cultural phantasms about a hierarchy of culture that I will also discuss later.

3. Recall from chapter 3 that the GRIOT system was the basis for the *Living Liberia Fabric* and other works of computational narrative and poetry.

4. The fact that "classics" tend to focus on ancient Greece and Rome in many cultural contexts, even diverse European ones with their own rich heritages, further reveals this bias.

5. This may also be, in part, because the concept of "Western civilization" is a cultural phantasm that is longer standing and more pervasive than the concept of "Africa" as a cultural, civilizational, or conceptual unit.

6. The term is used to refer to role-playing videogames that include strongly developed predesigned characters, linear narratives, and turn-based, often random, combat encounters. Interestingly, the phrase "Japanese role-playing game" (sometimes abbreviated JRPG) is most often used in U.S. gaming periodicals to contrast with "Western role-playing games." Interestingly, this binary division usually is written as "Japanese" versus "Western" role-playing games in U.S. gaming media—as if open-ended world exploration is a Western value and strong linear narrative is a specifically Japanese quirk.

7. The term "spaghetti western" reflects another association of culture with a particular cultural system, in this case blending Hollywood and Italian cinematic styles.

8. At the same time, the violin itself has been said to have historical origins in bowed instruments of diverse cultural origins, including Middle Eastern and Central Asian.

9. Level-grinding is a style of play, necessary for successful completion of some games, in which players must perform some action (usually fighting) repetitively so that the player character can advance in ability. It also refers to exploiting the same play style in order to achieve more highly powered characters earlier in a game, reducing the difficulty of the game overall.

10. This observation comes from personal experience.

11. Besides seeming unfamiliar, attempting to use phrasing that avoids cultural generalization might seem to some scholars to be the gesture of an apologist at best, a nod to the regime of "political correctness," or as words of appeasement from hegemonically privileged researchers who would balk at open discussion of "ethnic" cultural forms. Here, I take the view that even our most radical activist colleagues should be aware that a diversity of anti-oppression strategies should be used, including the approach here that exposes the imaginative nature of many social categories that are often treated as "real."

12. As Verran puts it:

> Contemporary numeral systems associated with Indo-European languages have ten as the base of their numeral system; in other words, ten is the point in the series that marks the end of the basic set of numerals. As each ten is reached, the basic series is started again, each time recording in the numeral how many tens have been passed by. The rule by which new elements are devised is addition of single units and units comprising multiples of ten. (Verran 2001, 53)

13. The specific origin of the term "griot" is still subject to controversy. Suggestions that the term originates from French are largely disputed, yet suggestions that the term originates from similar words in Wolof, Fulbe, Mandé, or even Portuguese have not been definitively substantiated (Hale 1997).

14. The "middle passage" is the common name given the voyage across the Atlantic Ocean in the holocaust of the Atlantic slave trade roughly between the sixteenth and twentieth centuries. Although the Atlantic slave trade involved not just West Africa, in North America a preponderance of enslaved peoples can from that region—a story that has been popularized in the mainstream media via works such as Alex Haley's book (and the television series it spawned) *Roots*.

15. Ngugi uses "cyberspace" as a blanket term for computational media involving spatial and social performance.

16. GRIOT was one outcome of my Ph.D. dissertation project in computer science and engineering.

17. The song was translated by the author.

18. In this case, the historic location is the Paraná river in South America. The river became a tragically notable emblem of the War of the Triple Alliance for capoeiristas because many oppressed Brazilians of African descent were among those sent across it to fight.

19. In terms of the GRIOT architecture, we would say that the system performer took the role of the event structure machine in addition to the role of user.

7   AGENCY PLAY

1. Interactive narrative research is an area of increasing importance. Some of the dreams of early interactive narrative may now seem passé, such as that the hypertext novel will supersede the traditional novel, but upon close inspection many dreams of interactive narrative have been realized in unexpected ways. We all read hypertext via the Internet daily, but not primarily hypertext fiction; interactive narratives are avidly consumed in the forms of many computer games, although the centrality of narrative to the experience of games remains a controversial topic.

2. For example, Peter Weyhrauch developed an adversarial search algorithm (a type of algorithm often used in order to implement competitive game-playing AI systems such as chess-playing agents) to address this problem in his Ph.D. dissertation work (Weyhrauch 1997).

3. Sengers uses the terms "signs" and "signifiers" in ways that depart from their more well-known uses in semiotics. For Sengers, a sign is an arbitrary label (and possible descriptive information about that label) that can be attached to a set of behaviors. When agents perform behaviors, they emit signs so that the system ends up outputting a record of "what the user is likely to interpret." In contrast, Sengers's signifiers are behaviors composed of an agent's physical actions, mental actions, and signs that are "explicitly intended to be communicated" to users.

4. Woodshedding is when musicians go to a private place to intensely practice alone (proverbially in a woodshed) with the aim of coming back to perform with other musicians with significantly enhanced skills or even a new conception of playing.

8   CRITICAL-COMPUTATIONAL EMPOWERMENT

1. The phrase is a Romanization of the Arabic "الشعب يريد إسقاط النظام."

2. A note regarding the use of these charged phrases as examples: it is inflammatory to describe the oppositional perspectives behind these ideologies in a symmetrical way, as if perspectives that oppress should be given equal representation as those that empower, or even to suggest parallels between the ideologies. In practice, even while recognizing that there are multiple points of view on many issues, one must realize that treating some viewpoints equally serves to further oppress. At the same time, critical awareness is required to assess which perspectives serve to empower and which serve to oppress and how to best represent complicated perspectives that may do both simultaneously.

3. There are other cases in which power is wielded at the expense of those without power, such as in parent-child relationships.

4. For example, *The Elder Scrolls III: Morrowind* and *IV: Oblivion* computationally implement existing stigmatizing social identity constructions related to intelligence. In these games, females of some races begin ten points more intelligent than their male counterparts, and individuals of the ostensibly French "race" (Bretons) are twenty points more intelligent than their Norwegian (Nords) or black (Redguards) counterparts, regardless of gender. In contrast, *The Elder Scrolls V: Skyrim* associates race with skill bonuses, an improvement because skills are not innate characteristics like intelligence, although it would be even better if skills were associated with cultures rather than races.

5. Many examples and variations of these counterarguments can be found in the comments sections of popular media interviews I have given or articles I have written (Harrell 2010b; Soep 2010).

6. Denial-of-service attacks consist of depriving users of access to computing systems and networks.

7. The idea of intertextual systems draws upon the notion of *intertextuality* from literary theory introduced by Julia Kristeva. Intertextuality is the idea that texts are connected through reference, allusion, and a type of dialogic exchange between authors' and readers' prior engagements with multiple texts (Kristeva 1980). In literary theory, this idea does not typically refer to actual structural references such as footnotes, quotations, plagiarism, or hyperlinking, though early hypertext research did apply the idea in this manner, to some criticism (Landow 2006). The usage of the term "intertextual" in this chapter is an intentional deviation from the literary theoretic usage of the concept of intertextuality.

8. "Formalist" approaches are related to, and one could say subsumed by, later structuralist approaches.

9. Loyer was gracious enough to share the design notes leading up to the system's implementation for purposes of this analysis. The close reading of the system's operation to follow, however, was performed before scrutinizing these documents.

10. With each repeated play of the system, I noticed later, more words appear at the top of the screen. The first time using the system, only "1:NEWORLEANS" appears, then "2:PREFERENCES" is added on the second play-through, such as is described. This proceeds until twenty-four words are added—the design of the system's arguments, to be discussed later, explains this progression.

11. In object-oriented programming, a "class" encapsulates associated data structures and procedures. Elements of classes can inherit from, and be inherited by, other classes.

12. Coincidentally with the title of this book, the music playing in the background, which was composed by Liu Scola, has the phantasmal name of "apparition." "Apparition" is also a type of argument in the work.

13. In personal communication, Loyer conveyed that playing with words (such as rhyming, alliteration, and constructing multiple words from the same stem root) is a value inherent in Goldberg's writing that they incorporated in the system's architecture.

REFERENCES

Aarseth, Espen J. 1997. *Cybertext: Perspectives on Ergodic Literature*. Baltimore, MD: Johns Hopkins University Press.

Abu-Lughod, Lila. 1990. The Romance of Resistance: Tracing Transformations of Power through Bedouin Women. *American Ethnologist* 17 (1): 41–55.

Addams, Shay. 1989. *Quest for Clues II*. Austin, TX: Origin Systems, Inc.

Agre, Philip E. 1997. *Computation and Human Experience*. Cambridge: Cambridge University Press.

Ahearn, Laura M. 2001. Language and Agency. *Annual Review of Anthropology* 30:109–137.

Akutagawa, Ryunosuke. 1999. *Rashomon and Other Stories*. New York: Liveright.

Alelo Inc. 2008a. *Tactical Language & Culture Training System*. YouTube. http://www.youtube.com/watch?v=zUr8k73D8zY (accessed August 6, 2012).

Alelo Inc. 2008b. *Operational Language and Culture Training*. http://www.alelo.com/tactical_language.html (accessed August 6, 2012).

America's Army 3, 2012. *Media Viewer*. http://www.americasarmy.com/media/ssViewer.php?xmlImageName=screenshots (accessed August 6, 2012).

Armah, Ayi Kwei. 2000. *Two Thousand Seasons*. Popenguine, Senegal: Per Ankh Books.

Ashcraft, Brian. 2010. "Protesting Japanese Role-Playing Games." *Kotaku*. http://kotaku.com/5604049/protesting-japanese-role+playing-games (accessed December 7, 2012).

AtariAge. 1978. Atari 2600 Screenshots—Superman (Atari). http://www.atariage.com/screenshot_page.html?SoftwareLabelID=532 (accessed December 30, 2011).

Aylett, Ruth, and Sandy Louchart. 2003. Towards a Narrative Theory for Virtual Reality. *Virtual Reality* 7 (1): 2–9.

Bakhtin, M. M. 1982. *The Dialogic Imagination: Four Essays*. Austin: University of Texas Press.

Baldwin, James. 1955. *Notes of a Native Son*. Boston: Beacon Press.

Ball, Randy. 2000. *Game Chambers Interview with John Dunn*. Game Chambers. http://www.mindspring.com/~rhball/gcDunn.htm (accessed January 12, 2011).

Barad, Karen. 2003. Posthumanist Performativity: Toward an Understanding of How Matter Comes to Matter. *Signs: Journal of Women in Cultural and Society* 28 (3): 801–831.

Baraka, Amiri Imamu. [1968] 1998. *Black Music*. Cambridge, MA: Da Capo Press.

Barker-Plummer, David. 2011. *Turing Machines.* http://plato.stanford.edu/archives/spr2011/entries/turing-machine (accessed February 7, 2012).

Barthes, Roland. 1967. *Elements of Semiology*. New York: Hill and Wang.

Barthes, Roland. [1957] 1972. *Mythologies*. Translated by Jonathan Cape. New York: Noonday Press.

Barwise, Jon, and John Perry. 1983. *Situations and Attitudes*. Cambridge, MA: MIT Press/Bradford Books.

Bates, Joe. 1992. Virtual Reality, Art, and Entertainment. *Presence: The Journal of Teleoperators and Virtual Environments* 1 (1): 133–138.

Baudrillard, Jean. 1983. *Simulations*. New York: Semiotext.

Berg, Alban. 1995. *Chamber Concerto; Three Orchestral Pieces, Op. 6; Violin Concerto.* Sony. Audio Recording.

Best, M. L., D. Serrano-Baquero, H. Abbasi, C. L. Pon, D. L. Roberts, and T. N. Smyth. 2008. "Design of Video-Sharing Kiosks for Liberian Post-Conflict Reconciliation." *Proceedings of the CHI 2008 HCI4D Workshop*, Florence, Italy.

Biakolo, Emevwo. 1999. On the Theoretical Foundations of Orality and Literacy. *Research in African Literatures* 30 (2): 42–65.

Blumberg, Bruce M., and Tinsley Galyean. 1995. "Multi-Level Direction of Autonomous Creatures for Real-Time Virtual Environments." *Proceedings of the 22nd Annual Conference on Computer Graphics and Interactive Techniques*, Los Angeles, CA.

Blumer, Herbert, 1986. *Symbolic Interactionism: Perspective and Method*. Berkeley: University of California Press.

Boellstorff, Tom, Bonnie Nardi, Celia Pearce, and T. L. Taylor. 2012. *Ethnography and Virtual Worlds: A Handbook of Method.* Princeton, NJ: Princeton University Press.

Bogost, Ian. 2007. *Persuasive Games: The Expressive Power of Videogames*. Cambridge, MA: MIT Press.

Bolter, Jay David, and Richard Grusin. 1999. *Remediation: Understanding New Media*. Cambridge, MA: MIT Press.

Bowker, Geoffrey C., and Susan Leigh Star. 1999. *Sorting Things Out: Classification and Its Consequences*. Cambridge, MA: MIT Press.

Bozon. 2007. "Etrian Odyssey Review." http://www.ign.com/articles/2007/05/16/etrian-odyssey-review (accessed August 7, 2012).

Brathwaite, Kamau. 1995. *Black + Blues*. New York: New Directions.

Brooks, Rodney A. 1991. "Intelligence without Representation." *Artificial Intelligence* 47:139–159.

Butler, Judith. 1990. *Gender Trouble: Feminism and the Subversion of Identity.* New York: Routledge.

Callon, Michel. 1986. "Some Elements of a Sociology of Translation: Domestication of the Scallops and the Fishermen of St Brieuc Bay." In *Power, Action and Belief: A New Sociology of Knowledge*, ed. John Law, 196–223. London: Routledge & Kegan Paul.

Calvino, Italo. 1982a. *If on a Winter's Night a Traveler.* San Diego, CA: Harvest/HBJ Books.

Calvino, Italo. 1982b. *The Uses of Literature.* San Diego, CA: Harcourt Brace and Co.

Cavazza, Marc, Fred Charles, and Steven J. Mead. 2001. Characters in Search of an Author: AI-Based Virtual Storytelling. In *Virtual Storytelling: Using Virtual Reality Technologies for Storytelling*, ed. Olivier Badet, Gérard Subsol, and Patrice Torguet, 145–154. Heidelberg: Springer Verlag.

Chalmers, D. J., R. M. French, and D. R. Hofstadter. 1992. High-level Perception, Representation, and Analogy: A Critique of Artificial Intelligence Methodology. *Journal of Experimental & Theoretical Artificial Intelligence* 4 (3): 185–211.

Chandler, Daniel. 1994. *Biases of the Ear and Eye: "Great Divide" Theories, Phonocentrism, Graphocentrism & Logocentrism.* http://users.aber.ac.uk/dgc/Documents/litoral/ (accessed January 5, 2012).

Chow, Kenny K. N. 2010. "An Embodied Cognition Approach to the Analysis and Design of Generative and Interactive Animation." Dissertation, Digital Media Program, School of Literature, Communication, and Culture, Georgia Institute of Technology, Atlanta, GA.

Chow, Kenny K. N., and D. Fox Harrell. 2009a. "Active Animation: An Approach to Interactive and Generative Animation for User-Interface Design and Expression." *Proceedings of the 2009 Digital Humanities Conference*, College Park, MD.

Chow, Kenny K. N., and D. Fox Harrell. 2009b. "Material-Based Imagination: Embodied Cognition in Animated Images." *Proceedings of the Eighth Digital Arts and Culture Conference*, Irvine, CA.

Chrisley, Ronald. 2000. "Introduction: The Development of the Concept of Artificial Intelligence–Historical Overviews and Milestones." In *Artificial Intelligence: Critical Concepts*, vol. 1, ed. Ronald Chrisley, 7–24. New York: Routledge.

Chun, Wendy Hui Kyong. 2011. *Programmed Visions: Software and Memory.* Cambridge, MA: MIT Press.

Clark, Kenneth B., and Mamie P. Clark. 1947. "Racial Identitifcation and Preference in Negro Children." In *Readings in Social Psychology*, ed. T. M. Newcomb and E. L. Hartley, 169–178. New York: Holt, Rinehart & Winston.

Clausner, Timothy C., and William Croft. 1999. "Domains and Image Schemas." *Cognitive Linguistics* 10 (1): 1–31.

Claxton, Guy. 1999. *Hare Brain, Tortoise Mind: Why Intelligence Increases When You Think Less.* New York: Harper Perennial.

Cohen, Harold. 2002. "A Self-Defining Game for One Player: On the Nature of Creativity and the Possibility of Creative Computer Programs." *Leonardo* 35 (1): 59–64.

Collins, Allan, and William Ferguson. 1993. "Epistemic Forms and Epistemic Games: Structures and Strategies to Guide Inquiry." *Educational Psychologist* 28 (1): 25–42.

Comic Vine. 2011. *Image of Superman (Superman in Flight)*. http://www.comicvine.com/superman/29-1807/all-images/108-218958/superman_fly1/105-1673558/ (accessed December 30, 2011).

Cope, David. 2004. *Virtual Music: Computer Synthesis of Musical Style*. Cambridge, MA: MIT Press.

Cortázar, Julio. 1966. *Hopscotch*. New York: Random House.

Coulson, Seana, and Todd Oakley. 2000. "Blending Basics." *Cognitive Linguistics* 11 (3/4): 175–196.

Critical Art Ensemble. 1993. *The Electronic Disturbance*. New York: Autonomedia.

Davidson, Donald. 2001. *Essays on Actions and Events: Philosophical Essays*. Oxford: Oxford University Press.

Delany, Samuel R. [1979] 1993. *Tales of Nevèrÿon*. Middletown, CT: Wesleyan University Press.

Delany, Samuel R. 1994a. *Flight from Nevèrÿon*. Hanover, CT: Wesleyan University Press.

Delany, Samuel R. 1994b. *Return to Nevèrÿon*. Hanover, CT: Wesleyan University Press.

Deleuze, Gilles. 1990. *The Logic of Sense*. New York: Columbia University Press.

Descartes, René. [1641] 1996. *Meditations on First Philosophy: With Selections from the Objections and Replies*. Trans. John Cottingham. Cambridge: Cambridge University Press.

Descartes, René. [1637] 2008. *Discourse on the Method of Rightly Conducting One's Reason and of Seeking Truth in the Sciences*. Project Guttenberg. http://www.gutenberg.org/files/59/59-h/59-h.htm (accessed July 28, 2012).

Di Donato, Pasquale. 2010. "Geospatial Semantics: A Critical Review." In *Computer Science and Its Applications—ICCSA 2010*, ed. David Taniar, Osvaldo Gervasi, Beniamino Murgante, Eric Pardede, and Bernady O. Apduhan, 528–544. Berlin: Springer-Verlag.

Domike, Steffi, Michael Mateas, and Paul Vanouse. 2003. "The Recombinant History Apparatus Presents: Terminal Time." In *Narrative Intelligence*, ed. Michael Mateas and Phoebe Sengers, 155–173. Amsterdam: John Benjamins Press.

Dourish, Paul. 2001. *Where the Action Is: The Foundation of Embodied Interaction*. Cambridge, MA: MIT Press.

Dreyfus, Hubert L. 1992. *What Computers Still Can't Do: A Critique of Artificial Reason*. Cambridge, MA: MIT Press.

Du Bois, W. E. B. 1903. *The Souls of Black Folk*. Chicago: A. C. McClurg & Co.

Eglash, Ron. 1995. "African Influences in Cybernetics." In *The Cyborg Handbook*, ed. Chris Hables Gray, 17–28. London: Routledge.

Ellison, Ralph. [1947] 1995. *Invisible Man*. New York: Random House.

Eshun, Kodwo. 1998. *More Brilliant than the Sun: Adventures in Sonic Fiction*. London: Quartet Books.

Evans, Vyvyan, Benjamin K. Bergen, and Jörg Zinken. 2006. "The Cognitive Linguistics Enterprise: An Overview." In *The Cognitive Linguistics Reader*, ed. Vyvyan Evans, Benjamin K. Bergen, and Jörg Zinken, 1–35. London: Equinox Press.

Everett, Anna, and S. Craig Watkins. 2008. "The Power of Play: The Portrayal and Performance of Race in Video Games." In *The Ecology of Games: Connecting Youth, Games, and Learning*, ed. Katie Salen, 141–166. Cambridge, MA: MIT Press.

Fauconnier, Gilles. 1985. *Mental Spaces: Aspects of Meaning Construction in Natural Language*. Cambridge, MA: MIT Press/Bradford Books.

Fauconnier, Gilles. 1999. "Methods and Generalizations." In *Cognitive Linguistics, Foundations, Scope, and Methodology*, ed. T. Janssen and G. Redeker, 95–127. The Hague: Mouton De Gruyter.

Fauconnier, Gilles. 2004. "Pragmatics and Cognitive Linguistics." In *Handbook of Pragmatics*, ed. Laurence R. Horn and Gregory Ward, 657–674. Malden, MA: Blackwell Publishing Ltd.

Fauconnier, Gilles. 2006. "Rethinking Metaphor." In *Cambridge Handbook of Metaphor and Thought*, ed. Ray Gibbs, 53–66. Cambridge: Cambridge University Press.

Fauconnier, Gilles, and George Lakoff. 2011. *On Metaphor and Blending*. http://www.cogsci.ucsd.edu/~coulson/spaces/GG-final-1.pdf (accessed February 7, 2012).

Fauconnier, Gilles, and Eve Sweetser. 1996. *Spaces, Worlds, and Grammar*. Chicago: University of Chicago Press.

Fauconnier, Gilles, and Mark Turner. 2002. *The Way We Think: Conceptual Blending and the Mind's Hidden Complexities*. New York: Basic Books.

Fellbaum, Christiane. 1998. *WordNet: An Electronic Lexical Database*. Cambridge, MA: MIT Press.

Fillmore, Charles J. 1985. "Frames and the Semantics of Understanding." *Quaderni di semantica* 6 (2): 222–254.

Finnegan, Ruth. 1988. *Literacy and Orality: Studies in the Technology of Communication*. Oxford: Basil Blackwell.

Flanagan, Mary. 2009. *Critical Play: Radical Game Design*. Cambridge, MA: MIT Press.

Forbus, Kenneth D. 2001. "Exploring Analogy in the Large." In *The Analogical Mind: Perspectives from Cognitive Science*, ed. Dedre Gentner, Keith J. Holyoak, and Boicho N. Kokinov, 23–58. Cambridge, MA: MIT Press.

Fortin, Marie-Eve. 2007. Interview with Abderrahmane Sissako: Director of Bamako. *Offscreen* 11 (6). http://www.offscreen.com/index.php/pages/essays/abderrahmane_sissako/ (accessed February 7, 2012).

Foucault, Michel. 1971. *L'Ordre du discours*. Paris: Gallimard.

Foucault, Michel. 1977. *Discipline and Punish*. New York: Pantheon.

Foucault, Michel. 1978. *An Introduction*, vol. I. The History of Sexuality. New York: Pantheon.

Foucault, Michel. 1982. *The Archaeology of Knowledge & The Discourse on Language*. New York: Vintage Books.

Free Software Foundation. 2012. *Free Software Foundation (Core Work)*. http://www.fsf.org/about (accessed February 12, 2012).

Frost, Robert. 1920. *Mountain Interval*. New York: Henry Holt and Company.

Gallaway, Brad. 2010. "Brink: No Girls Allowed." *Kotaku*. http://www.kotaku.com.au/2010/05/brink-no-girls-allowed/ (accessed October 14, 2011).

Galloway, Alexander R., and Eugene Thacker. 2007. *The Exploit: A Theory of Networks*. Minneapolis, MN: University of Minnesota Press.

GAMBIT Singapore—MIT Game Lab. 2011. *A Closed World.* http://gambit.mit.edu/loadgame/aclosedworld.php (accessed February 7, 2012).

Gates, Henry Louis, Jr. 1988. *The Signifying Monkey: A Theory of African-American Literary Criticism.* New York: Oxford University Press.

Gee, James P. 2007. *What Video Games Have to Teach Us about Learning and Literacy.* New York: Palgrave Macmillan.

Geertz, Clifford. 1973. *The Interpretation of Cultures.* New York: Basic Books.

Gentner, Dedre. 1983. "Structure-Mapping: A Theoretical Framework for Analogy." *Cognitive Science* 7 (2): 155–170.

Gibbs, Raymond W., Jr. 1994. *The Poetics of Mind: Figurative Thought, Language, and Understanding.* New York: Cambridge University Press.

Gibbs, Raymond W., Jr. 2000. "Making Good Psychology out of Blending Theory." *Cognitive Linguistics* 11 (3/4): 347–358.

Gibson, James J. 1977. "The Theory of Affordances." In *Perceiving, Acting, and Knowing: Toward an Ecological Psychology*, ed. Robert Shaw and John Bransford, 67–82. Hillsdale, NJ: Erlbaum Associates.

Goguen, Joseph. 1998. "An Introduction to Algebraic Semiotics, with Applications to User Interface Design." *Proceedings of the Computation for Metaphors, Analogy, and Agents Conference*, Yakamatsu, Japan.

Goguen, Joseph. 2001. *Notes on Narrative.* http://www.cse.ucsd.edu/~goguen/papers/narr.html (accessed October 10, 2010).

Goguen, Joseph. 2003. "Theories of Technology and Science Course Notes Section 6." http://www-cse.ucsd.edu/goguen/courses/275/s6.html (accessed October 7, 2010).

Goguen, Joseph. 2004. *Semiotic Morphisms.* UCSD. http://cseweb.ucsd.edu/~goguen/papers/sm/node5.html#SECTION3-2 (accessed October 7, 2010).

Goguen, Joseph. 2005a. "Sample GRIOT Output for 'November Qualia.'" http://www.cs.ucsd.edu/~goguen/projs/haibun05.html (accessed October 4, 2010).

Goguen, Joseph. 2005b. "November Qualia." *Journal of Consciousness Studies* 12 (11): 73.

Goguen, Joseph, and D. Fox Harrell. 2004. "Information Visualization and Semiotic Morphisms." In *Multidisciplinary Study of Visual Representation and Interpretations*, ed. Grant Malcolm, 83–98. Oxford: Elsevier.

Goguen, Joseph, and D. Fox Harrell. 2005. *The Griot Sings Haibun.* La Jolla, CA: Computational Poetry and Free Jazz.

Goguen, Joseph, and D. Fox Harrell. 2009. "Style as a Choice of Blending Principles." In *The Structure of Style: Algorithmic Approaches to Understanding Manner and Meaning*, ed. Shlomo Argamon, Kevin Burns, and Shlomo Dubnov, 291–317. Berlin: Springer.

Goguen, Joseph, and Grant Malcolm. 1996. *Algebraic Semantics of Imperative Programs.* Cambridge, MA: MIT Press.

Goldberg, David Theo, Erik Loyer, and Stefka Hristova. 2008. "Blue Velvet: Re-dressing New Orleans in Katrina's Wake." *Vectors: Journal of Cultural and Technology in a Dynamic Vernacular* 3 (1). http://vectors.usc.edu/projects/index.php?project=82 (accessed July 14, 2012).

Goldman, Alvin. 2010. "Social Epistemology." *The Stanford Encyclopedia of Philosophy 2010*, ed. Edward N. Zalta. http://plato.stanford.edu/entries/epistemology-social/ (accessed October 9, 2011).

Gómez-Peña, Guillermo. 1998. *The Virtual Barrio @ The Other Frontier.* http://www.zonezero.com/magazine/articles/gomezpena/gomezpena.html (accessed October 21, 2011).

Gómez-Peña, Guillermo, and Ali Dadgar. 2004. *The Chica-Iranian Project.* http://www.pochanostra.com/chica-iranian/ (accessed October 21, 2011).

Grady, Joseph E., Todd Oakley, and Seana Coulson. 1999. "Blending and Metaphor." In *Metaphor in Cognitive Linguistics*, ed. Gerard Steen and Ray Gibbs, 101–124. Amsterdam: John Benjamins.

Gramsci, Antonio. 1971. *Selections from the Prison Notebooks.* New York: International Publishers.

Greimas, Algirdas. 1971. "Narrative Grammar: Units and Levels." *Modern Language Notes* 86 (6): 793–806.

Gruber, Tom. 1995. "Toward Principles for the Design of Ontologies Used for Knowledge Sharing." *International Journal of Human-Computer Studies* 43 (5–6): 907–928.

Halberstam, Judith. 1991. Automating Gender: Postmodern Feminism in the Age of the Intelligent Machine. *Feminist Studies* 17 (3): 439–460.

Hale, Thomas A. 1997. From the Griot of Roots to the Roots of Griot: A New Look at the Origins of a Controversial African Term for Bard. *Oral Tradition* 12 (2): 249–278.

Haraway, Donna J. 1991. "A Cyborg Manifesto: Science, Technology, and Socialist-Feminism in the Late Twentieth Century." In *Simians, Cyborgs, and Women: The Reinvention of Nature*, 149–181. New York: Routledge.

Hardy, Thomas. 1932. "The Convergence of the Twain." In *Collected Poems of Thomas Hardy*, 288–289. London: Macmillan and Co.

Harrell, D. Fox. 2004. "Speaking in Djinni: Media Arts and the Computational Language of Expression." In *Life in the Wires: The CTHEORY Reader*, ed. Arthur Kroker and Marielouise Kroker, 277–284. Victoria, Canada: New World Perspectives/CTheory Books.

Harrell, D. Fox. 2005. "Shades of Computational Evocation and Meaning: The GRIOT System and Improvisational Poetry Generation." *Proceedings of the Sixth Digital Arts and Culture Conference*, Copenhagen, Denmark.

Harrell, D. Fox. 2006. "Walking Blues Changes Undersea: Imaginative Narrative in Interactive Poetry Generation with the GRIOT System." *Proceedings of the AAAI 2006 Workshop in Computational Aesthetics: Artificial Intelligence Approaches to Happiness and Beauty*, AAAI Press, Boston, MA.

Harrell, D. Fox. 2007a. "Cultural Roots for Computing: The Case of African Diasporic Orature and Computational Narrative in the GRIOT System." *Fibreculture* 11. http://eleven.fibreculturejournal.org/fcj-069-cultural-roots-for-computingthe-case-of-african-diasporic-orature-and-computational-narrative-in-the-griot-system/ (accessed December 7, 2012).

Harrell, D. Fox. 2007b. "GRIOT's Tales of Haints and Seraphs: A Computational Narrative Generation System." In *Second Person: Role-Playing and Story in Games and Playable Media*, ed. Noah Wardrip-Fruin and Patrick Harrigan, 177–182. Cambridge, MA: MIT Press.

Harrell, D. Fox. 2007c. "Theory and Technology for Computational Narrative: An Approach to Generative and Interactive Narrative with Bases in Algebraic Semiotics and Cognitive Linguistics." Dissertation, Department of Computer Science and Engineering, University of California, San Diego, La Jolla.

Harrell, D. Fox. 2008. "Algebra of Identity: Skin of Wind, Skin of Streams, Skin of Shadows, Skin of Vapor." In *Critical Digital Studies: A Reader*, ed. Arthur Kroker and Marilouise Kroker, 158–174. Toronto: University of Toronto Press.

Harrell, D. Fox. 2009a. "Computational and Cognitive Infrastructures of Stigma: Empowering Identity in Social Computing and Gaming." *Proceedings of the Seventh Association for Computing Machinery (ACM) Cognition and Creativity Conference*, Berkeley, CA.

Harrell, D. Fox. 2009b. "Toward a Theory of Phantasmal Media: An Imaginative Cognition- and Computation-Based Approach to Digital Media." *CTheory*. http://www.ctheory.net/articles.aspx?id=610 (accessed December 7, 2012).

Harrell, D. Fox. 2010a. "Designing Empowering and Critical Identities in Social Computing and Gaming." *CoDesign* 6 (4): 187–206.

Harrell, D. Fox. 2010b. "Identity and Online Avatars: A Discussion." *Kotaku*. http://kotaku .com/5523384/identity-and-online-avatars-a-discussion (accessed April 30, 2010).

Harrell, D. Fox. 2010c. "Toward a Theory of Critical Computing: The Case of Social Identity Representation in Digital Media Applications." *CTheory*. http://www.ctheory.net/articles.aspx?id=641 (accessed December 7, 2012).

Harrell, D. Fox, Chris Gonzalez, Hank Blumenthal, Ayoka Chenzira, Natasha Powell, Nathan Piazza, and Michael Best. 2010. "A Cultural Computing Approach to Interactive Narrative: The Case of the Living Liberia Fabric." *Proceedings of the AAAI Fall Symposium on Computational Models of Narrative*, AAAI Press, Arlington, VA.

Harrell, D. Fox, Greg Vargas, and Rebecca Perry. 2011. "Steps toward the AIR Toolkit: An Approach to Modeling Social Identity Phenomena in Computational Media." *Proceedings of the International Conference on Computational Creativity*, April 27–29, Mexico City, Mexico.

Harrell, D. Fox, and Jichen Zhu. 2009. "Agency Play: Expressive Dimensions of Agency for Interactive Narrative Design." *Proceedings of the AAAI 2009 Symposium on Interactive Narrative Systems II*, AAAI Press, Stanford, CA.

Harrigan, Patrick, and Noah Wardrip-Fruin. 2007. *Second Person: Role-Playing and Story in Games and Playable Media*. Cambridge, MA: MIT Press.

Havasi, C., R. Speer, and J. Alonso. 2007. "ConceptNet 3: A Flexible, Multilingual Semantic Network for Common Sense Knowledge." *Proceedings of Recent Advances in Natural Languages Processing*, Borovets, Bulgaria.

Hayles, N. Katherine. 1993. "The Materiality of Informatics." *Configurations* 1 (1): 147–170.

Hayles, N. Katherine. 2002. *Writing Machines*. Cambridge, MA: MIT Press.

Higginson, William J. 1985. *The Haiku Handbook: How to Write, Share, and Teach Haiku*. Tokyo: Kodansha International.

Higginson, William J. 1996. *The Haiku Seasons: Poetry of the Nature World*. Tokyo: Kodansha International.

Higginson, William J. 2006. *Renku Home.* http://www.2hweb.net/haikai/renku/ (accessed December 7, 2012).

Hiraga, Masako K. 2005. *Metaphor and Iconicity: A Cognitive Approach to Analysing Texts.* New York: Palgrave Macmillan.

Hodges, Andrew. 2012. *Alan Turing: The Enigma.* Princeton: Princeton University Press.

Hofstede, Geert. 2001. *Culture's Consequences: Comparing Values, Behaviors, Institutions and Organizations Across Nations.* 2nd ed. Thousand Oaks, CA: Sage Publications.

Hofstede, Geert. 2011. *Culture.* http://www.geerthofstede.nl/culture.aspx (accessed October 10, 2011).

Hutchins, Edwin. 1996. *Cognition in the Wild.* Cambridge, MA: MIT Press.

Hutchins, Edwin. 2005. "Material Anchors for Conceptual Blends." *Journal of Pragmatics* 37 (10): 1555–1577.

Ibarretxe-Antuñano, Iraide. 2004. "What's Cognitive Linguistics? A New Framework for the Study of Basque." *Cahiers de l'Association for French Language Studies* 10 (2): 3–31.

Interplay. 1988. Manual from *The Bard's Tale III.* Electronic Arts.

Jahn, Manfred. 2005. *Narratology: A Guide to the Theory of Narrative.* English Department, University of Cologne. http://www.uni-koeln.de/~ame02/pppn.htm (accessed February 8, 2010).

Jainism Global Resource Center. 2006. *Jainism Global Resource Center.* http://jainworld.com (accessed April 7, 2010).

Jakobson, Roman. 1981. *Selected Writings: Poetry of Grammar and Grammar of Poetry.* The Hague, The Netherlands: Mouton de Gruyter.

Jenkins, Henry. 2004. "Game Design as Narrative Architecture." In *First Person: New Media as Story, Performance, Game,* ed. Noah Wardrip-Fruin and Pat Harrigan, 118–133. Cambridge, MA: MIT Press.

Jenkins, Henry. 2006. *Convergence Culture.* New York: New York University Press.

Johnson, Mark. 1987. *The Body in the Mind: The Bodily Basis of Meaning, Imagination and Reason.* Chicago: University of Chicago.

Johnson, Mark. 2007. *The Meaning of the Body: Aesthetics of Human Understanding.* Chicago: University of Chicago Press.

Johnson, Steven. 1999. *Interface Culture.* New York: Basic Books.

Juul, Jesper. 2001. "Games Telling Stories?" *Game Studies* 1 (1). http://www.gamestudies.org/0101/juul-gts/ (accessed December 7, 2012).

Juul, Jesper. 2013. *The Art of Failure: An Essay on the Pain of Playing Video Games.* Cambridge, MA: MIT Press.

Kafka, Franz. [1915] 2002. *The Metamorphosis.* Translated by David Wyllie. Project Gutenberg eBook. http://www.gutenberg.org/files/5200/5200-h/5200-h.htm (accessed December 27, 2012).

Kalata, Kurt. 2008. *A Japanese RPG Primer: The Essential 20.* Gamasutra. http://www.gamasutra.com/view/feature/3581/a_japanese_rpg_primer_the_.php (accessed November 28, 2011).

Keltner, Dacher, Deborah H. Gruenfeld, and Cameron Anderson. 2003. "Power, Approach, and Inhibition." *Psychological Review* 110 (2): 265–284.

Kirschenbaum, Matthew. 2008. *Mechanisms: New Media and the Forensic Imagination*. Cambridge, MA: MIT Press.

Kluckhohn, Florence R., and Fred L. Strodtbeck. 1961. *Variations in Value Orientations*. Evanston, IL: Row, Peterson, and Company.

Kristeva, Julia. 1980. *Desire in Language: A Semiotic Approach to Literature and Art*. New York: Columbia University Press.

Kroeber, Alfred, and Clyde Kluckhohn. 1952. *Culture: A Critical Review of Concepts and Definitions*. New York: Vintage Books.

Kroker, Arthur, and Marilouise Kroker, eds. 2008. *Critical Digital Studies: A Reader*, Toronto: University of Toronto Press.

Kurosawa, Akira. 1950. Rashomon. Daiei.

Labov, William. 1972. *Language in the Inner City*. Philadelphia: University of Pennsylvania Press.

Lakoff, George. 1987. *Women, Fire, and Dangerous Things: What Categories Reveal about the Mind*. Chicago: University of Chicago Press.

Lakoff, George, and Mark Johnson. 1980. *Metaphors We Live By*. Chicago: University of Chicago Press.

Lakoff, George, and Mark Johnson. 1999. *Philosophy in the Flesh: The Embodied Mind and Its Challenge to Western Thought*. Cambridge, MA: MIT Press.

Lakoff, George, and Rafael E. Núñez. 2000. *Where Mathematics Comes From: How the Embodied Mind Brings Mathematics into Being*. New York: Basic Books.

Lakoff, George, and Mark Turner. 1989. *More than Cool Reason—A Field Guide to Poetic Metaphor*. Chicago: University of Chicago Press.

Landow, George P. 2006. *Hypertext 3.0: Critical Theory and New Media in an Era of Globalization*. Baltimore: Johns Hopkins Press.

Laplanche, Jean, and J. B. Pontalis. 1964. "Originary Phantasms, Phantasms of Origins, Origins of the Phantasm" (revised and abbreviated translation). *Les temps modernes* 19 (January–June). http://courses.essex.ac.uk/lt/lt948/phantasm.htm (accessed December 4, 2011).

Latour, Bruno. 1988. *Science in Action: How to Follow Scientists and Engineers Through Society*. Cambridge, MA: Harvard University Press.

Latour, Bruno. 2005. *Reassembling the Social: An Introduction to Actor-Network-Theory*. Oxford: Oxford University Press.

Lave, Jean, and Etienne Wenger. 1991. *Situated Learning: Legitimate Peripheral Participation*. Cambridge, UK: Cambridge University Press.

Lechte, John. 1994. *Fifty Key Contemporary Thinkers: From Structuralism to Postmodernity*. London: Routledge.

Lenoir, Tim, and Henry Lowood. 2005. "Theaters of War: The Military-Entertainment Complex." In *Collection, Laboratory, Theater: Scenes of Knowledge in the 17th Century*, ed. Helmar Schramm, Ludger Schwarte, and Jan Lazardzig, 427–456. Berlin: Walter de Gruyter Publishers.

Lewis, George E. 1995. "Singing the Alternative Interactivity Blues." *Front* 7 (2): 18–22.

Lewis, George E. 2000. "Too Many Notes: Computers, Complexity and Culture in Voyager." *Leonardo Music Journal* 10:33–39.

Liu, Hugo, and Push Singh. 2004. "ConceptNet: A Practical Commonsense Reasoning Toolkit." *BT Technology Journal* 22 (4): 211–226.

Louchart, Sandy, and Ruth Aylett. 2003. "Solving the Narrative Paradox in VEs—Lessons from RPGs." *Proceedings of the Intelligent Virtual Agents: Fourth International Workshop*, Kloster Irsee, Germany.

Magrino, Tom. 2007. *Etrian Odyssey Review.* Gamespot. http://www.gamespot.com/sekaikinomeikyuu/reviews/6171652/etrian-odyssey-review (accessed January 2, 2011).

Manovich, Lev. 2001. *The Language of New Media*. Cambridge, MA: MIT Press.

Manovich, Lev. 2005. *Soft Cinema: Navigating the Database*. Cambridge, MA: MIT Press.

Mateas, Michael. 2001. "Expressive AI: A Hybrid Art and Science Practice." *Leonardo* 34 (2): 147–153.

Mateas, Michael. 2002. "Interactive Drama, Art and Artificial Intelligence." Dissertation, Computer Science Department, Carnegie Mellon University, Pittsburgh, PA.

Mathews, Harry, and Alastair Brotchie. 1998. *Oulipo Compendium*. Los Angeles: Make Now Press.

McCloud, Scott. 1993. *Understanding Comics: The Invisible Art*. New York: HarperPerennial.

McCulloch, Warren S., and Walter Pitts. 1943. "A Logical Calculus of the Ideas Immanent in Nervous Activity." *Bulletin of Mathematical Biophysics* 5:115–143.

McGinn, Colin. 2004. *Mindsight: Image, Dream, Meaning*. Cambridge, MA: Harvard University Press.

McLuhan, Marshall. 1964. *Understanding Media: The Extensions of Man*. New York: McGraw Hill.

Meehan, James. 1976. "The Metanovel: Writing Stories by Computer." Dissertation, Department of Computer Science, Yale University, New Haven, CT.

Melville, Prem, and Vikas Sindhwani. 2010. "Recommender Systems." In *Encyclopedia of Machine Learning*, ed. C. Sammut and G. Webb, 829–838. Berlin: Springer-Verlag.

Mills, Charles Wright. 1958. *The Causes of World War Three*. New York: Simon and Schuster.

Mills, Charles Wright. [1956] 2000. *The Power Elite*. Oxford: Oxford University Press.

Mingus, Charles. 1960. *Charles Mingus Presents Charles Mingus*. Candid Records. Audio Recording.

Minsky, Marvin. 1975. "A Framework for Representing Knowledge." In *The Psychology of Computer Vision*, ed. Patrick Winston, 211–277. New York: McGraw-Hill.

Mitchell, W. J. T. 1987. *Iconology: Image, Text, Ideology*. Chicago: University of Chicago Press.

Montfort, Nick. 2007. "Ordering Events in Interactive Fiction Narratives on Intelligent Narrative Technologies." *Proceedings of the AAAI 2007 Fall Symposium on Intelligent Narrative Technologies*, AAAI Press, Arlington, VA.

Montfort, Nick, and Ian Bogost. 2009. *Racing the Beam: The Atari Video Computer System*. Cambridge, MA: MIT Press.

Murray, Janet H. 1997. *Hamlet on the Holodeck: The Future of Narrative in Cyberspace*. Cambridge, MA: MIT Press.

Nabokov, Vladimir. 1962. *Pale Fire*. New York: Putnam Publishing Group.

Nakamura, Lisa. 2002. *Cybertypes: Race, Ethnicity, and Identity on the Internet*. New York: Routledge.

Narayanan, Srini. 1999. "Moving Right Along: A Computational Model of Metaphorical Reasoning about Events." *Proceedings of the National Conference on Artificial Intelligence*, Orlando, FL.

Neruda, Pablo. 1947. "Walking Around." In *Anthology of Contemporary Latin American Poetry*, ed. Dudley Fitts, 311–312. Norfolk, CT: New Directions.

Ngugi, wa Thiong'o. 1998. *Penpoints, Gunpoints, and Dreams: Towards a Critical Theory of the Arts and the State in Africa*. Oxford: Oxford University Press.

Ong, Walter. 1982. *Orality and Literacy: The Technologizing of the Word*. London: Methuen.

Owusu, Kwesi. 1988. *Storms of the Heart*. London: Camden.

Palmer, Colin. 1998. "Defining and Studying the Modern African Diaspora." *Perspectives* 39 (6). http://www.historians.org/perspectives/issues/1998/9809/9809VIE2.CFM (accessed December 7, 2012).

Peirce, Charles Saunders. 1965. *Collected Papers of Charles Saunders Peirce*. 6 vols. Cambridge, MA: The Belknap Press of Harvard University Press.

Penny, Simon. 1997. "The Virtualization of Art Practice." *Art Journal* 56 (3): 30–38.

Pérez y Pérez, Rafael, and Mike Sharples. 1999. "MEXICA: A Computer Model of a Cognitive Account of Creative Writing." *Proceedings of the AISB Symposium on Creative Language: Humour and Stories*, Edinburgh, Scotland.

Perlin, Ken. 1998. *Sid and the Penguins*. http://mrl.nyu.edu/~perlin/experiments/sid/ (accessed June 17, 2011).

Perlin, Ken, and Athomas Goldberg. 1996. "Improv: A System for Scripting Interactive Actors in Virtual Worlds." *Proceedings of the 23rd Annual Conference on Computer Graphics and Interactive Techniques*, New Orleans, LA.

Perlroth, Nicole. 2012. "Hackers Step Up Attacks after Megaupload Shutdown." *New York Times*. http://bits.blogs.nytimes.com/2012/01/24/hackers-step-up-attacks-after-megaupload-shutdown/ January 24, 2012 (accessed December 4, 2012).

Petty, Richard E., and John T. Cacioppo. 1986. *Communication and Persuasion: Central and Peripheral Routes to Attitude Change*. New York: Springer-Verlag.

Pickering, Andrew. 1995. *The Mangle of Practice*. Chicago: University of Chicago Press.

Piper, Adrian. 1986–1990. *My Calling (Card) #1 (for Dinners and Cocktail Parties)*. Collection Davis Museum of Wellesley College. © APRA Foundation Berlin.

Piper, Adrian. 1999. *Out of Order, Out of Sight,* vols. 1 and 2. Cambridge, MA: MIT Press.

Poe, Edgar Allan. [1846] 2009. "The Philosophy of Composition." In *Edgar Allan Poe: Critical Theory*, ed. Stuart Levine and Susan F. Levine, 55–76. Chicago: University of Illinois Press.

Propp, Vladimir. 1928. *Morphology of the Folktale*. Austin: University of Texas Press.

Republic of Liberia Truth and Reconciliation Commission. 2009. Volume II: Consolidated Final Report.

Reticker, Gini. 2008. *Pray the Devil Back to Hell*. Balcony Releasing.

Reynolds, Craig. 2001. *Boids (Flocks, Herds, and Schools: a Distributed Behavior Model)*. http://www.red3d.com/cwr/boids/ (accessed August 30, 2008).

Rizzolatti, Giacomo, and Corrado Sinigaglia. 2008. *Mirrors in the Brain: How Our Minds Share Actions and Emotions*. Oxford: Oxford University Press.

Roberts, Sonya. 1997. *Sonya Roberts—Female Skin Pack Excerpts*. http://switch.sjsu.edu/CrackingtheMaze/sonya.html (accessed August 17, 2012).

Rohrer, Jason. 2007. "What I Was Trying to Do with *Passage*." http://hcsoftware.sourceforge.net/passage/statement.html (July 7, 2011).

Rosch, Eleanor. 1975. "Cognitive Representations of Semantic Categories." *Journal of Experimental Psychology* 104 (3): 192–233.

Rose, David. 1995. "Official Social Classifications in the UK." *Social Research Update*, July (no. 9). http://sru.soc.surrey.ac.uk/SRU9.html (accessed December 7, 2012).

Russell, Stuart, and Peter Norvig. 1995. *Artificial Intelligence: A Modern Approach*, 1st ed. Upper Saddle River, NJ: Prentice Hall.

Russell, Stuart, and Peter Norvig. 2002. *Artificial Intelligence: A Modern Approach*, 2nd ed. Upper Saddle River, NJ: Prentice Hall.

Ryan, Marie-Laure. 2001. "Beyond Myth and Metaphor: The Case of Narrative in Digital Media." *Game Studies* 1 (1). http://www.gamestudies.org/0101/ryan/ (accessed December 7, 2012).

Sadan, Elisheva. 2004. *Empowerment and Community Practice*. http://www.mpow.org (accessed August 12, 2011).

Santa Ana, Otto. 2002. *Brown Tide Rising: Metaphors of Latinos in Contemporary American Public Discourse*. Austin: University of Texas Press.

Saussure, Ferdinand de. 1959. *Course in General Linguistics*. New York: The Philosophical Library, Inc.

Searle, John. 1980. "Minds, Brains and Programs." *Behavioral and Brain Sciences* 3: 417–457.

Segal, Jerome M. 1991. *Agency and Alienation: A Theory of Human Presence*. Lanham, MD: Rowman & Littlefield.

Sengers, Phoebe. 1998. "Anti-Boxology: Agent Design in Cultural Context." Dissertation, Computer Science Department and Program in Literary and Cultural Studies, Carnegie Mellon University, Pittsburgh, PA.

Sengers, Phoebe. 2004. "Schizophrenia and Narrative in Artificial Agents." In *First Person: New Media as Story, Performance, Game*, ed. Noah Wardrip-Fruin and Pat Harrigan, 95–116. Cambridge, MA: MIT Press.

Sengers, Phoebe, Kirsten Boehner, Shay David, and Joseph "Jofish" Kaye. 2005. "Reflective Design." *Proceedings of* the *Fourth Decennial Conference on Critical Computing*, Aarhus, Denmark.

Sherry, Lorraine, and Maggie Trigg. 1996. "Epistemic Forms and Epistemic Games." *Educational Technology* 36 (3): 38–44.

Shneiderman, Ben. 2002. *Leonardo's Laptop: Human Needs and the New Computing Technologies*. Cambridge, MA: MIT Press.

Siegel, Nick, Keith Goolsbey, Robert Kahlert, and Gavin Matthews. 2004. *The Cyc System: Notes on Architecture.* Cycorp, Inc. http://cyc.com/copy_of_technology/whitepapers (accessed December 7, 2012).

Sissako, Abderrahmane. 2006. *Bamako.* Les Films du Losange.

Smith, Arthur David. 2003. *Routledge Philosophy Guide Book to Husserl and the Cartesian Meditations.* New York: Routledge.

Smith, Brian K. 2002. MIT Media Lab: Critical Computing. http://www.media.mit.edu/explain/ (accessed December 1, 2011).

Snow, C. P. 1959. *The Two Cultures.* Cambridge: Cambridge University Press.

Soep, Elisabeth. 2010. "Chimerical Avatars and Other Identity Experiments from Prof. Fox Harrell." *boingboing.* http://boingboing.net/2010/04/19/chimerical-avatars-a.html (accessed December 1, 2010).

Someformofhuman. 2008. "File:Petronas Panorama II.jpg." *Wikipedia.* http://en.wikipedia.org/wiki/File:Petronas_Panorama_II.jpg (accessed December 30, 2011).

Sowa, John F. 2010. *Ontology.* http://www.jfsowa.com/ontology/ (accessed July 14, 2012).

Speer, Robert, Catherine Havasi, and Henry Lieberman. 2008. "AnalogySpace: Reducing the Dimensionality of Common Sense Knowledge." *Proceedings of the Twenty-Third AAAI Conference on Artificial Intelligence*, AAAI Press, Chicago, IL.

Spence, Ryan. 2007. Who's Talking? Who's Listening? Toward a Better System of Communication in Abderrahmane Sissako's Bamako. *Offscreen* 11 (6). http://www.offscreen.com/index.php/pages/essays/whos_talking/ (accessed July 18, 2012).

Stevens, Tyler. 1996. "'Sinister Fruitiness': Neuromancer, Internet Sexuality and the Turing Test." *Studies in the Novel* 28 (3): 414–433.

Su, Xiaoyuan, and Taghi M. Khoshgoftaar. 2009. "A Survey of Collaborative Filtering Techniques." *Advances in Artificial Intelligence* 2009:1–19.

Suchman, Lucy A. 1983. "Office Procedure as Practical Action: Models of Work and System Design." *ACM Transactions on Office Information Systems* 1 (4): 320–328.

Talmy, L. 1988. "Force Dynamics in Language and Thought."*Cognitive Linguistics* 12 (1): 49–100.

Team Ico. 2011. *The Team Ico Wiki.* http://teamico.wikia.com/wiki/Ico (accessed June 17, 2011).

Toomer, Jean. [1923] 1969. *Cane.* New York: Harper & Row.

Torrens, Paul M. 2012. *Geosimulation.* http://www.geosimulation.org/riots.html (accessed February 7, 2012).

Torrens, Paul M., and Aaron W. McDaniel. 2013. "Modeling Geographic Behavior in Riotous Crowds." *Annals of the Association of American Geographers* 103 (1): 20–46.

Trilling, Lionel. 1978. *Beyond Culture: Essays on Literature and Learning.* New York: Harcourt Brace Jovanovich.

Turing, Alan M. 1950. "Computing Machinery and Intelligence." *Mind* 59:433–460.

Turkle, Sherry. 2004. "Whither Psychoanalysis in Computer Culture?" *Psychoanalytic Psychology* 21 (1): 16–30.

Turner, Mark. 1996. *The Literary Mind: The Origins of Thought and Language*. New York: Oxford University Press.

Turner, Mark. 2001. *Cognitive Dimensions of Social Science: The Way We Think About Politics, Economics, Law, and Society*. New York: Oxford University Press.

Turner, Mark. 2003. "Double-Scope Stories." In *Narrative Theory and the Cognitive Sciences*, ed. David Herman, 117–142. Stanford, CA: CSLI Publications.

Turner, Mark. 2004. "The Origin of Selkies." *Journal of Consciousness Studies* 11 (5–6): 90–115.

Turner, Mark. 2006. *The Artful Mind: Cognitive Science and the Riddle of Human Creativity*. New York: Oxford University Press.

T.V. Tropes Wiki. 2011. *Eastern RPG*. http://tvtropes.org/pmwiki/pmwiki.php/Main/EasternRPG (accessed November 28, 2011).

Unknown. n.d. Suparshvanath. http://www.jainworld.org/general/prem/JAIN TEMPLES OF INDIA/images/T idols/Suparshvanath.jpg (accessed December 4, 2012).

Varela, Francisco, Evan Thompson, and Eleanor Rosch. 1991. *The Embodied Mind: Cognitive Science and Human Experience*. Cambridge, MA: MIT Press.

Varenne, Hervé. 2002. *The Culture of CULTURE.* http://varenne.tc.columbia.edu/hv/clt/and/culture_def.html (accessed October 11, 2011).

Verran, Helen. 2001. *Science and an African Logic*. Chicago: University of Chicago Press.

Vizenor, Gerald. 2008. *Aesthetics of Survivance: Narratives of Native Presence*. Lincoln: University of Nebraska Press.

Von Neumann architecture.svg. 2006. http://en.wikipedia.org/wiki/File:Von_Neumann_architecture.svg (accessed October 14, 2011).

von Neumann, John. 1945. *First Draft of a Report on the EDVAC*. Philadelphia: Moore School of Electrical Engineering, University of Pennsylvania.

Wardrip-Fruin, Noah. 2009. *Expressive Processing: Digital Fictions, Computer Games, and Software Studies*. Cambridge, MA: MIT Press.

West, Cornel. 1990. "The New Cultural Politics of Difference." In *Out There: Marginalization and Contemporary Cultures*, ed. Russel Ferguson, Martha Gever, Trinh T. Minh-ha, and Cornel West, 19–38. Cambridge, MA: MIT Press.

Weyhrauch, Peter. 1997. "Guiding Interactive Drama. Computer Science." Dissertation, Computer Science Department, Carnegie Mellon University, Pittsburgh, PA.

Whitney, John. 1975. *Arabesque*.

Williams, Raymond. [1958] 1989. *Resources of Hope: Culture, Democracy, Socialism*. London: Verso.

Winograd, Terry, and Fernando Flores. 1986. *Understanding Computers and Cognition: A New Foundation for Design*. Norwood, NJ: Albex Corporation.

Wittgenstein, Ludwig. 1965. *The Blue and Brown Books*. New York: Harper Torchbooks.

Yee, Nicholas, and Jeremy Bailenson. 2007. "The Proteus Effect: The Effect of Transformed Self-Representation on Behavior." *Human Communication Research* 33:271–290.

Young, R. Michael. 2007. "Story and Discourse: A Bipartite Model of Narrative Generation in Virtual Worlds." *Interaction Studies: Social Behaviour and Communication in Biological and Artificial Systems* 8 (2): 177–208.

Young-Hae Chang Heavy Industries. 2008. *The Sea*. http://www.yhchang.com/THE_SEA.html (accessed June 17, 2011).

Youth Against Racism in Europe. 2006. *Youth Against Racism in Europe*. http://www.yre.org.uk (July 16, 2012).

Zbikowski, Lawrence M. 2002. *Conceptualizing Music: Cognitive Structure, Theory, and Analysis*. New York: Oxford University Press.

Zhu, Jichen. 2009. "Intentionality and the AI Hermeneutic Network: Agency and Intentionality in Expressive Computational Systems." Dissertation, Digital Media Program, School of Literature, Communication, and Culture, Georgia Institute of Technology, Atlanta, GA.

Zhu, Jichen, and D. Fox Harrell. 2008. "Daydreaming with Intention: Scalable Blending-Based Imagining and Agency in Generative Interactive Narrative." *Proceedings of AAAI 2008 Spring Symposium on Creative Intelligent Systems*, AAAI Press, Stanford, CA.

Zorn, John. 2012. Tzadik. http://www.tzadik.com (accessed July 10, 2012).

GAMES

Airport Insecurity. 2005. Persuasive Games.

Alternate Reality: The Dungeon. 1987. Datasoft.

America's Army. 2002. U.S. Army.

Angry Birds. 2009. Rovio Entertainment.

Call of Duty: Black Ops 2—Strike Force Yemen—2 Up, 2 Down. 2012. Activision.

Captain Goodnight. 1985. Broderbund.

Civilization IV. 2005. Firaxis Games.

Disaffected! 2006. Persuasive Games.

Elder Scrolls III: Morrowind. 2002. Bethesda Softworks.

Elder Scrolls IV: Oblivion. 2006. Bethesda Softworks.

Elder Scrolls V: Skyrim. 2012. Bethesda Softworks.

Escape from Monkey Island. 2001. LucasArts.

Etrian Odyssey. 2007. Atlus.

Façade. 2004. Michael Mateas and Andrew Stern (Procedural Arts).

Fallout 3. 2008. Bethesda Softworks.

Final Fantasy III (Nintendo Entertainment System). 1990. Square.

Grim Fandango. 1998. LucasArts.

ICO. 2001. Sony Computer Entertainment.

Legend of Mana. 2000. Square.

Neuromancer. 1988. Mediagenic (Interplay).

Pac-Man 2: The New Adventures. 1994. Namco.

Passage. 2007. Jason Rohrer.

Shadow of the Colossus. 2005. Sony Computer Entertainment.

Shenmue II. 2001. Sega.

Shenmue. 2000. Sega.

Star Wars: Knights of the Old Republic. 2003. LucasArts.

Superman. 1978. Atari.

The Bard's Tale III. 1988. Electronic Arts (Interplay).

Wasteland. 1988. Electronic Arts (Interplay).

Wizardry: Proving Grounds of the Mad Overlord. 1981. Sir-Tech.

INDEX